THE CAMBRIDGE COMPANION TO RACE AND AMERICAN LITERATURE

Race is central to American history. It is impossible to understand the United States without understanding how race has been defined and deployed at every stage of the nation's history. Offering a comprehensive and accessible introduction to the history of race, *The Cambridge Companion to Race and American Literature* shows how this history has been represented in literature, and how those representations have influenced American culture. Written by leading scholars in in African American, Latinx, Asian American, Native American, and white American studies, the essays in this volume address the centrality of race in American literature by foregrounding the conflicts across different traditions and different modes of interpretation. This volume explores the unsteady foundations of American literary history, examines the hardening of racial fault lines throughout the nineteenth century and into the twentieth, and then considers various aspects of the multiple literary and complexly interrelated traditions that emerged from this fractured cultural landscape.

JOHN ERNEST is the Judge Hugh M. Morris Professor and Department Chair of English at the University of Delaware. He is the author of more than forty-five essays, and the author or editor of thirteen books, including *Chaotic Justice: Rethinking African American Literary History* (2009) and *The Oxford Handbook of the African American Slave Narrative* (2014). With Stephanie Lee, he is the coeditor of *Elements in Race and US Literature and Culture*, a series published by Cambridge University Press.

A complete list of books in the series is at the back of the book.

THE CAMBRIDGE COMPANION TO RACE AND AMERICAN LITERATURE

EDITED BY

JOHN ERNEST

University of Delaware

Shaftesbury Road, Cambridge CB2 8EA, United Kingdom

One Liberty Plaza, 20th Floor, New York, NY 10006, USA

477 Williamstown Road, Port Melbourne, VIC 3207, Australia

314–321, 3rd Floor, Plot 3, Splendor Forum, Jasola District Centre, New Delhi – 110025, India

103 Penang Road, #05–06/07, Visioncrest Commercial, Singapore 238467

Cambridge University Press is part of Cambridge University Press & Assessment, a department of the University of Cambridge.

We share the University's mission to contribute to society through the pursuit of education, learning and research at the highest international levels of excellence.

www.cambridge.org
Information on this title: www.cambridge.org/9781108835657

DOI: 10.1017/9781108891189

First published 2024

A catalogue record for this publication is available from the British Library

Library of Congress Cataloging-in-Publication Data
NAMES: Ernest, John, editor.
TITLE: The Cambridge companion to race and American literature / edited by John Ernest.
DESCRIPTION: Cambridge ; New York, NY : Cambridge University Press, 2024. | Series: CCL Cambridge companions to literature | Includes bibliographical references and index.
IDENTIFIERS: LCCN 2023051980 | ISBN 9781108835657 (hardback) | ISBN 9781108812993 (paperback) | ISBN 9781108891189 (ebook)
SUBJECTS: LCSH: American literature – History and criticism. | American literature – Minority authors – History and criticism. | Race in literature. | Racism in literature | Minorities in literature.
CLASSIFICATION: LCC PS169.R28 C36 2024 | DDC 810.9/3552–dc23/eng/2023
LC record available at https://lccn.loc.gov/2023051980

ISBN 978-1-108-83565-7 Hardback
ISBN 978-1-108-81299-3 Paperback

For Charles W. Mills

Contents

Figures

Contributors

JOSÉ ANTONIO ARELLANO is Associate Professor of English and Fine Arts at the United States Air Force Academy. Some of his recent essays appear in the edited volume *Race in American Literature and Culture* (2022) and the journal *Teaching American Literature*. His art criticism appears in art magazines, including the Denver-based *DARIA*. He is currently working on two manuscripts: *Race Class: Reading Mexican American Literature in the Era of Neoliberalism, 1981–1984*, and *Life in Search of Form: 20th Century Mexican American Literature and the Problem of Art*.

VALERIE BABB is Andrew Mellon Professor of Humanities at Emory University, where she teaches in the departments of African American Studies and English. Her publications include *The Book of James: The Power, Politics, and Passion of LeBron* (2023), *A History of the African American Novel* (2017), and *Whiteness Visible: The Meaning of Whiteness in American Literature and Culture* (1998). She coauthored *Black Georgetown Remembered* (2022), a tribute to the little-known history of the Georgetown, Washington, DC Black community from the colonial period to the present, and developed the concept for and produced a video by the same name (1989). She is currently working on a book entitled *"Who Ain't a Slave?": How the Story of Slavery Shaped Ideas of American Belonging*.

MITA BANERJEE is Professor and Chair of American Studies at the Obama Institute for Transnational American Studies at Johannes Gutenberg University Mainz, Germany. She specializes in comparative ethnic American literature, with a particular emphasis on issues of immigration, health justice, and citizenship. She is the author of six monographs, including *Color Me White: Naturalism/Naturalization in American Literature* (2013), *Medical Humanities in American Studies* (2018), and *Biologische Geisteswissenschaften* (2020). She is a member of the collaborative research unit Human Differentiation and cospeaker for the research training group Life Sciences, Life Writing: Boundary Experiences of Human Life between Biomedical Explanation and Lived Experience, which is funded by the German Research Foundation.

RENÉ DIETRICH is a senior lecturer in American studies at the Catholic University of Eichstätt-Ingolstadt and was a visiting scholar at the American Indian Studies Center, University of California, Los Angeles. He is the author of *Revising and Remembering (after) the End: American Post-Apocalyptic Poetry since 1945 from Ginsberg to Forché* (2012), the coeditor of *Biopolitics, Geopolitics, Life: Settler States and Indigenous Presence* (2023), the editor of the *American Indian Culture and Research Journal* special issue "Settler Colonial Biopolitics and Indigenous Lifeways," and has published in venues such as *Amerikastudien/American Studies*, *Anglia Cultural Studies↔Critical Methodologies*, and the *Journal of Transnational American Studies*. Currently he is working on a monograph on US settler colonial biopolitics and Indigenous life writing.

JOHN ERNEST, the Judge Hugh M. Morris Professor and Chair of the Department of English at the University of Delaware, is the author of more than forty-five essays and the author or editor of thirteen books, including *Liberation Historiography: African American Writers and the Challenge of History, 1794–1861* (2004), *Chaotic Justice: Rethinking African American Literary History* (2009), *The Oxford Handbook of the African American Slave Narrative* (2014), and *Race in American Literature and Culture* (2022).

BRIGITTE FIELDER is an associate professor at the University of Wisconsin–Madison, the author of *Relative Races: Genealogies of Interracial Kinship in Nineteenth-Century America* (2020), and the coeditor of *Against a Sharp White Background: Infrastructures of African American Print* (2019). Fielder also coedits *J19: The Journal of Nineteenth-Century Americanists*.

TRAVIS M. FOSTER is Associate Professor of English and Academic Director of Gender and Women's Studies at Villanova University. He is the author of *Genre and White Supremacy in the Postemancipation United States* (2019), editor of *The Cambridge Companion to American Literature and the Body* (2022), and coeditor of "American Women's Writing and the Genealogies of Queer Thought," a special issue of *Legacy* (2020). He has published articles in, among other places, *American Literature*,

American Literary History, *ESQ*, *The History of the Present*, and *The Edith Wharton Review*.

CHRISTOPHER FREEBURG is currently the John A. and Grace W. Nicholson Professor of English at the University of Illinois Urbana-Champaign. He has authored three scholarly books and numerous articles, including *Melville in the Idea of Blackness* (2012), *Black Aesthetics and the Interior Life* (2017), and *Counterlife: Slavery after Resistance and Social Death* (2021). His book currently in progress, *Soul: A Brief History of Black Cultural Life*, is the culmination of his life's work in teaching African American history and culture.

RENEE HUDSON is an assistant professor at Chapman University. She specializes in hemispheric studies, multiethnic literature, speculative fiction, genre studies, and histories of revolution and resistance. She has published in *Modern Fiction Studies* and *CR: The New Centennial Review*, and has an essay in the forthcoming Cambridge volume *Latinx Literature in Transition Vol. 2*. She edited a cluster on Latinx speculative fiction for *ASAP/J*, and her book reviews can be found in the *Los Angeles Review of Books*, *MELUS*, and *ASAP/J*. Her first book project, *Latinx Revolutionary Horizons: Form and Futurity in the Americas*, is forthcoming from Fordham University Press and examines how contemporary Latinx literature illustrates the hemispheric convergence of Latin American independence movements and the long history of US occupations and interventions. She is currently developing a second project on Latinx girlhood.

STEPHANIE LI is the Lynne Cooper Harvey Distinguished Professor of English at Washington University in St. Louis. She has published six books, including the award-winning *Something Akin to Freedom: The Choice of Bondage in Narratives by African American Women* (2010) as well as *Signifying without Specifying: Racial Discourse in the Age of Obama* (2011), *Playing in the White: Black Writers, White Subjects* (2015), and *Signifyin(g) Immigrants: Twenty-First Century Pan-African American Literature* (2018). She has also written short biographies of Toni Morrison and Zora Neale Hurston and has a forthcoming book from the University of Minnesota Press entitled *Ugly White People: Whiteness in Contemporary American Literature*. She is the coeditor of the Cambridge University Press Series Race in US Literature and Culture, and has coedited several special issues of *American Literary History* and *Black Camera*.

DREW LOPENZINA is Professor of English at Old Dominion University and teaches in the intersections of Early American and Native American literatures. He is the author of three books: *The Routledge Introduction to Native American Literature* (2020), *Through an Indian's Looking Glass: A Cultural Biography of William Apess, Pequot* (2017), and *Red Ink: Native Americans Picking up the Pen in the Colonial Period* (2012). His studies focus on the presence of Indigenous peoples in the colonial Northeast.

KINOHI NISHIKAWA is Associate Professor of English and African American Studies at Princeton University. He is the author of *Street Players: Black Pulp Fiction and the Making of a Literary Underground* (2018), and is currently writing *Black Paratext*, a history of modern African American literature and book design. Nishikawa's essays have appeared in *PMLA*, *American Literary History*, *MELUS*, *Chicago Review*, and other journals.

FRANK OBENLAND is a senior lecturer in American studies at the Johannes Gutenberg University Mainz, Germany. His dissertation was published as *Providential Fictions: Nathaniel Hawthorne's Secular Ethics* in 2010. His postdoctoral research focuses on the social construction of racial identities in American theater and drama. He has published essays on transnational Black politics, revolutionary traditions, and subversions of racial stereotypes in African American drama in *Theatre Annual: A Journal of Theatre and Performance of the Americas*, *Amerikastudien/American Studies*, and the *Journal of Transnational American Studies*.

CLAIRE PARFAIT is Professor Emerita at Sorbonne Paris Nord University. Her research focuses on African American historiography and print culture. Among others, she authored *The Publishing History of Uncle Tom's Cabin, 1852–2002* (2007), and coedited *Writing History from the Margins: African Americans and the Quest for Freedom* (2016) and *Creative Margins: Afro-Descendant and Indigenous Intellectuals in the Americas of the 19th and 20th Centuries* (2020).

JEAN PFAELZER is the author of *California, A Slave State* (2023), *Driven Out: The Forgotten War Against Chinese Americans* (2008; which has been optioned for a four-part television series), and four other books. Forthcoming books include *California Slave Narratives: 1769–Present, A Reader* and *Muted Mutinies: Slave Revolts on Chinese Coolie Ships*. Pfaelzer was on curatorial teams for *I Want the Wide American Earth: An Asian Pacific American Story* for the Smithsonian Museum of

American History. She appears in the PBS documentary *1882: Chinese Exclusion Act* and was featured in the CSPAN interview "African American Slavery in California" (2015). Currently Professor Emerita at the University of Delaware, Pfaelzer was Executive Director of the National Labor Law Center and Senior Legislative Analyst in the US House of Representatives, focusing on immigration, labor, and women.

SWATI RANA is the author of *Race Characters: Ethnic Literature and the Figure of the American Dream* (2020), which links characterization and racialization, mapping the interrelation of literary persona and social personhood. Her writing has appeared in *American Literature, American Literary History, Asian American Literary Review, The Brooklyn Rail, Granta, Journal of Asian American Studies, The Paris Review, Wasafiri*, and elsewhere. She is Associate Professor of English at the University of California, Santa Barbara.

MALINI JOHAR SCHUELLER is a professor in the Department of English at the University of Florida. She is the author of several books, including *US Orientalisms: Race, Nation, and Gender in Literature, 1790–1890* (1998), *Locating Race: Global Sites of Post-Colonial Citizenship* (2009), and *Campaigns of Knowledge: US Pedagogies of Colonialism and Occupation in the Philippines and Japan* (2019). She coedited, with Ashley Dawson, *Exceptional State: Contemporary US Culture and the New Imperialism* (2007) and *Dangerous Professors: Academic Freedom and the National Security Campus* (2009). She is the director of an award-winning documentary, *In His Own Home* (2015), about police brutality and campus militarization. Currently she is working on a book project, *Building Solidarity Politics Through Critical Race Reading*, and an essay collection, *From Palestine to You*. Her essays have appeared in scholarly journals such *American Literature, Signs, Cultural Critique, American Quarterly*, and *Genders*. She has been the faculty advisor for SJP (Students for Justice in Palestine) on her campus for many years and is a member of the organizing collective for USACBI (United States Campaign for the Academic and Cultural Boycott of Israel).

SIOBHAN SENIER is Professor and Chair of the Department of Women's and Gender Studies at the University of New Hampshire. She is the editor of *Dawnland Voices: An Anthology of Writing from Indigenous New England* (2014) and dawnlandvoices.org. Her other publications include

Voices of American Indian Assimilation and Resistance (2001), *Sovereignty and Sustainability: Indigenous Literary Stewardship in New England* (2020), and essays in journals including *American Literature*, *American Indian Quarterly*, *Studies in American Indian Literatures*, *MELUS*, *Disability Studies Quarterly*, and *Resilience*.

Acknowledgments

As I've said before, any attempt to study race in American history reminds one of the necessity of collaborative work, and I could not have completed this project without the help of a number of people. Above all, I am grateful to the contributors, from whom I've learned so much. Working with the outstanding scholars represented in this volume has been a great honor, and I will continue to benefit from their work.

I am grateful beyond measure to Ray Ryan at Cambridge University Press for suggesting this project and for working with me through all of its stages. Through Cambridge, I also had the pleasure of working with Edgar Mendez, who was a great help as I edited this volume and prepared the final manuscript.

I'm indebted to and grateful for my colleagues at the University of Delaware. Dean John Pelesko has been very supportive as I've addressed scholarship while also serving as chair of the English Department, and I continue to learn and benefit from my astounding colleagues in the English Department and beyond. The university has provided an incredibly supportive environment for this work – both as it pertains to this book and as it pertains to all of the institutional work called for, directly and indirectly, by the chapters in this book.

This is the second collection of essays on this subject I have published with Cambridge University Press, and in both cases I've benefitted enormously from the help of a great research assistant and scholar, Darbyshire Witek. Darby helped me assemble this volume, and conversations with her have helped me think through my approach to this and other projects. For this volume, I'm indebted as well to two great rising scholars: Erica Quinones and Hannah Steele.

I could not say enough about how much I am inspired and supported by Denise Eno Ernest. All that I do and all that I am can be traced back to her guiding influence, many years ago and still today.

Chronology

1773	Phillis Wheatley's *Poems on Various Subjects, Religious and Moral* published
1776	Declaration of Independence
1790	Benjamin Franklin petitions Congress to abolish slavery Naturalization Act of 1790 limits citizenship to whites
1820	Missouri Compromise:allows the expansion of slavery into western territories and prohibits slavery north of the 36° 30′ latitude, except in Missouri
1823	In *Johnson* v. *M'Intosh*, Supreme Court Chief Justice John Marshall rules "that the principle of discovery gave European nations an absolute right to New World lands"
1824	Bureau of Indian Affairs established
1830	Indian Removal Act, relocating Native Americans of various tribes from US states to territories west of the Mississippi River
1845	Frederick Douglass's *Narrative of the Life of Frederick Douglass, an American Slave. Written by Himself* published
1848	Treaty of Guadalupe Hidalgo signed, with Mexico ceding half of its land to the USA. The treaty also presumably granted US citizenship to Mexican citizens who chose to stay in the USA. The USA removes Article X of the Treaty, which would honor all land titles held by Mexicans in the USA
1850	Fugitive Slave Act of 1850, requiring US citizens to assist in the return of escaped slaves to their owners
1852	Harriet Beecher Stowe's *Uncle Tom's Cabin* published
1854	Kansas–Nebraska Act, repealing the Missouri Compromise to allow slavery in the northern territories
1857	*Dred Scott* v. *Sanford* declares that Black Americans are not citizens of the United States
1861	Civil War begins
1861	Publication of Harriet Jacobs's *Incidents in the Life of a Slave Girl, Written by Herself*
1862	Federal emancipation of slaves in the District of Columbia
	Passage of "An Act to Prohibit the 'Coolie Trade' by American Citizens in American Vessels," designed to discourage Chinese migration to California
1863	The Emancipation Proclamation
1865	Civil War ends
	Thirteenth Amendment to the US Constitution abolishes slavery
	Act to Establish a Bureau for the Relief of Freedmen and Refugees

On June 19, or Juneteenth, Black people of Galveston Island, Texas, learn of the Emancipation Proclamation

Founding of the Ku Klux Klan (KKK), dedicated to maintaining white supremacy through intimidation and violence

1865–6 "Black Codes" enacted in southern states to restrict the rights of African Americans

1866 The Civil Rights Act declares that all people born in the United States are citizens, "without distinction of race or color, or previous condition of slavery or involuntary servitude"

1868 The Fourteenth Amendment, granting citizenship rights to those who were formally enslaved

1870 The Fifteenth Amendment, granting voting rights to African American men

Enforcement Act, an attempt to keep organizations like the KKK from harassing or violating the rights of American citizens

1875 Civil Rights Act, guaranteeing all citizens, regardless of race, access to accommodations, theaters, public schools, churches, and cemeteries, prohibiting as well any exclusion from jury service on the basis of race

The Page Act, prohibiting the immigration of Chinese women

1879 Establishment of the Carlisle Indian Industrial School, which served as a template for numerous other schools to force cultural assimilation on the Native American children who had been removed from their homes to board at the school

1882 Chinese Exclusion Act, prohibiting immigration of Chinese laborers

1883 Civil Rights Cases, five legal cases with a single ruling by the Supreme Court, declared the Civil Rights Act of 1875 to be unconstitutional

1887 Dawes General Allotment Act, which divided tribal lands into individually owned parcels, discouraging the continuation or development of Native American communal cultures, and opened "surplus" lands to non-Native Americans and use by railroad companies

1888 Scott Act, an expansion of the Chinese Exclusion Act, prohibiting Chinese laborers who had left the United States from returning

1891 José Martí publishes "Our America"

1892 Geary Act, extending the Chinese Exclusion Act for ten years, now requiring Chinese residents to carry a certificate of residence

José Martí founds the Partido Revolucionario Cuban (the Cuban Revolutionary Party) in New York in 1892

1896 *Plessy* v. *Ferguson*, a Supreme Court decision that upheld the constitutionality of a Louisiana statute that required railroads to provide "equal but separate accommodations for the white and colored races," a principle then extended to other public accommodations and institutions

1898 The USA signs the Treaty of Paris, thus ending the Spanish–American War. Spain cedes ownership of Puerto Rico, Guam, and the Philippines to the USA and allows them temporary control of Cuba, thus beginning the first US occupation of Cuba

Annexation of Hawaii

1899 Beginning of the Philippine–American War

1902 Cuban finally granted independence, but only according to the stipulations outlined in the Platt Amendment. One of the main stipulations was that the USA retained the right to intervene in Cuba

1905 Niagara Movement, led by W. E. B. Du Bois, that included roughly thirty Black men who vowed to fight for school integration, voting rights, and African American political representation

Japanese and Korean Exclusion League established (later called the Asiatic Exclusion League) committed to the extension of the Chinese Exclusion Act to include Japanese and Koreans, exclusion of Japanese employees and the hiring of firms that employ Japanese by those in the league, pressure to segregate schools, and development of a national campaign

1907 Gentlemen's Agreement of 1907, an informal arrangement between the United States and Japan, agreeing that the USA would not impose restrictions on Japanese immigrants in the USA, and Japan would not allow further emigration to the USA

In the Bellingham Riots, white laborers attacked Indian immigrants

1909 Creation of the National Association for the Advancement of Colored People (NAACP), extending the work of the Niagara Movement through an interracial organization committed to civil rights

1912 Publication of Sui Sin Far's *Mrs. Spring Fragrance*

1913 María Cristina Mena publishes "The Gold Vanity Set," in *American Magazine*

1915 Publication of W. E. B. Du Bois's *The Negro*, a history of Africans and African Americans

D. W. Griffith's film *The Birth of a Nation*, based on the white supremacist fiction of Thomas Dixon, Jr., presents the Ku Klux Klan as saviors of white American civilization

USA begins occupation of Haiti

1916 USA begins occupation of the Dominican Republic

1917 The Jones Act establishes English as the official language of Puerto Rico and also establishes that only US ships could carry goods and passengers from one US port to another, and that every ship must be built, crewed, and owned by US citizens. Foreign vessels must pay high tariffs, fees, and taxes to dock at Puerto Rican ports. This negatively impacts the Puerto Rican economy as tariffs and fees are passed down to Puerto Rican consumers

1920 Nineteenth Amendment gives women right to vote

1921 Zitkála-Šá's *American Indian Stories* published

1922 *Ozawa* v. *United States* Supreme Court decision affirming the 1790 Nationality Act's prohibition against naturalization for Asians

1923 *Thind* v. *United States* decides that Bhagat Singh Thind, an Asian Indian, could not be considered white, and therefore was ineligible for citizenship. This decision leads to the denaturalization of other Asian Indian Americans

1924 Indian Citizenship Act, granting national citizenship to Native Americans born in the USA

Labor Appropriation Act established the Border Patrol

1925 Arturo Alfonso Schomburg founds the Schomburg Center for Research in Black Culture

1929 Beginning of Great Depression, which extended to 1939 – especially hard on nonwhite populations in the USA

Beginning of Mexican Repatriation, including US citizens of Mexican descent.

1930 Pedro Albizu Campos elected president of the Puerto Rican Nationalist Party

1935 Río Piedra massacre occurs at the University of Puerto Rico. Police open fire on supporters of the Puerto Rican Nationalist Party. Four party members killed

1936 Pedro Albizu Campos imprisoned on sedition charges after he organized Puerto Rican workers

1937 Zora Neale Hurston's *Their Eyes Were Watching God* published

Law 116 made sterilization legal and free for women in Puerto Rico. No other forms of birth control were made available to them and women were misinformed (many did not realize the procedure was permanent)

1940 Richard Wright's *Native Son* published

Congress confers birthright citizenship on people born in Puerto Rico

1941 The Kansas Act of 1940, granting state jurisdiction over most criminal offenses committed by or against Indians on Indian reservations – considered part of the Indian Termination Policy designed to force Native American assimilation into the dominant US culture. Similar Acts followed in the 1940s

1942 Bracero Program allows Mexican citizens to work temporarily in the USA

Congress of Racial Equality (CORE) established to fight for civil rights

President Roosevelt authorizes internment of more than 120,000 Japanese–American citizens and documented immigrants

1946 Carlos Bulosan's *America is in the Heart* published

Miné Okubo's *Citizen 13660* published

School of the Americas founded to train soldiers and police (mostly from Latin America) in counterinsurgency

Philippines gains independence from the USA

1948 President Harry Truman issues Executive Order 9981, ending racial segregation in the US military.

Public Law 53 (the "Gag Law") enacted, making it a crime to support Puerto Rican independence

1950 Puerto Rican nationalists Oscar Collazo and Griselio Torresola attempt to assassinate President Truman

Pedro Albizu Campos release from prison, returns to Puerto Rico and attempts to organize an armed revolt that did not come to fruition

1952 Ralph Ellison's *Invisible Man* published

The Cuban dictator Fulgencio Batista mostly revokes the privileges outlined in the progressive Constitution of 1940 and is backed by the USA

1953 House Concurrent Resolution 108, a formal statement of the Indian Termination Policy, calling for the termination of reservations and federal aid for the Flathead, Klamath, Menominee, Potawatomi, and Turtle Mountain Chippewa, as well as all tribes in the states of California, New York, Florida, and Texas.

Public Law 280 gives state governments jurisdiction over any Indian reservations which had previously been excluded from state jurisdiction.

Cuban Revolution begins with the attack on the Moncada Barracks in Santiago

James Baldwin's *Go Tell It on the Mountain* published

1954 *Brown* v. *Board of Education*: Supreme Court overturns the principle of "separate but equal"

Immigration and Naturalization Service institutes "Operation Wetback," deporting undocumented Mexicans living in the USA

Puerto Rican nationalists, including Lolia Lebrón, attack the US House of Representatives

1955 Rosa Parks refuses to give up her seat on a bus in Montgomery, Alabama, leading to an organized bus boycott in that city that last over a year, ending when the Supreme Court upholds a lower court's ruling that segregated seating is unconstitutional

Emmett Till murdered for offending a white woman

1956 The Indian Relocation Act passed, encouraging Native Americans to relocate from reservations to urban areas

Birth control tested on Puerto Rican women. Women did not know they were participating in a drug trial. Three women died, but autopsies were not performed, so it is unclear if the drug played a part in their deaths. The dosage given to the women was three times higher than it is today

1957 Civil Rights Act, establishing the Civil Rights Commission (CRC) to protect an individual's rights to equal protection

President Dwight Eisenhower sends US Army troops to Little Rock, Arkansas, to enforce the desegregation of schools

Southern Christian Leadership Conference (SCLC) founded to coordinate civil rights efforts

John Okada's *No-No Boy* published

1959 First wave of Cuban immigration to the USA begins, composed primarily of Batista supporters

1960 Sit-in at the F. W. Woolworth lunch counter in Greensboro, North Carolina

Student Nonviolent Coordinating Committee (SNCC) founded to coordinate student-led efforts to end segregation

Civil Rights Act reaffirms voting rights for all Americans

Harper Lee's *To Kill a Mockingbird* published

Law 116, which made sterilization legal and free to women in Puerto Rico, repealed

Operation Pedro Pan begins, in which unaccompanied Cuban minors are sent to the USA (this is called the "1.5 immigration wave" from Cuba)

1963 Roughly 250,000 people attend the March on Washington, where Martin Luther King Jr. delivers his "I Have a Dream" speech

The KKK bombs the 16th Street Baptist Church in Birmingham, Alabama, killing four black girls in Sunday school

John Rechy's *City of Night* published

1964 Civil Rights Act, outlawing discrimination in public facilities and employment based on race, color, religion, sex, national origin

24th Amendment outlaws poll taxes for national elections

Civil rights workers Michael Schwerner, James Chaney, Andrew Goodman murdered by Klansmen in Mississippi

1965 Voting Rights Act, prohibiting discriminatory laws and practices in voting

Malcolm X assassinated

Martin Luther King, Jr., organizes a march from Selma, Alabama, to the state's capital, Montgomery, to press for federal protection for African Americans voters in the South

USA begins second occupation of the Dominican Republic

Second wave of Cuban immigration to the USA begins with freedom flights in which Cubans who had become dissatisfied with the revolution immigrate to the USA

1966 Founding of Black Panther Party

Samuel R. Delany's *Babel-17* published

President Lyndon B. Johnson signs the Cuban Adjustment Act into law, which grants work authorization permits and lawful permanent residency (green card status) to any

Cuban native or citizen who settled in the USA for at least one year

1967 *Loving* v. *Virginia* Supreme Court ruling that laws prohibiting interracial marriage are unconstitutional

Known as the Long Hot Summer of 1967, more than 150 race riots occur in cities across the USA

Thurgood Marshall becomes the first African American appointed to the Supreme Court

Piri Thomas's *Down These Means Streets* published

1968 Civil Rights Act of 1968, or Fair Housing Act prohibiting discrimination in sales, rentals, or financing of housing

Assassination of Martin Luther King, Jr.

The Third World Liberation Front (TWLF) – a coalition of the Latin American Student Organization (LASO), the Black Student Union (BSU), the Intercollegiate Chinese for Social Action (ICSA), the Mexican American Student Confederation, the Philippine American Collegiate Endeavor (PACE), La Raza, the Native American Students Union, and the Asian American Political Alliance – strikes in response to Eurocentric education and the lack of diversity on the campuses of San Francisco State College (now San Francisco State University) and the University of California, Berkeley

1969 President Richard Nixon issues Executive Order 11478, requiring equal opportunity and affirmative action programs in all federal agencies

The Sociedad de Albizu Campos (SAIC) forms. SAIC and other progressive Latino groups in New York turn to the Young Lords Organization in Chicago as a model. Chicago grants the New York Young Lords an official charter

First National Chicano Liberation Youth Conference held, which gathered together Mexican American youth to organize against issues of oppression, discrimination, and injustice. Rodolfo "Corky" Gonzales performs "I am Joaquín." El Plan Espiritual de Aztlán adopted

	The Young Lords Party writes the "13 Point Program of the Young Lords Party"
	N. Scott Momaday's *House Made of Dawn* published
1970	Voting Rights Act of 1965 renewed
	Young Lords Party splits from the Young Lords Organization and operates independently
1971	*The New Cavalcade: African American Writing from 1760 to the Present* published
	Pedro Pietri's Puerto Rican Obituary published
1972	The Equal Opportunity Act amends the Civil Rights Act of 1964 to apply to local, state, and federal governments
	The Way: An Anthology of American Indian Literature published
	First and last Young Lords Party Congress held
1973	Oscar Zeta Acosta's Revolt of the Cockroach People published
	Nuyorican Poets Café opens
1974	*Aiiieeeee! An Anthology of Asian American Writers* published
1975	Indian Self-Determination and Education Assistance Act, increasing tribal control over reservations
1976	Maxine Hong Kingston's *The Woman Warrior* published
1977	Leslie Marmon Silko's *Ceremony* published
1979	Lolita Lebrón granted clemency by President Jimmy Carter
1980	Toni Cade Bambara's *The Salt Eaters* published
	The Mariel Boatlift or third wave of Cuban immigration to the USA. In a fit of anger, Fidel Castro opened the port of El Mariel to anyone who wanted to leave Cuba. The majority of those who left were working class. Castro also used the Mariel Boatlift as an opportunity to deport criminals and people who were mentally ill
1981	Oscar Lopez Rivera sentenced to fifty-five years in prison for his involvement with FALN (Fuerzas Armadas de Liberación Nacional, the Armed Forces of National Liberation)
	This Bridge Called My Back, edited by Cherríe Moraga and Gloria Anzaldúa, published
1982	Theresa Hak Kyung Cha's *Dictee* published
	Alice Walker's *The Color Purple* published
1983	President Ronald Reagan issues a statement on American Indian policy supporting explicit repudiation of the termination policy
1984	Sandra Cisneros's *The House on Mango Street* published
1987	Toni Morrison's *Beloved* published
	Gloria Anzaldúa's *Borderlands/La Frontera: The New Mestiza* published
1988	Louise Erdrich's *Tracks* published
1989	Oscar Hijuelos's *The Mambo Kings Play Songs of Love* published
1991	Clarence Thomas appointed to the Supreme Court
	Gerald Vizenor's *The Heirs of Columbus* published
	The Fourth wave of Cuban immigration to the USA (balseros). With the collapse of the Soviet Union in 1991, Castro allowed anyone who wanted to leave Cuba to do so
	Julia Alvarez's *How the García Girls Lost Their Accents* published

1992 Toni Morrison's *Playing the Dark* published

The Recovering the US Hispanic Literatary Heritage Project founded. Publishes their first recovered work, María Amparo Ruiz de Burton's *The Squatter and the Don*

Cristina García's *Dreaming in Cuban* published

1993 Toni Morrison awarded the Nobel Prize in Literature

Ernest J. Gaines's *A Lesson Before Dying* published

1994 USA begins second occupation of Haiti

1995 The Million Man March, organized by Louis Farrakhan, the leader of the Nation of Islam, in Washington, DC

Wet Foot, Dry Foot Policy revised the 1966 Cuban Adjustment Act to allow any Cuban who touched US soil to not only stay in the USA, but also to be fast-tracked through the citizenship process

1996 *The Norton Anthology of African American Literature* published

1997 Charles W. Mills's *The Racial Contract* published

1999 Jhumpa Lahiri's *Interpreter of Maladies* published

2001 *Herencia: The Anthology of Hispanic Literature of the United States* published

School of the Americas changes name to the Western Hemisphere Institute for Security Cooperation (WHINSEC)

2003 Immigration and Customs Enforcement (ICE) created according to the Homeland Security Act of 2002

2007 Junot Diaz's *The Brief Wondrous Life of Oscar Wao* published

2009 Sonia Sotomayor becomes first Latina Supreme Court justice

2013 US Supreme Court limits the Voting Rights Act, ending the requirement for federal preclearance of voting law changes for states with a history of voter discrimination

2013 George Zimmerman is acquitted in the shooting death of African American teen Trayvon Martin

Black Lives Matter movement begins

2014 *Schuette* v. *Coalition to Defend Affirmative Action* upholds a Michigan referendum banning affirmative action in admissions at publicly funded state colleges

2015 Viet Thanh Nguyen's *The Sympathizer* published

2016 Colson Whitehead's *The Underground Railroad* published

2017 Unite the Right, a white supremacist rally, takes place in Charlottesville, Virginia

Oscar Lopez Rivera Freed

Hurricane Maria hits Puerto Rico

President Barack Obama ends Wet Foot, Dry Foot Policy, thus reversing his previous efforts to re-establish ties with Cuba

Carmen Maria Machado's *Her Body and Other Parties* published

2019 Ocean Vuong's *On Earth We're Briefly Gorgeous* published

El Centro de Periodismo Investigativo publishes 889 pages of private chats between Ricardo Roselló and his inner circle that includes racist, misogynist, homophobic, transphobic, and ableist comments. The investigation leads to historic #RickyRenuncia protests in Puerto Rico

	Mass shooting at an El Paso Walmart kills twenty-three people and injures twenty-three others; shooter cites the "Hispanic Invasion of Texas" as his rationale
2020	Breonna Taylor killed by Louisville Metro Police Department officers, one of several such killings over the next few years
	George Floyd killed by police officers during his arrest in Minneapolis, one of several such killings over the next few years
	Karla Cornejo Villavicencio's *The Undocumented Americans* published
	Natalie Diaz's *Postcolonial Love Poem* published
2022	Javier Zamora's *Solito* published

Introduction

John Ernest

Race is everywhere in American literature, sometimes seeming to enter by way of an apparently insignificant detail – a word, a face, a shadowy reference – and sometimes more dramatically – the rushing horses of the Ku Klux Klan in a white supremacist novel. In the pages of American fiction and poetry, on American stages, in American film – indeed, in every genre on every platform – the literary and cultural history of the United States is sure to include regular references to race. In works written by white writers, race is generally assumed to enter the work only when someone who is not white enters the story. In works by African American writers, or Asian American, or Latinx, or Native American writers, many readers have been prepared to assume that the work is *all* about race, regardless of whatever else it might address. But race in the literature of the USA – what we call "American literature" – is inarguably there in every work, even those novels, poems, plays, or other books that deal exclusively with white characters. Race is everywhere in US literature, but the story of how it gets there, where it came from, and what to make of it is complicated.

There's a relatively easy version of the story to tell, though, about the centrality of race in American literature. One could simply follow the emergence of a series of novels through the years that have had a huge impact on American culture in ways that reveal a great deal about American attitudes about race, and especially white understandings of American racial history. This story might begin with Harriet Beecher Stowe's *Uncle Tom's Cabin*, the 1852 novel about slavery that inspired an industry of novels, plays, and a range of games, household items, and other products that would make even the managers of the Harry Potter brand jealous. Wallpaper that features a scene of people escaping slavery? You've got it. The two-headed Topsy and Eva doll, white on one end and black on the other? A popular item. Card games based on the novel's characters? Certainly.[1] It's almost difficult to trace the many manifestations of the ongoing cultural presence of this problematic but influential novel. And from the middle of the nineteenth century we could move to the century's later decades, a time when white supremacist thought was asserting itself throughout the culture. Stowe's novel inspired a writer from this time, Albion Tourgée, to turn to fiction in his campaign against the Ku Klux Klan, and the resulting novel, *A Fool's Errand* (1879) was a great sensation, if not quite as broadly or deeply influential as Stowe's earlier work. Arguably more influential, and also inspired in part by Stowe's great success a half-century earlier, was the trilogy published by Thomas Dixon, Jr. at the beginning of the twentieth century. Like *A Fool's Errand*, Dixon's trilogy was also about the Ku Klux Klan, but Dixon presented the KKK as civilization's salvation. The three novels – *The Leopard's Spots: A Romance of the White Man's Burden* (1902), *The Clansman: A Historical Romance of the Ku Klux Klan* (1905), and *The Traitor: A Story of the Fall of the Invisible Empire* (1907) – were broadly influential, inspiring the film *The Birth of a Nation* (1915), and influencing a writer who produced yet another sensational novel dealing with race and slavery: Margaret Mitchell's *Gone With the Wind* (1936), romanticizing the white South and promoting stereotypes of Black southerners. *Gone With the Wind* has been an enduring cultural presence from the time of its publication to the creation of a legendary film of the same name in 1939, and still to the present day, eventually provoking a novel that attempts to respond to that story's tremendous cultural presence, Alice Randall's *The Wind Done Gone* (2001). What does it mean that some of the most significant, influential novels in American literary history deal directly with race, some of them inspiring films that are also considered to be among the most popular and iconic movies in American film history? What does it mean, too, that, aside from Alice Randall, all of these writers are white and virtually all the representations of Black people we encounter in these works are deeply problematic?

Of course, the story of US racial history is not limited to white and Black Americans, for white writers have regularly written about a broad range of ethnic and racial others, sometimes in well-intentioned ways and sometimes in ways that can only be accounted for by racism or white supremacy, whether consciously or not. Charlie Chan, a fictional Honolulu police detective, was created by Earl Derr Biggers for a series of mystery novels in the 1920s and 1930s. Biggers believed that the character was a strongly positive alternative to existing Asian American stereotypes, but he succeeded in replacing those stereotypes with new ones that influenced a great many film and television portrayals of Asian Americans for years to come.

Perhaps influenced by such portrayals was Mickey Rooney, a white actor who played an extravagantly stereotyped Japanese character in the 1961 film *Breakfast at Tiffany's*. Pearl S. Buck, born in West Virginia but raised for many years in China, similarly thought she was fighting against prejudice when she wrote *The Good Earth* (1931) and other works that portrayed village life in China – works for which she earned the Pulitzer Prize and the Nobel Prize for Literature. Most readers today would almost certainly find reason to question her authority over the subject, despite her many years in China and her clear devotion to its people.

Native Americans have encountered equally problematic representations. Early on, commentators on the United States talked of the "three races" – white, Native American, and Black – and many assumed that Native Americans would simply fade from the scene over time. Indeed, white government policy seemed determined to make that happen over the years. One can see this vision of history rather directly in white historian George Bancroft's ten-volume *History of the United States* (1834–74). In his second volume, Bancroft sets the scene: "The three races, the Caucasian, the Ethiopian and the American, were in the presence of one another on our soil. Would the red man disappear entirely from the forests, which, for thousands of years, had sheltered him safely?" (II 464); but he has already offered his answer in the first volume: "It might have seemed that the European and the native races were about to become blended; yet no such result ensued. The English and the Indians remained at variance, and the weakest gradually disappeared" (I 148). The process of understanding this disappearance was played out with some regularity in American fiction. While Native Americans were sometimes presented as a noble but sadly vanishing people in early white American writing, as is generally the intention in the work of James Fenimore Cooper, they were also regularly presented as a violent threat to white civilization. Robert Montgomery Bird was among those who countered the noble though uncivilized stereotype early on in his 1837 novel *Nick of the Woods*, which portrays Native Americans as murderous savages. At best, white writers presented Native Americans as a people close to nature, and they looked to them to learn lessons about the natural order that could then be applied to refining white civilization. At worst, Native Americans were reduced to stock figures, the stereotypes that eventually dominated the American western genre in film.

White writers took on Mexican history and identity as well. Before he wrote *Nick of the Woods*, Bird offered the world *Calavar; or, The Knight of the Conquest* (1834), which he presents as the product of an American who inherits a large manuscript about Mexico's history, which he edits and, in effect, folds into the history and destiny of the United States. This was a subject that drew other writers as well, usually involving similar acts of historiographical conquest and cultural appropriation. Bird continued his journeys into the subject in *The Infidel: Or, the Fall of Mexico. A Romance* (1835), which was later joined by Joseph Holt Ingraham's *Montezuma, the Serf* (1845) and Edward Maturin's *Montezuma: The Last of the Aztecs* (1845). Whether positive or negative in their attempts at representing Mexican life, many works finally represented the assumed superiority of white US culture. Coming at the time of the annexation of Texas, approved in 1844 and accomplished in 1845, these and other works reflected a vested interest in the expanding United States, an expansion that was cultural as well as geographical. This, at least, was the point made by a reviewer of Maturin's novel for the *American Whig Review*, arguing that Maturin had "introduced his readers to what should be claimed by appropriation, as an exclusively American field." "The legendary and historical wealth of this entire hemisphere," the review continued, "should be made ours by the bloodless conquest of the Pen."[2] The conquest of the pen continued over the years, as white writers looked both to and beyond Mexico to create a range of Latinx characters to populate their fictional worlds and their social imaginations.

My point is not that white writers are inherently racist or simply incapable of representing other cultural traditions thoughtfully and fairly, but rather that what we see in these and other literary works are representations of white America. Among the various stories of race in American history is that about the process by which white people became, in effect, white; how it came to matter to identify as white; and how one's association with white culture shapes one's understanding of those who were identified as racial others. A novel, poem, play, essay, or history doesn't need to focus on slavery or Chinese immigrants or Mexican history or the conquest of Native lands to be *about* race. Even in the absence of stereotypical Indians, Chinese cooks, Mexican gardeners, or African American servants, white literature is about race, just as much as works of Asian American, Native American, African American, or Latinx literature are understood to be about race even when they make no point about it at all. One could hardly avoid writing about life in the United States, in fact, without in some way writing about race, whether or not one addresses it deliberately.

What is race? It is not a biological reality. Quite simply, race is a matter of placing great significance on observable differences. If those differences speak as well about dramatic differences in geographic background, ancestral traditions, and cultural perspectives and practices, then it can be even more seductive to account for those differences, and for the anxieties inspired by such differences, by understanding it in terms of fundamental racial distinctions, and then placing those differences in a hierarchy, one that allows one racial category to claim natural dominance over another. Race, then, is conceptualized and created over time. Laws are passed to separate those who are different; the laws, and the social separations they enforce, lead to the development of social attitudes and cultural practices. Consider, for example, the 1790 Naturalization Act, which limited naturalization to "free white persons." Or look at the complex legal, economic, and political system of slavery, including the Dred Scott Supreme Court decision in 1857, in which Chief Justice Roger B. Taney, speaking for the majority decision, declared that African Americans had "no rights which the white man was bound to respect." Consider as well the process by which the Irish and other social groups transitioned from being members of an inferior race to being accepted, at least peripherally, as white. Add to this history the 1909 court decision that rendered Armenians white, or the 1923 Supreme Court decision that Asian Indians were nonwhite. The legal history of race is amazingly intricate, often contradictory, and frequently absurd. And for those living under such murderously and frankly fictional legal distinctions, mundane fears and prejudices are reinforced, given increasing authority, and are taken as natural and right. Fictions overrule even obvious realities, absurdities become real; and the difference of even one drop of blood is given great significance, making the difference between great opportunities and oppressive conditions. It matters whether one is white, and most white Americans barely notice the most fundamental racial privileges they enjoy – that is, until they feel that those privileges are threatened, or until someone suggests that there is such a thing as white privilege. As Charles W. Mills, a philosopher who has studied race carefully, has explained, "whites ... take their racial privilege so much for granted that they do not even see it as *political*, as a form of domination."[3]

Let's pause over this statement, for when this book you're reading was first planned, Charles W. Mills was going to write the opening chapter.[4] His book *The Racial Contract* is one of the best considerations of race available, and it focuses on the privileges and operations of whiteness, or what he calls "global white supremacy," which he presents as "a political system, a particular power structure of formal or informal rule, socioeconomic privilege, and norms for the differential distribution of material wealth and opportunities, benefits and burdens, rights and duties."[5] Drawing from the philosophical concept of the Social Contract, Mills suggests that whiteness functions as a *racial* contract – in effect, an agreement (conscious or unconscious) to accept the terms of the racial order, to accept that the ruling fictions are real, and that absurd and oppressive legal and social distinctions actually make sense. By the terms of this racial contract, Mills argues, "one has an agreement to *mis*interpret the world. One has to learn to see the world wrongly, but with the assurance that this set of mistaken perceptions will be validated by white epistemic authority, whether religious or secular."[6] One needs to see a world ordered according to racial distinctions while believing that those distinctions are either natural or virtually nonexistent, and it is important that one is surrounded by others who believe that the racial distinctions are real. One needs to see injustice and turn it back on the victims. One needs to be able to avoid the signs all around that one's world is, in fact, *about* race, and that one is basing one's life on a fundamentally invented and unjust set of superficial distinctions. "Nonwhites," Mills observes, "find that race is, paradoxically, both everywhere and nowhere, structuring their lives but not formally recognized in political/moral theory." "In a racially structured polity," he continues, "the only people who can find it psychologically possible to deny the centrality of race are those who are racially privileged." This has become, in fact, a distinctive feature of whiteness: the assumption that all is right with the world aside from a few isolated racial issues. "The fish does not see the water," Mills explains, "and whites do not see the racial nature of a white polity because it is natural to them, the element in which they move."[7]

This is about whiteness as an ideological force, I should emphasize; whiteness as a set of attitudes and practices built into the system. If you are born white, then the privileges of whiteness will be quietly seductive for you, and the habits of operating in a world that facilitates your development will seem natural. But you do not *naturally* come to see things a certain way; you gradually become a white person. As Mills suggests, those who are included in "the racial contract" accept "an inverted epistemology, an epistemology of ignorance."[8] You come to accept that the world around you makes sense, you adopt "a particular pattern of localized and global cognitive dysfunctions" which are reinforced by those around you, quietly and daily assuring you that your world, and your own sense of identity, are firmly founded and make sense – all of which produces, Mills insightfully observes, "the ironic outcome that whites will in general be unable to understand the world they themselves have made."[9] Such limitations of perception and understanding naturally shape the literature white writers produce, even when those writers try to struggle against their limitations.

And this emphasis on whiteness, at once everywhere and nowhere, creates challenges for a great many US writers who have been identified as racial because they are not white, because they are not members of the nation's dominant racial group. Finding themselves so deeply written into the pages of American literature, accordingly, writers from various US cultural traditions worked to create their own literature. These cultures – the most prominent of which are African American, Laxinx, Asian American, and Native American – are themselves tremendously diverse, and the large labels barely manage to account for the many communities they represent – communities that have emerged from a variety of national origins, cultural traditions, tribes, communities, and religions. While the larger labels indicate attempts at collective self-representation and political power, they also represent a history of white supremacist control that has defined other racial groups broadly, and so they do as much to obscure as to reveal the lives and communities they are used to represent. Not all people grouped under the heading of *Latinx* come from the same national or cultural backgrounds, and not all even support the use of the term Latinx. Not all African Americans come from the same origins. The terms *Native American* or *Indigenous* don't begin to account for the great number of tribes, cultural traditions, and histories it represents. *Asian American* similarly covers enough national, historical, and cultural ground to be virtually useless as a defining term. But however they understood their association with these larger labels, writers have understood the need to represent broadly interrelated and deeply intertwined communities – those who in some ways looked like them, those most prepared to understand life from their perspective – and appreciated the need to recognize themselves in stories that went against the grain and worked against the stereotypes promulgated by the dominant culture. Are such writers any more successful in their representations than white writers? Certainly, as some of the chapters in this volume will suggest, there are disagreements in every field of study, and no one would argue that representing Japanese Americans is the same as representing Chinese Americans, let alone all of those included as Asian Americans, and few would argue that it is possible to represent all Native Americans by focusing on a single tribe. It's useful, though, to return to Mills's observation that nonwhites "find that race is, paradoxically, both everywhere and nowhere, structuring their lives but not formally recognized in political/moral theory." Those who are not white, Mills suggests, cannot help but recognize the centrality of race in American culture, though they might well understand and address the realities of race in a broad variety of ways. They bring deep and painful experience to the subject of US racial history.

Just as there have been important and controversial "race" books by white writers through the years, so have there been books that have revealed the limits of established representations of American history and culture, books that have spoken profoundly to specific communities. American literary history has been influenced by novels and other works by a broad range of writers representing literary and cultural traditions that speak from and to communities that developed in resistance to the oppression and exclusions of the dominant culture, and one can learn a great deal about US history and culture by focusing on these works and the literary traditions they represent. Among African American writers, it would be difficult to miss the profound impact of novels such as Richard Wright's *Native Son* (1940), Ralph Elison's *Invisible Man* (1952), Alice Walker's *The Color Purple* (1983), Toni Morrison's *Beloved* (1987), or Colsen Whitehead's *The Underground Railroad* (2016), among many other works. Focusing on Asian American writers, one could turn to Sui Sin Far's *Mrs. Spring Fragrance* (1912), Carlos Bulosan's *America is in the Heart* (1946), John Okada's *No-No Boy* (1957), Maxine Hong Kingston's *The Woman Warrior* (1976), or Amy Tan's *The Joy Luck Club* (1989). Reading Latinx traditions, one is likely to find one's way to *The House on Mango Street*, a 1984 novel by Sandra Cisneros, Piri Thomas's *Down These Mean Streets* (1967), Giannina Braschi's *Yo-Yo Boing!* (1998), or Junot Díaz's *The Brief Wondrous Life of Oscar Wao* (2007). A reading of Native American literature might well involve works such as N. Scott Momaday's *House Made of Dawn* (1969), Leslie Marmon Silko's *Ceremony* (1977), Gerald Vizenor's *The Heirs of Columbus* (1991), or Louise Erdrich's *The Round House* (2012). I'm offering here a rather conventional listing of the "best of" these traditions, which I actually do not present as the best of or anything that should be taken as wholly representative of the cultures and literary traditions one would want to explore. Many of these works have been greatly celebrated, with numerous Pulitzer prizes and other awards represented here; some have challenged how we think about literature, or how we read literature; some have challenged readers' understandings of the geographical and historical boundaries that define the United States; and virtually all have challenged what a great many readers thought they understood about American history and culture. Together, they offer an understanding of the nation's history and culture, and of the practice and priorities of literary reading, that would have been virtually unthinkable through a reading of what was presented as American literature in most English classes even in the 1970s and '80s, when some of these works were just beginning to break into the conventional wisdom about what "we," as Americans, should teach and what "we" should read.

The highly selective listing of books I've presented here speaks of long and difficult struggles to establish stable and supportive cultures in a deeply destabilizing nation, including attempts to establish identifiable literary traditions – and then subsequent struggles to draw readers, publishers, teachers, and students to those traditions. Today, someone taking a course on American literary history will encounter glimpses into these various traditions in the major anthologies for the field: the *Norton Anthology of American Literature* and the *Heath Anthology of American Literature*. But even before these dominant anthologies were published (and then revised to be more inclusive), anthologies devoted to specific traditions attempted to represent specific literary traditions and influence the teaching of American literary history. Influential early anthologies include *The New Cavalcade: African American Writing from 1760 to the Present* (1971), *The Way: An Anthology of American Indian Literature* (1972), and *Aiiieeeee! An Anthology of Asian American Writers* (1974), with the more recent addition of *Herencia: The Anthology of Hispanic Literature of the United States* (2001). Through these anthologies – joined by a range of other publications, including important reprintings of early literature, and other collections of fiction, poetry, and drama – both students and the broader reading public have had the opportunity to follow important literary movements, creative interventions in established literary conventions, and writing that gives voice to communities that have been represented only incidentally and problematically in previous anthologies of American literature. From exclusions, struggles, and imposed identities emerged expressive possibilities that spoke of newly recovered histories and open futures, and we have benefitted from the rich and diverse literary tradition created by writers who realized these possibilities.

With the emergence of literary traditions came as well scholarly books, literary handbooks, and biographies to address the importance of coming to just understandings of these literary works. One of the things many readers – not just white readers – discover when reading in these expansive literary traditions is that Americans do not enjoy a shared understanding of history, and that many Americans, of any background, have little to draw from when trying to follow the historical context and pointed references they encounter in literature that challenges the terms of "the racial contract." In a country that has long promoted "invented Orients, invented

Africans, invented Americas," as Mills has observed, what does one have to bring to a work about Chinese Americans, African Americans, Native Americans, Mexican Americans, or any number of racial and ethnic communities misrepresented in or wholly excluded from the accounts of American history and culture taught in US schools and featured in our textbooks? Moreover, that same dominant culture has developed its own approach to reading and assessing the value of literary works, and the standards of the dominant culture are sometimes ill-equipped to lead one to an appreciation of literature that challenges or wholly dismisses those standards. Accordingly, scholarship developed in these marginalized fields – often, at first, scholarship devoted to piecing together histories, biographies, and communities, or even simply devoted to discovering and publishing works that have been long ignored. Over time, scholars worked to develop appropriate approaches to this literature, new ways of reading, new ways of understanding what literature has to say and how it says it. Today, readers can readily find anthologies for all of these literary traditions, and they can also find guidance through those traditions by way of very prominent essay collections by such presses as Oxford University Press and Cambridge University Press – which, as this volume suggests, has made the representation of Asian American, African American, Native American, and Latinx literary traditions (along with broader considerations of race, ethnicity, and religion) a priority. Writers addressing the pressures of a white supremacist culture learned to write against the grain so that we could learn, in turn, how to *read* against the grain and take in the broader and more complex story of American literature and culture.

The Cambridge Companion to Race in American Literature is an attempt to represent that broader history by accounting for these various literary traditions while also accounting for whiteness as a central racial category in American literary and cultural history. Doing so, though, as I hope this introduction helps to explain, is no simple task. It's simply not possible present a straightforward, chronological history of race in American literature. What one encounters when one looks for such a history is overwhelming complexity that leads to multiple narrative lines, several stories to tell, and no simple way to bring them all together. Accordingly, this volume is committed to a deliberately messy story. It makes no claims to full historical coverage, either of American literary history in general or of the specific literary traditions that emerged within that larger framework. Rather, this volume places the reader directly in a series of traditions, each of which is well underway. It might be disorienting at first to immerse oneself in a focused study of Native American literature and then turn to a consideration of a particularly important moment in Chicano history and literature – but the disorientation, I would argue, is part of the point, as is the sense that one is always catching up with a story already well in progress. The contributors to this volume have all attempted to make their work accessible to those who are just entering the conversation, just getting accustomed to a particular literary tradition and the historical, cultural, or interpretive questions it raises. However, the contributors have also been encouraged to attend to the integrity of their own fields of study, and accordingly they make (manageable) demands on their readers. In effect, the reader is asked to move through this book by conceptual steps (and, hopefully, relatively few leaps), taking in one tradition, one set of issues, one set of texts to consider, and then moving on to another, and in this way gradually appreciating the diversity of American literary history, along with the complex history it represents.

This volume is divided into five parts – Foundations, Backgrounds, The Dynamics of Race and Literary Dynamics, Rethinking American Literature, and Case Studies – that should make that conceptual journey more manageable. The different sections take the reader from considerations of race to introductions to different literary traditions, then to explorations of the operations and implications of those traditions, and finally to case studies that attempt to bring this journey to a purposeful conclusion. Following those steps, the reader might well begin to apprehend an underlying coherence to the volume, something that connects the chapters in the absence of any overt, narrative, or narrowly logical connection: the untellable story of race in American history and literature that still asks to be heard.

Notes

1. For background on *Uncle Tom's Cabin* and its tremendous cultural presence, see Thomas F. Gossett, *Uncle Tom's Cabin and American Culture* (Dallas: Southern Methodist University Press, 1985), E. Bruce Kirkham, *The Building of Uncle Tom's Cabin* (Knoxville: The University of Tennessee Press, 1977), Claire Parfait, *The Publishing History of Uncle Tom's Cabin*, 1852–2002 (Hampshire: Ashgate Publishing Limited, 2007), Joy Jordan-Lake, *Whitewashing Uncle Tom's Cabin: Nineteenth-Century Women Novelists Respond to Stowe* (Nashville: Vanderbilt University Press, 2005), Sarah Meer, *Uncle Tom Mania: Slavery, Minstrelsy and Transatlantic Culture in the 1850s* (Athens: The University of Georgia Press, 2005), Audrey Fisch, *American Slaves in Victorian England: Abolitionist Politics in Popular Literature and Culture* (Cambridge: Cambridge University Press, 2000), and Marcus Wood, *Blind*

Memory: Visual Representations of Slavery in England and America, 1780–1865 (New York: Routledge, 2000).

2. Qtd. in Jesse Alemán, "The Invention of Mexican America," in Russ Castronovo, ed., *The Oxford Handbook of Nineteenth-Century American Literature* (Oxford: Oxford University Press, 2012), 86.
3. Charles W. Mills, *The Racial Contract* (Ithaca: Cornell University Press, 1997), 1.
4. Sadly, Charles W. Mills passed away before he was able to contribute this volume. He is greatly missed, but his work and his vision have guided me in my work on this project, in my teaching, and in my life.
5. Mills, *The Racial Contract*, 3.
6. Ibid., 18.
7. Ibid., 76.
8. Ibid., 18.
9. Ibid.

PART I

Foundations

CHAPTER 1

Tracing Race

Travis M. Foster

The presence of race in American literary texts might seem obvious – far too obvious for a volume like this to include an entire chapter on tracing it. In text after text, American literature invites readers to notice race. It provides opportunities to explore which characteristics have racial salience, to look for effects and histories of racial meaning, and to ask how race positions characters and communities. Readers of American literary texts have been taught how to notice race not only by other readers, our teachers, and our students, but also by those very texts. My goal here is to argue that such an education has been, for many of us, insufficient. Specifically, the work of this chapter is twofold: first, to delineate the reasons readers often overlook and misunderstand race; second, to suggest methods for more accurately analyzing racial meaning.

Misapprehending Race

There are at least four overlapping reasons why many students and critics of American literature too frequently overlook and misidentify the presence of race in the texts we study. In this section, I describe each of these reasons, drawing from scholars working within fields related to ethnic literary studies who have brought them to readers' attention. As I hope becomes clear, all four emerge as outcomes of the strategies white supremacy (the belief that whites constitute a superior race and should maintain control over others) and settler colonialism (the displacement and erasure of Indigenous people by settlers who steal land for use in perpetuity) have used to maintain dominance within American life. While it may be too hopeful to say that the analysis of race in American literature serves an antiracist or decolonial agenda, it is no doubt true that the misapprehension of race frequently advances racist and colonialist ones.

The first reason many have overlooked race is that the modus operandi of whiteness is to cloak itself, hiding behind a façade of racial neutrality or racelessness. White Americans (I include myself) have become magicians of a sort. Whites reproduce the privileges of white supremacy in ways that seemingly leave no trace of them and of their fellow whites, rendering white supremacy – and whiteness itself – so invisible that whites often remain oblivious to their own consent. Such ignorance arguably constitutes white supremacy's most characteristic and defining tactic: "as a general rule," philosopher Charles Mills writes, "*white misunderstanding, misrepresentation, evasion, and self-deception on matters related to race* are among the most pervasive mental phenomena of the past few hundred years, a cognitive and moral economy psychically required for conquest, colonization, and enslavement."[1] Hence, when reading texts by white authors about white characters living in white communities, white readers frequently stop seeing race, despite the fact that whiteness, in many of these texts, constitutes the setting's dominant characteristic. Paradoxically, the ubiquity of whiteness in much of American literature stymies analysis of whiteness. It's been more than two decades since Toni Morrison insisted that readers of American literature pay attention to race, especially in texts predominantly featuring white characters,[2] yet not many whites have heeded Morrison's advice. As Christine Okoth notes, this pattern means that "the foundational gestures of literary study do not just reflect race and racism as they exist in the world but actively produce racial hierarchies," structured as they are "around the assumption that some bodies can and should be read more closely and more readily than others."[3] The failure to fix whiteness as an object for attention has led many white teachers, students, and critics to thematize or reference race only when reading novels, plays, or poems representing characters who are not white.[4] Race, for many white readers, has become a characteristic solely attached to others.

Even when analyzing race in texts that do feature a multiracial or nonwhite cast of characters, white misunderstanding can lead to faulty interpretations. Racist bias leads white readers either to filter all representations of characters of color through the logics of racial violence, ignoring other themes in the text they're interpreting, or to fundamentally misunderstand otherwise evident aspects of the worlds being represented.[5] These failures of apprehension occur when whites' experiences and ways of knowing the world have left them without adequate tools to know what they're reading, seeing, and experiencing. Building on the work of the sociologist Pierre Bourdieu, historian Michel-Rolph Trouillot describes these gaps in white knowledge as "the unthinkable" – a realm of meaning that sits outside readers' common sense understanding of how the world works.[6] Trouillot's paradigmatic example is the Haitian Revolution, an event of mass Black resistance to slavery and colonialism. Because it transpired through Black strategies, intellects, and desires that challenged the very framework shaping how white Europeans and Americans understand Blackness, whites examining Haiti have either willfully misinterpreted its history or been forced to revise their previously held notions.[7]

A second source of misapprehension can be found in the tendency for many students and critics of American literature to see all histories of racism and racialization through the Black–white binary. To be sure, this is in part because many readers have come to recognize the exceptional nature of antiblackness. Students growing up during the advent of Black Lives Matter have learned how to connect images of state violence and police murders to the long history of US slavery and re-enslavement. They've begun understanding antiblackness as a vast, originating pattern of bigotry that continues to shape not only other modes of American racialization, but also how we understand gender, class, disability, sexuality, and region.[8] If anything, the scope of the afterlife of slavery has been understated within social and cultural histories of American life.

However, this emphasis on antiblackness can also obfuscate when it becomes the primary lens through which to understand other forms of bigotry – that is, when the exceptional nature of antiblackness is mistaken as paradigmatic. Moves to abstract or generalize the history of antiblackness, treating it as an analog for all racisms (or even bigotries such as ableism, misogyny, homophobia, and transphobia), end up occluding the singularity of that very history. Such thinking, as Jared Yates Sexton understands it, "cuts its teeth on the denial of this fundamental social truth: . . . antiblackness . . . is unlike other forms of racial oppression in qualitative ways – differences in kind, rather than degree."[9] While we can craft usefully overarching definitions of racism – such as when Ruth Gilmore Wilson describes it as "the state-sanctioned or extralegal production and exploitation of group-differentiated vulnerability to premature death" – we also need to learn how to identify qualitative differences in how that racism impacts people's lives, both in our communities and in our literature.[10]

Put differently, antiblackness falters as a conceptual model when used as the readymade approximation for histories of anti-Latinx or anti-Asian racisms or to assess the ongoing effects of settler colonialism and the afterlives of the genocide of Indigenous people. Nor does a one-size-fits-all model of antiblackness grounded in the afterlives of slavery account for differences within the bigotry and systemic racism targeting Black people, particularly the distinctions between racisms affecting more recent Black immigrants and racisms affecting Black Americans whose ancestors survived the Middle Passage two or more centuries ago. Histories of racism find their genealogies not only in slavery, but also in US imperialism, xenophobia, and settler colonialism. Rather than treating racisms and racializations as parallel phenomena, then, scholars engaged in critical race studies encourage us to historicize distinctions, divergences, and crossings.

The third reason readers too frequently misunderstand race is a historicization of the second: concepts of race and racial identity mean different things at different times in different places and to different groups of people. The processes Michael Omi and Howard Winant famously describe as "racial formation" – in which "racial categories are created, inhabited, transformed, and destroyed" – have transpired through different social structures, scientific debates, and cultural representations: "The processes of racial formation we encounter today . . . are merely the present-day outcomes of a complex historical evolution."[11] It's striking, for instance, that late-eighteenth-century Americans largely conceived of race as an exterior trait "produced," as Katy L. Chiles puts it, "by environmental factors (such as climate, food, and mode of living) and continuously subject to change."[12] It was only in the early nineteenth century that Americans began to formulate the notion of race as a fixed biological category. Tracing race in any given literary text is often only possible after historicizing what race and racial identity even means in that text's particular setting.

Briefly comparing the early-twentieth-century histories of Black and Indigenous racialization provides a case in point. During the institutionalization of Jim Crow definitions of Blackness were in flux. In most states, the so-called one-drop rule defining Black racial identity as any degree of Black ancestry continued to reign. In others, definitions changed, even if just for a period. In 1910, for instance, Virginia changed its definition of Blackness to anyone with at least one Black grandparent, only to then revert to the one-drop rule in 1930.[13] At the same time, the federal government was imposing a "blood quantum" system for adjudicating and racializing fractions of American Indian identity, demanding increasing proportions of Indigenous ancestry before counting an individual as such. As C. R. Kelly puts it, the ideological inconsistency of "one drop" and "blood quantum" mattered less than that both systems served white supremacy and settler colonialism: "Whereas the irreducible degree of African blood ensured perpetual enslavement and segregation, the diminished nature of Indian blood guaranteed legal extinction. American Indians' historical claims to sovereignty made assimilation, rather than segregation, the prevailing practice of institutional racism."[14] What counts as race or racial identity shifts both within and across various moments in history. Because of this variability, when we analyze texts we first need to determine just what systems of definition are operational within their pages and which modes of racialization are informing how characters think of themselves and others.

The fourth reason tracing race has proven more of a critical stumbling block than we might think pertains to how histories of racialization incorporate a multitude of histories that may at first seem to have little or no relation to race, allowing race to remain just below the surface of analyses that remain ostensibly about something else. Race, as David L. Eng and Shinhee Han argue, is more "a verb than a noun": it exists as "a continuous modulating *relation* between object and subject."[15] American literature reflects what Eng and Han refer to as the dynamic movement between histories of race and other phenomena, and, for this reason, the presence of race in American literary texts often exists as a structuring presence that students and critics leave in the background. We can find a well-known example of how this works in Hortense J. Spillers's 1987 article, "Mama's Baby, Papa's Maybe: An American Grammar Book." There, Spillers outlines a rationale for understanding why discussions of gender will always also be discussions of race. As Spillers details, "gendering takes place within the confines of the domestic," which in the US has been constituted as an exclusive domain of white heterosexuality.[16] For those outside those confines, "gendering is a tale writ between the lines and in the not-quite spaces of American domesticity."[17] As Spillers so compellingly argues, then, gender does not merely intersect with race. It is a function of race.[18] To trace race in texts representing white American domesticity, from Louisa May Alcott's *Little Women* (1869) to Alice Walker's *The Color Purple* (1982), is to read racial content through the representation of gender roles, gendered spaces, and the home.

Such a pattern extends far beyond how texts represent gender or identity. Most (if not all) of the discussions in American literature classrooms, in student papers on American literature, and in professional Americanist criticism are *about race* even when race is never mentioned.[19] A paper on the American Dream in *The Great Gatsby* is about race. A paper on the nature writing of the 1960s is about race. A discussion of how recent US novels have represented climate change is about race. Essays on modernism, on Beat writing, on lyric poetry, on transcendentalism – all of these are about race. Too often, though, such discussions and papers, from the essays in first-year seminars to the publications in peer-reviewed journals, leave unspoken the racial content that, upon even brief examination, might be revealed as a crucial dimension within the essay's argument.

For readers of American literature, to correct the misapprehension of race is to approach texts with a degree of humility – to think of interpretation and analysis as modes of learning something new rather than exemplifying something already known. It is to identify and name whiteness and to unsettle what Grace Kyungwon Hong and Roderick A. Ferguson term the "received categories and modes of categorization" that make us think we already understand what race is and how it operates.[20] In this vein, Linda Martín Alcoff calls on us to "seek the operative meaning of identity terms, and not merely their conceptual or abstract meaning."[21] How do racial identities operate alongside one another? How do they operate when placed against characters' cultural settings? What histories do they evoke and require us to understand? The answers to these questions will sometimes come in the form of comparisons more complex than mere parallels. And they will require us to think outside of received schemes of racial classification, which frequently get taken to constitute a kind of "common sense" that gets taken for granted.

At the same time, to trace race is to trace racialization's only constant: its service on behalf of white supremacy and settler colonialism. As Adrienne Brown puts it: "Racial categorizations rely on processes of recognition historically rooted in feeling, genealogy, and visual perception that have allowed whiteness to be conferred upon some and figured as needing defense from the encroachments – spatial, sexual, social – of others."[22] Indeed, white supremacy and settler colonialism have been so successful precisely for their ability to reproduce themselves through endless adaptation and complexity. And so, as Sexton emphasizes, tracing race requires plural conceptualizations of racisms and racializations, accounting for unlikeness as least as much as for areas of overlap or similarity.

The rest of this chapter aims to provide readers of American literature with critical tools to trace race. Specifically, it suggests how the terms and methods developed in literary studies and the literature classroom – especially those pertaining to reading for genres and reading for tropes – can help readers perceive, historicize, and differentiate the presence of race in the texts we read. I've opted to emphasize genres and tropes for how they index larger systems of meaning. Both allow readers to track patterns of meaning within a single text and patterns of meaning binding texts into relationship. Both operate through repetition, tapping into the interplay between cultural representations and the reproduction of social structures. Both, when examined carefully, emerge as key devices through which race and racial meaning enter literary texts and through which literary texts, in turn, come to inform how their readers think about and perceive race.

Race and Genre

Critics have come to realize that genres constitute far more than classificatory schemes, and to see how inquiry into genres increases knowledge about race and racism. Genres shape our experiences with race, providing an interchange between aesthetic objects and social life. They present us with readymade ideas about how scenarios play out and what outcomes we can expect. The conventions of contemporary cop shows, to take one example, help inform our expectations not only about what we'll encounter when we turn on the latest episode of *Law & Order*, but also about what to expect during our encounters with the police. As Mark C. Jerng writes, "we *participate in genres* in order to form and organize our sense of the world."[23] Moreover, genres usher us into this sense of the world at the level of everyday experience. When we pay attention to texts' participation in genres, we pay attention to how literature participates in and enacts ordinariness. Doing this is key to the tracing of race because it's precisely in the register of the ordinary that we enact what Omi and Winant term "our ongoing interpretation of our experience in racial terms."[24] Moreover, because everydayness so often slips by unnoticed, it's precisely through ordinariness that so many tactics of white supremacy and resistance to white supremacy merge into the ambience of everyday life. Through attention to genre, we turn ordinariness into an object for inquiry and critique.

Texts connect to genres by incorporating conventions and thereby marking themselves as participants within a larger kinship of, say, romance novels or literary fiction. Readers interested in tracing race through genre need first to identify which patterns in the text link it into the wider relationship of genre. Doing so leads to a second step: asking how generic conventions in the text influence our perception of racial meaning. A third step involves making cultural speculations about what purpose that influence is serving and requires more explanation. We know that genres come and go. New genres emerge when they fulfill a function for their moment and their audience, and they fade once that function loses urgency. There are, as Bruce Robbins puts it, "social tasks that cause a genre to be seized on at a given moment."[25] Readers need to ask "Why *this* genre at *this* time?"

Often, after identifying those conventions through which the text participates in a specific genre, this third step – asking what function those conventions serve in any given moment – will enable an interpretation particularly telling about the salience of race.

Jerng's *Racial Worldmaking* provides a useful model for this sort of reading. The book traces several generic conventions in prominent storytelling from the twentieth century and demonstrates how such analysis can better reveal white supremacy's capacity to organize what we anticipate, experience, and perceive in our everyday lives. Arguing that we misread popular genres when we view them as derivative reinforcements of "already existing modes of racial discrimination," Jerng reveals genres to be interactive and constitutive. They shape how and when race becomes noticeable, a process Jerng calls "worldmaking." So, for example, future war stories such as H. G. Wells's *The War in the Air* (1908) and Jack London's "The Unparalleled Invasion" (1910), which use existing anti-Asian stereotypes to depict future global conflict as inevitable, impact readers "not solely through the representation of Asiatic persons but through convincing us that we live in a world in which the yellow peril is a present and future reality."[26]

Yet even as Jerng reveals genre to be white supremacy's able coconspirator for white-authored texts such as *Gone with the Wind*, he also suggests that the politics of race and genre cannot be determined in advance. The book shows as well how writers of color, including Frank Yerby and Samuel Delany, have taken up the conventions of popular genres to remake worlds, in part by rendering racial worldmaking newly visible. For example, Cherokee writer Daniel Heath Justice's epic fantasy novel, *The Way of Thorn and Thunder: The Kynship Chronicles* (2011), critiques its genre's tendency to present Indigenous people as a vanishing race while also using the conventions of fantasy fiction to provide readers with new models for kinship, reciprocity, and transforming a painful past into redemptive potential.[27] By studying race through genre, we can learn why certain stories emerge about racial histories, trace the presence of race within the phenomenology of everyday experience, and see how within literary texts various racial futures – those both resisting and reaffirming white supremacy – compete for readers' attention.

Race and Tropes

If genres enter social worlds by creating expectations for readers, regularizing everyday life into predictable patterns, tropes enter the world as peripatetic voyagers, traveling promiscuously across highbrow and lowbrow art, literary and nonliterary texts. An emphasis on genre underscores the conventionality of racial phenomena such as white supremacy. An emphasis on tropes underscores their ubiquity.

Yet for critics and students of American literature, it can be particularly vexing to identify and analyze tropes. This is in no small part because critics tend to use the term to refer to two overlapping yet distinct occurrences. On the one hand, critics influenced by cultural studies tend to think of tropes as common themes or figures recurring in the cultural imaginary. So, for example, David Ikard titles his 2017 book *Loveable Racists, Magical Negroes, and White Messiahs* after the three popular white supremacist tropes he examines. On the other hand, critics influenced more by formalist literary criticism and rhetorical analysis tend to think of tropes as instances where a shift in language transforms the meaning of a word or phrase. So, for example, Elda E. Tsou organizes her 2015 book, *Unquiet Tropes: Form, Race, and Asian American Literature*, around linguistic features such as apophasis (mentioning an issue by claiming you won't mention it). For our purposes, what these distinct uses of *trope* have in common is that both refer to identifiable aspects within the texts we study where racial phenomena can be tracked and analyzed.

The tropological analysis of racial themes and figures tends to work best with broader archives. Ikard's range is characteristically prodigious, shifting rapidly and productively from his own experiences to Solomon Northup's *Twelve Years a Slave* (both the 1853 text and the 2013 film) to Harriet Beecher Stowe's 1852 *Uncle Tom's Cabin* to Hollywood's 1999 Stephen King adaptation *The Green Mile* to white backlash over depictions of Black Jesus and Black Santa. This widespread attention allows Ikard to demonstrate the full breadth of his thesis that the "seemingly innocuous tropes" of white supremacy "not only perpetuate various forms of willful white blindness but also operate as real and symbolic currency in pushing the whitewashed cultural narratives of American exceptionalism, white redemption, self-determination, and racial inclusivity."[28] In "Gender, Ethno-Nationalism, and the Anti-Mexicanist Trope," anthropologist Alex E. Chávez similarly tracks one racial and racist trope across multiple cultural texts, aiming to show how racial nationalism depends on racial tropes. As he puts it, "the cultural work" of race and racialization works through "tropes, or figures of thought in social life, which bear the capacity to align subjectivities, space, and time to notions of assumed tradition or shared history."[29] Chávez tracks a racist trope of "the Mexican" as a criminal outsider as it appears in white American discourse, from Walt

Whitman's 1840s journalism to the political speech of Donald Trump. Such an analysis allows him to demonstrate both the durability and the ubiquity of anti-Mexican tropes transforming Mexican masculinity into "an exoticized poetics of fear and desire."[30] Arguably, the paradigmatic tactic of settler colonialism has been the transformation of North America's indigenous people into tropes: mascots, stock Hollywood figures (bloodthirsty warriors, stoic representatives of the past, and beautiful maidens eager for the embrace of their white lovers), and logos. As writer Tommy Orange observes in the prologue to his 2018 novel *There, There*, "Indians were removed then reduced to a feathered image."[31] From local media depictions of Black Santas to Walt Whitman's journalism to the caricatured mascots affixed to the walls of high school gyms, tracing race through thematic and figural tropes allows for wide-ranging analyses demonstrating just how ubiquitously racism and settler colonialism manifest in American cultural and literary texts.

A tropological approach more aligned with literary and rhetorical analysis asks how racialization and racism appear in figures of speech and patterns of language. Just as ubiquitous as their thematic variation, identification and analysis of rhetorical tropes allows readers of literature and other media to examine the nontransparency of language – the multiple meanings in which racial presence affects how things are said just as much as what things are said. One classic rhetorical trope of white supremacy, for example, is the euphemism, in which words and terms writers deem too off-putting for easily offended white audiences (say "racist" or "white supremacist") find themselves replaced with words and terms whites will find more palatable (say "racially charged," "racially motivated," or, cringiest of all, "racially tinged"). So common has this pattern been in recent years that in 2019 the AP Stylebook commonly used by journalists felt compelled to intervene with a statement that otherwise seems so grossly self-evident it should go without saying: "Do not use euphemisms for racist or racism when the latter terms are truly applicable. *Mississippi has a history of racist lynchings, not a history of racially motivated lynchings. He is charged in the racist massacre of nine people at a Black church, not the racially motivated massacre of nine people at a Black church*" (emphasis in original).[32] By apprehending these patterns in the use of language and asking what purpose they serve, we can better understand how white supremacy maintains its stranglehold over US life, continuing to shape how Americans understand and talk about their present-day realities.

Literary critics have devoted most of their energies not to the rhetorical tropes of white supremacy, but instead to how racialized and minoritized writers use patterns in language and speech to unsettle white supremacy. Doing so, they've tracked the power of language to reveal and unsettle dominant worldviews. Elda Tsou's *Unquiet Tropes* provides a powerful model. In it, she argues for "reconceptualizing Asian American literature as a set of rhetorical tropes taking shape around highly specific historical problematics."[33] This allows her to trace racial themes and meanings beyond what she calls the "referential representation" of more explicitly racialized content.[34] In one chapter, for instance, Tsou examines the prominence of apophasis within Maxine Hong Kingston's 1980 short-story cycle, *China Man*. By repeatedly leaving aspects of her narrative unspoken – for instance refusing to assign a racial identity to key characters – Kingston represents Asian American experience and history while simultaneously making that representation trickier and less immediately legible than it at first appears. Such apophasis allows Kingston to replicate in the form of her prose the strategies that the Chinese Exclusion Laws enacted in law. Put into place from the late nineteenth through the mid-twentieth centuries, these laws operated through their own apophasis in which Chinese people were legally recognized only in the naming of their exclusion from US immigration or citizenship policies.[35] By tracking the trope of apophasis in Kingston's text, Tsou reveals how we might trace racial content past racial references and into the figures of speech and errant turns in language that render literary representations thick with meaning.

The most well-known example of this kind of a tropological reading practice, one invested in antiracist interpretive strategies, comes in Henry Louis Gates's 1989 monograph, *The Signifying Monkey: A Theory of African-American Literary Criticism*. "Signifyin(g)," Gates argues, "is the black trope of tropes," a practice of "repetition and revision" and "black double voicedness" that allows expression in a language that has been "decolonized" and divested of its capacity to enact or reproduce white supremacy.[36] Gates's primary example is the Monkey, a trickster character found in Black storytelling traditions whose doubled use of language enables him to convince his powerful rival, the Lion, to take his figurative speech literally and thereby misread his intended meaning. For our purposes – for the purposes of learning how to read and interpret race – what most matters here is that the ability to understand signifyin(g) texts turns on our capacity to identify the strategies they engage to double their meaning. By doing so, we can achieve what Gates calls "mastery of reading," tracking both layers (what the Monkey intends and what the Lion understands) simultaneously and locating the strategies – "including metaphor, metonymy, synecdoche, and irony" – through which meaning has been doubled.[37] Failure to achieve such mastery can lead to grotesque misunderstandings. Without seeing its double voicedness, for instance, readers interpret Phillis Wheatley's 1773 "On Being Brought from Africa to America" as a poem of gratitude for the transatlantic slave trade rather than what it really is: a complex and thorough critique of the entire system of chattel slavery, the plantation economy, and white cruelty. Like Tsou, Gates insists on valuing minoritized and racialized writers not only for what has come to be called "representation," but just as much for their use of literary form to unsettle dominant worldviews and propose alternatives.

Conclusion

I suggested at the outset of this chapter that we should be cautious about the extent to which reading and interpreting literature advances antiracism and decolonization. And, indeed, change requires far more than reading, researching, studying, and discussing literature. Yet literature still has a vital role to play. Interpretation of race, racism, and racialization in American literary texts serves as one of the best possible ways, first, to critique the present, coming to know it more fully, and second, to use that knowledge in order to undo systems of oppression and forge new worlds based on principles of real justice. Speaking to a Kalamazoo College audience in 1960, James Baldwin described such work as the first step in any antiracist, decolonial politics: "before we can do very much in the way of clear thinking or clear doing as relates to the minorities in this country, we must first crack the American image and find out and deal with what it hides."[38] The work I've described in this chapter is twofold: first, identifying and undoing the misunderstandings that prevent the tracing of race in American literary texts, and, second, finding strategies successfully to perform such interpretation. While on its own this work won't make a substantive difference, it's precisely through it that we can reckon with what America hides, crack its façade, and teach ourselves and each other how to do the clear thinking and clear doing Baldwin describes.

Notes

For their invaluable suggestions on this piece, I am indebted to this volume's editor, John Ernest; to my writing group: Angie Calcaterra, Greta LaFleur, Caroline Wigginton, Michele Currie Navakas, Wendy Roberts, and Abram Van Engen; and to my Villanova colleagues Yumi Lee and Kimberly Takahata.

1. Charles W. Mills, *The Racial Contract* (Ithaca: Cornell University Press, 1997), 19 (emphasis in original).
2. Toni Morrison, *Playing in the Dark: Whiteness and the Literary Imagination* (New York: Vintage Books, 1993), 46–47.
3. Christine Okoth, "The Black Body and the Reading of Race," in *The Cambridge Companion to American Literature and the Body*, ed. Travis M. Foster (New York: Cambridge University Press, 2022), 227–228.
4. See Richard Dyer, *White: Essays on Race and Culture* (New York: Routledge, 1997). My emphasis here follows from critical race frameworks of whiteness such as Dyer's while differing from that in the field of "whiteness studies" that became prominent 1990s. Texts like Noel Ignatiev's *How the Irish Became White* and Theodore Allen's *The Invention of the White Race* focus primarily on the social construction of whiteness: – how certain groups, such as the Irish or Jews, came to see themselves and be seen by others as white, thereby securing a place atop the racial hierarchy. My emphasis aligns more with work in critical race studies, which instead tends to conceptualize whiteness as a key mechanism in structures of domination and privilege anchored by the legacies of enslavement and dispossession. So, for example, within the framing of this latter scholarship, it is of course still accurate to say that European immigrants were assimilated into whiteness, but we get closer to the underlying nature of the process when we observe, as does Morrison in *Playing in the Dark*, that European immigrants came to understand "their 'Americanness' as an opposition to the resident black population" (47).
5. On the importance of avoiding interpretive methodologies that replicate forms of racial violence, see Katherine McKittrick, "On Plantations, Prisons, and a Black Sense of Place," 12 *Social and Cultural Geography* (2011): 947–963; and Peter James Hudson and Katherine McKittrick, "The Geographies of Blackness and Anti-Blackness: An Interview with Katherine McKittrick," 20 *The CLR James Journal* (2014): 233–240.
6. Michel-Rolph Trouillot, *Silencing the Past: Power and the Production of History* (Boston: Beacon Press, 1995), 82.
7. Ibid., 82–83.
8. On the exceptional nature of antiblackness, see Saidiya Hartman, *Lose Your Mother: A Journey Along the Atlantic Slave Route* (New York: Farrar, Straus, and Giroux, 2007); and Christina Sharpe, *In the Wake: On Blackness and Being* (Durham: Duke University Press, 2016).
9. Jared Yates Sexton, *Amalgamation Schemes: Antiblackness and the Critique of Multiculturalism* (Minneapolis: University of Minnesota Press, 2008), 245.
10. Ruth Wilson Gilmore, *Golden Gulag: Prisons, Surplus, Crisis, and Opposition in Globalizing California* (Berkeley: University of California Press, 2007), 28.
11. Michael Omi and Howard Winant, *Racial Formation in the United States from the 1960s to the 1990s*, 2nd ed. (New York: Routledge, 1994), 56, 61.
12. Katy L. Chiles, *Transformable Race: Surprising Metamorphoses in the Literature of Early America* (New York: Oxford University Press, 2014), 2. See also Roxann Wheeler, *The Complexion of Race: Categories of Difference in*

Eighteenth-Century British Culture (Philadelphia: University of Pennsylvania Press, 2000).

13. Jerrold M. Packard, *American Nightmare: The History of Jim Crow* (New York: Macmillan, 2003), 98–99. See also Adrienne Brown, *The Black Skyscraper: Architecture and the Perception of Race* (Baltimore: Johns Hopkins Press, 2018), 17–20.
14. Casey Ryan Kelly, "Blood-Speak: Ward Churchill and the Racialization of American Indian Identity," 8 *Communication and Critical/Cultural Studies* (2011): 244. See also Kimberly TallBear, *Native American DNA: Tribal Belonging and the False Promise of Genetic Science* (Minneapolis: University of Minnesota Press, 2013); Kimberly Tallbear, "DNA, Blood, and Racializing the Tribe," 18 *Wicazo Sa Review* (2003): 81–107; and Desi Rodriguez-Lonebear, "The Blood Line: Racialized Boundary Making and Citizenship among Native Nations," 7 *Sociology of Race and Ethnicity* (2021): 1–16.
15. David L. Eng and Shinhee Han, *Racial Melancholia, Racial Dissociation: On the Social and Psychic Lives of Asian Americans* (Durham: Duke University Press, 2018), 12 (emphasis in original).
16. Hortense J. Spillers, "Mama's Baby, Papa's Maybe: An American Grammar Book" 17 *Diacritics* (1987): 72. See also C. Riley Snorton : *Black on Both Sides: A Racial History of Trans Identity* (Minneapolis: University of Minnesota Press, 2017); and Kyla Schuller, *Biopolitics of Feeling: Race, Sex, and Science in the Nineteenth Century* (Durham: Duke University Press, 2018).
17. Ibid., 77.
18. Ibid., 77 (emphasis in original).
19. For a useful analysis of how "aboutness" shapes thinking about race, see Kandice Chuh, "It's Not about Anything," 32 *Social Text* (2014): 125–134.
20. Grace Kyungwon Hong and Roderick A. Ferguson, eds., *Strange Affinities: The Gender and Sexual Politics of Comparative Racialization* (Durham: Duke University Press, 2011), 18.
21. Linda Martín Alcoff, "Comparative Race, Comparative Racisms," in *Race or Ethnicity?: On Black and Latino Identity*, ed. Jorge J. E. Gracia (Ithaca: Cornell University Press, 2007), 177.
22. Brown, *Black Skyscraper*, 21.
23. Mark C. Jerng, *Racial Worldmaking: The Power of Popular Fiction* (New York: Fordham University Press, 2018), 9 (emphasis in original). See also Virginia Jackson, "The Function of Criticism at the Present Time," *Los Angeles Review of Books* (April 12, 2015); Lauren Berlant, *The Female Complaint: The Unfinished Business of Sentimentality in American Culture* (Durham: Duke University Press, 2008), 4; Lauren Berlant, *Cruel Optimism* (Durham: Duke University Press, 2011), esp. pp. 6–9; and Travis M. Foster, *Genre and White Supremacy in the Postemancipation United States* (New York: Oxford University Press, 2019), 14–17.
24. Omi and Winant, *Racial Formation*, 60.
25. Bruce Robbins, "Afterword," 122 *PMLA* (2007): 1650.
26. Jerng, *Racial Worldmaking*, 67.

27. See Kathleen Washburn, "Review of *The Way of Thorn and Thunder: The Kynship Chronicles*," 37 *The American Indian Quarterly* (2013): 400–403.
28. David Ikard *Loveable Racists, Magical Negroes, and White Messiahs* (Chicago: University of Chicago Press, 2017), 19, 9.
29. Alex E. Chávez, "Gender, Ethno-Nationalism, and the Anti-Mexicanist Trope," 134 *Journal of American Folklore* (2021): 4.
30. Ibid., 10.
31. Tommy Orange, *There* (New York: Vintage, 2018), 7.
32. "Race-Related Coverage," in *AP Stylebook* (entry updated and expanded April 2, 2022). www-apstylebook-com.ezp1.villanova.edu/villanova_edu/ap_stylebook/race-related-coverage. See also Doris Truong, "AP Stylebook Update: It's OK to Call Something Racist When It's Racist," Poynter, March 29, 2019: www.poynter.org/reporting-editing/2019/ap-stylebook-update-its-ok-to-call-something-racist-when-its-racist/.
33. Elda E. Tsou, *Unquiet Tropes: Form, Race, and Asian American Literature* (Philadelphia: Temple University Press, 2015), 5.
34. Ibid., 70, 99.
35. Ibid., 97.
36. Henry Louis Gates, *The Signifying Monkey: A Theory of Afro-American Literary Criticism (Twenty-Fifth Anniversary Edition)* (New York: Oxford University Press, 2014), 56–57, 56, 55.
37. Ibid., 84, 57.
38. James Baldwin, "In Search of a Majority: An Address," in *Nobody Knows My Name: More Notes of a Native Son* (New York: Dell Publishing, 1962), 132.

CHAPTER 2

Racial Management and Technologies of Care

Malini Johar Schueller

In June 2020, three weeks after the murder of George Floyd by the Minneapolis police department, Kennedy Mitchum, a young African American college graduate, wrote to the editors of the Merriam-Webster dictionary requesting changes in their definition of racism. Mitchum was frustrated by Webster's entry, which defined racism primarily as a belief in the inherent superiority of a particular race without adequate attention to racialized power structures. The editors concurred with Mitchum and revised the entry to reflect the convergence of racial prejudice with "social and institutional oppression."[1] Columnist Leonard Pitts similarly described racism not as "a loathsome character defect" but rather "the water in which we swim."[2] Mitchum and Pitts both emphasized racism as a structure than an individual affect. Racism informs the economic, social, cultural, and political structures through which we live and is therefore the water in which we swim. Thus, while the category of race is scientifically specious, its deployment in managing the lives of populations through policies, and its workings in everyday life, have had profound consequences. Race is not simply a social construct; it is a power construct.[3]

In the USA, forms of racial control have been pivotal in preserving the sociopolitical order. What Achille Mbembe has argued about late-modern colonial occupation combining disciplinary, biopolitical, and necropolitical power[4] is particularly applicable to the USA's racial management of its population within both the nation and its colonies, territories, and areas of occupation. However, while disciplinary and necropolitical technologies like the carceral system have received attention – most brilliantly in Michelle Alexander's *The New Jim Crow* – less attention has been paid to pervasive biopolitical technologies of governmentality, such as surveys of populations and their habits, and management of welfare through policies of health and schooling, all of which have been important forms of racial control. Michel Foucault sees governmentality as a complex form of power "which has as its target population, as its principal form of knowledge

Figure 2.1 Uncle Sam (to his new class in Civilization): Now, children, you've got to learn these lessons whether you want to or not! But just take a look at the class ahead of you, and remember that, in a little while, you will feel as glad to be here as they are! Illus. from Puck, v. 44, no. 1142, (1899 January 25), centerfold. © Keppler & Schwarzmann, 1899.

political economy, and as its essential technical means apparatuses of security."[5] Exercised at the level of population, governmentality, unlike disciplinary power, works through mechanisms that provide populations with the structures they require in order to live, to feel secure about their lives, and to reproduce their social conditions.

Control of racialized populations through governmentality was particularly apt for the post-Reconstruction USA because these means could be seen as (and often were) productive for racialized populations. The late nineteenth and the early twentieth centuries are therefore particularly important in analyzing the tactics of racial governmentality and their continuance. As the USA moved from a settler colonial and slave-owning nation to a settler colonial and imperial nation of overseas colonies, a politics of violence was followed by a pedagogy of recovery through different benevolent technologies of welfare such as childrearing, education, and health. In this chapter I will focus on health and education and show how these became mobile sites through which the lives of racialized populations could be "improved" as they learned the values of Protestant Christianity, capitalist meritocratic equality, the work ethic, self-reliance, and individualism. Although the specific ways in which these technologies worked varied according to the particular racial group, these strategies were pervasively deployed in the name of the savior nation.

Education

By far the most ubiquitous strategies for racial management have involved education. Louis Dalrymple's 1899 cartoon forcefully dramatizes education's role in containing and ruling its racial others. The cartoon depicts a threatening Uncle Sam as teacher, ready with a cane to discipline his "students" from newly acquired territories. The lesson presented to the sulking students from the Philippines, Hawai'i, Puerto Rico and Cuba is clear: they will be tutored (governed) by the US. Students from the new states of Texas, California, Alaska, New Mexico, and Arizona, respectably dressed and earnestly learning, have integrated into the nation and Uncle Sam intimates that those from overseas territories could be similarly integrated. The Native American in the corner, marked by feathers and a blanket, reading a book he holds upside down suggests his special position in, yet apart from, the national body and the futility of book-learning for him. The African American is in the classroom but in a position of servitude, doing menial labor to which he is more suited. Finally, the pigtailed Chinese, book in hand, stands outside the classroom suggesting that the nation is not quite ready to absorb him.

Louis Althusser famously argued that schooling was an ideological state apparatus drumming the ruling ideology into children and finally ejecting them into production to occupy their roles in class society.[6] But in the USA schooling was more importantly designed for children to take their roles in raced society. In the antebellum South the proscription of education was deemed essential to the maintenance of slavery. The brief period of Reconstruction saw a flourishing of Black education but also the burning of Black schoolhouses and intimidatory tactics dissuading Blacks from pursuing education.[7] As Ronald E. Butchart states, by the end of the nineteenth century, "a triumphalist white supremacy reunited the North and South. Thereafter, the northern and southern white elite began to work together to shape black education to serve their ends."[8]

Although there were different types of schools for Blacks post-Reconstruction, educational establishments remained segregated and often capitulated to ideologies of the racial status quo by promoting industrial education over higher learning. The Hampton Institute, founded by the American Missionary Association, was first led by Samuel Chapman Armstrong, whose mission was to school African Americans "not only in book knowledge, but in practical industry ... not for an ideal future, but for the real life before them."[9] Arguably, it was his success in distinguishing Hampton from academic schools that made it palatable to Southern whites and Northern philanthropists. Hampton alumnus Booker T. Washington continued stressing vocational training when hired as principal of Tuskegee in 1881.

While schooling for Blacks worked to maintain their separation from other races (Hampton had started admitting Native Americans but stopped because of objections to racial intermixing with Blacks), schooling for Native Americans was directed at cultural transfiguration and assimilation. Shortly after the 1871 Congressional Act deeming Native Americans wards of the USA, reformers began discussing education and congress allocated funds. Ignoring indigenous diversity, reformers lumped Indians into one category and sought to transform them from savages to civilized beings.[10] David Wallace Adams has deemed the project of education an education for extinction. White observers saw Indians as "savages because they lacked the very thing whites possessed – civilization. And since ... civilized ways were destined to triumph over savagism, Indians would ultimately confront a fateful choice: civilization or extinction."[11] It was a method of "saving Indians by destroying them."[12]

But while paternalistic and racist, Indian education also reflected the faith of reformers that Native Americans could actually learn and advance if they underwent complete cultural change. Thus, boarding schools which separated children from their tribes were promoted both in and off reservations. Such an education was not mandated by law but rather presented as a form of care – a classic form of colonial governmentality. Indeed, writer Zitkála-Šá, who would go on to teach at Carlisle, wrote about her mother's decision to send her to a boarding school as one premised on the idea of education as reparation: "The palefaces, who owe us a large debt for stolen lands, have begun to pay a tardy justice in offering some education to our children . . . Go tell them [the missionaries] that they may take my little daughter, and that the Great Spirit shall not fail to reward them."[13]

The nexus between the violence of removal and the civilizational mission of education was made clear in the work of Richard Henry Pratt, the founder of Carlisle boarding school, who began teaching prisoners of war under his command at Fort Marion, St Augustine, Florida, and tellingly titled his memoir *Battlefield and Classroom*. In boarding schools, the process of cultural conversion was absolute: children were given haircuts, dressed in Western clothes, assigned European names, taught English and forbidden to speak in other languages or perform tribal rituals. "Before" and "after" student photographs demonstrated to the public the assimilation of Indians into white America. Although many students formed affectionate bonds with teachers, they also resisted deculturation by running away and defying their teachers. As David Wallace Adams puts it, children recognized "white education for what it was: an invitation to cultural suicide."[14] And like Hampton and Tuskegee, schools emphasized physical labor: students spent half the time learning practical skills. These boarding schools continued to operate till the 1970s, when activism led to their closure.

By the time of the US colonization of the Philippines in 1898, educational efforts on behalf of Indians were seen as evidence of the successful "saving" of an erstwhile warlike, savage culture doomed to perish. Ann Paulet argues that the treatment of Indians rather than Blacks provided a model for the nation's future dealings with the Philippines because laws regarding Blacks were sectional rather than federal; Indians were not citizens but "wards"; Indians had wars waged against them; and Blacks were already "Americanized" through years of slavery.[15] However, schooling in the Philippines was far more imbricated in violence, and educators drew on both Native American and Black examples. American soldiers opened the first school in Corregidor in 1898 and the Department of Public Instruction which stipulated English as the language of instruction was established under the army. In 1901 the *USA Transport Thomas* brought 500 American teachers to the Philippines and another 600 next later. All this happened while the USA engaged in a bloody war with Filipinos who had proclaimed independence in 1898 and formed the Philippine Republic in 1899, a war in which anywhere from 250,000 to a million Filipino lives were lost. Trying to subdue an intransigent rebellion, military governor General MacArthur wrote, "I know nothing . . . that can contribute more in behalf of pacification than the immediate institution of a comprehensive system of education . . . the matter is so closely allied with the exercise of military force in these islands that . . . [I] suggested a rapid expansion of educational facilities as an exclusively military measure."[16]

The teachers (called Thomasites) recognized their role as the new soldiers of empire, but significantly as carrying out the task of sentimental imperialism. Thomasite Adeline Knapp wrote of the "educational army," which would soon be "scattered over the insular field, fighting each his battle . . . Each member of the new army must carry into his work in the wilderness, the spirit of love."[17] Managing Filipinos through education marks what Laura Wexler has called the "tender violence" of US imperialism, a term coined by General Armstrong, the founder of Hampton, as a descriptor of the spirit of tutelage to educate ex-slaves and Indians.[18] Wondering how to manage a racially different, backward population, educators of Filipinos turned to Black and Indian examples. Thus Fred Atkinson, the first General Superintendent of Public Instruction, visited Carlisle, Hampton, and Tuskegee before leaving for the Philippines. Atkinson wrote to Booker T. Washington for advice and argued for agricultural schools because Filipinos needed to be taught "those things for which they have a capacity, i.e., industrial and mechanical pursuits."[19] Not surprisingly, when in 1901 Estelle Reel developed the Uniform Course of Study for Indian schools, 6,000 copies were sent to Puerto Rico and the Philippines.[20]

Educational techniques in the Philippines included the imposition of English, a standard curriculum with hagiographies of American presidents (and of Filipinos such as Jose Rizal, who had fought for Philippine independence but from the Spanish), and abundant use of the American flag. Classrooms were decorated with portraits of Washington, Lincoln, Magellan, Columbus, and Rizal. School holidays celebrated not only American social and political culture but also colonization. Included among the holidays were Independence Day on July 4th; Thanksgiving; Washington's birthday; and Occupation Day on August 13th, marking the American occupation of Manila.[21]

As subjects of the USA, Filipinos were schooled to aspire to American democracy, liberty, and equality, but on a personal rather than a sociopolitical level. They were to believe that as "little brown brothers" these rights were best available to them through American rule. In a 1906 article titled "The Kindergarten as an Americanizing Influence," the author Austin Craig recounted this episode: "A visitor to our provincial capital school the other day asked of one of the pupils, 'Why do you come to school?' The answer was: 'To learn.' 'To learn what?' 'To learn American ways.' 'And why do you want to learn American ways?' 'Because they are the best ways.'"[22] Such displays of deference to the USA, while initially encouraged as a means for quelling opposition, became part of the school culture of the Philippines and a salient feature of historical memory.

Education was also seen as a means of inculcating capitalist individualism. The landmark 1925 Survey of the Educational System of the Philippine Islands, while severely critical of schools, was clear about the importance of disseminating capitalist values. It contrasted family and community as loci of value for Filipinos with the valorizing of individualism in the West and saw a major objective of American education as being to teach Filipinos to change social organizations based on "community possessions and customs" to the "complex" and highly individualized Western culture. The absence of a fully developed sense of property rights was responsible, it was felt, for the "too common trait of dishonesty among the school pupils."[23] A clearer statement about the role of schooling in managing a people through a normalization of property as central to character can hardly be found.

The schooling practices of Blacks, Native Americans, and Filipinos are representative examples of the biopolitical managing of racialized and colonized populations. Overseas, this biopolitical technology has been exercised in diverse ways to buttress and consolidate US imperialism: in Hawai'i, Puerto Rico, Haiti, Cuba, the Dominican Republic, South Korea, and arguably now in Afghanistan and Iraq. Indeed, military personnel are well versed in theories of hegemony and continue to look at schooling in the Philippines as an exemplary instance of counterinsurgency that should be followed today.[24]

Health

Nowhere is the salubrious management of populations more evident than in the fields of public health, where doctors, health workers, and sanitation experts worked in tandem with missionaries, teachers, and administrators to improve the lives of colonized and racialized peoples. Indeed, as medical historians have suggested, in colonial medicine natives were not persons, but simply populations to be observed, studied, and treated.[25] Imperial hygiene viewed the habits of nonwhite subjects as contributing to contagions that menaced Anglo-American civilization.[26] Nineteenth-century tropical medicine had used climatology to argue that the white man's burden could become the "white man's grave" due to the "burning heat, fever-laden swamps, [and] swarming insects."[27] But by the early twentieth century germ theory had changed explanations of disease from climate to microbes carried by natives. The observation and surveillance of native bodies thus became central to colonialism, while simultaneously their well-being was part of the colonial burden. The native was both contaminant and reformable but always different from the white colonizer. Colonial medical practices reified these distinctions.

Reynaldo C. Ileto writes that in the Philippines the "conquering soldier" soon transformed into the "crusading sanitary inspector."[28] This move from sovereignty to governmentality via health was linked with the project of education: schoolteachers often doubled as sanitary inspectors. For instance, H. C. Theobold's *The Filipino Teacher's Manual*, a teacher-training text used by the Board of Education, points to the intimacy between school-teaching and health-teaching. Teachers are instructed to visit students' homes to ensure that children are being adequately fed and housed, to inspect homes for adequate sanitation and cleanliness, and to examine parents for signs of disease. Furthermore, teachers are advised to inform Filipinos about the dangers of a diet of rice and fish and instruct them about healthy American-style diets of vegetables, meat, and bread.[29] Lamenting the Filipino practice of inculcating adult behavior too young, Theobold urged teachers to delay play and physical activities and to advise parents against the habit of introducing infants to a variety of foods too early.[30] Filipino women were warned against indulging their children by rocking and picking them up when they cried, or to sleep with a child because that is what cattle did, and were advised not to engage in promiscuous kissing.[31] Thus, the promotion of healthy practices involved what Ann Laura Stoler has called a "politics of intimacy . . . where colonial regimes of truth were imposed, worked around, and worked out."[32]

Because Filipinos were seen as purveyors of disease threatening white Americans, discourses of health emphasized distinctions between clean and unclean bodies, hygienic and unhygienic behaviors, and, ultimately, moral and immoral lifestyles. For Victor Heiser, commissioner of health, the filthy, disease-ridden Filipino, a threat to the "Occidental," required the use of "sanitary-squads" to inspect the homes of natives.[33] But hygiene reform was also a civilizing process. For instance, a Bureau of Health update on water closets in Manila stated firmly that each public closet was under the direction of a caretaker who "enforces a set of regulations which prohibit any misuse of closets . . . standing on the seats is prohibited, and the prohibition is strictly enforced."[34] Thus, concludes Warwick Anderson, "Racial type was manifested in bodily function and pathological potential, on which medicos put a gloss of civilizational status. If they wanted recognition from the public health department, Filipinos were expected to confess their uncleanliness . . . and to make themselves available for hygienic salvation."[35] The Philippines became a laboratory of hygienic modernity wherein Filipinos, triaged as "infantile, immature subjects, unready yet for self-government,' were subject to "medico-moral uplift."[36]

Health practices in the Philippines might be taken as modular for other US colonized and racialized groups, but with differences arising due to strategic needs. Strikingly similar discourses of contagion, paternalism, and racial difference marked the health policies in Guam, where the US Navy controlled the island from 1898 till 1941 when the Japanese came. Guam's first naval governor, Captain Richard Leary, saw the US Navy as "champions in succoring the needy, aiding the distressed and protecting the honor and virtue of women."[37] Chamorros were interpellated as a pathetic people in need of US support, and the name "Department of Health and Charities" conveyed the idea of Chamorros as "beneficiaries of American colonial philanthropy."[38]

Chamorro bodies were also seen as vehicles of contagion and their salubrious health a necessity for the colonial project which targeted Chamorro lifestyles and maintained a clear separation between medical treatment of Americans and Chamorros. Colonial racial difference demarcated who would be treated as populations (natives) and who as individuals (American soldiers). This demarcation was easy in Guam, where colonizers were not present in large numbers. Thus, in the treatment of hookworm, soldiers were treated only if diagnosed with the parasite, whereas Chamorro schoolchildren were subject to annual treatment without diagnosis.[39] Similarly, during the Allied occupation of Japan, which was, for all intents and purposes, a US occupation,[40] Japanese school children were routinely sprayed with DDT. Japanese recall being taught lessons about communicable diseases and singing the DDT song on the day of spraying.[41] However, DDT was not recommended for human application in the USA, and studies in 1945 pointed out potential health hazards.[42]

Perhaps no disease marked native difference in two US colonies – Guam and Hawai'i – as did Hansen's disease or leprosy. Although leprosy is among the least contagious of diseases, requiring two distinct genetic markers and prolonged contact, Western belief in leprosy as a contagious disease was prevalent till the 1860s. Only in 1867 was a major British scientific study published proving that the disease was hereditary and isolation unnecessary.[43] The point, though, is not whether Americans were acting upon known scientific information but rather how the disease was racially marked and changed native perceptions of the disease and community. In Hawai'i, although the disease had been present from the time of Western contact, it was only in the 1860s, with the involvement of American advisors, that "leprosy became essentially a criminal act which could result in . . . permanent exile or incarceration."[44] Treated more like inmates than patients, the deviant, disease-ridden bodies of Chamorros and Hawaiians were virtually imprisoned in isolation. In Hawai'i, the facility for isolated patients in Kalaupapa, Molokai, was cut off from the rest of the island by steep cliffs, and people described it as a "living tomb."[45] In Guam, patients were isolated in a compound enclosed by barbed wire, housed in rooms with bars on windows, and locked by a supervisor to prevent escape.[46] In the long run, this racialized treatment affected native cultural practices, demonstrating that American colonialism had changed native epistemologies. As Anne Hattori demonstrates, Chamorros had viewed leprosy patients as those who needed comfort and care, as signified by the term for the disease – *atektok* – which translates as "to hug each other." A decade into American rule, Chamarros associated the disease with *mamahlao* or "shame."[47]

Just as Filipinos, Chamorros, and Hawaiians were educated on health measures so that they would not endanger white Americans, treaty agreements with Indian tribes often provided health services in exchange for land and agreements to remain on reservations.[48] By the early twentieth century, the reservation system became a site for the surveillance and scrutiny of a population that was seen as declining and in need of intervention. Nowhere was this scrutiny more apparent than in the concern for infant mortality. Brianna Theobald notes the contrast between Europe, where public health officials measured infant mortality by socioeconomic position, and the USA, where it was measured according to race. "As a result," she argues, "mortality rates functioned to buttress and reify racial stereotypes."[49] Thus, birthing methods, childrearing practices, and maternal and infant care, all of which were tied to cultural behaviors, could be subject to scientific inquiry, critique, and well-intentioned calls for change in the name of infant health. Ultimately, these changes would further the settler colonial project of cultural extinction by assimilating Native Americans to the norms of white America. For instance, during the Office of Affairs' (OIA) Save the Babies campaign of 1912–18, field matrons visited childbearing women, instructing them on scientific motherhood; Native American women were discouraged from putting children in cradleboards which were referred to as tight containers; they were to display more concern for their children by caring for them exclusively instead of allowing tribe members to look after them; and they were to consult physicians rather than Native healers or female elders.[50] Similarly, in Guam the practice of burying the child's umbilical cord under the house to prevent the child from straying too far was seen as evidence of backward superstition.

Post-Reconstruction care of Blacks, on the other hand, followed the principles of Jim Crow. Although Blacks, like Filipinos and Chamorros, were seen as sources of contagion, it was felt that they would be best served by their own race. The highly influential Flexner report of 1910 stated that Blacks doctors should serve Blacks alone, and that Black patients could contaminate white doctors. Further, it warned that an "untrained negro wearing an MD degree is dangerous."[51] On the basis of the report, the number of Black medical schools decreased from seven to two. As with Filipinos, Chamorros, and Hawaiians, Black health was considered important more because it could imperil the health of whites than for the health of Blacks. However, unlike other racial minorities, the impetus to maintain racial separation, even if it meant a degree of healthcare provided by Blacks, was paramount. In his 1920s novel *Dark Princess*, W. E. B. Du Bois documents this racism through Matthew Townsend, a brilliant doctor rejected by the white medical profession.

I have focused on education and health as technologies of racial governmentality rather than on overt dominance such as Jim Crow laws, the sterilization of Native American women, the Tuskegee syphilis experiments, or the unauthorized use of Blacks for research because the rhetoric of American imperialism and multiculturalism has drawn upon these technologies of care as evidence of the nation's exceptionalism in caring for its Others. Such exceptionalist rhetoric emerged particularly in 1898 when arguments about the benevolence of taking over territories were made both to differentiate the nation from European colonial powers and to mollify anti-imperialists. But these technologies of care reveal how both settler and extractive colonial projects were threatened by racial–cultural differences which had to be managed by translating them into the lexicon of Anglo-American racial intelligibility.

By the mid-twentieth century anticolonial movements were strong, and the USA's moral authority was being challenged by countries which pointed to de jure racism as evidence of the unsuitability of the USA as hegemon. In this scenario, the nation's ability to demonstrate its smooth and democratic absorption of nonwhite racial groups was important. The technologies of care used in the US occupation of Japan during its reverse course phase (1948–52) illustrate how racial–cultural differences could be refashioned in order to uphold the racial order of post–World War II USA. Early in the occupation, the Japanese, despite their technological modernity, were Orientalized as inherently conformist, bound to outdated familial ties, obsequious, and feudalist. Their re-education involved not simply teaching them the dangers of militarism and ultranationalism, but civilizing them. As Douglas MacArthur stated, "Supposedly, the Japanese were a twentieth-century civilization. In reality, they were more nearly a feudal society, of the type discarded by Western nations some four centuries ago."[52] However, during the reverse course of occupation, when the Japanese had accepted defeat and were compliant with US authorities, they began to be viewed as potential partners in a hegemonic alliance and the racialization correspondingly shifted; the status of Japanese was upgraded to that of "honorary whites and an ally."[53]

Brides Schools for wives of American GIs in Japan, run by the American Red Cross at the behest of the government, are perfect examples of how a technology of care functioned to create subjects that would demonstrate American racial democracy. Topics taught ranged from US culture, history, religion, cooking, social life, and fashion to instructions on hygiene, child care, and travel. The end of each session was marked by a formal ceremony, and the "schooling" of these wives was filmed by the Department of Defense as well as by broadcasting networks, to be shown in propaganda movies which proclaimed the suitability of these wives for America. The wives were seen as racially assimilable beings who could be brought into the orbit of American discursive legibility. Women were urged to use their "Japanese womanly qualities of gentleness, patience, [and] thoughtfulness" for their husband's comfort and to maintain "respect for him as the head of [their] little household."[54] Thus, Japanese cultural traits could harmonize with and bolster the image of the ideal family of 1950s' America. In addition, brides also functioned as model minority subjects constructed out of stereotypes of Japanese culture: negatively stereotyped as lacking spontaneity and being fatalistic and imperturbable, and positively as methodical, courteous, respectful of authority, and with a penchant for "ignoring the unpleasant."[55] Both stereotypes were used to create the ideal subject of Cold War capitalist America: the model minority subject who didn't question her racialized position and would become an invisible minority in a racially charged America seeking to suppress Black unrest.[56]

While control of the United States' racialized and colonized populations is not limited to biopolitical projects of health and education, such ventures illuminate the extent to which race has been central not only to punitive, racist institutions or segregationist practices such as redlining, but also to the seemingly unraced policies of care. Toni Morrison brilliantly stages the trauma of epistemicide through schooling via the character Schoolteacher in *Beloved*. In this powerful novel about memory and slavery, Morrison depicts Sethe, the central character who has fled from slavery at Sweet Home Plantation in Kentucky to her mother-in-law's home in Cincinnati, as haunted by Beloved, the ghost of the baby girl she killed while escaping in order to save her from being enslaved. But the key figure who clinches Sethe's determination to leave is the character known only as "Schoolteacher" who runs the plantation. For Schoolteacher, Sethe is not only a racially abject being to be punished but an object to be studied and a source of "knowledge." Morrison makes clear that Sethe's decision to flee comes when she hears Schoolteacher tell his nephews to meticulously note down her human and animal characteristics after she is whipped.[57] As Paul D ruminates about Miss Bodwin, a schoolteacher sympathetic to Sethe's daughter: "Watch out. Watch out. Nothing in the world more dangerous than a white schoolteacher."[58]

Notes

1. www.nytimes.com/2020/06/10/us/merriam-webster-racism-definition.html.
2. www.sltrib.com/opinion/commentary/2020/06/13/leonard-pitts-dont-say-i/.
3. See Ibram X. Kendi, *How to Be an Antiracist* (New York: One World, 2019), 201.
4. Achille Mbembe, "Necropolitics," *Public Culture* 15, I (2003), 27.
5. "Governmentality," in *The Foucault Effect: Studies in Governmentality*, ed. Graham Burchell, Colin Gordon, and Peter Miller (Chicago: University of Chicago Press, 1991), 102–103.
6. Louis Althusser, "Ideology and Ideological State Apparatus," in Ben Brewster (trans.), *Lenin and Philosophy, and Other Essays* (London: New Left Books, 1971), 155–156.
7. Ronald E. Butchart, "Black Hope, White Power: Emancipation, Reconstruction and the Legacy of Unequal Schooling in the US South, 1861–1880," *Paedagogica Historica* 46, 1–2 (2010), 38.
8. Ibid., 36.
9. *Catalogue of the Hampton Normal and Agricultural Institute for the Academic Year 1870–71*, 18; *The Southern Workman*, XXIV: 9. Sept., 1895, 145.
10. Elisabeth M. Eittreim, *Teaching Empire: Native Americans, Filipinos, and US Imperial Education, 1879–1918* (Lawrence: University Press of Kansas, 2019), 69.
11. David Wallace Adams, *Education for Extinction: American s and the Boarding School Experience, 1875–1928* (Lawrence: University of Kansas Press, 1995), 5–6.
12. Ibid., xi.
13. Zitkala-Sa, "Impressions of an Childhood," *Atlantic Monthly*, 85, DVII (Jan., 1900), 47.
14. Adams, *Education for Extinction*, 212.
15. Anne Paulet, "The Only Good Is a Dead : The Use of United States Policy as a Guide for the Conquest and Occupation of the Philippines, 1898–1905," unpublished PhD dissertation, Rutgers University, New Brunswick, New Jersey, 1995.

16. *Report of the War Department*, 1901, part 4, p. 258. Cited in W. Cameron Forbes, *The Philippine Islands vol. 1* (Boston: Hougton Mifflin, 1928), p. 423.
17. Adeline Knapp, "A Notable Educational Expedition," Ronald P. Gleason, ed., *The Log of the Thomas, July 23 to August 21*, 1901 (S.I: S.N.), 11–12.
18. Laura Wexler, *Tender Violence: Domestic Visions in an Age of US Imperialism* (Chapel Hill: University of North Carolina Press, 2000), 52.
19. Fred Atkinson, *Education in the Philippine Islands* (Washington: Government Printing Office, 1902), 1327.
20. K. Tsianina Lomawaima, "Estelle Reel, Superintendent of Schools, 1898–1910: Politics, Curriculum, and Land," *Journal of American Education* 35, iii (May 1996), 12.
21. See *Philippine Education*, 8, iv (July 1911), 10.
22. Austin Craig, "The Kindergarten as an Americanizing Influence," *The Philippine Teacher* 2, viii (1906), 26–27.
23. *A Survey of the Educational System of the Philippine Islands by The Board of Educational Survey*; created under Acts 3162 and 3196 of the Philippine Legislature (Manila: Bureau of Printing, 1925), 96.
24. See Louis John Loius Ruscetta's Master's thesis (unpublished), "Education for Philippine Pacification": https://apps.dtic.mil/sti/citations/ADA569855.
25. Jeremy Greene, Marguerite Thorp Basilico, Heidi Kim and Paul Farmer, "Colonial Medicine and Its Legacies," in *Reimagining Global Health: An Introduction* (Berkeley: University of California Press, 2013), 42.
26. Ibid., 39.
27. P. D. Curtin, "'The White Man's Grave': Image and Reality, 1780–1850," *Journal of British Studies* 1, 1 (Nov., 1961), 94.
28. Reynaldo C. Ileto, "Outlines of a Non-Linear Emplotment of Philippines History," in *The Politics of Culture in the Shadow of Capital*, ed. Lisa Lowe and David Lloyd (Durham: Duke University Press, 1997), 110.
29. Harry Crouch Theobold, *The Filipino Teacher's Manual* (New York: World Book Company, 1907), 66.
30. Ibid., 68, 90.
31. Bonnie McElhinny, "Kissing a Baby Is Not at All Good for Him": Infant Mortality, Medicine, and Colonial Modernity in the US-Occupied Philippines," *American Anthropologist* 107, ii (2005), 188.
32. Ann Laura Stoler, "Tense and Tender Ties: The Politics of Comparison in North American History and (Post)Colonial Studies," *Journal of American History* 88 (2001), 843.
33. Cited in Warwick Anderson, "Where Every Prospect Pleases and Every Man Is Vile," *Critical Inquiry* 18, iii (1992), 526.
34. Cited in Victor Roman Mendoza, *Metroimperial Intimacies: Fantasy, Racial-Sexual Governance, and the Philippines in US Imperialism, 1899–1913* (Durham: Duke University Press, 2015), 46.
35. Warwick Anderson, *Colonial Pathologies: American Tropical Medicine, Race, and Hygeine in the Philippines* (Durham: Duke University Press, 2006), 106.
36. Ibid., 3.

37. Naval Government of Guam, Annual Report 1900 (Washington, DC: Government Printing Office, 1900), 1.
38. Anne Perez Hattori, "'The Cry of the Little People of Guam': American Colonialism, Medical Philanthropy, and the Susana Hospital for Chamorro Women, 1898–1941," *Health and History* 8 I (2006), 7–8.
39. Kerri A. Inglis "Disease and the 'Other': The Roles of Medical Imperialism in Oceania," in *Native Diasporas: Indigenous Identities and Settler Colonialism in the Americas*, ed. Gregory D. Smithers and Brooke N. Newman, 396–397.
40. John Dower, *Embracing Defeat: Japan in the Wake of World War II* (New York: Norton, 1999), 23.
41. Yoshikuni Igarashi, *Bodies of Memory: Narratives of War in Postwar Japanese Culture, 1945–1970* (Princeton: Princeton University Press, 2000), 68.
42. See James Erwon Schmitt, "From the Frontlines to Silent Spring: DDT and America's War on Insects, 1941–1962," *Concept* XXXIX (2016), 1–29, 18.
43. Emily Kern, "Sugarcane and Lepers: Health Policy and the Colonization of Hawaii (1860–1900)" *Penn History Review* 17 ii (2010), 83.
44. Ibid., 78.
45. Inglis, "Disease and the 'Other,'" 400.
46. Inglis, "Disease and the 'Other,'" 398.
47. Anne Perez Hattori, *Colonial Dis-Ease: US Navy Health Policies and the Chamorros of Guam, 1898–1941* (Honolulu: University of Hawaii Press, 2004), 60, 86.
48. Betty Pfefferbaum, Rennard Strickland, Everett R. Rhoades, and Rose L. Pfefferbaum. "Learning How to Heal: An Analysis of the History, Policy, and Framework of Health Care," *American Law Review* 20, 2 (1995/1996), 369.
49. Brianna Theobald, *Reproduction on the Reservation: Pregnancy, Childbirth, and Colonialism in the Long Twentieth Century* (Chapel Hill: University of North Carolina Press, 2019), 47.
50. Ibid., 50–51, 54.
51. Cited in Roger Koppl, Expert Failure (New York: Cambridge University Press, 2018), 207.
52. Douglas MacArthur, *Reminiscences: General of the Army* (New York: McGraw Hill, 1964), 283.
53. Yukiko Koshiro, *Trans-Pacific Racisms and the US Occupation of Japan* (New York: Columbia University Press, 1999), 16.
54. *Far East Asia American Red Cross Brides School*, 1959, National Archives Records of the American Red Cross, 1947–1964, RG200. National Archives, College Park, Maryland, 27.
55. *Camp Kokura Brides School October 1956, American Red Cross*. National Archives Records of the American Red Cross, 1947–1964. RG200. National Archives, College Park, Maryland, "Culture, Customs and Manners," 2.
56. See Masako Nakamura, "Families Precede Nation and Race? Migration and Integration of Japanese War Brides after World War II." 2010. University of Minnesota. Unpublished PhD dissertation, 133.
57. See Justine Tally, *Toni Morrison's Beloved: Origins* (New York: Routledge, 2009), 18.
58. Toni Morrison, *Beloved*, New York: Alfred A. Knopf, 266.

PART II

Backgrounds

CHAPTER 3

Still Looking for the Meaning of Whiteness in American Literature

Valerie Babb

When I first wrote *Whiteness Visible* in 1998, the systematic study of whiteness as a racial construct was just hitting its stride with Theodore Allen's *The Invention of the White Race, Volume 1* (1975), Peggy McIntosh's essay "White Privilege: Unpacking the Invisible Knapsack" (1989), Mike Hill's *Whiteness: A Critical Reader* (1997), and David Roediger's *The Wages of Whiteness* (1991) among the works undertaking this inquiry.[1] My contribution examined eighteenth- and nineteenth-century American literature's involvement in constructing whiteness as a racial identity that unified a population of white ethnics with diverse political and social aspirations. In this chapter I would like to offer a review of earlier American literature's role in building whiteness and consider the afterlives of this construction in subsequent selected literature. Such an exercise seems particularly appropriate in a cultural moment when the premises of whiteness still vex questions of American social justice.

Surveying the emergence of whiteness in American literature must begin with the prenational period, for it is here that the parameters of whiteness are set. As the survival and expansion of early English settlements necessitated the dispossession of Indigenous peoples, the creation of a slave-for-life caste, and the push to expand national boundaries westward and southward, early American documents midwifed the binary of white–nonwhite through prenational colonial histories, religious treaties, and, significantly, what became two of the seventeenth century's most popular genres: captivity and criminal narratives. In this early archive both the preexistence of whiteness and its germinating formulations of racial difference are evident.

Stemming from public executions that often generated crowds in the thousands, criminal narratives might be seen as the popular literature of their time, reaching a vast audience. Magistrates recorded the last moments of condemned criminals' lives and used them as cautionary tales in jeremiads warning of moral decay and painting the perdition awaiting those not heeding the warning. In *Pillars of Salt* (1993), Daniel Williams observes that these popular narratives were not only a means of reinforcing religious ideology, as their broad audience made them an ideal venue for conveying racial and gender mores as well. Through print, audiences who might not have attended actual executions were also exposed to increasingly consistent ideas on race and gender that began to cohere a community imagined around an idealized whiteness. In etching moral failings on criminals who were poor, female, not English, or Black, the narratives limned an ideal identity as economically privileged, masculine, "white," and preferably English. As the genre became mass-marketed so too were these notions.

Sketches of the Life of Joseph Mountain, a Negro (1790), the narrative of a Black subject, is one illustration of how the terms "Black" and "white" fused race and morality.[2] The full title of the work is *Sketches of the Life of Joseph Mountain, a Negro, Who Was Executed at New-Haven, on the 20th Day of October, 1790, for a Rape, Committed on the 26th Day of May Last. [The Writer of This History Has Directed That the Money Arising From the Sales Thereof, After Deducting the Expence of Printing, &c. Be Given to the Unhappy Girl, Whose Life Is Rendered Wretched by the Crime of the Malefactor.].* "Sketches," "Life," "Joseph Mountain," "a NEGRO," and "For a Rape" all have typographical emphasis that implies an equivalency. After Mountain has told his story (in which he professes his innocence of rape), the following inclusion from the sentencing magistrate appears:

> The crime which you are convicted, is of a *deep dye*, very heinous in the sight of God and man, and in most if not all the civilized nation punishable with death . . .
>
> The female sex are weak and feeble in their frame, timid and unable to resist the force and strength of man, who was designed for their protection . . . but instead of protecting, you, regardless of the all-piercing eye of God . . . wholly inattentive to human discovery, or the detection of your *dark designs*, meeting the harmless and innocent maid . . . urged on by *worse than brutal lust*, and *more than savage barbarity* . . . with force and violence ravished her of what to a female is as dear as life.[3]

The addendum is as concerned with titillation as it is with salvation. Entwining color and morality continues here as the terms "Deep dye" and "dark designs" are accompanied by "brutal lust," serving to color sexual perversion as black. Associating "weak" and "feeble" with "female" genders moral frailty in a foreshadowing of what would become the use of the white female figure to embody ideas of racial purity. The two portraits – one of a defiled woman, the other of a demonized black man – combine to show the need for white maleness to secure moral and social order.

Captivity narratives, also a widely popular genre of this time, went hand in hand with criminal narratives in constructing whiteness. Mary Rowlandson's archetypal *A Narrative of the Captivity and Restoration of Mrs. Mary Rowlandson* (1682), for instance, reveals a formula no Puritan father could find fault with. The daughter of one of the town's founders and the wife of Reverend Joseph Rowlandson, a Lancaster clergyman, her narrative is full of biblical typology as commentary on every thought. It is also full of instances of whiteness forming a racial identity against the backdrop of an imagined enemy, and the combination sanctifies racial whiteness.

Of the "First Remove," Rowlandson writes, "Now away we must go with those barbarous creatures, with our bodies wounded and bleeding, and our hearts no less than our bodies .... Oh the roaring, and singing and dancing, and yelling of those black creatures in the night, which made the place a lively resemblance of hell." Rowlandson's confederation of blackness, the Devil, and Indigenous peoples solidifies their deviance from Christian whiteness. She extends this portrait of indigenous deviance in "The Nineteenth Remove," where a passage discussing "Praying Indians" implies that this term is an oxymoron:

> It was a praying Indian that wrote their letter [communication about the amount of Rowlandson's ransom] for them. There was another praying Indian who told me that he had a brother that would not eat horse; his conscience was so tender and scrupulous (though as large as hell for the destruction of poor Christians) .... There was another praying Indian who, when he had done all the mischief that he could, betrayed his own father into the English hands thereby to purchase his own life .... There was another praying Indian so wicked and cruel as to wear a string about his neck strung with Christians' fingers.[4]

The juxtaposition of so many non-Christian acts with so many converted Christians of another race undermines the integrity of "praying Indians," racializes salvation, and intimates that color prevents even baptized Indians from being "real" Christians among the chosen ones. Such representation has secular implications as well, as the concept of the "chosen" starts to utilize race, gender, and class as measurements of one's distance from or approximation to an idealized spiritual state that encodes whiteness.[5]

The written matter of prenational New England began to aggregate racial representations, making whiteness normative and all else aberrant, and implicitly gendering ideal whiteness as male; however, American literature's cementing of whiteness blossoms fully in the nineteenth century as colonies became a country in search of tropes signifying national identity. Among texts that provide insight into the nineteenth-century workings of whiteness are James Fenimore Cooper's *The Last of the Mohicans* (1826), Herman Melville's *Moby-Dick* (1851), and Harriet Beecher Stowe's *Uncle Tom's Cabin* (1852).

The Last of the Mohicans utilizes characterization and frontier contestations to firmly set the boundaries of racial identity. The American landscape is virgin forest ripe for the right kind of settlers – that is, white. Indigenous people can be "good," such as the Grecian-chiseled Uncas, or "bad," such as the too-eloquent Magua, depending on how well they facilitate the white mission of conquest. "Good" or "bad," there is no place for Indigenous or mixed-raced characters in Cooper's vision of a future America. Uncas and Cora, who turns out to have African antecedents, both die, symbolically married in death, not life, because such a union is anathema to Cooper's vision of whiteness. Chingachgook is a broken father who dies in prequel fashion in Cooper's *The Pioneers* (1823). "Bad" Indians, such as Magua, who uses his words to fight dispossession, have been vanquished. The characters that remain to populate the new nation are the white Duncan Heyward, who denies being bigoted when learning of Cora's background yet is "at the same time conscious of such a feeling," and Alice of the "dazzling complexion, fair golden hair, and bright blue eyes." The scout Hawkeye, a transitional figure whose frontier immersion makes him a little too native to be part of the procreative future, is their guide through this new landscape. Cooper ensures that a "pure" white lineage continues. In a work whose title frames Indigenous peoples as artifacts, the final lines read "The pale-faces are masters of the earth, and the time of the red-men has not yet come again."[6]

In contrast to Cooper, Herman Melville is an example of an author deconstructing whiteness to discover its meaning and its cultural power. The "Etymology" and the "Extracts" that open his most famous novel, *Moby-Dick* (1851), signal a prescient critique of the dangers ideologies can pose. The sections' allusions to literature, art, history, philosophy, theology, and pseudoscience query how disciplines convey not just knowledge but also values that privilege the primacy of whiteness.

In "Unspeakable Things Unspoken," Toni Morrison describes the boldness of Melville's unmasking whiteness in the novel:

> But to question the very notion of white progress, the very idea of racial superiority, of whiteness as privileged place in the evolutionary ladder of

> humankind, and to meditate on the fraudulent, self-destroying philosophy of that superiority, to "pluck it out from under the robes of Senators and Judges," to drag the "judge himself to the bar," – that was dangerous, solitary, radical work. Especially then. Especially now.[7]

The means to this "dangerous, solitary, radical work" is the white whale. In a chapter titled "the Advocate," while analyzing what might be termed anti-whaleness, the narrator Ishmael's comments are resonant with rationales behind American discrimination: "The whale has no famous author, and whaling no famous chronicler . . . . [W]halemen themselves are poor devils; they have no good blood in their veins . . . . [S]omehow whaling is not respectable . . . . The whale himself has never figured in any grand imposing way."[8] Although referencing whales or whaling, each of these statements rings with values often used to affirm the preeminence of ideological whiteness: "chronicler" evokes the ways written discourse and its culture are privileged; "whalemen" as "poor devils" without "good blood" ties privilege to biology; "grand" or "imposing" are subjective and justify dispossessing or enslaving people who do not matter. Intertwining whales and social observations allows Moby Dick to signify both cetological and human systems of taxonomy. A novel whose ocean setting defies land boundaries and their social orders, whose whaling crew represents multiracialism writ large, puts the lie to privileging whiteness through biased taxonomy and canonization. In 1851 it broached what took more than 100 years to be forthrightly discussed: the need for whiteness to be named and examined.

Melville was indeed an outlier. Even works deemed radical in their political messaging did not offer the far-reaching critique of an ideology that threatens American multiracial parity. The woman whose book was said to have started the Civil War, for instance, penned a passionate antislavery tome that nonetheless reinforced notions of whiteness.[9] Harriet Beecher Stowe's *Uncle Tom's Cabin* has far more in common with *The Last of the Mohicans* than it does with *Moby-Dick*, but rather than a frontier, Stowe selects the domestic sphere as her site for feminized white privileging.

That Stowe centers the domestic space, commonly seen in the nineteenth century as the domain of women, is evident in the introductions of major characters. Each begins with an analogy between domestic space and humane morality. We hear of Aunt Ophelia's "large farmhouse, for instance, with its clean-swept grassy yard" where "everything is once and forever rigidly in place," and the description foretells her inability to empathize with those different from her. True humanity is represented through Quaker Rachel Halladay's home, a respite for the novel's fugitive slaves and a "quiet scene" with a chair "motherly and old, whose wide arms breathed hospitable invitation." Spiritual decadence, on the other hand, is represented through the suspect syncretism of New Orleans epitomized by the St. Clares' "ancient mansion, built in that odd mixture of Spanish and French style, . . . built in the Moorish fashion." Abolition may be desirable but not racial hybridity. The objectifying naturalism Stowe associates with her fully Black characters is seen in the description of Tom's cabin as "a small log building . . . where, every summer, strawberries, raspberries, and a variety of fruits and vegetables, flourished under careful tending," while the evilness in Simon Legree is foretold by the description of a "wild, forsaken road . . . through dreary pine barrens, where the wind whispered mournfully," through "doleful trees" to a house with a "ragged, forlorn appearance."[10] These images stress the importance of home in building human decency, and, significantly, the importance of women in this endeavor. Within this sphere sentiment and affect are used to elicit sympathy toward the enslaved, but ideological whiteness prevents a fully realized vision of Black equality. One reason for the lack of such vision might be Stowe's inability to see greatness in Blackness, except in the figures of self-liberating mulatto characters or the messianic humbleness of Tom. In both instances biology governs who deserves full social equality.

We are introduced to Tom, a "large, broadchested, powerfully-made man, of a full glossy black" with a face of "truly African features," as he learns to write at the tutelage of the son of his master, George. As Tom and his wife Chole watch, George shows Tom the difference between "g" and "q" by writing a trail of "g's," and they marvel at "How easy white folks al'us does things!" Here biology is used to explain a difference in capability. When it comes time for him to be sold, biology is again implicitly referenced in his choosing to remain loyal to his master. Shortly after Eliza, described as having the "natural graces in the quadroon . . . united with beauty of the most dazzling kind," informs Tom and Chole that she must run to avoid the sale of her son, Tom responds in the following manner when Chloe suggests he do the same:

> Tom slowly raised his head, and looked sorrowfully but quietly around, and said, "No, no – I an't going. Let Eliza go – it's her right! I wouldn't be the one to say no – 'tan't in natur for her to stay . . . If I must be sold, or all the people on the place, and everything go to rack, why, let me be sold. I s'pose I can b'ar it as well as any on 'em."[11]

"'[T]an't in natur for her to stay" implies that Eliza's lineage and its approximation to whiteness gives her a "natural" desire for freedom that the "fully black" Tom does not share. Further, "I can b'ar it as well as any on 'em" echoes specious arguments that Blacks were naturally, biologically suited to enslavement because of their higher tolerance for suffering.

Ultimately, in *Uncle Tom's Cabin*, Black characters seeking the privileges of full citizenship must go abroad, and the work's "Concluding Remarks" reveal Stowe's inability to conceive of full Black citizenship:

> Let the church of the north receive these poor sufferers in the spirit of Christ; receive them to the educating advantages of Christian republican society and schools, until they have attained to somewhat of a moral and intellectual maturity, and then assist them in their passage to those shores, where they may put in practice the lessons they have learned in America.[12]

Stowe seeks the end of slavery, but the next steps are not so clear-cut in her novel. A key component in ideological whiteness is the notion that America is fundamentally a "white" nation, and these closing remarks hint of this notion. Stowe's solution isn't inclusion, but its opposite.

One need only look at the novel of a Black nineteenth-century woman writer to see the whiteness of Stowe's vision. While detailing the life of the protagonist Frado, a biracial indentured servant abandoned by her mother and employed by the white Bellmont family, Harriet Wilson's *Our Nig* (1859) offers a profound dissection of a sisterhood undone by whiteness.

A part of *Our Nig*'s subtitle describes its setting: *In a Two-Story White House, North, Showing that Slavery's Shadows Fall Even There*. Here Wilson signals a direct challenge to Stowe's idea of moral domesticity and enlightened white womanhood. In keeping with traditions of nineteenth-century women's writing, the male characters in *Our Nig* are peripheral. Mr. Bellmont, the head of the household, and his son, the ill James, witness violence and racism directed at Frado, and offer sympathy or bromides, but no meaningful alleviation of her suffering. The other two brothers of the Belmont household, Lewis and Jack, move away. As Mr. Bellmont observes, throwing up his hands, "How am I to help it? Women rule the earth, and all in it." This ceding of masculine accountability squarely places responsibility for Frado's being in the hands of white women: the "she-devil" Mrs. Bellmont; her daughter and eager protegee, Mary; and Aunt Abby and Jane, both of whom are sympathetic and influence her spiritual evolution, yet are unable to materially affect her well-being.

Wilson critiques the way human characteristics become articles of trade in her description of Mrs. Belmont's desire to maintain a visible color line. No matter the exposure to sun and heat in agrarian work, she forbids Frado's wearing a hat. The source of Mrs. Bellmont's prohibition is fear of the loss of whiteness: "She was not many shades darker than Mary now; what a calamity it would be ever to hear the contrast spoken of." The line between constructed whiteness and all other races must be vigilantly, and cruelly, maintained. Wilson's domestic space is a social economy where Mary's whiteness needs to be preserved to secure her privilege over Frado, where her mother Mag's virginity is a "priceless gem" and her white skin is a "prize," and where her mother's Black rescuer speaks of a white wife as a "treasure."[13] Instead of an idealized morality, white women characters represent the supports of a racial system that commodifies human traits for market. In this market, whiteness is a prized item, but a costly one to social parity.

The foregoing selected texts illustrate the ways the first two centuries of American writing helped to construct and solidify whiteness in response to enslavement, demands for gender equality, migrations to and settlement in the West, contestations over southern national borders, and continued Indigenous dispossession. What inheritance does this body of writing leave to more contemporary works? Is ideological whiteness now more visible than before? Toni Morrison's *A Mercy* (2008), Mat Johnson's *Pym* (2011), and a "barbaric yawp of a book," Jack Kerouac's *On the Road* (1957), provide insight into these questions.[14]

For all of its edginess of language, rhythms of jazz, and manifestations of beat, *On the Road* is in many ways a replica of eighteenth- and nineteenth-century literary engagements with whiteness.[15] It is a romantic escape for a white male, and in its construction we see what might be considered an aesthetics of whiteness: portraits of whites as the only constructors of Americanness, representations of those not deemed white framed through a white gaze, and the appropriation of forms not created by whites to encourage white vicarious pleasure without complex emotional understanding. *On the Road* enacts the cultural imperialism of whiteness while hiding behind the veil of aesthetic experimentation.

The novel is a paean to American traditions and is not as counter-culture as it might appear. Kerouac's Sal embodies a pioneer in contemporary times. The route to his escape in the mid-twentieth century is not as evident as Cooper's frontier or Melville's sea, so he invents his unknown territory at the same time he invents himself:

> I thought all the wilderness of America was in the West till the Ghost of the Susquehanna showed me different. No, there is a wilderness in the East; it's the same wilderness Ben Franklin plodded in the oxcart days when he was postmaster, the same as it was when George Washington was a wildbuck Indian-fighter, when Daniel Boone told stories by Pennsylvania lamps and promised to find the Gap, when Bradford built his road and men whooped her up in log cabins.[16]

Kerouac offers four white men as pillars of American cultural history: George Washington, president and slaveholder; Benjamin Franklin, who embodied the ideal of white male individualism; Daniel Boone, a scout similar to Cooper's Hawkeye, making the frontier and indigenous peoples legible to whites; and engineer Sam Bradford, who exploited Chinese, Mexican, and Black laborers to build the transcontinental railroad. Kerouac does not frame these white men as agents who made space for slavery in the constitution, facilitated dispossession, or created labor conditions that caused the deaths of thousands. They are simply American heroes.

Kerouac's narrator, Sal, can only see the lives and cultures of those not defined as white through his own white gaze. Upon arrival in Mexico he observes that "Just across the street Mexico began. We looked with wonder. To our amazement, it looked exactly like Mexico."[17] Here we see white identity imposing its expectations on the world it encounters. Sal is enthusiastic not to encounter Mexico but to encounter his *idea* of Mexico. He never examines his racial positionality because he moves through the world as if whiteness is universal, synonymous with just being human. This unexamined whiteness is as mobile as the characters in *On the Road* and inhibits true seeing of a varied cultural landscape. Sal's portrait of a black couple picking cotton is an example. "There was an old Negro couple in the field with us," Sal observes:

> They picked cotton with the same God-blessed patience their grandfathers had practiced in ante-bellum Alabama; they moved right along their rows, bent and blue, and their bags increased. My back began to ache. But it was beautiful kneeling and hiding in that earth. If I felt like resting I did, with my face on the pillow of brown moist earth. Birds sang in accompaniment.

Sal's whiteness frames the couple in his own nostalgia. "God-blessed patience" implies that divine order has given them the strength needed to carry out the duties of their caste. The word "slavery" is not used, just the euphemistic "antebellum." Cotton picking is devoid of its links to Black enslavement and the racist legacies that evolved from it. The passage closes with a statement clearly showing Sal's white privilege: "If I felt like resting

I did with my face on the pillow of brown moist earth. Birds sang in accompaniment. I thought I had found my life's work." With the soundtrack of birds singing, this Disney-like evocation shows Sal to have a freedom the black couple does not: the freedom to rest, find fulfillment in picking cotton, or grow weary of the work and hit the road.

In many moments in the novel Sal expresses white cultural discontent. As he slums through Denver, he seeks to consume Blackness, Latinidad, and Asianness to achieve some sort of redemptive euphoria:

> At lilac evening I walked with every muscle aching among the lights of 27th and Welton in the Denver colored section, wishing I were a Negro, feeling that the best the white world had offered was not enough ecstasy for me, not enough life, joy, kicks, darkness, music, nor enough night . . . . I wished I were a Denver Mexican, or even a poor overworked Jap, anything but what I was so drearily, a "white man" disillusioned.[18]

The trope of a white identity dissatisfied and anxious in its privilege indicates the ways American writing both fabricates whiteness and responds to its intrinsic nothingness. Whites have no culture that has not been appropriated from others, Kerouac implies, only social power.

It is the pattern of not naming whiteness, not showing it constituting a threat to multiracial democracy, that Toni Morrison's *A Mercy* questions. The novel is her rewriting of the American origins narrative to re-place the racial, gender, and class complexities lost in creating American whiteness. While telling the story of Florens, a young Black woman traversing various spaces seeking a remedy for her ailing mistress, Morrison makes pronounced allusions to prenational laws and events, such as the suppression of Bacon's Rebellion, to show how lines of race, gender, and class were enlisted to fabricate whiteness.

Willard and Scully, white indentured servants, are Morrison's most direct means of dissecting the hollowness of white privilege. Their lives are described in terms showing the tenuousness of the line separating "indentee" from "slave-for-life":

> Willard was getting on in years and was still working off his passage. The original seven years stretched to twenty-some, he said, and he had long ago forgotten most of the mischief that kept extending his bondage . . . . Scully, young, fine-boned, with light scars tracing his back, had plans. He was finishing his mother's contract. True, he didn't know how long it would take but, he boasted, unlike Willard's or Lina's his enslavement would end before death.

Willard has aged in indenture with no future end to his servitude in sight. Scully dreams of receiving his "freedom fee" – money to help establish himself once his stint is completed – and even this terminology shows how closely indenture aligned with enslavement. Other indentees convey the same message. At one point, Florens is a passenger in a wagon along with "A boy with a yellow pigtail" who "sits on the wagon floor, his hands tied to his ankles."[19] Morrison describes the boy not as white, but by his physical attributes, which also include his tied hands. By doing this she breaks what is assumed to be a natural equivalency between racial designation and physical appearance to disclose the artificiality of racial categories. In this prenational moment, the boy's white skin and yellow hair are only beginning to be associated with white privilege. They do not protect him from social caste but provide an illusion of social privilege. *A Mercy* deracinates freedom and enslavement to lessen the biological rationales of racial privilege. Races are enslaved for political, social, and economic reasons, and biology follows as a justification.

While wearing the hat of cultural critic, Toni Morrison produced one of the most trenchant analyses of whiteness in American literature, and its impact is seen when Mat Johnson makes a literary allusion to it in *Pym*. The narrator, Chris, introduces himself as "Professor of African American Literature. Professional Negro" who offers the course "Dancing with the Darkies: Whiteness in the Literary Mind." The course title is a clear pun on Morrison's *Playing in the Dark: Whiteness and the Literary Imagination* (1992), and the novel offers a tripartite critique of slavery's exploitation as a subject, the exclusionary nature of the American literary canon, and whiteness. It is fitting to end a consideration of whiteness in American literature with a work that explicitly engages whiteness's relationship to literature to show how one supported the other.

After a series of mishaps, including not receiving tenure at Bard College, Chris's luck seems to change when he acquires the narrative of Dirk Peters, Arthur Gordon Pym's Black partner in mutiny, exploration, and survival in the original Poe work, *The Narrative of Arthur Gordon Pym* (1838). Dirk tells his story to Poe, hoping the latter might facilitate public recognition; instead, Poe appropriates Dirk's experience for his own ends. Chris seeks to use this newly discovered complement to Poe's novella to restart his academic career.

Johnson's erasing of the temporal and stylistic lines between his novel and Poe's novella accentuates the ways Black experience informed American literature, even as white writers devalued Blackness and Black creativity. In Chris's view, Black life and white writing are inextricable:

> I like Poe, I like Melville, I like Hemingway, but what I like the most about the great literature created by the Americans of European descent is the Africanist presence within it. I like looking at myself in the whitest of pages. I like finding evidence of myself there, after being told my footprints did not exist on that sand.

Chris's search for evidence of his own existence in white pages is an intervention into the ways whiteness shapes literature and, subsequently, knowing. He seeks to read between the lines, discovering what lies within the silences and gaps of the literary record.

Pym defines ideological whiteness in the following terms: "Whiteness isn't about being something, it is about being no thing, nothing, an erasure."[20] This nothingness of whiteness is precisely its most threatening quality. It allows whiteness to mutate to serve the needs of racial dominance in different cultural contexts and periods. In the eighteenth century it was the rallying point that cohered white ethnics into a "race" to justify the dispossession and enslavement of others; in the nineteenth century it rationalized American imperialism, continued enslavement, and deepening class inequity; and in the twentieth and twenty-first centuries it fuels the values that force repeated racial "reckonings."

Increasingly, ideological whiteness has spread beyond its original referent: white skin. It is evolving into a system of unstated signifiers that now allows members of other racial groups to partake of its ideals of hierarchy, capitalism, exclusion, and consumption. The Afro-Latin Enrique Tarrio, a leader of the far-right group Proud Boys, can now participate in spreading white supremacist ideology because such ideology is masked as patriotism or a fight to save American traditions. Advocacy to change exclusionary practices and institutions has resulted not in a disavowal of whiteness as an ideology, but rather in granting some who are deemed nonwhite to participate in its privileges. This latest iteration of whiteness may be the most harmful yet to what Ralph Ellison termed "the principle on which the country was built," one that was "greater than the men, greater than the numbers and the vicious power and all the methods used to corrupt its name."[21] Ideological whiteness's penchant for classification dehumanizes; its discourse of conquest creates perpetual adversaries; and its defining a single racial group as the inheritors of American rights and privileges guarantees undemocratic social stratification and contestations.

As I wrote in 1998, "The ideology that has created a race and allowed it to exist in a space of social privilege, will keep a nation of the verge of a remarkable cultural experiment from asking the right questions and following the correct course to realizing its full potential."[22]

Notes

1. Theodore Allen, *The Invention of the White Race, Volume 1* (New York: Verso, 1994–7), 2 volumes; Peggy McIntosh, "White Privilege: Unpacking the Invisible Knapsack," *Peace and Freedom Magazine*, July/August, 1989, 10–12; Mike Hill, *Whiteness: A Critical Reader* (New York: New York University Press, 1997; David R. Roediger, *The Wages of Whiteness: Race and the Making of the American Working Class* (New York: Verso, 1991).
2. Joseph Mountain, *Sketches of the Life of Joseph Mountain, a Negro* (1790), in Daniel E. Williams, *Pillars of Salt: An Anthology of Early American Criminal Narratives*, 1st ed. (Madison: Madison House, 1993).
3. Qtd. in Williams, *Pillars of Salt*, 305. Italics mine.
4. Mary Rowlandson, *Narrative of The Captivity and Restoration of Mrs. Mary Rowlandson* (1682), www.gutenberg.org/files/851/851-h/851-h.htm.
5. Rowlandson's narrative is itself framed. The extratextual elements, presumed to be written by Increase Mather, can be seen as containing her voice, countering the text's depiction of her increasing familiarity with her Indigenous community and its economy. Mather's words represent a guarantee that she has been restored and there was no cultural slippage. A study considering this aspect of Rowlandson is Rebecca Bievins Faery, *Cartographies of Desire: Captivity, Race, and Sex in the Shaping of an American Nation* (Norman: University of Oklahoma Press, 1999).
6. James Fenimore Cooper, *Last of the Mohicans* (New York: Viking Penguin, 1986), 159, 18, 350.
7. Toni Morrison, "Unspeakable Things Unspoken: The Afro-American Presence in American Literature. The Tanner Lectures on Human Values, October 7, 1988, 18. https://tannerlectures.utah.edu/_resources/documents/a-to-z/m/morrison90.pdf.
8. Herman Melville, *Moby-Dick, or The Whale*. Ed. Harrison Hayford, et al. (Evanston: Northwestern University Press and the Newberry Library, 1988), 111.
9. The phrasing here alludes to an oft-told story that upon meeting Stowe, Abraham Lincoln said "So you're the little woman who wrote the book that made this great war!" For an examination of the significance(s) of this anecdote see, Daniel R. Vollaro, "Lincoln, Stowe, and the 'Little Woman/Great War' Story: The Making, and Breaking, of a Great American Anecdote," *Journal of the Abraham Lincoln Association*, 30, 1, Winter 2009, 18–34. http://hdl.handle.net/2027/spo.2629860.0030.104.
10. Harriet Beecher Stowe, *Uncle Tom's Cabin: Or, Life Among the Lowly* (1852), 227, 196, 236, 14, 177; http://utc.iath.virginia.edu/uncletom/uthp.html.
11. Beecher Stowe, *Uncle Tom's Cabin*, 42, 28, 65, 319.
12. Beecher Stowe, *Uncle Tom's Cabin*, 319.
13. Harriet E. Wilson, and Henry Louis Gates Jr. , *Our Nig: Or, Sketches from the Life of a Free Black, in a Two-Story White House, North: Showing That Slavery's Shadows Fall Even There* (New York: Vintage Books, 1983), 44, 12, 39, 6, 11, 14.

14. "Books: The Ganser Syndrome." *Time Magazine*, September 16, 1957, http://content.time.com/time/subscriber/article/0,33009,809932,00.html.
15. In "Specters in the Rear-View: Haunting Whiteness in Jack Kerouac's On the Road," Justin Thomas Trudeau also analyzes whiteness in the novel and focuses on its performativity via "Kerouac's spontaneous prose": *Text & Performance Quarterly*, 31, 2, Apr. 2011, 149–168. *EBSCOhost*, https://doi.org/10.1080/10462937.2010.549238.
16. Jack Kerouac, *On the Road* [1957] (New York: Penguin, 1999), 97.
17. Kerouac, *On the Road*, 261.
18. Kerouac, On the Road, 89, 170.
19. Toni Morrison, *A Mercy*, 1st ed. (New York: Alfred A. Knopf, 2008), 57, 39.
20. Mat Johnson, *Pym: A Novel*, 1st ed. (New York: Spiegel & Grau, 2011), 27, 225.
21. Ralph Ellison, *Invisible Man* [1952] (New York: Vintage, 1989), 574.
22. Valerie Babb, *Whiteness Visible: The Meaning of Whiteness in American Literature and Culture* (New York: New York University Press, 1998), 177.

CHAPTER 4

From Plymouth Rock to Standing Rock
Hospitality, Settler Colonialism, and 400 Years of Indigenous Literary Resistance

Drew Lopenzina

On a sunny morning in mid-November 2016, I found myself standing alongside a heavily trafficked roadway outside the Statehouse in Bismarck, North Dakota, part of a large group gathered there to protect the water rights of the Standing Rock Sioux tribe. We had left the reservation early that morning – a gleaming convoy of cars, vans, jeeps, and pick-up trucks snaking its way through rolling Dakota ranchlands, each vehicle packed with as many as it could hold. The plan was to separate into four groups upon nearing the city, in order to throw the state police (who were monitoring our every movement) off our trail, and then to converge again at the downtown Federal Building to demand the release of detainees arrested on trumped-up charges during the months-long movement. Many of us were strangers, hailing from different states, different countries, different nations. But all of us were united in common cause as "water protectors" standing in opposition to the construction of the Dakota Access Pipeline (DAPL), a 1,712-mile-long energy infrastructure project meant to channel crude oil from the Bakken fields of northern North Dakota to existing pipeline networks in Illinois. At this particular moment, the pipeline was all but completed, awaiting only the drilling of a tunnel beneath the Missouri River to connect its two separate ends. Where the pipeline crossed the river was, not coincidentally, on unceded treaty lands belonging to the Standing Rock Tribe, making the pipeline's construction a violation of their sovereign space and a direct threat to their drinking water as well as to the well-being of all life downriver from the crossing.

As we prepared for our march downtown, a steady stream of jeers flew from the windows of passing cars, including an oft-repeated call for us to "go back where you came from," – a particularly ironic request under the circumstances. Despite the fact that many, like me, had travelled long distances to be there, a considerable number of the assembled "protectors" were Indigenous, either as members of the Oceti Sakowin (the seven council fires of the Lakota), or, more broadly, Indigenous to the North American continent. Representatives of roughly 100 different tribes had journeyed to Standing Rock over the course of the year to contest the construction of the pipeline. The idea that they should all *go back where they came from* made little or no sense. They had always already been there.

As a straight white male, I am rarely on the receiving end of such targeted animosity, so it provoked not only a profound sense of unease, but a – perhaps predictable – cognitive dissonance. Were the cries to "go back where you came from" directed at me and the other non-Indigenous "allies" present? Or were they directed at the Indigenous peoples themselves whose lands, the very lands on which we were standing, had been stolen out from under them? Of course, attempting to decipher the logics of racism is always a thankless endeavor. Its rationale is never rooted in logic so much as in the raw assertion of power – the power to claim one's own reality regardless of logic, science, justice, or any other attempt at mutually agreed-upon truth. Logic is an insult to racism – particularly the brand of "blood and soil" nativism resurfacing that election year, with its hyperbolic mix of xenophobia, misogyny, and a toxic, sentimentalized sense of entitlement to the land. Few of those passing by that day were prepared to entertain the idea that perhaps they were the ones who should return to their place of origin

This particular strain of incongruity has deep roots in the USA, tracing back to the origins of settler colonialism and its rhetorical imperative to make Native people disappear. Dina Gilio-Whitaker of the Colville Confederated Tribe of Indians observes that, just as with DAPL, such impulses are invariably connected to the colonial commodification and exploitation of Indigenous resources. "Colonization was not just a process of invasion and eventual domination of Indigenous populations by European settlers," she writes, "but also the eliminatory impulse" built up around structures of "environmental injustice."[1] Telling Native people to go back where they came from was a time-honored means for colonists to assert illogical claims to lands and commodities that never belonged to them in the first place, while insisting upon the impermanence of Indigenous peoples.

If, on the other hand, the jeers *were* directed at me, then perhaps worth noting is that I am from Massachusetts, a place of origin for many of the traditions surrounding the history of colonization in the USA and, as I write this, it has been 400 years since a small band of English separatists first attained these shores, extending themselves from the deck of the

Mayflower onto Plymouth Rock and one small step from there to manifest destiny. These "pilgrims" presumed that the Indigenous peoples occupying the site of their landing, the Patuxet, had been wiped out by disease a few years prior, leaving the region free for them to claim as their own. As was reported by one Plymouth settler, "all of the inhabitants died of an extraordinary plague, and there is neither man, woman, nor child remaining, as indeed we have found none, so as there is none to hinder our possession, or to lay claim unto it."[2] Early English settlers were anxious, in their manner, about proper land claims and patents, but curiously, when the famed interpreter Squanto, a Patuxet himself, appeared on the scene a few months later, it wasn't assumed that he or his direct kin should inherit the title to Patuxet lands. He was viewed instead by Plymouth Colony's governor, William Bradford, as "a special instrument, sent of God" to instruct the colonists on the lay of the land and teach them how to sow fish with the corn.[3]

Taking the Plymouth anniversary as a timely launching-off point, this chapter seeks to highlight Indigenous strategies of diplomacy, engagement, and resistance stretching over a 400-year period, noting the significance of Indigenous scholarship and its methodologies (the one resource left untapped by settler colonial acquisitiveness) and marking a continuum of traditional responses (as opposed to isolated eruptions of reactionary violence), leading up to the #NoDAPL movement at Standing Rock. Although Indigenous nations of this continent have vastly different traditions, languages, spiritual concerns, and practices, they also can be said to share a certain cultural and linguistic orientation bespeaking a sense of responsibility to the land and the beings occupying it. When colonizers made treaties with *Indians*, these agreements were interpreted from a settler perspective as power alignments marking the politicized boundaries between civilization and savagery – an expediency designed to provide legal cover for the containment of Indigenous peoples. But as Dakhóta scholar Christopher Pexa observes, the Dakhóta had a more expansive notion of such diplomatic exchanges. In their translation of treaty relations, the Dakhóta and the colonists were "hold[ing] each other's hearts," signifying layers of commitment and care unimagined by their cosigners.[4]

Indigenous peoples recognized responsibilities of shared space that conferred obligations on either end, a kind of hospitality extending beyond the immediate human contractors to a larger animated world that included rock, wind, lightning, and water, alongside flora and fauna. Similarly, water protectors at Standing Rock saw themselves responsible not only for halting a pipeline project, but to all of the beings endangered by its construction – a sense of shared responsibility to human and nonhuman worlds that succinctly translates into the NoDAPL catchphrase "water is life."

Assistance received from Squanto and other Indigenous allies in those early years of English settlement should be understood within a consistent pattern of absolute hospitality practiced by Native peoples. Although conflict occasionally erupted in these highly fraught cultural encounters, the initial terms of engagement, from Columbus's 1492 landfall onward, were nearly always peaceful. Instead of insisting settlers go back where they came from, as they might easily have done, Indigenous peoples more often than not created the conditions for survival that allowed poorly equipped European colonies to thrive. Europeans depended on Native peoples for sustenance throughout their first years of settlement and could not have persisted without the surplus produce of Native communities that were generally willing to share or barter their resources.

A typical example of this tradition of hospitality can be gleaned from an early excursion to Nemasket, an area neighboring Plymouth, recounted in *Mourt's Relation*, a journal of the Puritans' first year of settlement. The authors (the text is believed to be a collaborative effort between Bradford and Edward Winslow), recorded meeting with the "Namascheuks" who "welcomed us also, gave us of their fish, and we them of our victuals, not doubting but we should have enough where'er we came." The river they were exploring is described as having "many towns" alongside it where "the ground is very good on both sides, it being for the most part cleared."[5] This brief passage anticipates countless others like it in the colonial archive in which early settlers are met with extraordinary good will, so assured of hospitable encounters that they were persuaded to share their own meager rations as there was no fear but that they should "have enough where'er we came." But this acknowledgment of hospitality is accompanied by an acquisitive estimation of the landscape, described as replete with villages and cleared fields. The colonists, despite having been met with Indigenous hospitality, remain covetous of their lands and keep a weather eye out for prime real estate. Patuxet itself was chosen because it was on "high ground, where there is a great deal of land cleared, and hath been planted with corn three or four years ago."[6]

Native hospitality was not performed, as some might presume, out of cultural simplicity or a sense of obligation to a superior civilization. It was an ethos embedded in long-established practices of Indigenous diplomacy, kinship, and land management. Abenaki historian Lisa Brooks observes how this practice, far from being an altruistic ideal,

> was necessary to human survival. Sharing space meant sharing resources, and . . . communities relied on equal distribution to ensure social stability and physical health. All inhabitants of the pot [Brooks uses the Indigenous metaphor of the "common pot" to define the land and its resources] were fed from the pot and were part of the pot. Every part affected the whole.[7]

Such beliefs were cemented by the sharing of food and resources and by social structures organized around kinship networks that kept communities bound together in both actual and metaphorical relations of connectivity.

Despite the many ways the colonial archive offers glimpses into Indigenous structures of kinship, diplomacy, and hospitality, the prevailing mindset concerning this period (and all that follows) holds Native peoples in primitive lockdown, incapable of acknowledging their condition and complexity as civilized peoples with customs standing in equal relation to those of the settlers to whom they played host. It is the great trick of colonial reporting that, even as it presents brief windows into the complexity of Indigenous lives, it swiftly walks back those claims, performing acts of rhetorical erasure that transform this well-ordered village world into a negative space, "a vast and empty chaos . . . spacious and void" where the inhabitants are "few and do but run over the grass, as do also the foxes and wild beasts. They are not industrious, neither have art, science, skill, or faculty to use either the land or the commodities of it."[8] Clear from their own accounts, however, is that what they truly encountered were village spaces replete with sustainable agricultural practices and traditions of governance and diplomacy that often put the settlers themselves to shame.

Cognitive dissonance.

We see one thing with our own eyes, but are then compelled somehow to believe another. I call this process *unwitnessing*: the passive acts of deference to settler colonial power by which a history made eminently knowable from archival postings is, nevertheless, collectively disavowed. *Unwitnessing* is not only the process that renders Native civilization inert within the colonial scene, it also effectively renders inoperative radical acts of colonial violence that became the normative response to Indigenous hospitality. This can be seen in accounts of the 1636–7 Pequot War, in which the archive makes transparent how colonial violence was, in fact, the precursor to the construction of "empty" space. The Pequot War reached its climax in 1637 when an estimated 600–800 Pequots were burned to death in their village – an act likened by Bradford to an offering of incense to God, or a "sweet sacrifice" for giving "so speedy a victory over so proud, and insulting an enemy."[9] It was decreed upon victory that the Pequot name never be spoken again as the Lord was "pleased to give us this land as an inheritance."[10] In *Newes from America*, Captain John Underhill's 1637 account of the conflict, the title page doubles as an advertisement for newly *discovered* lands "that as yet have very few or no inhabitants" and will "yield further accommodation to such as will plant there."[11] The lands in question were, of course, those territories belonging to the Pequots prior to their near-annihilation by colonial forces.

One of the major objectives of the Pequot War was to control the manufacture and trade of wampum. Controlling resources and commoditizing the land and its people is always part of the settler colonial agenda and wampum, as it turns out, was a precious commodity in that Native peoples of the Northeast placed great ceremonial value on it. Wampum lay at the center of most important Indigenous rituals, played a role in the documenting of histories, and, as it turns out, was integral to the maintenance of diplomatic relationships. Controlling the source of wampum shells, along what had been Pequot lands between the mouths of the Thames and the Connecticut Rivers, meant controlling the wampum trade into inland territories in exchange for valuable furs. The New England colonists fully understood this and, indeed, wampum quickly became the currency of the colony, proving more valuable than the English pound.

Disregarding control of the wampum trade as the catalyst leading to the attempted genocide of the Pequots is like ignoring the significance of oil in the US wars in the Middle East over the last few decades. Despite the US government's official stated objectives to "promote democracy" in unstable parts of the globe, there would be few incentives for involvement if not for the oil-rich deposits defining the region.[12] Likewise, colonial violence was justified by the oft-stated endeavor to promote the civilizing light of Christianity among the "heathen," but settler actions resulted instead in continuous ripples of destruction as control of the wampum trade gave way to control of the fur trade, resulting in the near extinction of beavers, otters, and other beings whose furs proved valuable commodities on the European markets. The surviving Pequots, mostly women and young children, were rendered into commodities themselves, either bonded into service in the colonial settlements or sold into slavery in Bermuda. The first laws concerning slavery on the North American continent were subsequently codified in the 1641 Massachusetts Body of Liberties to justify the "spoils of war" and normalize how violently commandeered Pequot lands suddenly became "empty" spaces for expanded colonial settlement.

This widespread erasure that rendered thriving Pequot villages into vacant lands, continues to be enabled by scholarly practices that privilege colonial print history over the traditional beliefs and representational practices of Indigenous peoples. There is a prevailing belief that Native peoples, in their presumed cultural infancy, did not possess the tool of literacy, so that their narratives evaporated into thin air just as they themselves ceased to exist as a viable cultural force. Many are surprised to learn that Indigenous societies do, in fact, have their own recorded forms of history-keeping, including wampum belts, birchbark scrolls, winter counts, and many other types of nonalphabetic writings. Native peoples also quickly adapted to western literacy as a form of resistance to the inhospitable policies of the colonists. A 1752 petition written in the Algonquian language by the Mashpee Indians of what is today Cape Cod defiantly decreed to the Massachusetts Bay Colony's General Court that "this Indian land ... was conveyed to us by these former sachems of ours. We shall not give it away, nor shall it be sold, nor shall it be lent, but we shall always use it as long as we live, we together with all our children, and our children's children, and our descendants, and together with their descendants."[13] Acquiring the skill of alphabetic literacy became a strategic necessity for Indigenous peoples of the Northeast as, more and more, their claims to land were contested in English courts.

The Mashpee, who had been in the crosshairs of settler colonial policies since the colonists first "set foot on Plymouth Rock," were subject to all the rhetorical and physical violence defining colonial agendas. Despite the 1752 insistence of the Mashpees that the land would remain theirs in perpetuity, the settler state devised its own claims to inheritance, imbuing that which was taken by conquest with a kind of birthright privilege, a title divine, transcendent of law or right, but embedded in highly sentimentalized frameworks of belonging. Note how, in 1820, the statesman Daniel Webster stood at the location of Plymouth Rock, asserting his veneration for those forefathers (Bradford, Underhill, etc.) who "encountered the dangers of the ocean, the storms of heaven, the violence of the savages" in order to bequeath their "great inheritance" to future generations "unimpaired."[14] Orations such as this were common in the early nineteenth century and designed to almost magically bestow upon settler colonial populations an uncontested "inheritance," employing a set of ritualized themes that traced the origins of civilization and Christianity on this continent back to a constructed marker, a touchstone, a sacred site like Plymouth Rock from which all further claims to the land might be justified. In this settler purification ritual, it was not enough to claim a site of origin – the "eliminatory impulse," referred to by Gilio-Whitaker, needed to be fully engaged as well, including its monetized agenda. As Webster asserted of the Pilgrims, "they came to a new country. There was, as yet, no lands yielding rent, and no tenants rendering service. The whole soil was unreclaimed from barbarism."[15]

There were few who cared to contest such claims in this flush of early US nationhood. In 1833, however, William Apess, a Pequot, came to Mashpee on Cape Cod, in his capacity as Methodist minister, and joined with the Mashpees to resist the oppressive conditions under which Natives of New England were forced to live at this time. Although the Mashpees had managed to retain a portion of the territory to which they had laid claim in their 1752 petition, like other New England tribes they lived under the "protective" rule of court-appointed "overseers" who held tight social and economic control over every aspect of Indigenous life. The Mashpees were suffered to live on their own land, but overseers retained the right to "improve and lease the lands of the Indians, and their tenements; regulate their streams, ponds, and fisheries; mete out lots for their particular improvement; [and] control and regulate absolutely, their bargains, contracts, wages, and other dealings."[16] In other words, Indigenous lives and resources were treated as "lawful spoil" to those in the white community.[17] Native people came to be considered, in fact, as foreigners on their own lands. As Apess would write of Massachusetts Governor Levi Lincoln, "he seems to consider the Marshpees as strangers and thinks they ought to be driven to the wilds of the far west."[18]

Apess, too, was labelled an "intruder," a "disturber" both "riotous and seditious" for his efforts to organize the Mashpees in pursuit of their rights.[19] He recalled how, upon first arriving in the predominately white town of Barnstable, he and his young family were turned away from the inns and forced to sleep in a stable for a dollar a night. "We certainly owe them small thanks on the score of hospitality," Apess wrote, maintaining that "if any white man should come to Marshpee and ask hospitality for a night or two, I do not believe that one of the whole tribe would turn him from his door, savages though they be."[20] Apess, as a nineteenth-century Indigenous intellectual, fully understood how the laws of hospitality, and their presumptive connections to Christian civilization, were upended, perverted, by settler colonial practice. The irony, of course, was that it was the supposedly "savage" Natives who acted as practitioners of absolute hospitality and, in their persecution, were more Christ-like than any settler example. Following the civil disobedience actions he orchestrated at Mashpee that summer, Apess was himself persecuted and jailed for the alleged crimes of "trespassing" (on Indigenous lands) and "inciting a riot" (although the movement remained peaceful from start to finish). Apess would ultimately regain his freedom and continue to advocate for the rights of Natives until the Mashpee were finally guaranteed the right to limited self-governance the following year.

As part of his famous 1821 *Travels through New-England and New-York*, Timothy Dwight, a former president of Yale, visited Plymouth and, reflecting on its most famous landmark, wrote that no New Englander "willing to indulge his native feelings, can stand upon the rock, where our ancestors set the first foot after their arrival on American shores, without experiencing emotions very different from any common object of the same nature. No New Englander could be willing to have that rock buried and forgotten."[21] What Dwight's claim failed to entertain was the continued existence of *Indigenous* New Englanders in the region. For him, Native communities didn't matter or, even worse, simply didn't exist. In his 1836 "Eulogy on King Philip," however, Apess spoke directly back to Yale's former president in an emphatic reminder of the continued presence of Native peoples. From the stage of Boston's Odeon Theater, he proclaimed that we must "bury the hatchet, and those unjust laws, and Plymouth Rock together" for war, unlawfulness, and Plymouth Rock, including everything it symbolized to settler presence, were understood to be inseparable components of settler colonial violence and inhospitality.[22] Apess asserted how in 1620 "the Pilgrims landed at Plymouth, and without asking liberty from anyone they possessed themselves of a portion of the country . . . This, if now done, it would be called an insult and every white man would be called to go out and act the part of a patriot, to defend their country's rights."[23] "Go back where you came from," they would likely say. In the 1830s, Apess, an early practitioner of critical race theory, wrote books and gave speeches condemning settler colonial inhospitality. But his message of peace and reconciliation largely fell on deaf ears, and even today there are few who mark his words or understand them to be part of a long-standing continuum of Indigenous resistance and a direct provocation to his more influential white contemporaries.

Indigenous hospitality abounded in the colonial world, but settler colonialism, by its very nature, is the precise opposite of hospitality. It acts like a cancer, occupying the host body and proceeding to multiply and destroy. While the Indigenous ethos of the common pot valued sustainable ecological and human relationships, settler colonialism, at least in its 400-year history on this continent, has proven an extremely hostile guest. Few realize how deeply embedded are prevailing racialized notions of Indigenous identity in our collective understanding, for these notions have been carried forward, inscribed in history books, movies, poems, novels, paintings, and every other medium by which cultural narratives are advanced over time, until they have accrued an undeniable weight and mass resembling authenticity. Native people rarely surface in national conversations on race, even when they are the communities being hardest hit along the racial fault lines running through American society.

This legacy of neglect bleeds directly into our current pedagogical practices, where not only is Indigenous history whitewashed and elided by our continued cultural addiction to overtly biased colonial reporting, but even dynamic Native writers and intellectuals such as William Apess remain in obscurity or are misread and misrepresented in the classroom. And so persuaded are we that Native contributions to literature, history, and scholarship don't matter that we routinely exclude them from our theoretical practices and conversations concerning race and intersectionality. For example, Wiley Blackwell's third edition of *Literary Theory: An Anthology* came out in 2017. Part Eight is subtitled "Ethnic, Indigenous, Post-Colonial and Transnational Studies," but boasts not a single North American Indigenous Studies author or critic. Norton's third edition of *Theory and Criticism*, released in 2018, includes African American, Latinx, LGBTQ, and Asian scholars, but not one Indigenous author, thinker, or scholar. The most recent critical anthologies by Routledge and Broadview suffer from similar absences, leading one to suppose that Indigenous intellectuals either don't exist or that their thought stands somewhere outside the tradition of racial theory and criticism. Prominent Indigenous Studies scholars – including high theorists such as Gerald Vizenor (Anishinaabe) and Jodi Byrd (Chickasaw), rhetorical studies scholars like Robert Warrior (Osage) and Scott Lyons (Haudenosaunee), scholars specializing in Native feminisms such as Mishuana Goeman (Seneca) and Sarah Deer (Muskogee), authors dealing in Queer Studies including Mark Rifkin (white) and Daniel Heath Justice (Cherokee), religious studies scholars such as Jace Weaver (Cherokee) and George Tinker (Osage), environmental justice scholars such as Dina Gilio-Whitaker (Colville) and Kyle White (Potawatomie), and Indigenous historical scholars including Jean O'Brien (White Lake Ojibwe) and the 2019 Bancroft Prize winner Lisa Brooks (Abenaki) – have been effectively erased for the next generation of students delving into the field of critical theory, leaving Native scholars to carve out their own critical spaces – to locate their own intellectual homes in a land that was once theirs entirely.

"Go back where you came from": this rude assertion of settler belonging persisted at Standing Rock in 2016, where the conditions were, in many ways, similar to those in Mashpee 183 years earlier. Once again, just as in Mashpee, Native peoples effectively organized around principles of civil disobedience to protect their resources and livelihoods from being illegally exploited. And once again, just as with William Apess, who was absurdly charged with "trespassing and inciting a riot," Native peoples were treated as intruders, unlawful trespassers on their own lands, with the Morton County Police Department declaring conditions at Standing Rock an "ongoing riot."[24] The 1868 Fort Laramie Treaty, alongside subsequent court orders such as the 1980 *United States* v. *Sioux Nation of Indians* decision, expressly forbade any major projects running through Lakota territories, waterways, and sacred burial grounds without the consultation and approval of the Lakotas themselves. But the US government did not understand itself to be bound by its own laws when dealing with Indians. As Apess had already forcefully stated in 1836, "look at the treaties made by Congress, all broken . . . yea, every charter that has been given was given with the view of driving the Indian out of the states, or dooming them to become chained under desperate laws."[25]

Those who came to Standing Rock in 2016 were welcomed as guests, given a space to sleep, and offered three free meals a day. Like the Pilgrims at Patuxet, water protectors never had reason to doubt "but we should have enough where'er we came." Many of us reciprocated that hospitality where we could, helping around camp, chopping wood for fires, bringing meals to the elderly, and participating as "protectors" in the ongoing demonstrations. The key Lakota phrase of the #NoDAPL movement, "Mni Wiconi" (water is life), rose up in response to cries of "go back where you came from." "Mni Wiconi" expresses the Lakota belief that all life is sacred and that we have a common purpose to protect the resources that make life possible. As Nick Estes of the Lower Brule Sioux Tribe elaborates, "Mni Wiconi" speaks to how "Indigenous ways of relating to human and other-than-human life exist in opposition to capitalism, which transforms both humans and nonhumans into labor and commodities to be bought and sold," and also in opposition to settler colonialism, "which calls for the annihilation of Indigenous peoples and their other-than-human kin."[26]

The notion of Indigenous hospitality must not be construed as a romantic or essentialized character trait depicting Natives as hapless victims inviting further intrusion and disruption on their lands. The Standing Rock movement exists as part of a continuum of Indigenous resistance to settler colonial inhospitality – what Pexa deems just "the latest face of a centuries-long struggle against colonization," stretching all the way back to Apess and beyond.[27] Recognizing the long chain of Indigenous intellectuals advocating for Native rights in previous centuries is, in and of itself, a decolonizing strategy, reminding us of a persistent resistant Native presence during times when Native peoples were presumed to have been conquered, extinguished, become politically and intellectually inert.

In mid-November of 2016, we were 700 strong marching into downtown Bismark – the largest single action of the #NoDAPL movement. I was among those on the front line who locked arms and faced down the officers, with their batons and tear-gas canisters, who had aligned themselves with corporate forces over constitutional law. Almost without a doubt, I was the only one there thinking of Willam Apess that day. Nevertheless, behind our ranks, the Indigenous organizers of our march held ceremony – a set of spiritual invocations inclusive of everyone, red, white, black, and blue, in their plea to protect the waters that give life. This is why they called themselves "protectors" rather than "protesters." The rhetorical aim of the movement was not to set itself against a hostile force, a stranger, a foreigner, a pilgrim, but to once again draw upon traditional Indigenous frameworks of absolute hospitality to protect all that life included in the space of the common pot. These struggles persist today as DAPL continues to be contested in court and protectors hold space in places like Bears Ears, Utah, the Line 3 Pipeline in Minnesota, the Atlantic Coastal Pipeline in Virginia, and countless other less visible, but equally important, struggles, with still more struggles to come, where Indigenous peoples reflect traditions of absolute hospitality by demonstrating responsible stewardship of the lands that sustain us all.

Notes

1. Dino Gilio-Whitaker, *As Long as Grass Grows: The Indigenous Fight for Environmental Justice, from Colonization to Standing Rock* (Boston: Beacon Press, 2019), 12.
2. *Mourt's Relation: A Journal of the Pilgrims at Plymouth* (Bedford: Applewood Books, 1963), 51.
3. *Mourt's Relation* 133.
4. Christopher Pexa, *Translated Nation: Rewriting the Dakhóta Oyate* (Minneapolis: University of Minnesota Press, 2019), 24.
5. *Mourt's Relation*, 63.
6. Ibid., 41.
7. Lisa Brooks, *The Common Pot: The Recovery of Native Space in the Northeast* (Minneapolis: University of Minnesota Press, 2008), 5.
8. *Mourt's Relation*, 91–93.

9. William Bradford, *Of Plymouth Plantation: Along with the Full Text of the Pilgrims' Journals for Their First Year in Plymouth*, Ed. Caleb Johnson (Bloomington: Xlibris Corporation, 2006), 355–356.
10. John Mason, "A Brief History of the Pequot War: Especially of the Memorable Taking of Their Fort at Misitck in Connecticut I 1637," *History of the Pequot War*, Ed. Charles Orr (Cleveland: Helman-Taylor Co., 1980), 40–44.
11. John Underhill, *Newes from America* (New York: De Capo Press, 1971).
12. Caryl Christian, "The Democracy Boondoggle in Iraq." *Foreign Policy*, March 6.
13. Kathleen J. Bragdon and Ives Goddard, *Natve Writings in Massachusett* (Philadelphia: American Philosophical Society, 1988), 373.
14. Daniel Webster, *A Discourse, Delivered at Plymouth, December 22, 1820. In Commemoration of the First Settlement of New England.* Ed. Paul Roster (Lincoln: Zea Books, 2022), 10.
15. Webster, *A Discourse*, 71.
16. William Apess, "Indian Nullification." In Barry O'Connell, Ed., *On Our Own Ground: The Complete Writings of William Apess, a Pequot* (Amherst: University of Massachusetts Press, 1992), 209.
17. Apess, "Nullification," 181.
18. Ibid., 225.
19. Ibid., 227.
20. Ibid., 178.
21. Quoted in James Thacher, *History of the Town of Plymouth from Its First Settlement in 1620, to the Year 1832* (Boston: Marsh, Capen & Lyon, 1832), 169.
22. William Apess, "A Eulogy on King Philip," *On Our Own Ground: The Complete Writings of William Apess, a Pequot, Ed. Barry O'Connell* (Amherst: University of Massachusetts Press, 1992), 306.
23. Apess, "Eulogy," 280.
24. Pexa, *Translated Nation*, x.
25. Apess "Eulogy," 306.
26. Nick Estes, *Our History Is the Future: Standing Rock versus the Dakota Access Pipeline, and the Long Tradition of Indian Resistance* (New York: Verso, 2019), 16.
27. Pexa, *Translated Nation*, ix.

CHAPTER 5

Racing Latinidad

Renee Hudson

The driving issue behind who counts as Latinx and who does not revolves around the paradox of *latinidad* (typically understood as Latinxness, the essence of what it means to be Latinx) as a category that unifies a group of people but one that is also fundamentally incoherent. For example, in *The Trouble with Unity: Latino Politics and the Creation of Identity* (2010),[1] Cristina Beltrán critiques "unity" as a framework for latinidad, arguing that the terms Latinx and latinidad can obscure difference through an alignment with white supremacist logics of identity. José Esteban Muñoz puts the problem of Latinx identity succinctly when he writes that the term "has *not* developed as an umbrella term that unites cultural and political activists across different national, racial, class, and gender divides. This problem has to do with its incoherence, by which I mean the term's inability to index, with any regularity, the central identity tropes that lead to our understandings of group identities in the United States."[2] For Muñoz, such incoherence stems from the term's failure "to enable much-needed coalitions between different national groups,"[3] leading Muñoz to resolve the impasse between identity and politics through the shared affects and affinities he traces among different Latinx groups.[4]

The questions and concerns that subtend such theorizations of latinidad – whether stated explicitly or not – form the complicated relationship between latinidad and race. Beltrán's "trouble with unity" emerges from her observations of failures of solidarity, while Muñoz focuses on the lack of coalition-building among such diverse national-origin groups. As I detail later in this chapter, such failures are historically grounded in appeals to rights-based whiteness and how many Latinx groups are excluded from this approach. Thinking outside of identity as ostensibly biological and cultural facts toward affinity and solidarity, which are political positions that emphasize relationality on the one hand and action on the other, are potential next steps for the futures of latinidad; however, my contention in this chapter is that such work is impossible without acknowledging the complicated racial history of Latinxs in the United States and the ramifications of that history for present understandings of latinidad. I want to suggest that what are typically seen as the problems with the categories Latinx and latinidad are not problems at all, but an opportunity for contending with Latinxs' complicated racial history.

Retaining both terms allows them to continue to be messy signifiers that, as I demonstrate in this chapter, are open to change and adaptability and are thus able to evade institutionalization and disrupt the state. If the terms Latinx and latinidad are to offer anything in terms of a politically useful category, it must hinge on irresolvable difference rather than try to assimilate different Latinx groups into one umbrella term. When we say "Latinx," rather than try to summon a *people* we should focus on summoning a *politics*. My thinking here relies on the Chicano Movement, which attempted to conjure a people out of a politics. Crucially, the Chicano Movement created a bridge out of an impasse: to identify as Chicanos rather than Mexican Americans, Chicanos had to subscribe to a politics that emphasized embracing cultural values and uplifting the community. While there are many critiques to be had regarding the Chicano Movement's relationship to indigeneity, the focus on Indigenous heritage is one of the many facets that set the movement apart from the assimilationist mode of the Mexican American, captured in Ruben Salazar's famous formulation that "[a] Chicano is a Mexican-American with a non-Anglo image of himself."[5]

Recently, scholars in the field have offered substantial critiques of latinidad, but they have also imagined a latinidad that centers what Marta Caminero-Santangelo describes as "*commitment* – not just to an exploration of conditions that encourage pan-ethnic collectivity but also to an exploration of those conditions (including differences) which potentially inhibit it."[6] Rather than seeing the diversity and incoherence of latinidad as a problem, Caminero-Santangelo suggests we examine it as a feature. Or, to use her words: "At its best, identifying as Latina or Latino also allows us to express, to ourselves and to others, our *commitment* to attending to the historical and present differences among Latinos, as well as to the sometimes overlapping or analogous histories and current structural problems – which is another way of saying our commitment to solidarity" (219). Although in many ways solidarity returns us to Muñoz's suggestion of affinity, I want to emphasize that solidarity is affinity coupled with action.

In many ways, this chapter is conceived as a response to the backlash against the neologism "Latinx," which seems to also extend into how people conceptualize latinidad and its presumed whiteness.[7] Here, I examine Manuel Muñoz's *What You See in the Dark* (2011)[8] to illuminate how the logic of inclusion enforces the logic of the state in determining who counts as a citizen regardless of citizenship status. I also read Dahlma Llanos-Figueroa's *Daughters of the Stone* (2009)[9] to demonstrate how excavating racial histories outside of the logic of the state is one method for summoning a politics to imagine a people – in this case, a latinidad that embraces incoherence rather than striving for an inclusion model that will inherently be exclusionary. While my focus is on the United States, I do want to acknowledge how in places like the Southwest, particularly California, this logic overlaps with the racial logics of Spanish colonization in Mexico which created *el sistema de castas* (the caste system) based on a complex taxonomy of racial classification and the mandate to improve the race (*mejorar la raza*) through marriage to a lighter-skinned person. Assuming that Latinxs are white or that latinidad itself is a whitening process mistakes the racial processes of the state (first Spain, then the USA) for the project of creating community among Latin American-descended people. Before turning to the novels, I briefly examine how the USA adjudicated race following the US–Mexico War (1846–8) and the Spanish–American War (1898) to track the USA's racial logic in these instances.

I focus on Chicanxs and Puerto Ricans because, historically, they were foundational to the formation of Latinx Studies precisely because of their close ties with the USA given the US acquisition of Mexican and Puerto Rican territories. While I do not want to replicate the dominance of these two groups within the field, I do want to explore how the legal cases adjudicating the racial status of each of these groups has implications for how latinidad is conceptualized racially. These two groups have particularly illuminating histories within the USA as Mexicans were presumably declared white by treaty after the US–Mexico War (1846–8) and the signing of the Treaty of Guadalupe Hidalgo. Meanwhile, after the Spanish–American War (1898), the USA decided to maintain Puerto Rico as a colony without the prospect for statehood, and race played a significant role in the Insular Cases that made this determination.

Adjudicating Race: Mexican Whiteness and Puerto Rican Blackness

Latinidad and Latinx are burdened by the history of racialization in both the USA and Latin America, which Laura E. Gómez calls "double colonization."[10] The issue of Mexicans' racial status arose as soon as the language for the Treaty of Guadalupe Hidalgo was drafted. As Juan F. Perea notes, the acquisition of Mexican and Puerto Rican territories posed a threat to the USA's presumed Anglo-Saxon whiteness.[11] Indeed, the Treaty of Guadalupe Hidalgo, which outlined the terms of Mexico's surrender of land, introduced a paradox in that only white men could be citizens at the time, but Mexicans who chose to stay in the lands newly acquired by the USA would be considered citizens. California explicitly addressed this paradox in the 1849 California constitutional convention, where it was decided that "[e]very white male citizen of the United States, *and every white male citizen of Mexico* . . . shall be entitled to vote at all elections" (150; emphasis Perea's). As Perea observes, this also posed a problem by leaving out "who was a 'white Mexican male' and entitled to vote" (150). Thus, the legal fiction of Mexican whiteness was created and, as numerous cases following the treaty demonstrate, the issue of Mexican whiteness was far from settled.

As Laura E. Gómez outlines in *Inventing Latinos: A New Story of American Racism*,[12] Mexicans often appealed to their supposed whiteness as a strategy to gain rights, often at the expense of other people of color. Among the key cases she examines is *Hernandez* v. *Texas* (1954), wherein "[t]he *Hernandez* lawyers walked a tightrope between claiming their Mexican American client's rights were violated because Mexican Americans were excluded from the jury pool in his case and maintaining that Mexican Americans were White under Texas law" (103). That said, not all cases sought to appeal to whiteness, as demonstrated by *Mendez* v. *Westminster* (1946), which "also represented a turning point in that Latino and African American civil rights groups collaborated on the case" (107), which ruled that the segregation of Latino children was unconstitutional.[13]

Yet, while in the case of northern Mexico the USA was able to put aside its concerns about absorbing a nonwhite population because of the sparse population and the ability to delay full enfranchisement, according to Perea the acquisitions of Puerto Rico and the Philippines extended the logic at play during the US–Mexico War, but with the conclusion that these populations would be unassimilable into the nation. As Perea notes, quoting Rubin Weston's *Racism in US Imperialism* (1972), "Puerto Rico's population, 'composed of a mixture of Negro, Indian, and Spanish ancestry . . . rendered the island incapable of independent self-government' in the eyes of Americans" (156). One of the key Insular Cases (the set of court opinions following the Spanish–American War that determined the status of US territories), *Downes* v. *Bidwell* (1901), held that the constitution did not necessarily apply to US territories and that such territories would be governed by Congress. Thus, "[i]n *Downes*, the Court demonstrates its ideological commitment to an Anglo-Saxon conception of United States citizenship" (159), reinforcing the Teutonic origins thesis of American government, which viewed "Anglo-Saxons as a people with a special genius for law and for state-building; they described the state and legal order itself as Anglo-Saxon in character; and they portrayed dark-skinned peoples as incapable of legality and thus essentially criminal."[14] I dwell on the racist views that informed the Insular Cases and the acquisition of US territories in places populated by people of color to emphasize how the construction of Latinx as a racial category in the USA positioned Latinxs as nonwhite (even if Mexicans presumably had a kind of white status) while explicitly creating frameworks for Latinxs to appeal to whiteness for the acquisition of rights. While this was more explicit in court cases such as *Hernandez* v. *Texas*, relegating Puerto Ricans to second-class status (they only became US citizens in 1917, and only mainland Puerto Ricans have the right to vote in presidential elections) because of their racial mixture[15] illuminates the powerful prowhite messaging of the USA. Thus, when celebrities such as Indya Moore, who is Puerto Rican and Dominican, refuse to identify as Latinx because of its presumed whiteness, I suggest that this rhetorical move is one that ignores the role whiteness plays in conceptions of Latinx identity construction, from the pressure to *mejorar la raza* under Spanish colonization to the desire to gain rights, if not equality, in the USA. Acknowledging this history and turning away from whiteness is how we can mobilize latinidad as a politically useful formation.

Surveilling Mexicanidad

Manuel Muñoz's *What You See in the Dark* examines the perils of turning toward whiteness as a strategy for equality as the policing of the identity of Teresa Garza, a Mexican American woman, replicates the whitening logic of the state and how it monitors identity. The novel juxtaposes the murder of Teresa and the filming of Alfred Hitchcock's *Psycho* (1960) in Bakersfield, California, to explore racial tensions in a small town. Teresa's murder is initially framed as a consequence of her supposed mixed-race relationship with a white man, Dan Watson. The character Candy, who is Teresa's coworker at a shoe store, polices Teresa's identity as she monitors her movements and the mixed-race spaces available in Bakersfield in the 1950s. Indeed, *What You See in the Dark* is a novel about watching and being watched, and I suggest that this focus on watching is also an emphasis on how Candy surveils Teresa's race, monitoring the unfolding miscegenation romance between Dan and Teresa. While Teresa would seemingly be a part of the community, given the fact that her mother worked at the diner with Dan's mother and that Teresa mostly grew up there, Candy's policing of Teresa's identity illuminates how the logic of inclusion depends upon exclusion. Thus, even though Teresa's identity would seem to potentially be fluid, as exemplified by her relationship with Dan, what the novel emphasizes is Teresa's vulnerable status as not only does Dan murder her, he also gets away with it.

Candy underscores the exclusionary logic of the community when she comments upon her perception that Teresa and Dan are an incompatible match, noting that Dan "was the most handsome man in town for sure" (3) and "would be a good man to marry" (4), before remarking:

> And yet the one to grab his attention was that skinny brown girl who lived above the bowling alley. Always on foot, always staring into the windows of the record shop, of the TG&Y, of the furniture store, of the Rexall, even of the shoe store where you worked, as if she hadn't set up the displays herself. A very plain girl, not too tall, with slender hips, and hair as dark as her mother's. Her mother had worked at the café too – with his mother, in fact – almost eight or nine years ago. No doubt his mother remembered. (4)

Teresa's brown skin and dark hair rankle Candy, who focuses on how "skinny" Teresa is, noting her "slender hips" as if to suggest that Teresa is ill-equipped for having children. Candy imbues her racialized critique of Teresa with overtones of class disparities, as she comments on the fact that Teresa is "[a]lways on foot, always staring into the windows" of various stores, clearly imagining a better life for herself and unable to afford a car.

Teresa's internalization of the town's racial politics becomes clear when Dan offers to give her a ride home one day after meeting her outside the bar where he works, Las Cuatro Copas. Initially intending to audition at El Molino Rojo with Cheno, the Mexican fieldworker she has started to date, Teresa ends up singing for Dan instead and agreeing to sing at Las Cuatro Copas. While she eventually accepts Dan's offer of a ride, she at first refuses, thinking "about the people in town, how a ride through the afternoon streets with the windows rolled down was far different from Cheno's careful, tiptoeing courtship" (85). Teresa is right to be worried, as the next day Candy confronts her:

> "I saw you yesterday, too. Riding in Dan Watson's truck." She looked up at Teresa, and the tone in her voice was unmistakable: accusatory, yet not

> mean spirited, a flat statement that dared to be denied, as if she were confronting Teresa with an empty cashbox, wordless, yet with the facts in hand, a fact that needed to be explained. (119)

No longer the Mexican girl who was hired for Spanish-speaking customers and stayed squarely in her part of town – over the bowling alley, near the corner where the Mexican day laborers sought work – Teresa is now the girl in Dan Watson's car, a fact that Candy treats like a crime. Teresa's relationship with Dan thus reveals the cracks in the small-town camaraderie.

The complex racial dynamics of Bakersfield are further illuminated by Las Cuatro Copas, a bar that "welcomes everyone" (8). As Candy describes the scene at Las Cuatro Copas on Teresa's opening night, it's clear that Teresa and Dan are actually a synecdoche for mixed relationships that are largely kept on the down-low. According to Candy,

> [s]ome of the Mexican men have even come with blond American women, heedless of the hard glares. These couples have little to say to each other, though sometimes the women jabber on to fill the quiet space between them. Here, everyone is out in the open – it is clear who brought whom, who is being distracted, who is being worn away by jealousy, and who is going to be brokenhearted. (16)

Teresa and Dan's relationship seems to have encouraged other couples to be "out in the open," but it's clear that the tolerance for a Mexican woman and a white man does not extend to Mexican men with white women, demonstrating how Mexican women are able to move between the two racial groups more fluidly than their male counterparts.

Candy proves to be the most faithful documentarian of "that girl" Teresa. While no one contests that Dan beat her to death, the motive remains unclear until the end of the novel, when Candy "put[s] it all together" (236). She observes that a week before Dan murdered Teresa, Cheno and a group of other fieldworkers showed up at Las Cuatro Copas. As Candy reports, "That night, there was another man in the back. You could tell by the way that girl brought her voice inward, her eyes squinting as if to confirm what she had recognized, and her easy flirtation with Dan Watson hardened into a forced gesture" (234). Seeing Cheno shifts something within Teresa, within her relationship with Dan. In Candy's reimagining of how the murder unfolded, Dan beats Teresa for her relationship with Cheno: "*Did you?* Dan Watson asked. Because that is the question everyone wanted to know about that girl. Had she, with that Mexican boy?" (250). Yet Cheno's quiet courtship of Teresa before she met Dan would hardly seem worthy of such jealousy, punctuated as it is with his small gifts of Gerber baby-food jars filled with delicacies from the fields – toasted pumpkin seeds, shelled walnuts – and bottles of soda.

Part of what makes Cheno's courtship ritual so threatening is its untranslatability from the courtship rituals practiced by the white people in the town. As we learn from Candy, Teresa and Dan go to the drive-in and the Jolly Kone. As Candy comments, "None of the ladies who came to the shoe store ever knew about the Jolly Kone. They never knew about the drive-in. The things that went on in both places. You never said a word about the boyfriend taking you there" (242). Cheno never takes Teresa to either place; he maintains respectability rather than the illusion of respectability that Candy cultivates. While the town is titillated by Teresa and Dan's public courtship – with their sexual relationship implied by their presence at the drive-in and the Jolly Kone – Cheno's courtship is more private, more confined to the Mexican community within the town rather than the town at large. Teresa is killed, then, not for daring to date someone outside of her community, but for having the potential to choose her community over the possible future that Dan represents. We never learn where Dan disappears to, but we do learn that Cheno is deported, "[even] though everyone knew he had had no involvement in the death whatsoever" (195). Teresa's death and Cheno's deportation thus mark a return to the white fantasy of normality, exemplified by Candy, where Mexican women do not date white men and Mexicans are sent back to Mexico.

Where *What You See in the Dark* starts to imagine a California without the threat of Mexican sexuality or a white man's desire for a Mexican woman, *Daughters of the Stone* illuminates how Puerto Rican writers such as Dahlma Llanos-Figueroa engage with Puerto Rico's conflicted racial history by directly addressing the sexual violence of the slave past. Ultimately, I argue that returning to the slave past is a way to imagine not only a future for Afro Puerto Ricans, but also a politics rooted in a latinidad that does not seek to erase such histories.

Racial Excavations

In October 2020, Jennifer Lopez came under fire for using the term *negrita* in her song "Lonely." The lyric in question is "[y]o siempre seré tu negrita del Bronx," which translates to "I'll always be your little Black girl from the Bronx." As the *Miami Herald* reported at the time, "[t]he term 'negrita' is used in many Latino cultures as a term of endearment, kind of like the word 'gorda,' which doesn't equate to 'fat,' but 'cutie.' Or 'mama,' which can be even used on small children in place of 'honey.'" Tellingly, the article does not offer a translational equivalent for negrita in the way it does for gorda and mama, leaving the direct translation – little Black one – as the meaning behind the term. The brouhaha behind Lopez's usage is contextualized within the fact that, as Tanya K. Hernández notes, "[a]t no other time has Lopez personally identified herself with Blackness" and she has a "history of whitening her appearance and hair." [16] As this example demonstrates, the term negrita/o has a contested history within Puerto Rico which, I would argue, has much to do with the island's conflicted relationship with Blackness.

Dahlma Llanos-Figueroa centers the issue of Puerto Rican Blackness in her novel *Daughters of the Stone*, which tells the story of an enslaved African's descendants across five generations.[17] The story begins in the mid-1800s, and tells the story of Fela, an enslaved woman who is brought to Puerto Rico from Africa. Fela carries with her a childstone, which carries the soul of her unborn child with Imo, her partner in Africa. To "finish the work of the stone" (37), Fela sleeps with her enslaver, Don Tomás. The resulting child, Mati, regards Don Tomás as her biological father and Imo as her "*soul* father" (95). Although Fela dies shortly after delivering Mati, she leaves her with the stone, which continues to be passed from woman to woman through the generations: from Mati to Concha to Elena to Carisa. Concha moves to New York in the 1950s and Carisa is subsequently born there.

After her professors ridicule her writing as "a mass of superstitious nonsense" (270), Carisa returns to Puerto Rico to heal her "bruised spirit" (274) with her Abuela Concha's remedies. While there, Carisa becomes interested in the stories of her abuela's friends, one of whom entreats her to "make sure you write down the stuff that's usually left out" (279). Eventually, Carisa seeks out the broader history of Puerto Rico, beyond her abuela's house. She enrolls in a class at university, only to learn that the university is not a place for an Afro Puerto Rican like Carisa. Carissa observes,

> [t]he words "*esclavos*" and "*esclavitud*" were rarely mentioned and then only in passing – like an unfortunate disease. Slavery was referred to as a regrettable period in our history. Much was made, however, of the glory of the cane and coffee that was the mainstay of colonial society. Who actually worked the cane and coffee fields was not the issue. We learned about all the great Puerto Rican abolitionists who became great statesmen, but nothing of the slaves themselves. The times I brought up the question of race, I was assured

repeatedly that all Puerto Ricans were treated equally and racism simply didn't exist in Puerto Rico. Looking around the campus, my eyes told me differently. (292)

Carisa's empirical experience, as well as her family history, does not resonate with the version of Puerto Rican history and culture she learns at the university. While scholars such as Ileana M. Rodríguez-Silva have pointed out the many ways that the issues of racial difference and racism are "silenced" on the island, what Carisa observes is a Puerto Rico that still hasn't fully accounted for its African (and Indigenous) roots.[18] Her history and culture class lacks a structural critique of the plantation legacy, and attempts to recover the voices of the enslaved are clearly not underway.

Carisa's university experiences thus motivate her to excavate the larger history of Afro Puerto Ricans on the island, which she does once she meets an Afro Puerto Rican photographer, María Luisa Campos, at a protest. Carisa accompanies her across the island as María Luisa seeks out "socially invisible communities, or the quickly disappearing past" (307). The first such place Carisa sees with María Luisa are the ruins of a former coffee plantation. Explaining her mission, María Luisa says, "I wanted to listen for the voices of ghosts. I wanted to try to find them before all our progressive leaders sanitize it too much and put it on display for a buck or two" (304). In this way, María Luisa listens for the voices of the ancestors, "people with no public voices" (306). Moreover, she seeks out this history before it can be folded into the mainstream history of Puerto Rico. Describing María Luisa's photographs, Carisa remarks, "Not one of the pictures I had seen was like those of the San Juan socialites, beauty queens, cotillions, or political leaders that hung framed and prominently displayed in the university administration building. We already had a disproportionate number of their stories" (306). In joining María Luisa in her work, Carisa helps recover the lost histories of Afro Puerto Ricans, in contrast to the received history represented by the pictures in the university administration building. Recovering such histories means looking outside of institutions toward ruins – toward the spaces that are not maintained and valorized, and that testify to a starkly different history.

The novel ends hopefully, with Carisa on a plane to Lagos, Nigeria, to continue her work of recovery by seeking out her African roots. While the novel doesn't portray Carisa's experiences in Nigeria, we know based on Richard Wright's and Saidiya Hartman's portrayals of returning to Africa to excavate the past that it can lead to a less than enthusiastic welcome, if not outright hostility.[19] The novel evades this potential outcome and instead offers a vision of Oshun while Carisa is on the plane. Carisa narrates the scene as follows:

> She walks a path that is clearly marked. She knows her way. She remembers the markers. The *griot*'s stool is abandoned on the hill. She picks it up, dusts it off, and takes a seat. She grinds her hips into it. It fits well. It is her journey's companion. She opens her mouth and starts to sing. She knows I am watching. When she turns her face to me I see that the Lady has my face. (323)

By merging with Oshun, Carisa takes up the role of griot, or storyteller. We know from the prologue that the stories in *Daughters of the Stone* are Carisa's, and her section narrates how she comes to be the storyteller of the family and how taking on such a role stems explicitly from the desire to tell the stories that aren't told, the histories that aren't commemorated. In short, *Daughters of the Stone* imagine a Blackness that hasn't been forgotten, but that has a history that must actively be remembered and maintained to persist. While it potentially offers a romanticized view of Africa, where it succeeds is in centering Blackness as part of the Latinx experience while also acknowledging the work that must be done to continue centering Blackness.

The Latinx Turn

As *What You See in the Dark* illuminates, state models of inclusion will always necessarily be exclusionary in a hierarchical model that historically places whites at the top. Moreover, Candy's policing of Teresa's identity illustrates how the logic of who belongs in the category of whiteness resonates with the ongoing issue of who belongs in latinidad. Rather than focusing solely on issues of belonging, I suggest that for latinidad and Latinx to be useful categories, we must embrace their incoherence. Thus, when Llanos-Figueroa excavates the racial histories that the state would rather forget in *Daughters of the Stone*, she highlights how operating outside the logic of the state is a way to imagine latinidad as a political orientation rather than an identity marker.

By emphasizing how notions of latinidad can reproduce the logic of the state, both novels point to the potential of the term "Latinx," which has been the subject of countless debates.[20] On its most basic level, the x signals the embrace of a wide range of gender expressions, including binary, trans, and genderqueer subjectivities. It has also been the occasion for a rethinking of the kind of latinidad the x signifies. As Alan Pelaez Lopez argues, "'Latinx' is not for everyone" and it's an opportunity to reflect that "violence against Lesbian, Gay, Bisexual, Transgender, Intersex, Asexual + (LGBTQIA+) Latin Americans has been accepted by Latin American people to the point that LGBTQIA+ Latinxs have had to create a linguistic intervention in the hopes that they can live a livable life."[21] Pelaez Lopez thus explores "the visible wound that the 'X' forces the Latin American diaspora to confront," wounds that they identify as "settlement, anti-Blackness, femicides, and inarticulation." Pelaez Lopez argues for a powerful politics around the × that moves beyond simply signaling solidarity or inclusion. As *What You See in the Dark* and *Daughters of the Stone* make clear, the issues Pelaez Lopez underscores are issues that Latinx literature confronts directly as Latinx authors contend with the legacy of double colonization.

Literature offers a unique opportunity to offer different imaginaries for latinidad, a future orientation that, as Claudia Milian argues, emphasizes that the term Latinx "shows that Latino/a imaginations are not extinguished, that the terms Latin and Latino are not so 'common sense' and complacent, after all."[22] I would add that latinidad's lack of coherence is an advantage that resists legibility and visibility and thus state management. As Laura E. Gómez's extensive analysis of how the census counts Latinxs exemplifies, Latinxs defy easy categorization and disrupt the Black–white binary upon which the USA was founded.[23] I see the ever-shifting terminology for Latinxs – from Latino to Latin@ to Latina/o – as part of the way that Latinxs evade institutionalization. Quite simply, the confusion over what to call us – and how to name our departments at universities – becomes an occasion to teach the complexities of Latinx identities, on the one hand, and an opportunity to reflect on who we are and what values we represent on the other. Pelaez Lopez offers one such reflection that centers a particular politics – one that critiques the settler colonialism, anti-Blackness, and misogyny that characterizes both Latin America and the USA and uses the x to articulate the unspeakable violence enacted by these three wounds. However, I would argue that Latinx literature is explicitly a project to articulate that violence and, in so doing, write against the three wounds Pelaez Lopez describes.

While Pelaez Lopez is right to insist that Latinx is not for everyone, and to worry about the normalization of the term, I argue that using "Latinx" means signaling the kind of politics Pelaez Lopez outlines, particularly because their framework foregrounds Indigeneity and Blackness to the Latinx formation. In other words, much like Chicanxs use the term to distinguish their politics from Mexican Americans, Latinxs can also use the x to signal their commitment to a latinidad that foregrounds the experiences of Indigenous and Afro Latinxs such that these Latinx populations do not have to qualify their latinidad. What I'm calling for is a latinidad that's not quite here yet: a decolonial latinidad that takes a critical stance toward the history of double colonization in the United States and foregrounds the ramifications of colonial logic on Latinx thinking. Thus, one of the unknowns that the × signals is Latinx futures, particularly the kind of future where a politics becomes synonymous with a people.

Notes

1. Published by Oxford University Press.
2. José Esteban Muñoz, "Feeling Brown: Ethnicity and Affect in Ricardo Bracho's The Sweetest Hangover (and Other STDs)," *Theatre Journal* 52, no. 1 (March 2000): 67–79, 67.
3. Ibid.
4. For a fuller discussion of Muñoz 's ideas, see *The Sense of Brown* (Durham: Duke University Press, 2020).
5. See Ruben Salazar, *Border Correspondent: Selected Writings 1955–1970* (Berkeley: University of California Press, 2018), 235.
6. Marta Caminero-Santangelo, *On Latinidad: US Latino Literature and the Construction of Ethnicity* (Gainesville: University Press of Florida, 2009), 218 (hereafter, cited parenthetically in the text). For more on these critiques, see Maylei Blackwell, Floridalma Boj Lopez, and Luis, Urrieta Jr. (eds.), *Critical Latinx Indigeneities*. Special Issue of *Latino Studies*, vol. 15, 2017 and Miriam Jiménez Román and Juan Flores (eds.), *The Afro-Latin@ Reader: History and Culture in the United States* (Durham: Duke University Press, 2010).
7. Yara Simón, "'Pose' Star Indya Moore on Why They Don't Identify as Latino: 'I'm Not White'" in *Remezcla* (September 22, 2019). https://remezcla.com/film/indya-moore-emmys-red-carpet-interview/.
8. Published by Algonquin Books (hereafter, cited parenthetically in the text).
9. Published by Thomas Dunne Books (hereafter, cited parenthetically in the text).
10. Laura E. Gómez, *Manifest Destinies: The Making of the Mexican American Race* (New York: New York University Press, 2007).
11. Juan F. Perea, "Fulfilling Manifest Destiny: Conquest, Race, and the Insular Cases,' in *Foreign in a Domestic Sense: Puerto Rico, American Expansion, and the Constitution, Foreign in a Domestic Sense: Puerto Rico, American Expansion, and the Constitution*, ed. Christina Duffy Burnett and Burke Marshall (Durham: Duke University Press, 2001), 140–166 (hereafter, cited parenthetically in the text). For more on how the Anglo-Saxon character of the USA informed the Insular Cases, see Mark S. Wiener, "Teutonic Constitutionalism: The Role of Ethno-Juridical Discourse in the Spanish-American War" in *Foreign in*

a Domestic Sense: Puerto Rico, American Expansion, and the Constitution, ed. Christina Duffy Burnett and Burke Marshall (Durham: Duke University Press, 2001), 48–81. For a broader discussion of how the idea of Anglo-Saxonism became predominant in the nineteenth century, see Reginald Horsman, *Race and Manifest Destiny: Origins of American Racial Anglo-Saxonism* (Cambridge: Harvard University Press, 1981).

12. Laura E. Gomez, *Inventing Latinos* (New York: The New Press, 2020).
13. As Gómez notes, *Mendez* v. *Westminster* was also an important precedent for *Brown* v. *Board of Education* (1954), especially since the *Westminster* attorneys would "go on to argue *Brown* v. *Board of Education*" (107).
14. Mark S. Wiener, "Teutonic Constitutionalism: The Role of Ethno-Juridical Discourse in the Spanish-American War" in *Foreign in a Domestic Sense: Puerto Rico, American Expansion, and the Constitution*, ed. Christina Duffy Burnett and Burke Marshall (Durham: Duke University Press, 2001), 48–81, 49.
15. Perea, "Fulfilling Manifest Destiny," 160.
16. See "Latina Professors Discuss use of 'Negrito' and 'Negrita' in Latin Culture, after J.Lo Controversy," *San Diego Union Tribune*, Nov. 1, 2020. www.sandiegouniontribune.com/columnists/story/2020-11-01/latina-professors-discuss-use-of-negrito-negrita-in-latin-culture-after-j-lo-controversy.
17. For a useful discussion of corporeality and belonging in *Daughters of the Stone*, see C. Christina Lam, "Flipping the Script: Memory, Body, and Belonging in Dahlma Llanos-Figueroa's *Daughters of the Stone*" in *Label Me Latina/o*, vol. VII (Summer 2017), pp. 1–9.
18. See Illeana M. Rodríguez-Silva, *Silencing Race: Disentangling Blackness, Colonialism, and National Identities in Puerto Rico* (New York: Palgrave Macmillan, 2012).
19. See Richard Wright, *Black Power: Three Books from Exile: Black Power, The Color Curtain, and White Man, Listen!* (New York: Harper Perennial Modern Classics, 2008) and Saidiya Hartman, *Lost Your Mother: A Journey Along the Atlantic Slave Route* (New York: Farrar, Straus and Giroux, 2007).
20. See the following special issues: *Theorizing LatinX*, special issue of *Cultural Dynamics*, vol. 29, no. 3, August 2017; *Latinx Lives in a Hemispheric Context*, special issue of *English Language Notes*, vol. 56, no. 2, October 2018; and *LatinX Studies: Variations and Velocities*, special issue of *Cultural Dynamics*, vol. 31, no. 1–2, February–May 2019.
21. See "The X in Latinx Is a Wound, Not a Trend," www.colorbloq.org/article/the-x-in-latinx-is-a-wound-not-a-trend.
22. Claudia Milian, *LatinX* (Minneapolis: University of Minnesota Press, 2019), 4.
23. Gómez, *Inventing Latinos*.

CHAPTER 6

African American Literature's One Long Memory

Christopher Freeburg

What is African American literature – and is this a body of work that necessarily focuses on race and social injustice? African American literature can read like "one long memory."[1] At the time W. E. B. Du Bois wrote this phrase in *Dusk of Dawn* he surely did not have the future trajectory of African American literature in mind. But if one begins to study how the challenges of race shapes life in the USA, the words of Black writers, and the thoughts and memories of their characters, is a great place to begin. For most of its history the USA has been a nation dominated by powerful whites who have systematically and often violently excluded African Americans from any form of social and political equality. Looking backward, it is not surprising, then, that being treated like second-class citizens and other race-based political exclusions have become the subject of African American writing. In so much of African American prose and poetry, writers portray various senses of Black humanity to encourage the realization of opportunities for full citizenship and social equality. In this robust body of literature, Black writers tether together the subjects of racial inequality and explore what it means to be human together.

This tethering prompts a perennial question for critics and students alike: When it comes to examining African American literature's long memory, do we examine the history of racial inequality to find out more about what it means to be human, or do we look to rich humanistic social relations in fiction to reimagine and/or resolve any remaining concepts of racial inequality? To put it slightly differently, are ideas about what is valuable, meaningful, and purposeful in life, commonly referred to as humanistic and existential questions, significant insofar as they speak directly to solving racial inequality? Writers from Phillis Wheatley to Ta-Nehisi Coates creatively reimagine how to ask questions like "What is my life worth in world that devalues me" or "How do I define myself in a world where I feel I have no voice?" These questions permeate Black literary experience. What is more, across African American writing there are explicit ongoing debates about how to produce the human as if the stakes of doing it one way or another can weigh significantly in political outcomes toward racial progress. Not surprisingly, critics incorporate ideas of humanistic complexity and depth that can help society make evident alternative directions for living otherwise, or they imagine new equalities and ideas beyond current racial disparities (e.g., police brutality, prison reform or abolition, health disparities). In short, through its probing of what it means to be human, African American literature is often read for its commentary on the social order, and for its ability to present solutions to ongoing social problems.

Du Bois famously wrote that all Negro art should be written in this vein, as propaganda, and it is not a surprise that critics continue to mine literature for evidence of racial progress and sociopolitical transformation.[2] From a different perspective, Alain Locke, Sterling Brown, and Zora Neale Hurston advocated that Black writers produce beauty and interiority first and foremost, but still critics tend to read this aesthetic production on the beauty of interiority as a framework for conceptualizing political progress against white supremacist and patriarchal ideas, practices, and institutions. While certainly not beyond politics by any stretch of the imagination, these writers saw this beauty and interiority as part of the richness of human depth that works of art with too much emphasis on racial conflict failed to fully reveal. Ralph Ellison and James Baldwin carried this concept of richer and more complex humanity in their art through the bulk of the twentieth century.

At the center of African American literary history are incessant debates about how writers might achieve the highest levels of aesthetic achievement while also shaping American political consciousness in a way that makes a pivotal difference in the lives of African Americans. There is no debate, however, about the importance of the rhetoric of humanity to any discussion of race and African American literature. While I of course recognize the importance of studying the ongoing exploration of race in African American literary history, in this chapter I am more specifically interested in considering the ways in which Black humanity is revealed in African American literature. I submit that when studying African American writers and race, we should view Black humanity's significance as a discussion that is ongoing and remains unsettled.

At first glance this argument may seem to be a no-brainer, but critics and artists, directly or indirectly, emphasize that there are real stakes in precisely what kind of Black humanity is produced in and through writing. Thus, for this chapter I will explore the terms of the debates over how to represent Black humanity, and I will suggest that the debate has produced only ongoing and unanswered questions. Hence, I posit that it is in fact the irresolvability of human conflict that asks and re-asks questions about Black humanity, and I will suggest that it is this ongoing instability or tension that defines race's seminal role in African American literature.

The first section considers Black humanity as a topic of debate, provocation, and issue in African American writing. Subsequently, I look at Ta-Nehisi Coates and James Baldwin to compare how the former reveals a Black humanity defined as a subject of violence and how Baldwin portrays Black humanity as rooted in the force of self-revelation. The final section looks closely at how debates between critics about the political uses of Black writing further advance the idea of the irresolvability of the fundamental questions about Black humanity in African American literature. This ongoing dilemma is central to African American literature's unending quest to discover and rediscover humanity itself.

An Ongoing Crisis

In recent criticism, whether one focuses on Black human beings as animals or things, in rural or urban environments, critics cannot avoid the predominance of Black humanity as a subject. You'd think that there was some magic lever that said if you could figure which version of the human was right or the best expression of humanity, grasping that notion would ensure some profound social transformation. Anyone reading their way through African American literary history might think that Black writers are near-obsessed with the concept of humanity, as if the terms of humanity must be defined and explored again and again. This ongoing focus on what might seem a basic question, though, is hardly surprising, given the realities of African American history. And perhaps most importantly, because of centuries of Black people being dehumanized by whites in the USA, Black writers carry the heaviest burden of reclaiming what it means to be human. But as much as this burdensome occasion provides opportunities to intensely realize the human through portrayals of racial conflict in African American literature, this section asks: Is there either clarity or consensus on how humanity is reached or revealed most fully in African American literature? My answer here is no. The "no" is not an endpoint, however, but rather a point of departure to consider how the beauty and profundity of this question's insolvability shapes Black writers' attempts to grasp the problem of race.

In the late nineteenth century, progressive whites such as Henry Ward Beecher believed that African American people didn't deserve be lynched, but at the same time he believed that the descendants of slaves had yet to make a major contribution to modern society.[3] Thus, to convey their readiness for social equality, the first generation of Black writers after slavery used literature as a vessel to demonstrate the highest attributes of African Americans' sense of their rights to citizenship, their experience in entrepreneurship, their capacity for fair labor, and their extensive cultural contributions. Books such as Du Bois's *The Souls of Black Folk* (1903) portray the stinging devastation of segregation and racism, but also the insight and culture Black people contributed to the USA. Pauline Hopkins, Anna J. Cooper, Ida B. Wells, and Sutton Griggs also answered the calls by powerful whites to reveal Black cultural contributions and different guises of Black humanity. Decades later, writers we conventionally associate with the Harlem Renaissance, such as Claude McKay, Langston Hughes, and Zora Neale Hurston, emphasized the language of Black humanity and pride through modernistic techniques that incorporated the valence of Black culture in the USA and abroad. In his landmark essay "The New Negro," depicting the spirit of this moment in the 1920s, Alain Locke wrote that these writers rejected the concept of the "Negro Problem" of earlier generations and embraced instead "self-respect and self-dependence" – shaking off "imitation and implied inferiority."[4]

The correlation between prevailing beliefs in racial inferiority and Black inhumanity continued to preoccupy Black writers throughout the twentieth century, from the Harlem Renaissance writers of the 1920s through the 2000s. Zora Neale Hurston wrote that it was important for Black writers to make evident and reaffirm that, overall, African Americans were "very human and . . . just like everybody else."[5] Others, though, believed that recognition of this humanity would not be easy. "Until the art of black folk compels recognition," Du Bois wrote, "they will not be rated as human."[6] Decades later, when composing her most famous novel to date, *Beloved* (1987), Toni Morrison considered the fiction and nonfiction about slaves and felt the humanity of slaves needed further exploration and restoration. There was no mention in these sources of slaves' "interior life," Morrison wrote; "interior life," she continues, is something that helps us make sense of who we are as human beings.[7] Science fiction writer Octavia Butler reflected on the idea which animates her work that deals directly and indirectly with race, explaining, "I write about the different ways of being human."[8] My point in this very brief but telling catalog of references is that there is no period of African American writing thus far, where race is a focus, which escapes the important question of what it means to be human. This question has been and is central to African American literature's working through the social reality of racial difference.

Before the first half of the twentieth century was over, Richard Wright would look at the major writers before him and encourage newer generations of Black writers not to look obsequiously to white readership to accept Black humanity. Critical of older generations of Black writers, Wright wrote that instead of addressing the needs, sufferings, and aspirations of "the Negro himself," Black writers "went a-begging to white America."[9] Wright claims that while Negro writers have produced great "technical craftmanship and beauty," they were too focused on "pleading with white America for justice."[10]

Wright's polemic, "Blueprint for Negro Writing," published in the journal *New Challenge* (1937), offered a choice for the way forward: Black writers could either "address the Negro masses" or continue "begging the question of the Negroes' humanity."[11] On the one hand, in a rhetorical sense Wright is suggesting a feeling, an abstraction about what it means to beg for Black humanity to whites; on the other, it is entirely unclear what begging for humanity means. Still, according to Wright, presenting Black humanity a different way could shape the pursuit of Black social equality. With this concept, Wright presents the idea that it is not just being human but a particular kind of Black humanity that will be potentially advantageous in the fight for social equality.

Ironically, it was Wright who would soon be criticized by another great African American writer, James Baldwin, for being in a tradition of Black writing that portrayed the wrong type of Black humanity. Just over a decade after Wright's "Blueprint" appeared, Baldwin published "Everybody's Protest Novel" (1948). Baldwin argued that Wright, like other protest writers, presented sterile, mechanical, and predictable characters that reflected sociological data and categories more than the mysterious form of being human. Baldwin wrote that we should not prove or argue for Black humanity, but it should be assumed. Baldwin and Wright, though, agree here on two things: one, claiming humanity should not be an overt or flagrant act; two, there are social and political stakes in how Black humanity is presented. Baldwin, more so than Wright, did argue for an approach to representing Black humanity that revealed terror, instability, and ambiguity in social life, yet the concrete explanation of this humanity was left out of "Everybody's Protest Novel," and to most readers it is to be fully discovered not in this essay but in Baldwin's fiction.

What, precisely, does Wright mean by begging humanity, and what does Baldwin mean when he states that we have to assume it? Perhaps an easy target for Wright could have been something like Langston Hughes's "Theme for English B," wherein the speaker says "I guess being colored doesn't make me *not* like/ the same things other folks like who are other races"; "I feel and see and hear, Harlem, I hear you/ hear you, hear me – we two – you, me, talk on this page./ (I hear New York, too.) Me – who?"[12] The poem provokes the idea that even though we are racially different and may like different things, we also like similar things and should recognize both in a shared sympathetic identification and social equality. In the poem "If We Must Die," by Claude McKay, when the speaker proclaims "If we must die, let us not be like hogs/ . . . Like men we'll face the murderous, cowardly pack," he professes not only a sense of masculine self-preservation but a resolute realization that life itself is worthy of being defended, preserved, and even celebrated. In this poem, the idea of being willing to face death means seizing one's own human dignity and the willingness to fight for freedom. Readers of the poem often see these lines as demonstrating Black humanity and an affirmation that all human beings deserve freedom. In McKay's and Hughes's verse, we are reminded of the very basic need to recognize and affirm Black humanity. Is this the kind of begging that Wright warned about: a verse that asks or pleads for humanity rather than assumes it, as Baldwin suggests?

In a different vein, Sterling Brown's poem "Ma Rainey" depicts a gathering of Black folks listening to the eponymous legendary blues singer. There isn't an explicit cry of abuse or demand for human decency. The tone is bluesy, the language vernacular, and the surroundings immerse the reader in the folksy reality of the moment. The blues singer, the conditions of people, and the ethos of blues breathes in the rhythm of each line. When describing Ma Rainey's impact, the speaker says "she jes' gits hold of us dataway" (63).[13] The music experience makes manifest a tragicomic deep feeling in the scene of community. Brown often lectured Black middle-class audiences on their rectitude and respectability, and the tendency to only value Black art if it portrayed noble professions such as doctors, successful businesspeople, and politicians.[14] Brown emphasizes that the common man has all the profound mix of dignities and problems that many associate with the upper classes, and the overt whip and glare of whiteness is largely absent. This seems to be in line with assuming Black humanity, but it's not clear how Brown's mode of presentation could lend itself fruitfully to freedom's progress.

In Toni Morrison's *Beloved*, two characters who love one another split up after Paul D accuses Sethe of acting like an animal. You "got two feet, Sethe, not four," were the chilling words Paul D said when Sethe told him how she attempted to kill all her children rather than go back to slavery.[15] Morrison adds: "then a forest sprang up between them."[16] It was a moment where Paul D fails to give Sethe the sympathetic understanding she deserves. Then Paul D dehumanizes Sethe by not understanding how very human it was for a victim of slavery's violent trauma to want more than anything else to see her children dead rather than grow up under slavery's abuses. Paul D judges her and wounds her rather than helping her stretch beyond the boundaries of memory that gripped her life.

From McKay to Morrison, which type of Black humanity is more pertinent and necessary and why? Black writers in different historical contexts suggest that the answer to this question does indeed matter, and critics have followed suit, praising some artists and traditions over others and using oppositions to describe humanity's conditions: real versus romantic, the folk versus urban class conflict, modernist complexity versus naturalist simplicity. Is it possible to represent Black humanity in African American literature in such a way that avoids going "a-begging to white America"[17] or whatever pitfall could throw off the potential social and political impacts of Black writing?

When it comes to race and African American literature, writers working to honor this tradition struggle with the different demands of aesthetic gratification and potential political payoff. No one is going to say that one of these is right or wrong or exclusive of the other, but generations of Black artists debate what kind of humanity – assumed, overt, or understated – encourages, demands, even, moral elevation, social understanding, and social change in each historical moment. Today, various affirmations and critiques of concepts of the human, the posthuman, or the new humanism(s) make one thing clear: we have no intention of getting rid of humanistic thinking, humanistic relations, or analysis; we only attempt to reinvent, reimagine, and perfect humanism(s) lenses for our critical moments, intellectual explorations, and pressing needs to alleviate racist thinking and practices.

Human Inside Out

There are at least two ways Black protagonists demonstrate humanity in racist and dehumanizing conditions: the first is by way of various guises of self-revelation about the choices and guiding definitions they have over their own life; the second involves a protagonist or speaker who feels the constraints of anti-Blackness so thoroughly that they realize they're inescapably defined by and subjected to them. The former is rooted in the idea that despite the horrors of one's surroundings, one can change the way one sees oneself and act accordingly with this new lens. Change begins with revelations about self and world on the inside (spiritual or psychological). The latter is more naturalistic: one's built environment is overwhelmingly determinative of one's identity, to the degree that every glimpse of escape or relief only tightens the very grip one seeks to loosen or move beyond; thus, the outside world must be fixed, radically transformed, before any real self-revelation can take place. Both versions can tell us something powerful, a deepening of feeling and thinking about what it means to be human as a way of understanding how race works in African American literature.

Two writers – one from the past (Baldwin), the other a contemporary writer (Ta-Nehisi Coates) – reveal humanity powerfully but differently in their explorations of racial conflict. One finds it in self-revelation and the other reveals the impermeability and inescapability of an anti-Black world. I treat Baldwin and Coates here to explore how Black humanity operates differently in two writers who critics have compared to one another.

Coates points his readers toward the racist structures of environment that produce a climate of fear, precarity, and everyday violence against African Americans. Baldwin, who certainly does not disregard the horrors of American racism, highlights his characters' inner worlds for opportunities of revelation and self-definition. Coates's and Baldwin's work intensifies the connection between the pressures of racist social environments and a character's feeling of humanity and between a racist society and the significance of seizing one's own meaning in the most challenging circumstances. Yet, in the end, there are significant differences between these two, and these differences between them, especially concerning what kind of social and political change is possible and necessary, has implications for how we think about why Black writers repeatedly return to the question of Black humanity.

Baldwin burst onto the American writing scene with a blistering critique of Black writers who produced protest novels. He contended that the style and form of Black protest, its tone, opposition, and lack of creative variety followed too closely the formulas of sentimental romances such as Harriet Beecher Stowe's *Uncle Tom's Cabin* (1852). Stowe's novel, for all its success, contained a degraded and lifeless kind of humanity, according to Baldwin – an inhumanity that undermined the humanizing sense of identification that Stowe ultimately wanted to portray. Hence, Black writers, chief among them Wright, inherited this problematic legacy, espousing the clever aesthetic work of deepening Black humanity but, instead, undermining the profound humanity of Black fictional characters by containing them in neat categories based on race, environment, and social class.

Baldwin described this dilemma of the Black writer of protest fiction as ultimately one of perception. He writes: "We take our shape, it is true, within and against that cage of reality bequeathed us at our birth; and yet it is precisely through our dependence on this reality that we are most endlessly betrayed."[18] Baldwin says that we cling to this sense of reality, which Stowe and Black protest writers such as Wright ultimately reinforce, because we fear being "hurled into that void."[19] But it is precisely in "this void" where real "new acts of creation" take place, "which can save us" (32).[20] Baldwin's belief in a self that is capable of new acts of creation defines the very thing he believes cannot be found in Wright and Stowe's art: the full acceptance of "our humanity"[21] in a racist world.

Ta-Nehisi Coates characterizes his life and the lives of his family members as defined by an overwhelming sense of fear. Coates paints his upbringing in this way to expose racism in the USA. Wright also used fear as way of revealing the angst and suffering of African Americans. One of Baldwin's major problems with Wright's characters like Bigger Thomas is that "all of Bigger's life is controlled, defined by his hatred and his fear."[22] Ta-Nehisi Coates's world of writing doubles down, expands even, the very immovable sense of fear which drives Baldwin to criticize Wright. Ta-Nehisi Coates portrays his life and that of every significant Black person connected to his upbringing as drenched in fear. In *Between the World and Me*, Coates can be seen as a writer who exposes the racism that still plagues the USA, but in doing so falls into the narrow representational mode about which Baldwin warned us

This is not aesthetic flowering for Coates. It is social reality in the USA. Coates states that "Fear ruled everything around, and I knew, that this fear was connected to the Dream out there, to the unworried boys . . . to white fences and green lawns."[23] The Dreamers were not Martin Luther Kings Jr's progressives but plunderers of Black people's labors and the source of Black suffering and disenfranchisement. The Dreamers maintain a need for categories to create and maintain a social hierarchy, and racism came out of this need, bringing with it color and feature codes that whites use to humiliate, reduce, and destroy them.[24] Racism and its corresponding social hierarchy produce the climate of fear Coates depicts so eloquently. Racism,

Coates writes, denies "you and me the right to secure and govern our own bodies."[25] Coates's writing mixes the social history of racist oppression and violence with affect. He is unapologetic in his depictions of what means to be Black, educated, and impoverished.

Coates links his racial awareness to the violent death of a friend who was killed by police and the striking impact that death had upon Coates's own outlook. When reflecting upon the death, his friend's mother recalls Solomon Northup's *Twelve Years a Slave* (1853). Northup, an educated, upstanding, and prosperous Black man, is manipulated and snatched into slavery. Coates's friend was an upper-middle-class African American killed by the police. This, too, is a moment where humanity is brutally taken away.[26] This is precisely what Coates means when racism against Black people prevents them from securing and governing their own bodies. He goes on to conclude that the abundance of beauty shops, crumbling housing, churches, and liquor stores instill the old fear that he inherited, and he is doomed to perpetuate this feeling if the looming reality of one racist violent act continues to define Black life.

What would make this fear go away and get to a real sense of humanity that Coates says is missing or impoverished in Black social life? The complete elimination of the possibility of racist acts or acts that appear to be driven by racial bias? The total transformation of urban poverty centers or Black neighborhoods that remind Coates's of the fear that he says rules everything? These questions do not get answered in *Between the World and Me*, but the major distinction of Coates's indictment of society is that he gives the impression that the entire world needs to change to eradicate lethal racist acts. These are essays and not sociology, yet Coates does not make room for revelatory possibility beyond the racist sphere of fear without dramatic social transformation. Baldwin is the opposite, arguing that without revelations of one's humanity, we'll never get the necessary dramatic social change we need. Coates demonstrates how the constant threat of violence in a racist society obscures and obstructs Black humanity. Baldwin sees his writing as an invitation to discover unknown selves and new acts of creation. Coates's voice is powerful, but he leaves us in a sea of observations that do not lead to clear solutions, and he creates a loose historical tapestry that feels, to some readers, suffocating.

Among their writerly achievements, Baldwin's and Coates's compositions interrogate and expose the violent affects of US racism. Baldwin pushes for the best aesthetic version of remaking the self, the revisiting of Black humanity, the kind Coates portrays as crushed by the burdens of inhumanity with little or no way out of the nightmare created and run by the Dreamers. Both writers are interested in race and African American writing as firmly grounded in the interrogation of what it means to be human. But does it matter which kind of interrogation of race through the lens of Black humanity/inhumanity is right? Baldwin strongly implies that it does, and Coates, quiet on solutions, suggests that society needs to be overhauled. In their fundamental agreements about the nature of the problem and their equally fundamental differences in how to address the problem, these two writers help me to reiterate my argument, which is that instead of asking what concept of Black humanity best serves the needs of racial progress, we should focus on the rich and complex ways Black writers interrogated, reimagined, and rewrote Black humanity as a seminal feature of coming to grips with the USA's race problem.

I've tried to demonstrate and reaffirm something fundamental. When it comes to African American literature and the reality of race, the question of what it means to be human is central, and how to fully approach this question has yet to be resolved. And, further, this insolvability should be our focus, instead of looking for the best, most progressive humanistic portrayals. Cornell West, a major critical voice, popularized the strategic use of the term "Race Matters" as way of illustrating the undeniable importance of race to US social life and politics. Part of West's thinking about race is rooted in the importance of all Americans realizing our common humanity. In mapping out his political horizons, West did not draw on Martin Luther King Jr.'s speeches but rather from a spiritual gathering in Morrison's *Beloved.* West is interested in the politics of conversion shaped through a love ethic, which is why Morrison's work seems to fit. But what I am interested in is West's call for Morrison's novel and the work of other Black writers to squarely leverage political traction through the "critical affirmation of Black humanity." Responding to West's claims about *Beloved*, Kenneth Warren asks important questions about the relationship between the novel's scenes and concrete political goals. I want to use West's claims about Morrison's *Beloved* and Kenneth Warren's discussion of West to demonstrate an ongoing point about the relationship between Black humanity and the end game of addressing racial conflict and unrest in the USA.

In the moment in *Beloved* to which West refers, Morrison's character Baby Suggs calls a gathering of open, honest, truth of expression, where Black folks sing, shout, and moan, not as way of burying trauma but, rather, as a way of facing it as a community. West turns to Morrison to make sense of how to address dehumanizing racist violence, and while he's certainly not the only person to turn to literature for inspiration, West's

Race Matters is especially important because it figures so prominently in debates about race. Inside Morrison's prose, West finds "the bringing together" of "the loving yet critical affirmation of black humanity found in the best of black nationalist movements, the perennial hope against hope for trans-racial coalition in progressive movements, and the painful struggle for self-affirming sanity in history in which the nihilistic threat seems insurmountable."[27] Hence, West insists that African American literature matters to understanding race's import, just as he's insisting on the significance of race in general.

Warren was drawn to West's claims about *Beloved* because West saw democratic possibility in it. A definitive part of Warren's project in *So Black and Blue* questions the uses of Black vernacular culture for restoring Black politics or other pursuits of modern racial equality. In this vein, Warren, skeptical of West's reading of *Beloved* as a political guide, claims that Morrison's novel does not yield the democratic vision Wests sees, but instead produces "a religious, therapeutic community."[28] Warren doesn't deny the force of a love ethic as a humanistic need, but he sees it as an ineffective strategy for galvanizing momentum to end racialized social inequality. Even though West is not naïve and knows that progressive movements and grass roots organizing is required for political change, he does see the love ethic that Baby Suggs preaches about as important to it – perhaps a vision of what can sustain people through the gritty challenges of change. Suggs's sermons in the clearing about truth and realization are about how one sees oneself in the world in relation to communities' blessings and evils, crimes committed against people, and the damage those very people have caused in others. Sugg's sermons are moral, existential, in *Beloved*, and Warren does not deny this, yet he doesn't see the pragmatic possibility of democratic order in Morrison's representations. But does the right kind of critical affirmation of Black humanity exist for Warren, as it does for Baldwin or Richard Wright?

Warren and West's disagreement is a cautionary reminder about the importance of considering carefully our approaches to the topic of race in African American literature. Does the realization of Black humanity bring us closer to everyday political solutions about race, or does it make us more aware of the widening gaps between spiritual and psychological affirmation and political agency? The existential and political ideas about race should be teased apart, analyzed together, pitted against each other, in causal relation and simultaneous opposition, but one cannot get around the ever-present question of humanity in African American writers' sustained dialogues. Evocations of post-Black or posthuman, wild fantastical varies of human, alien, and other imaginative correlations flourish in the era of the Black Lives Matters movement and still come back to the originator of all the concepts: the human. And while it can be transformed, it cannot be fully transcended.

I do not think race in African American literature is a matter of competing humanities, such as complex ambiguity versus accessible simplicity, mysterious interiority versus mechanical interiority, real people versus fake people, where ultimately at some point we settle for the winner in our historical moment. However, these oppositions are a critical part of aesthetic judgment and the politics of how critics read and evaluate Black humanity in its historical context. Additionally, these oppositions have too long dominated how we approach Black humanity in discussions of race in American literature, superseding more interesting lines of questions. It is in our very inability to resolve the issues raised by this complicated history that we rediscover the genius of African American writing. This is a tradition that opens rather than closes complexity, and this is a tradition that discovers humanity in the struggle to make sense of life, sometimes against all odds, but always with determination and purpose.

Notes

1. W. E. B. Du Bois, *Dusk of Dawn, Du Bois: Writings* (New York: Library of America, 1986), 640.
2. Du Bois, "Crisis of Negro Art," *Crisis* 32, October 1926.
3. Anna Julia Cooper, "What Are We Worth," in *A Voice from the South* (New York: Oxford University Press, 1988) 231.
4. Alaine Locke, "The New Negro," *The New Negro: Voices of the Harlem Renaissance*, ed. Alain Locke (New York: Touchtone, 1997) 10.
5. Zora Neale Hurston, "What White Publishers Won't Print," *Negro Digest* 8, April 1950.
6. Du Bois, "The Criteria of Negro Art."
7. Toni Morrison, "Site of Memory," in *What Moves at the Margin: Selected Nonfiction* (Jackson: University of Mississippi Press, 2008) 74.
8. Octavia Butler, Interview with Charlie Rose, episode 9409, PBS, 2000. www.loa.org/news-and-views/1835-octavia-e-butler-i-could-become-a-writer-or-i-could-die-really-young.
9. Richard Wright, "Blueprint for Negro Writing," *New Challenge* 11, 1937.
10. Ibid.
11. Ibid., 57.
12. Langston Hughes, "Theme for English B," in *The Collected Poems of Langston Hughes*, ed. Arnold Rampersad (New York: Vintage Press, 1994), 410.

13. Sterling Brown, "Ma Rainey," *The Collected Poems of Sterling A. Brown* (Evanston: Triquartley Books, 2000) 63.
14. Sterling Brown, "Our Literary Audience," *Opportunity*, February 1930.
15. Toni Morrison, *Beloved* (New York: Vintage, 1987), 194.
16. Ibid., 194.
17. Wright, "Blueprint."
18. James Baldwin, "Everybody's Protest Novel," in *The Price of the Ticket: Collected Nonfiction 1948–1985* (New York: St. Martins, 1985) 32.
19. Ibid.
20. Ibid.
21. Ibid.
22. Ibid., 33.
23. Ta-nehisi Coates, *Between the World and Me* (New York: Spiegel and Grau, 2015), 29.
24. Ibid., 7.
25. Ibid., 8.
26. Saidiya Hartman, *Scenes of Subjection* (New York: Oxford University Press, 1997).
27. Cornel West, *Race Matters* (Boston: Beacon Press, 1991), 19.
28. Kenneth Warren, *So Black and Blue: Ralph Ellison and the Occasion of Criticism* (Chicago: University of Chicago Press, 2003), 78.

CHAPTER 7

Race and the Mythos of Model Minority in Asian American Literature

Swati Rana

"An Asian American reckoning," reads the summons of Cathy Park Hong's *Minor Feelings* (2020) when we are called upon to carry the memory of Asian and Asian American women murdered in the 2021 Atlanta spa shootings while wrestling with the inaction of Asian American police power on the sidelines of George Floyd's 2020 murder. Given these extremities of disincorporation and assimilation; the gendered violence of the US empire as it tracks into the diaspora; and the inheritance of slavery at the crossroads of white supremacy, police brutality, and Asian American concession, how can we fit Asian Americans to the racial history of the United States? "Asian Americans have yet to truly reckon with where we stand in the capitalist white supremacist hierarchy of this country," Hong writes.[1] Hong's exhortation is all the more resonant for being familiar. The word "reckoning" registers the sense of urgency renewed in each generation in which Asian American belonging is once again stripped away and the precariousness of Asian America as a construct – and as a US people – is exposed.

The work of reckoning is partly calculation or enumeration, a sum of determinable quantities through which scores, grievances, accounts, and differences are settled. But reckoning also involves expectation and anticipation, the estimation of chances or contingencies. It is contemplative, ponderous even, as likely to unsettle grievances and differences as to settle them.[2] How does literature contribute to this imaginative and speculative work of reckoning with race? This question guides the present chapter, which finds in literature and literary criticism tools for understanding Asian American racialization.

I first trace the emergence of the panethnic construct of Asian America out of the social movements of the civil rights era as a radical exercise of global, anticolonial imagination. In a context where Asian Americans are unevenly and unstably racialized as intermediaries within US liberal racial orders, Asian American literary criticism captures the dynamism of this construct. It brings us from myth to mythos, from tragic flaw to the flawed social world, bridging the disjunctures of Asian America and its relational possibilities. I then turn to Chang-rae Lee's novel *Native Speaker* (1995), which continues to captivate teachers and students of Asian American literature because it allegorizes so many of the contradictions of Asian American representation. From Lee's work and its criticism, I draw out an allegory for literary analysis, showing how the tragic characterization of the novel's protagonist – a spy cast as *analyst* – reorients the reader from a trajectory of assimilation and incorporation to the broader interpretive totality of US militarism and empire.

Asian American Construct

The making of Asian America as a construct took an imaginative leap, seeking to connect Asian immigrants with one another and to people of color in the USA and globally. Historians trace the origins of this construct to student and community organizations founded in the late 1960s as the Asian American movement took shape. Emma Gee and Yuji Ichioka co-organized the Asian American Political Alliance (AAPA) at the University of California, Berkeley, in 1968.[3] Reflecting on its formation in the context of the antiwar movement, Ichioka recalled in a 1988 interview: "There were so many Asians out there in the political demonstrations but we had no effectiveness. Everyone was lost in the larger rally. We figured that if we rallied behind our own banner, behind an Asian American banner, we would have an effect on the larger public. We could extend the influence beyond ourselves, to other Asian Americans."[4] Asian American panethnicity, following Yen Le Espiritu, was catalyzed in part by racialized opposition to the US war in Vietnam, as Asian Americans positioned themselves as Third World peoples in solidarity with Southeast Asians.[5] The historical regime of Asian exclusion, racial prerequisites to naturalization, entrenched discrimination, and nativist violence deepened the sense of joint Asian American racialization. Its specificity was sharpened by interracial coalitions (such as the Third World Liberation Front) where Asian Americans allied with Black, Chicana/o/x, Latina/o/x, and Native American communities from a position of shared yet differential subjection.[6]

"The paint on the Asian American label has not dried," Hong writes more than fifty years later: "Will 'we,' a pronoun I use cautiously, solidify into a common collective, or will we remain splintered, so that some of us remain 'foreign' or 'brown' while others, through wealth or intermarriage, 'pass' into whiteness?"[7] *Minor Feelings* signals the contradictions of this construct, its centrifugal force, and that race cannot be mapped evenly onto Asian America. For one, Asian Americans are racialized very differently as workers or capitalists, elites or subalterns, allies or enemies, or on the spectrum thereof in relation to US capitalism, colonialism, militarism, and empire. Also, their racialization is unstable. As recruits to ethnic assimilation, racial nativism, and settler colonialism, Asians Americans inflect white/Black, white/Brown, and settler/Indigenous binaries to stabilize white power.[8]

These contradictions can be parsed in terms of the tension between radicalism, articulated to race, and liberal racial regimes. Daryl Joji Maeda has traced the "racial radicalism" of the Asian American movement, which adapted and entwined the tenets and aesthetics of the Black Panthers with Third World radicalism and Maoism.[9] Alongside such radical affinities, "postwar race-liberal orders" also took hold in three phases (racial liberalism, liberal multiculturalism, and neoliberal multiculturalism), as Jodi Melamed demonstrates, channeling the materialist, decolonial internationalism of the social movements of the 1960s and 1970s into discourses of racial progress, reform, and pluralism that perpetuated white supremacy and secured US global, capitalist hegemony.[10] The model minority myth developed to manage the Cold War crisis of US racial inequality domestically and abroad. This ideological construct was deployed against African American and other racial minorities facing entrenched discrimination in order to obviate meaningful structural reforms. Stories of Chinese and Japanese success held out the promise of racial assimilation via ethnicization, representing "Asian Americans as a *racial* minority whose apparently successful *ethnic* assimilation was a result of stoic patience, political obedience, and self-improvement," as Robert Lee notes.[11] This "morphing of race into ethnicity," following Susan Koshy, would "ground the fiction of model minority and the refurbished American dream" in the post-civil rights era, incorporating "nonwhite capital-compatible ethnicities" as "whites-to-be."[12]

A Dynamic Conjunction

In this context, literary concepts do particular work to express the contradictions of Asian America, beyond the work literature does as representation. The title of a 2021 op-ed by Viet Thanh Nguyen, "The Beautiful, Flawed Fiction of 'Asian American,'" gestures to a 1996 essay by Koshy, entitled "The Fiction of Asian American Literature." Both pieces, in their distinct registers, and twenty-five years apart, underscore the fictionality of Asian America as an imagined, yet necessary, construct. Nguyen foregrounds the act of "self-conjuring" entailed in claiming "an identity that is inherently political, and must be chosen."[13] "'Asian American' offers us a rubric that we cannot not use," Koshy writes, "But our usage of the term should rehearse the catachrestic status of the formation."[14] This claim employs two rhetorical devices: litotes, or double negative, implicitly, to underscore the political imperative; and catachresis, or misnomer, to invite into the field of Asian American studies a conceptual richness around this construct.

Critics have answered Koshy's challenge by sustained recourse to literary tools. Kandice Chuh charts the "arbitrary but inscribed" nature of the term "Asian American" by describing it as a "*metaphor* for resistance and racism."[15] Parsing Chuh's arguments, Elda Tsou emphasizes the role that metaphor plays in "thinking the literary as figuring and therefore pulling away from identity" in the course of which metaphor is itself transformed: "in the place of identity, it indexes difference (racism), and instead of unity it registers contention and potential deviation (resistance)."[16]

Grounded in this understanding of "Asian American" *as* metaphor, and in the enlarged function of metaphor itself, we can appreciate the additional work metaphors do *for* Asian America. Hong renders "Asian American" as a "label" whose paint has not yet dried, figuring its relative newness, its susceptibility to appropriation and erasure. Ichioka presents "an Asian American banner" to be "rallied behind" as call, proclamation, or principle. These metaphors bring incommensurable, nonidentical yet communicating parts – a panoply of identities, or people marching apart – into precarious connection. Figuration encompasses disjuncture as well as relation. There is a "transference" or "turn" here (part of the etymology of metaphor and trope, respectively) between what Richard Lanham calls "normative 'reality'" and "metaphorical transformation." Despite its production of similitude, metaphor holds in tension identity and difference – what Lanham describes as "the essential bounded instability of a bistable illusion."[17] This instability is transformative. The transference of metaphor, the turn of trope, the leap of imagination between literal and figurative is also that of desire. The gap between Asian America and what the Asian American construct describes might well fall short of what is, but this construct also draws into relation – and therefore possibility – what might be.

Building from this conceptual understanding of metaphor for and as Asian America involves the practical work of literary analysis. By tracing the complex itineraries of figuration between literary and social worlds, we can grasp the metaphorical work of Asian American literature broadly. As Colleen Lye argues, this is "a question of the relationship between language ... and other material processes." Lye's work invites us to "Asiatic racial form" across literary and social registers, clarifying the role of literary critique in historicizing race and mapping its variability as "an active social relation."[18] The hope is that by becoming better readers of racial form, we become better readers of racial formations.

Model Minority Myth

In practice, the work of reading *Native Speaker* shows how these propositions play out. Part bildungsroman, part spy fiction, *Native Speaker* is narrated by Henry Park, a second-generation Korean American whose exemplary career as a corporate spy falls apart as he faces multiple crises of marriage, family, allegiance, and identity. As Lye points out, Lee is among Asian American authors "treated so often as 'representative' ... because their work is preoccupied with Asian American representation as a problem."[19] The wealth of critical and pedagogical engagement with *Native Speaker* follows partly from its paradigmatic representation of Asian American racialization via two, linked trajectories: assimilation and incorporation. The Park family's self-effacing upward mobility as Korean immigrants speaks to the first. Arriving from Seoul with his pregnant wife, Henry's father gets his start as a greengrocer living in a small apartment in Queens and works his way up to being a successful owner of a chain of grocery stores with a large house in the affluent, predominantly white suburb of Ardsley. As a beneficiary of the American dream, Henry makes a career of his assimilability; "the obedient, soft-spoken son," "the invisible underling," he is employed by a private intelligence firm that goes by the name of Glimmer & Company, serving a powerful global elite of wealthy individuals, foreign governments, and multinational corporations.[20] He marries a white woman, Lelia, a speech therapist and self-avowed "standard-bearer" of the English language, and his "assimilist sentiment" has him "hoping whiteness" for their son Mitt (12, 267, 285).

When Henry is assigned to infiltrate the offices of New York City Council member John Kwang, rumored to be running for mayor, we meet another Asian American protagonist of the American dream. Henry's dispatches chart John's hardscrabble rise and his transformation from a refugee, orphaned by the Korean War, into a self-made millionaire and a wildly popular politician. What draws Henry to John is his claim to the name and the language of everyman, and his assumption – as Korean – of the mantle of the representative American. "I had never conceived of someone like him. A Korean man, of his age, as part of the vernacular," Henry marvels, admiring John's apparent ease at being "effortlessly Korean, effortlessly American" (139, 328). John holds out the distinct promise of racial incorporation rather than racial assimilation. His appeal, unlike that of Henry and his father, is conditioned by liberal multiculturalism, hinging on the calculated revelation of race through a carefully crafted public persona.

The trajectories of these characters are shaped by the history of Korean migration and its intersection with the model minority myth. Delimited by Japanese colonialism, the Korean War, US occupation, and Cold War militarism, immigration from Korea in the first part of the twentieth century involved primarily military brides, students, and adoptees.[21] Dictatorial rule in South Korea, along with rapid industrialization, population growth, and emigration incentives, pushed more immigrants to the USA under the 1965 Immigration Act.[22] While large numbers of white-collar middle- and upper-class Koreans (Lee's father among them) were able to immigrate, not all found skilled work. Many Koreans settled in urban centers such as Los Angeles and New York where, supported by strong diasporic networks, they opened retail stores in low-income Black and Brown neighborhoods. These small-business owners were recruited to the individualist, triumphalist narrative of upward mobility. What this model minority script obscured was the nexus of imperialism, globalization, and deindustrialization that impoverished inner-city neighborhoods, eviscerated the Black middle class, and drove Korean immigrants into exploitative roles, sparking the 1990 Flatbush Boycott and the 1992 Los Angeles uprising.[23]

Published in the wake of these crises of racial capitalism, *Native Speaker* engages the Cold War history of Korean migration and its refraction through the model minority myth. As James Kyung-Jin Lee, Daniel Kim, Jodi Kim, and Amy Tang have shown, the complex triangulation of Korean and African American representation in *Native Speaker* both generates (and undermines) a radical multiracial imaginary, overdetermined by the failures of liberal multiculturalism and post–Cold War liberal democracy.[24] "When others construct and model you favorably, it's easy to let them keep at it, even if they start going off in ways that aren't immediately comfortable and right. This is the challenge for us Asians in America," John tells Henry, speaking to the solicitation of the model minority myth (193). They sit behind the sliding screen of a private room in a Korean restaurant, trading stories of Asian American privilege and anti-Black racism. This anecdotal history is framed by a litany of violence – brutal robberies, ruthless reprisals, grocer boycotts, looting, arson – that echo the Flatbush boycott and the Los Angeles uprising and the names of their dead, including fifteen-year-old Latasha Harlins, who was fatally shot in March 1991 by storeowner Soon Ja Du. As Henry apprehends, "perfect credit, being perfect, shooting black people, watching our stores and offices burn down to the ground" are successive clauses in the vicious grammar of Asian American Americanization (53).

Model Minority Mythos

Native Speaker's dynamic relationship to this history can be mapped through what I call model minority mythos. Generally, myth and mythos are overlapping concepts, evocative of folk tales and traditions. The term "myth" also signifies a false belief that calls for demystification because it is exaggerated, misconceived, or simply untrue. David Palumbo-Liu parses the particular intersection of the model minority myth and Asian American literature in terms of discourse and narrative, respectively: "'model minority discourse' is an ideological construct" that "has been naturalized" in model minority "narratives" that "constitute a specific model of assimilation."[25] The place where ideology and literature meet is unstable and contradictory, as Jinqi Ling and Nguyen have shown, analyzing the active "negotiations" and "flexible strategies" Asian American writers employ.[26] How, then, to further encapsulate the agency of literary narrative as it overlaps with and deviates from model minority discourse?

This relation can be recalibrated through the concept of mythos, an Aristotelian term for tragic plot that Northrop Frye adapts to narrative generally. In the dizzying relay between anatomized detail and totalizing schema in Frye's work emerges a useful articulation of method: "In literary criticism myth means ultimately *mythos*, a structural organizing principle of literary form."[27] There is an opening here to reimagine mythos capaciously to describe literary – characterological, figurative, narrative, thematic – elements that structure the rendering of the model minority myth in literature and society. Mythos, in other words, designates that place where the interpellation of the model minority myth meets the resistance of the text, a place where we might learn to better read our world through our books and vice versa. This counterposition of model minority mythos to model minority myth sharpens our sense of how literature engages with the historical conditions of its making and enables us to map out the particular work literature does in reimagining constructs of identity.

Focusing on mythos as plot, the trajectory of assimilation and incorporation that Lee's characters follow proves to be tragic as model minority success is entwined with gendered suffering. The Park family breaks down when Henry's mother dies of cancer and his father arranges for a housekeeper to be brought from Korea. Knowing neither her name nor the details of her past, Henry refers to her as Ahjuhma, using the generic Korean form of address for an older woman. Bearing scars and intimations of trauma, Ahjuhma disrupts the heteronormative model minority plot, assuring the family's upward mobility even as her work as surrogate wife and mother is stripped to its barest, exploitative function as sexual and domestic labor.[28] In the confines of racist suburbia, Mitt is crushed to death by a group of neighborhood children playing a game at his birthday party, a tacit culmination of the racism the family endures that unravels Henry and Lelia's marriage. John's career hopes are also eviscerated. When he discovers that one of his trusted workers (likely also working for Glimmer & Company) is a spy, John orchestrates his murder at his main offices. Shaken by this realization, Henry leaks the membership list of an informal, rotating community bank that John is running on the model of a Korean *ggeh*. Gripped by remorse, a flailing John is arrested when he has an accident driving drunk with an underage hostess; Chun Ji-yun is in the hospital in a coma even as the leak finds its way to immigration authorities and is spun out by the media as an illegal money-laundering racket.

Glib multiculturalism runs aground in the shallows of betrayal, violence, and misogyny as John's political career comes to a definitive close. Interracial and intraracial solidarity is eviscerated and the prospect of migrant self-sufficiency destroyed as the alternative underground economy of the *ggeh*, which empowers its members to shift the terms of their exploitation, is dismantled by the deportation apparatus of the national security state. As Kim argues, "John's *ggeh* is surveilled and criminalized as racialized undocumented capital precisely because it attempts a racial redistribution of economic and *political* capital and power."[29] The end of the novel recalls Mitt's death, as Henry rushes in to save John, this "broken child" besieged by a racist and nativist mob (343). The mythos of the model minority dismantles the myth of upward mobility and linear progress, ending in disincorporation and inassimilability – the tragic apotheosis of Asian American racialization.

Spy as Analyst

Shifting from the plot to its broader framing enables us to read other aspects of *Native Speaker*'s mythos. The novel is shaped by the genres in which it partakes: ethnic bildungsroman, spy thriller, and postmodern novel, for instance, not to mention tragedy.[30] Henry's first-person narration in the guise of a spy charged with supplying a "workaday narrative" of his surveillance activities puts his reliability into question, heightening the drama of deception and introducing a metafictional layer of commentary upon the narrative (170).

Henry's "double life" demands an allegorical reading, as Tsou argues, tracking through the "turning tropes" of the novel, its "looping and opacity," the "figurative activity" of Asian American racialization, whose "orientalist inscrutability" ultimately points to "a hegemonic whiteness imagining itself as racially transparent."[31] An allegory for reading race, following Tsou – and also for the hyphenation of Korean American identity (Tina Chen), the ethics of the minority intellectual (Crystal Parikh), the Asian American writer in the literary marketplace (Michelle Young-Mee Rhee), and the binary containment logics of the Cold War (Ju Young Jin) – this layering of Henry's narration upon the action of the novel also works as an allegory for literary analysis that cues strategies for interpretation.[32] The "daily register" that Henry proffers ("naming the who, the what, the where, when") is a kind of exegesis ("background studies, psychological assessments, daily chronologies, myriad facts and extrapolations") (170, 18). After all, "analysts" is another word for spies in the novel (164, 170).

Consider Henry's obsessive analysis of John, which reorients the reader from model minority to literary figure. Recording "one more version" of John's story for his employer, Henry arrives at the place "where he began to think of America as a part of him, maybe even his, and this for me was the crucial leap of his character, deep flaw or not, the leap of his identity no one in our work would find valuable but me" (210, 211). The word "character" layers meaning at two levels, signifying John's individual personality and his fictive persona both, as Lee foregrounds the craft of his own fiction. He associates John with America on the axis of metonymy, the one contiguous with the other. Through a succession of leaps, Lee then enlivens this symbolism, evoking metaphor to admit to the existence of a gap between John and America – and the daring ambition of their substitutability. Essentially, we are pulled from model to figure. *Native Speaker* shifts our attention from John as model minority, monadic, yoked to an individualistic notion of personality (character as something to be had or not) and susceptible to "flaw," understood as a tragedy of personality, toward a relational, implicated literary figure in an assembly of tenuous figures part of a larger whole.

Two conflicting modes of analysis are represented in this chapter, and in the novel more broadly. Henry is trained in the first by the head of the spy agency, Dennis Hoagland, who demands meticulously observed reports devoid of analysis. Henry must "simply know character," be "the scribe," the "eye," confined to the "rigorous present tense," build a "daily log," "present the subject in question like some sentient machine of transcription . . . and leave to the unseen experts the arcana of human interpretation" (203, 204). Henry struggles increasingly, and especially after Mitt's death, to follow Dennis's prerogative. This struggle is due in part to his sessions with Emile Luzan, a Filipino psychoanalyst in exile to whom Henry is assigned as patient to gather intelligence about Emile's involvement with a repatriation movement for Ferdinand Marcos. In the course of their sessions, Henry starts "unraveling," "stringing" his fabricated biography "back upon" himself, "looping it through the core" (181, 22). Focusing here on "textuality rather than identity," following Tsou, also opens up new prospects for analysis.[33] An analyst in his own right, Emile presents Henry with a different prerogative, asking that Henry inhabit his discomfiture, that he learn to "speak to him in skeins," to "take up story-forms," to look at his life "not just from a singular mode but through the crucible of a larger narrative" (206).

Thus Henry adds to his monadic, circumscribed "stills" of John "one more version," encompassing the "greater lore": how John was "born in Seoul before the last world war, a boy during the Korean one, his family not mercifully sundered or refugeed but obliterated, the coordinates of his home village twice removed from the maps," how "he stole away to America as the houseboy of a retiring two-star general" (210). A succession of *wheres* render the extremities of John's deprivation: "Where he saved enough money to leave the general's house in Ohio and go to New York. Where he named himself John. Where he was beaten nearly to death and robbed of all his savings. Where he worked in a Chinatown noodle shop and slept outside next to the steam vent and awoke one morning to see that his feet had turned almost black with the cold. Where he knew hunger again, that unforgettable taste of his other country" (210–211). In this breathless litany, Henry begins to entwine the interpretive strands that culminate in John's metonymic and metaphorical assumption of America.

It is no accident that Henry spins out these "story-forms" in the course of his session with Emile, which is cut short dramatically when Henry is drugged and escorted from the building by two Glimmer & Company associates. While Henry is contained, his latest "version" of John escapes containment. Emile has already taught Henry to read differently. The closing of the chapter is thick with contrast to Dennis's directives. Henry as analyst, rather than "scribe," does not generate a "log" but crafts a mythos, eschewing the "rigorous present tense" by plumbing John's past and conjuring his future.

Allegory for Analysis

As an allegory for literary analysis, Henry's reinterpretation of John points the way to a reinterpretation of *Native Speaker*. Trained to study character by Dennis, and then retrained by Emile, Henry doubles for readers working through their own character studies of the novel. "Is this what I have left of the doctor?" Henry ruminates, "That I no longer can simply flash a light inside a character, paint a figure like Kwang with a momentary language, but that I know the greater truths reside in our necessary fictions spanning human event and time?" (206). Dennis insists on disconnected, momentary revelations, a "flash" of light inside the hollow of character – models of minority, in effect, singular protagonists of the American dream blinkered by their own glare. But Emile pushes Henry outside this isolating view, evoking an "additional dimension," "a cultural one": "Cast it all, if you will, in a broad yellow light. Let us see where this leads you and me" (133).

Such invitations prompt us to refigure John's American dream as a nightmare of penury and to trace its origins to the wider ambit of racial capitalism and empire. *Native Speaker* encourages its readers to understand the novel as a "register" in itself, to read beyond a narrow formalism and link its tragic figures to the Korean War and its gendered, "refugeed" diaspora. What Henry leaves "nameless" in Ahjuhma and her past, we concretize as the masculinist subjection of Korean women in the diaspora (66).[34] The irony that this larger view is opened up by a Filipino American looking to reinstate a corrupt and brutal dictator buttressed by the USA enjoins us to read beyond Emile's and Henry's limited perception. That Emile and John as subjects of US empire are respectively murdered and banished due to Dennis's intelligence testifies to the role Glimmer & Company plays as an extension of imperial power. The breadth of John's representative character draws Black subjection into this totality, creating a transformative linkage. Speaking to a multiracial audience of his constituents, John exhorts Koreans and Korean Americans to view the structural impoverishment of African Americans through their collective memory of Japanese imperial violence in Korea: "Know that what we have in common, the sadness and pain and injustice, will always be stronger than our differences" (153).[35]

Native Speaker renders the tragic imperative as a social imperative, telling a bigger story in which the rise and fall of the model minority becomes a necessary feature of survival under US militarism and empire. The novel retells the story of success as a story of multiple failures. These are not necessarily the failures of John, or of Henry or Emile, in that the novel takes us from tragic flaw, imagined as a flaw of individual personality ("inside a character" where Dennis would have Henry dwell), into the flawed social world in which Asian American racialization takes shape, casting a "broad yellow light" that opens up structural and global understandings. This reach is encapsulated by the "crucial leap of his character" that draws Henry to John: the latter's daring to remake "America as a part of him," representing not only his narrow, blinding candidacy as an exemplary mayor for a multicultural New York but also his wider subjection to the geopolitics of imperialism. "I am here for the hope of his identity," Henry says, capturing the hope of figuration, its leap of desire toward a relational whole (328).

Remarkably, Henry chooses the alias of Mr. Dennis when he is entrusted with the work of managing the *ggeh*. There can be no doubt when he hands over the membership list to Glimmer & Company that he is a retainer for empire who shapes Emile's and John's tragic arcs: "For even Dennis Hoagland understands that in every betrayal dwells a self-betrayal, which brings you that much closer to a reckoning" (314). As the cipher for spy, *analyst* implicates the Asian American reader and the reader of Asian American literature as well. The second-person address, finally, draws "you" into the work of reckoning, asking how readers figure in the world they set out to analyze.

Thus, we come around once again to an Asian American reckoning. Even as the eschatology of reckoning anticipates an uncertain future it also summons the difficult past. Hong's exhortation draws us to the radical, global formation of Asian American studies and its call to reorient the model minority myth – and its trajectory of assimilation and incorporation – toward a broader interpretive totality. Asian American literature answers this call insofar as its "story-forms" render myth as mythos, enmeshing the singular model of minority in a broader narrative of interracial relations, war, militarism, and refugee displacement that upends the American dream. The *and* of race and literature is a dynamic conjunction. Literary analysis can inhabit this conjunction, especially when sharpened by methods of Asian American literary criticism attuned to the articulation of race and form. So, too, can literature as an allegory for analysis show us to read not for the representation of race but for its refiguration, to trace the cocreative relationship between social formations and literary forms.

Notes

I am very grateful to Stephen Hong Sohn for his thoughtful reading and encouragement, and to Maile Aihua Young for their steadfast help with research and proofreading.

1. Cathy Park Hong, *Minor Feelings: An Asian American Reckoning* (New York: One World, 2020), 86.
2. These definitions are adapted from the *Oxford English Dictionary (OED) Online*, s.v. "reckoning, *n.*," Oxford University Press, December 2021.
3. On these early Asian American organizations, see Daryl Joji Maeda, *Rethinking the Asian American Movement* (New York: Routledge, 2012), 9–26.
4. Yen Le Espiritu, *Asian American Panethnicity: Bridging Institutions and Identities* (Philadelphia: Temple University Press, 1992), 34.
5. Espiritu, *Asian American Panethnicity*, 1–52.
6. On the interracialism and internationalism of the Asian American Movement, see Maeda, *Rethinking the Asian American Movement*, 107–135.
7. Hong, *Minor Feelings*, 29.
8. On the complexity of Asian American racialization, see Junaid Rana, "Race," in *Keywords for Asian American Studies*, ed. Cathy Schlund-Vials, 202–207 (New York: New York University Press, 2015).
9. Daryl J. Maeda, *Chains of Babylon: The Rise of Asian America* (Minneapolis: University of Minnesota Press, 2009), 86.
10. Jodi Melamed, *Represent and Destroy: Rationalizing Violence in the New Racial Capitalism* (Minnesota: University of Minnesota Press, 2011), 1–50.
11. Robert G. Lee, *Orientals: Asian Americans in Popular Culture* (Philadelphia: Temple University Press, 1999), 145.
12. Susan Koshy, "Morphing Race into Ethnicity: Asian Americans and Critical Transformations of Whiteness," *boundary 2* 28, 1 (2001), 156, 165, 194, 187.
13. Viet Thanh Nguyen, "The Beautiful, Flawed Fiction of 'Asian American,'" www.nytimes.com/2021/05/31/opinion/culture/asian-american-AAPI-decolonization.html.
14. Susan Koshy, "The Fiction of Asian American Literature," *The Yale Journal of Criticism* 9 (1996), 342.
15. Kandice Chuh, *Imagine Otherwise: On Asian Americanist Critique* (Durham: Duke University, 2003), 27.

16. Elda E. Tsou, *Unquiet Tropes: Form, Race, and Asian American Literature* (Philadelphia: Temple University Press, 2015), 9, 10.
17. Richard A. Lanham, *A Handlist of Rhetorical Terms* (Berkeley: University of California Press, 1991), 101; see also Tsou, *Unquiet Tropes*, which extends these into "proper" and "improper" assignations of race (9).
18. Colleen Lye, "Racial Form," *Representations* 104, 1 (2008), 95, 99.
19. Colleen Lye, "Reading for Asian American Literature," in *A Companion to American Literary Studies*, ed. Caroline F. Levander and Robert S. Levine (Malden: Blackwell Publishing, 2011), 492.
20. Chang-rae Lee, *Native Speaker* (New York: Riverhead Books, 1995), 202. Subsequent references are cited parenthetically in the text.
21. On this history, see Crystal Mun-hye Baik, *Reencounters: On the Korean War and Diasporic Memory Critique* (Philadelphia: Temple University Press, 2020), 35–65.
22. On this history, see Shelley Sang-Hee Lee, "After the Watershed: Korean Migration since 1965," in *A Companion to Korean American Studies*, ed. Rachael Miyung Joo and Shelley Sang-Hee Lee, 21–46 (Leiden: Brill, 2018).
23. See, generally, Claire Jean Kim, *Bitter Fruit: The Politics of Black–Korean Conflict in New York City* (New Haven: Yale University Press, 2000); Lynn Mie Itagaki, *Civil Racism: The 1992 Los Angeles Rebellion and the Crisis of Racial Burnout* (Minneapolis: University of Minnesota Press, 2016); and Shelley Sang-Hee Lee, "Where Others Have Failed: Korean Immigrants and the Reinvention of Entrepreneurship in 1970s and 1980s America," *Journal of Asian American Studies* 21, 3 (2018): 341–366.
24. James Kyung-Jin Lee, "Where the Talented Tenth Meets the Model Minority: The Price of Privilege in Wideman's *Philadelphia Fire* and Lee's *Native Speaker*," *Novel* 35, 2–3 (2002): 231–257; Daniel Y. Kim, "Do I, Too, Sing America? Vernacular Representations and Chang-rae Lee's *Native Speaker*," *Journal of Asian American Studies* 6, 3 (2003): 231–260; Jodi Kim, "From *Mee-gook* to Gook: The Cold War and Racialized Undocumented Capital in Chang-rae Lee's *Native Speaker*," *MELUS* 34, 1 (2009): 117–137; Amy C. Tang, *Repetition and Race: Asian American Literature After Multiculturalism* (Oxford: Oxford University Press, 2016), 99–133.
25. David Palumbo-Liu, *Asian/American: Historical Crossings of a Racial Frontier* (Stanford: Stanford University Press, 1999), 396, 397.
26. Jinqi Ling, *Narrating Nationalisms: Ideology and Form in Asian American Literature* (New York: Oxford University Press, 1998), 11; Viet Thanh Nguyen, *Race and Resistance: Literature and Politics in Asian America* (New York: Oxford University Press, 2002), 5. See, relatedly, Eleanor Ty, *Asianfail: Narratives of Disenchantment and the Model Minority* (Urbana: University of Illinois Press, 2017) and James Kyung-Jin Lee, *Pedagogies of Woundedness: Illness, Memoir, and the Ends of the Model Minority* (Philadelphia: Temple University Press, 2021) on how narratives of failure and illness reframe model minority discourse.

27. Northrop Frye, *Anatomy of Criticism: Four Essays* (Princeton: Princeton University Press, 1957), 341.
28. See, generally, You-me Park and Gayle Wald, "Native Daughters in the Promised Land: Gender, Race, and the Question of Separate Spheres," *American Literature* 70, 3 (1998), 609.
29. Kim, "From *Mee-gook* to Gook," 128.
30. On how *Native Speaker* negotiates genre and the spy novel, see Betsy Huang, *Contesting Genres in Contemporary Asian American Fiction* (New York: Palgrave Macmillan, 2010), 1–10; and Tina Chen, *Double Agency: Acts of Impersonation in Asian American Literature and Culture* (Stanford: Stanford University Press, 2005), 152–183.
31. Elda E. Tsou, "'This Doesn't Mean What You'll Think': *Native Speaker*, Allegory, Race," *PMLA* 128, 3 (2013), 575, 582, 583. See also Tsou, *Unquiet Tropes*, 128–160.
32. Chen, *Double Agency*, 181; Crystal Parikh, *An Ethics of Betrayal: The Politics of Otherness in Emergent US Literatures and Culture* (New York: Fordham University Press, 2009), 96–128; Michelle Young-Mee Rhee, "'Greater Lore': Metafiction in Chang-rae Lee's *Native Speaker*," *MELUS* 36, 1 (2011): 157–176; and Ju Young Jin, "Spies in the Third Space: Spy as a Trope for Cultural Emplacement in Chang-rae Lee's *Native Speaker* and Kim Young-Ha's *Your Republic Is Calling You*," *Journal of Narrative Theory* 47, 2 (2017): 224–251.
33. Tsou, *Unquiet Tropes*, 146. Conversely, on the limits of Emile's hermeneutic, see Tsou, "This Doesn't Mean What You'll Think," 580; and Tang, *Repetition and Race*, 114–115.
34. See also Parikh, *An Ethics of Betrayal*, which argues that these characters allegorize "diasporic desire" for "some time and place other than the here and now of citizenship and national belonging" (128).
35. On the limits and possibilities of Kwang's solicitation, see Huang, "Citizen Kwang," 252–254; Kim, "Do I, Too, Sing America?," 239–241; and Min Hyoung Song, "A Diasporic Future? *Native Speaker* and Historical Trauma," *Lit: Literature Interpretation Theory* 12, 1 (2001), 81–83.

PART III

The Dynamics of Race and Literary Dynamics

CHAPTER 8

"Dramatic Race"

Democratic Lessons of Twenty-First-Century African American Drama

Frank Obenland

> It was not really dramatic. And then . . .
>
> F. Fanon[1]

Over the last decade, African American theater has witnessed an extraordinary flourishing of Black plays, playwrights, and performances innovating traditional theatrical forms and bringing to the stage a diversity of themes and facets of Black experience. The popularity of this formative cultural presence is attested by a number of noteworthy revivals and adaptations of well-known and well-received "classic" plays. Lorraine Hansberry's *A Raisin in the Sun* saw a new filmic adaptation for TV in 2008 and a subsequent prize-winning run on Broadway in 2014, with actor Denzel Washington starring as Walter Lee Younger.[2] In 2020, Netflix released a filmic version of *Ma Rainey's Bottom*, thus underlining Harry J. Elam's argument that Hansberry and Wilson exemplify "the social power and cultural capital of theater."[3] While theater and drama compete with other media and performing arts for cultural visibility, African American theater, Elam argues, acts "as a regenerative agent [. . . that] connect[s] African Americans with their African heritage, commenting on the past and present meanings of blackness as well as its possibilities."[4] With their works, Hansberry and Wilson thus continue to exert a formative influence on a new generation of twenty-first-century African American playwrights, such as Robert Alexander, Marcus Gardley, Robert O'Hara, Jeremy O. Harris, Branden Jacobs-Jenkins, Lynn Nottage, Dominique Morisseau, Tanya Barfield, Tarell Alvin McCraney, Jackie Sibblies Drury, and Claudia Rankine – to mention only a few of the most renowned contemporary African American playwrights.

In recent years, these writers have responded to an increasing proliferation of conflicts and debates over such issues as police violence, the public commemoration of the Civil War, the "New Jim Crow" of the prison-industrial complex and the mass incarceration of people of color, a white supremacist backlash in national politics, as well as the Black Lives Matter movement against the vulnerability of Black lives in an era of wide-ranging structural racism. The formation of emancipatory and intersectional movements in the wake of the violent deaths of Michael Brown, Freddie Gray, Tamir Rice, Tanisha Anderson, Trayvon Martin, Breonna Taylor, and others resulted in an increasing interest in the precarity of Black existence and the pervasiveness of Black deaths abetted by a structural racism endemic in American society and politics. In the face of such challenges, critics have lamented the absence of a clearly defined political agenda and orientation in contemporary Black activism in comparison to the Civil Rights Era, the Black Arts Movement, or the Black feminist movement.[5] While African American drama cannot be summarized or accounted for in the terms of a coherent political vision or agenda, the following attempt at mapping the politics of African American theater and drama at the beginning of the twenty-first century takes its cue from conceptualizations of Black theater and drama as an important democratic art form in the political struggle of making African American voices heard.

In 2004, playwright and dramatist Robert Alexander argued for the continuing importance of African American theater as an important cultural venue for addressing social injustices and racial inequalities. For Alexander, theater remains an important vehicle for protest and critique because it inserts "the agony and ecstasy of each and every social drama . . . in the kind of civil discourse that is ours."[6] Referring to theater as a special form of political speech, Alexander concurs with Black feminist critic bell hooks, who has also underlined the importance of voice in Black performance as "crucial in the struggle for liberation," arguing that "the spoken word, transformed into a performed act, remains a democratic cultural terrain."[7] For hooks, the performativity of the Black voice offers an oppositional instrument for challenging oppressive social structures and "white supremacist capitalist patriarchy."[8] Taken together, Alexander and hooks identify theater as an important democratic cultural force whose significance results from its potential for representing or raising awareness about pressing social issues.

This chapter proposes to read the plays *The White Card* by Claudia Rankine and *Fairview: A Play* by Jackie Sibblies Drury as dramatic interventions in a larger cultural conversation on the dramatic meaning of "race." Both plays will be discussed in light of recent developments in Black performance theory and with regard to Jacques Rancière's argument on the democratic and egalitarian potential of theatrical performance. It will be shown that both plays disrupt and intervene in contemporary theatrical and cultural performances of race by reconfiguring the meaning and operation of "dramatic race" in the twenty-first century. More particularly, Rankine's *The White Card* extends and revises the traditional protest and social issue play by reflecting on the theatrical representation of police brutality and its mediation through photography and art. Sibblies Drury's *Fairview* provides an example of how contemporary playwrights elaborate on a tradition of actor–spectator interaction in African American theater that is used as a means for destabilizing the social allocation of racial and spatial positions in society. In addressing the issue of "race" in the contemporary moment, these plays work toward a revision of how racial identities are configured in what Rancière has called the "distribution of the sensible."[9] In this sense, Rankine and Drury transform African American theater into an oppositional site that challenges the configuration of racial discourses in a variety of contexts and instances.

Black Performance and the (Re-)Distribution of the Sensible

For French philosopher Jacques Rancière, political art exposes the randomness and inherent inequality structuring the "distribution of the sensible," which is his term for the underlying perceptual categories governing political debates and artistic forms. Art is political in that it throws into relief the "political dissensus," which for Rancière is not "a quarrel over which solutions to apply to a situation but a dispute over the situation itself, a dispute over what is visible as an element of a situation."[10] In similar terms, contemporary African American plays can be understood as making "visible" specific racial and social injustices and concrete instances of racist behaviors, practices, and institutions. In doing so, Rankine and Drury protest reductionist notions of Blackness in contemporary political and cultural debates.[11] Their works expose a "gap in the sensible" in that they unmask the inconsistency between the promise of an egalitarian democratic order and the prolonged existence of exclusionary racist policies and modes of perception.[12]

Obviously, any account of contemporary African American theater as political art needs to be complemented by the rich scholarship on the intersection of Black performance and American discourses on race and racism. As Roderick Ferguson has argued, "race" impacts a wide range of social, political, economic, and cultural discourses that entail "a set of wide-ranging analyses of freedom and power," particularly regarding "academic and political notions of epistemology, community, identity, and the body."[13] Answering to Ferguson's analysis, critics in the field of Black performance theory have suggested that we understand "race" as a cultural performance and racial identities as reiterative and performative enactments of a "racial habitus."[14]

From the perspective of Black performance theory, then, dramatic performances of "race" offer not only mimetic and performative instantiations of racialized Black bodies for a limited period of time in a public, institutional setting; rather, Black performances and theatrical (re)presentations of race focus on "the details of black expressivities and transgressions within the abiding contexts of disciplinary histories and circulations of inequality."[15] This oppositional and transgressive potential of Black performance on and beyond the theatrical stage thwarts any attempts of solidifying a unified or even totalized Black identity in favor of "generating a multiplicity of positions from an intersectional perspective."[16] Cognizant of the multiplicity and intersectionality of Blackness, Black performance theory traces the rhizomatic connections between race, class, gender, and sexualities in the formation of Black subjectivities across national boundaries and continental divides. This dynamic and rhizomatic understanding of Black performance – what Nadine Georges-Graves has recently described as "a performativity in flux" – precludes any attempts at essentializing identities in the name of a monolithic Afrocentric diaspora.[17]

In a similar manner, performance scholar and theater historian Soyica Diggs Colbert insists on the creative and emancipatory potential of Black performance as a form of self-determined cultural expression. For Colbert, Black performance grows out of "black social life as the basis for artistic and political action."[18] She argues that Black performance traditions constitute a "mechanism to *create*, even within contexts of suffering and illegibility" (emphasis added).[19] Colbert thus describes Black performance as a creative alternative to Afro-pessimist "theorists of Black positionality who share Fanon's insistence that . . . the structure of the entire world's semantic field . . . is sutured by anti-Black solidarity."[20] For Afro-pessimists, Blackness does not denote a particular social or ethnic identity but demarcates "a structural position of noncommunicability" and a "silencing" in that Black individuals are sentenced to a "banishment from the Human fold."[21] In contrast to the Afro-pessimist argument that a history of anti-Black violence shapes contemporary conceptualizations of Blackness "in the afterlife of slavery,"[22] Colbert seeks to "affirm the ontology of black people as beings who resist, innovate, live, thrive, suffer, and die" by exploring the "archive and repertoire" of Black performance history.[23] Building on

Colbert's argument, the following discussion will consider the work of contemporary African American playwrights as being informed by the Black experience and echoing the diverse and long-standing history of Black performance culture. Making Black voices heard in theaters across the country gives these works a democratic function. As instances of Black performance, these works belong to a performative "counter-culture" or a "culture of resistance."[24]

The following discussion of two plays by contemporary female playwrights will take its lead from the rich scholarship in Black performance theory as well as from Jacques Rancière's argument about the democratic and egalitarian potential of theatrical performances. While questions of race and racism are obviously absent from his work, Rancière forcefully argues for the emancipatory cultural work of theatrical performances in that they constitute collective processes of meaning-making that cannot be dominated or monopolized by any of the participants. Instead, the communal experience of theatrical performance immerses actors and audiences in a shared process of interpretation and translation. Similarly, the plays under discussion here challenge their audiences to respond to and participate in the theatrical performance. As Rancière has observed, the dismantling of the fourth wall that separates the audience from the theatrical performance restructures the conventional spatial organization of theatrical performances, thus allowing for the experience of "the living, communitarian essence of theatre."[25] Instead of calling for an identification with a particular community or collectivity by all audience members, the egalitarian potential of theater consists in spectators realizing the performative quality of their own social roles and their individual participation in a simultaneous, yet not homogeneous, process of cultural translation.[26] As Rancière argues, this entails a "new form of allocating bodies to their rightful place."[27] Drawing on Rancière's egalitarian conceptualization of theatrical performance, Black theatrical performance can thus be understood to address existing and conflicted conceptualizations of "race" and "Blackness" without sacrificing its cultural specificity and relationship to a long history of African American theater and drama. Herein, the social function of contemporary Black plays such as *The White Card* and *Fairview: A Play* will be understood not as a form of intervening directly in political debates but more generally as a form of "democratic disruption," and they do so by innovating well-established genres in African American theater and drama and by attempting to reorganize how "race" is represented and perceived in theatrical performance.

Problematizing Police Violence and the White Gaze in Claudia Rankine's *The White Card* (2019)

Police brutality is not a new subject on the African American stage in the twenty-first century. In *Gem of the Ocean* and *Radio Golf*, the bookend plays to his ten-play cycle on the African American experience in the twentieth century, August Wilson speaks out against the detrimental impact of police violence on the African American community.[28] As Wilson shows in these two plays, police violence against African Americans is symptomatic of an ongoing history of racial violence and socioeconomic injustice spanning from the early twentieth to the early twenty-first century.

In contrast to Wilson's project of reconfiguring notions of history, temporality, and theatrical performance, Claudia Rankine's recent play *The White Card* more closely adheres to the conventions of dramatic realism in her theatrical critique of police brutality and systemic racism. In the preface to the play, Rankine recounts how *The White Card* originated from a real-life conversation about structural racism in the United States between her and an attendee of one of her poetry readings. Taking questions from the audience after a reading from her *Citizen: An American Lyric*, Rankine was startled by a white middle-class spectator offering his personal help to the poet. For Rankine this gesture signaled "an age-old defensive shield against identifying with acts of racism at the hands of liberal, well-meaning white people."[29] As a consequence, Rankine problematizes diverging social and racial perspectives in the commemoration of recent historical events, such as the violent clashes between the national guard and African American protesters in Ferguson in 2014. Thus, the play not only analyzes how social relations and hierarchies are structured by and around objects of (African American) art; it also exposes American liberalism's claims to "colorblindness" as a false and disturbing form of cultural appropriation.

Moreover, Rankine's *The White Card* relies on the conventions of dramatic realism in order to condemn the American infatuation with Black suffering and death. Echoing Teju Cole's trenchant critique of "The White Savior Industrial Complex," Rankine's protagonist eventually unveils her white liberal patrons' interest in and sympathies for the Black Lives Matter movement as an ill-directed and ineffective instance of "American sentimentalism."[30] Instead, *The White Card* culminates in the search for an alternative to the display and consumption of Black suffering and victimization in theater and art. In the preface to the play, Rankine expresses her hope that the translation of her real-life conversation with a spectator from her poetry reading into a theatrical performance will result in what could be described as a Rancièrian reorganization or "redistribution" of the sensible. Rankine anticipates the theatrical performance of her play as a means of redressing the hiatus in the American conversation about structural racism and anti-Black violence resulting from well-meaning white liberal patrons seeking to "retreat into the comfort of control" by placing Black individuals and their history and experience back into a pre-established conceptual or "imagined" place.[31] As a playwright, Rankine does not see herself in the role of a teacher conveying a superior or premeditated knowledge to an audience. Instead, Rankine, in a way reminiscent of Rancière's conceptualization of the theatrical performance in *The Emancipated Spectator*, envisions the staging of her play as a means of exposing an "invisible dynamic" which will only be rendered palpable in the theatrical event by "get[ting] in a room and act[ing] it out."[32]

This theatrical dynamic described by Rankine in her preface surfaces at a pivotal moment in the first act of the play, set in March 2017. Virginia and Charles, a well-to-do white couple and collectors of African American art, reveal their newest acquisition of a photograph entitled *An Anatomy of a Death*, depicting a diagram from Michael Brown's autopsy report.[33] The ensuing conversation between the white patrons and art collectors, their activist son Alex, and their guest Charlotte, a young and aspiring African American artist, derails once the "invisible dynamic" of the photography as an artistic representation of Black death becomes exposed. For one, Virginia's and Charles's consumerist appropriation of the photograph is challenged by their son Alex, an adolescent progressive activist who regularly participates in protests against the Trump administration and structural racism in American society. For him, his parents' acquisition of the photograph amounts to little more than an expression of white privilege, while his parents' treatment of Charlotte constitutes a performative enactment of "white supremacy."[34] Their inability to understand the implications of their consumption of Black death in the form of this particular photograph demonstrates their "internalized racism" and even amounts to an instance of "upper-class terrorism."[35]

More important than Alex's vocal critique of his parents' patronizing attitude, however, is the dissonance between Charlotte's and Charles's readings of the photograph. For Charles, the photograph documents the social realities protested by the Black Lives Matter movement and serves as a "memorial" to Michael Brown.[36] Charles attributes an immediacy and presence to the photograph that denies the mediated character of its representation when he asks "How can we get any closer to Brown's reality than this?"[37] For Charles, the diagram's representation of Black death offers a metaphorical reference to "the violence against Brown," becomes "a portal for the inhumanity," renders "the invisible visible," and thus effectively "gestures toward [the] structural racism" endemic in American society.[38] Charlotte, however, objects to Charles's reading, for several reasons. For her, the photograph does not add anything to the extant documentations of Michael Brown's dying. In its facticity, the photograph does not effectually challenge an entrenched view of anti-Black violence. Instead, the photograph effectively screens the spectator from a direct confrontation with the actual violence of Michael Brown's death. As a proxy for Brown's dead body, for Charlotte the photograph only establishes an indexical relationship that allows spectators to maintain an emotional and perceptual distance from the actual events. As Charlotte points out, Virginia and Charles respond to the horror they feel about the killing of Michael Brown by engaging in an act of capitalist consumption of a piece of art. As Charlotte also keenly observes, the photograph, as an official document from the police investigation, effectively obscures and effaces a Black perspective on the event by circling back to the white police officer directly responsible for Brown's death. The photograph thus does not point at a broader social reality but ultimately reaffirms the institutional context in which it has been produced and thus fails to evoke an appropriate emotional and moral response from its white privileged spectators.

Mistaking their affective response to the photograph for "Brown's reality" – in Charles's words – characterizes the sentimental appropriation of Michael Brown's death by Virginia and Charles. In the final scene of the play, set in March 2018, Charlotte effects a reversal of this previous scenario. When Charles visits her at her studio, Charlotte places him, the white, well-to-do art collector, in a position that exposes him more directly to the vulnerability and contingency of Black life in the United States. Asked to turn his bare back to the Black artist, he expects to be shot and killed. When nothing happens, he turns with an expression reflecting the existential insecurity he has just experienced only to face the "shot" of Charlotte taking his picture with her camera. While this "shot" metaphorically relates to the actual violence against Black bodies, it also captures the inherent violence of capturing and representing their objectification and victimization in media and art. Observing a self-determined and autonomous act of artistic representation, audiences witness how Charlotte's redistribution of the visible makes palpable a state of feeling and being in the world that moves beyond a "realistic" or documentary representation of contemporary events.

Audience Participation in Jackie Sibblies Drury's *Fairview: A Play*

In her Pulitzer Prize–winning *Fairview: A Play*, Sibblies Drury engages in a more radical strategy of effecting a reorganization of perceptual categories in the theater. In her soliloquy at the end of the three-act play, Keisha, the aspirational teenage daughter of an African American middle-class family, breaks the fourth wall and asks audience members who identify as white to come on the stage and take the place of the play's African American characters.[39] In contrast to other experimental and avant-gardist performances, *Fairview*'s bid for involving audience members does not – at least initially – entirely deconstruct the separation between audience and performance spaces. The reorganization of theatrical space affirms the spatial separation in the positioning of Black and white bodies in the theatrical space. Provided that most patrons of theaters in the United States identify as white and the protagonists in the play are Black, the soliloquy calls for a reorganization of theatrical space that would also transform and reverse the spatial and racial logic that has informed the theatrical performance up to that point.

With its postdramatic structure of overlapping performances and blending of individual characters, *Fairview* defies the classical structure of the well-made play as well as the realist tradition of protest plays in African American theater history. With its splicing of acts and the fluidity of individual characters, the play exhibits what Hans-Thiel Lehman has described as "parataxis" or the combining of contrasting or dissimilar images, concepts, or fragments.[40] The arrival and preparations of an African American family to celebrate the birthday of Keisha's grandmother in the first act blends with the conversation of white characters fantasizing about assuming different racial identities in the second. This postdramatic stylistic device of two simultaneous yet spatially, and racially, separated performances reveals not only a conceptual but also a social gap between the two different sets of characters. With the white characters being at liberty to comment on and judge the African American characters, the play addresses a fundamental problematic in the American conversation on race.

The play's second act exposes a series of stereotypical views and notions of Blackness held by the white characters. It features a lengthy monologue by Jimbo, one of the white characters, who turns the conventional horror movie into a medium for reflecting on race as a system of social domination. That Jimbo's vision is delimited by focusing on white characters underlines the shortcomings of his endeavor to think through "race." Eventually, Jimbo loses himself in a fantasy scenario he nurtures and embraces because it allows him to imagine himself in control and to deflect any challenges to his self-image. Apparently, Jimbo's monologue nods to Frank B. Wilderson's critical work on Hollywood films as the purveyors of narratives that stoke anti-Black solidarity. It is important to note, however, that the play does not leave this Afro-pessimist reading of American popular culture uncontested. Throughout Jimbo's monologue, the African American family can be seen dancing on the stage. This mismatch between the aural and visual codes of theatrical representation thus undergirds the play's argument for the importance of African American dance as an important theatrical art form for cultural and individual self-expression.

At the end of the play, Keisha emerges as the voice articulating this performative claim to autonomous self-expression. Hemmed in by the audience's white gaze, Keisha finds speaking her mind "[d]ifficult because I have heard so many stories. It's hard to find the one I wanted to tell."[41] The moment for her to articulate her own vision only arrives after the established categorical distinctions between the actors and viewers of the play have been overturned. By asking the audience "to switch" and to take the place of the characters on the stage, Keisha, as the secondary text informs us, effectively "steps through the fourth wall. It's as simple as that."[42] Aiming for a complete reversal and exchange of cast and spectators allows Keisha to assume a liminal position in between both spaces, and to reconstitute the audience as the interethnic community to which she refers as "all my colorful people."[43] Addressing and thus positioning a diverse and intersectional audience, Keisha overcomes culturally viable narratives that regulate how "race" is narrated and performed in theatrical spaces. At the same time, the spatial reorganization of the theatrical performance also gestures to the possibility of reversing the hierarchical relationships between a predominantly white audience and the predominantly Black cast. It is important to emphasize here that Keisha emerges as the speaker of a new and different story about race in America only after the fourth wall has been shattered. In her utopian outlook on a racially just society, Keisha's prophetic call for mutual recognition culminates in her vision of "A Person Trying" as the personification of individuals struggling for achievement, success, and progress. It would be too facile to read this as an affirmation of dominant narratives or ideologies of American individualism. In fact, Keisha only finds herself empowered to articulate her vision after the "switch" and the reorganization of the theatrical performance. In other words, Keisha's individualism only flowers after the egalitarian and emancipatory potential of theatrical performance has been realized. By making race the key factor in turning spectators into active participants, Keisha's intervention demarcates a move from post-dramatic theater's *parataxis* to *methexis*, a "communal 'helping-out' of the action by all assembled."[44] In contrast to the revolutionary theater of Amiri Baraka and Ed Bullins that was intended for an exclusively Black audience, Keisha's maneuver exposes the fluidity and volatility of racial identities in theatrical performances.

In their revisions of established dramatic forms, the works of Claudia Rankine and Sibblies Drury are joined by a host of works by other contemporary African American playwrights. In his various plays, Branden Jacobs-Jenkins, for example, has explored the transhistorical connections between contemporary stagings of Blackness and historical theatrical forms such as blackface, the minstrel show, and melodramatic performances of race. Similar to Rankine's critique of the lingering sentimentalist notions inflecting the white gaze institutionalized in theatrical performances, Jacobs-Jenkins's *An Octoroon* rewrites, revises, and restages Dion Boucicault's nineteenth-century melodramatic play set on a Louisiana plantation during the antebellum period. Like Boucicault's original play, *An Octoroon* pivots around a sequence of highly theatrical scenes that foreground the performative construction of racial identities in the staging of a slave auction, sentimentalist understandings of law and justice in the play's trial scene, as well as the violent history of lynchings that has shaped race relations in the USA. Jacobs-Jenkins's reworking of the slave auction scene stands out here since the play's secondary text demands involving theater audiences as bidders in the staging of the auction: "*maybe there's some clever way to force the audience into doing this*" (italics in original).[45] While this scene is intended to confront the audience with its complicity in the affective organization of melodramatic performance traditions, this strategy has received mixed reactions as regards its effectiveness.[46] Nevertheless, what Jacobs-Jenkins's play attests to is the continuing interest of contemporary African American playwrights in questioning and criticizing theatrical performances as social practices and institutions.

Considered alongside each other, Rankine's *The White Card* and Sibblies Drury's *Fairview* engage in a Rancièrian redistribution of the sensible with regard to theatrical performances of race. Critically exploring the intersection of spatial and racial categories in stage performances, these plays articulate the hope for a more democratic and egalitarian form of theater and drama. Race becomes "dramatic" in these plays as they aim at transforming the intellectual and emotional responses of their audiences. The accomplishments of these contemporary playwrights also stand in the tradition of August Wilson, who has criticized the paucity of African American professionals in major American theaters in his seminal lecture "The Ground on Which I Stand" in 1996. More recently, the debate on the necessity of a sustained critique of theater as a social institution has been forcefully propelled by playwright Dominique Morisseau. In her "Playwright's Rules for Engagement," Morisseau has penned a list of appreciated audience behavior that emphasizes the interactive and collective character of theatrical performance. First distributed in the context of a production of her play *Pipeline* at the Lincoln Center in 2017, these rules on proper "theater etiquette" call on spectators to "engage" and respond to the live performance on stage.[47] Read alongside the theatrical works of Rankine, Drury, and others, Morisseau's comments indicate that theater's engagement with race does not end with the exploration of the performative and theatrical aspects of racial identities. To make race not only "dramatic" but also more "democratic," playwrights, actors, and theatergoers will need to confront theater's organization of social relations and address society's struggles with forms of race-based discrimination and systemic racism.

Notes

1. Franz Fanon, *Black Skin, White Masks* (New York: Grove Press, 1967), 110.
2. Two years later, Denzel Washington costarred with Viola Davis in the film adaptation of August Wilson's *Fences* (2016), in which he played the lead role of Troy Maxon. *Fences* and *Jitney* also won the Tony Award for Best Revival of a Play in 2010 and 2017, respectively.
3. Harry J. Elam Jr., "Cultural Capital and the Presence of Africa: Lorraine Hansberry, August Wilson, and the Power of Black Theater," in *The Cambridge History of African American Literature*, ed. Maryemma Graham and Jerry W. Ward Jr. (Cambridge: Cambridge University Press, 2011), 680–702; 681.
4. Ibid.
5. Kenneth Warren, *What was African American Literature* (Cambridge, MA: Harvard University Press, 2011), 96. Influential manifestoes on what constitutes a "black play" in the twentieth century are: W. E. B. Du Bois, "Krigwa Players Little Negro Theatre," *Crisis* 32.3 (July 1926): 134–136; Alain Locke,

"Steps Toward the Negro Theatre" (1922), in *Lost Plays of the Harlem Renaissance, 1920–1940*, ed. James V. Hatch and Leo Hamalian (Detroit: Wayne State University Press, 1996), 440–445; Amiri Baraka, "The Revolutionary Theater." *The Norton Anthology of African American Literature*, ed. Henry Louis Gates and Nellie Y. McKay, (New York: Norton, 1997), 1899–1902; Ed Bullins, "The So-Called Western Avantgarde Drama" (1967), in *Ed Bullins: Twelve Plays and Selected Writings*, ed. Mike Sell (Ann Arbor: The University of Michigan Press, 2006), 284–287; August Wilson, "The Ground on Which I Stand," *Callaloo* 20.3 (1997), 493–503; Suzan-Lori Parks, "Elements of Style," in *The America Play, and Other Works* (New York: Theatre Communications Group, 1995), 6–18.

6. Robert Alexander, "American Pop and Why Plays Still Matter," in *The Fire This Time: African American Plays For the 21st Century*, ed. Harry J. Elam, Jr. and Robert Alexander (New York: Theatre Communications Group, 2004), xxvii–xxxiv; xxxiv.
7. bell hooks, "Performance Practice as Site of Opposition" in *Let's Get It On: The Politics of Black Performance*, ed. Catherine Ugwu (London: Institute of Contemporary Arts, 1995), 210–221; 211.
8. Ibid., 212.
9. Jacques Rancière, *The Politics of Aesthetics: The Distribution of the Sensible*, ed. and trans. Gabriel Rockhill (London: Bloomsbury, 2012), 12. For Rancière's understanding of politics as a struggle for recognizing the "voice" of groups or individuals marginalized or excluded from the political discourse altogether, see Rancière, *Disagreement: Politics and Philosophy*, trans. Julie Rose (Minneapolis: University of Minnesota Press, 1999), 2. While Rancière's theory does not provide a recipe for subverting or challenging particular ideologies, I take his account of the "emancipated spectator" as usefully describing a challenge to the dominant organization of social and theatrical spaces and practices along lines of racialized differences.
10. Jacques Rancière, "Introducing Disagreement." *Angelaki*, 9.3 (Dec. 2004), 3–9; 6.
11. While I rely on Rancière's conceptualization of the connection between politics and aesthetics, Rancière has been rightfully criticized for glossing over the categories of race, class, gender, and sexualities, as well as historical formations such as imperialism and colonialism. His model of political struggle is not only informed by the nineteenth and twentieth-century labor movements but is also restricted to a conceptualization of the social body in terms of the French nation state. While his work obviously needs to be supplemented by the work of scholars and critics on Black performance theory, his theories nevertheless offer themselves to a discussion of the intersection of politics and drama since for him the disruption of a dominant political order is inherently theatrical.
12. Jacques Rancière, *Dissensus: On Politics and Aesthetics*, trans. Steven Corcoran (London: Continuum 2009), 38.

13. Roderick A. Ferguson, "Race," in *Keywords for American Cultural Studies*, ed. Bruce Burgett (New York: New York University Press, 2014), 191–196; 191.
14. Harvey Young, *Theatre and Race* (New York: Palgrave Macmillan, 2013), 10.
15. D. Soyini Madison, "Foreword," in *Black Performance Theory*, ed. Thomas F. DeFrantz and Anita Gonzalez (Durham: Duke University Press, 2014), vii–ix; vii.
16. Jean-Paul Rocchi, with Anne Crémieux and Xavier Lemoine, "Introduction: Black Beings, Black Embodyings: Notes on Contemporary Artistic Performances and Their Cultural Interpretations," in *Understanding Blackness through Performance*, ed. Anne Cremieux, Xavier Lemoine, and Jean-Paul Rocchi (New York: Palgrave Macmillan, 2013), 1–22; 2.
17. Nadine George-Graves, "Diasporic Spidering: Constructing Contemporary Black Identities," in *Black Performance Theory*, ed. T. DeFrantz and A. Gonzalez (Durham: Duke University Press, 2014), 33–44; 37.
18. Soyica Diggs Colbert, *Black Movements: Performance and Cultural Politics* (New Brunswick: Rutgers University Press, 2017), 13.
19. Ibid., 13.
20. Frank B. Wilderson III., *Red, White & Black: Cinema and the Structure of U.S. Antagonisms* (Durham: Duke University Press, 2010), 59.
21. Ibid., 59, 9.
22. Saidiya Hartman, *Lose Your Mother: A Journey Along the Atlantic Slave Trade Route Terror* (New York: Farrar, Straus and Giroux, 2007), 6.
23. Colbert, *Black Movements*, 13.
24. Paul Gilroy, *The Black Atlantic: Modernity and Double Consciousness* (Cambridge, MA: Harvard University Press, 1993), 37; Dwight Conquergood, "Beyond the Text: Toward a Performative Cultural Politics," in *The Future of Performance Studies: Visions and Revisions*, ed. Sheron J. Dailey (Annandale: National Communication Association, 1998), 25–36; 28.
25. Jacques Rancière, *The Emancipated Spectator*, trans. Gregory Elliott (London: Verso, 2011), 16.
26. Ibid., 14–15, 16–17.
27. Ibid., 15.
28. Another example is Adrienne Kennedy's 1996 play *Sleep Deprivation Chamber*, which deals with a case of police brutality involving her son, with whom Kennedy wrote the play. The script includes dialogue lifted directly from the minutes of her son's trial for attacking a police officer. *Sleep Deprivation Chamber* received the Obie Award for best play in 1996.
29. Claudia Rankine, *The White Card: A Play in One Act* (Minneapolis: Graywolf Press, 2019), 7.
30. Teju Cole, "The White Savior Industrial Complex," in *Known and Strange Things: Essays* (London: Faber & Faber, 2016), 340–349.
31. Rankine, *White Card*, ix.
32. Ibid.
33. Ibid., 55.
34. Ibid., 59.

35. Ibid., 59, 60.
36. Ibid., 59.
37. Ibid., 60.
38. Ibid., 56, 57.
39. Jackie Sibblies, *Drury, Fairview: A Play* (New York: Theatre Communications Group, 2019), 102.
40. Hans-Thies Lehmann, *Postdramatic Theatre* (London: Routledge, 2006), 86; 88.
41. Drury, *Fairview*, 105.
42. Ibid., 101, 102.
43. Ibid., 105.
44. Kimberley W. Benston, *Performing Blackness: Enactments of African-American Modernism* (London: Routledge, 2000), 28.
45. Branden Jacobs-Jenkins, *An Octoroon* (New York: Dramatists Play Service, 2015), 43.
46. Carrie J. Preston, "Hissing, Bidding, and Lynching and the Melodramatics of American Racism," *TDR: The Drama Review* 62.4 (Dec. 2018), 64–80.
47. Dominique Morisseau, "Why I Almost Slapped a Fellow Theatre Patron, and What That Says About Our Theatres," *American Theatre* (Dec. 9, 2015), www.americantheatre.org/2015/12/09/why-i-almost-slapped-a-fellow-theatre-patron-and-what-that-says-about-our-theatres/.

CHAPTER 9

Beyond Humanization

Decolonization, Relationality, and Twenty-First-Century Indigenous Literatures

René Dietrich

This chapter seeks to trouble our understanding of the degree to which the category of the "human" plays a role and is articulated in the theory and literature concerning race, specifically in the differing contexts of Blackness and Indigeneity. Doing so, I particularly want to point out how one might view the category of the "human" and its import differently when the focus is shifted from Blackness to Indigenous literature and culture. While not meaning to oversimplify these positions, this chapter departs from the premise that Black studies and Black literature recurringly pose and examine the question of which bodies are assigned a fully human status in a white-dominated society and how the rights granted to a specific body change when constructed as either fully human or less-than-fully human. Inflected through its own particular perspective, one can find this pertinent question being asked in Indigenous studies as well. However, Indigenous literatures interrogating the category of the "human" oftentimes ask a question that, as I want to argue in this chapter, moves beyond dehumanization: namely, how the human is constructed or constituted in relation to other forms of life, sometimes called other-than-human or more-than-human, and sometimes including the land which is then conceived of as a form of life in itself.

Such literature thus invites us to ask what different political and social imaginaries can be articulated when we view the social as being made up of the relationships maintained between the human and other forms of life, including the land. Beyond literary articulation and theoretical interest, this question also has political import, as we can view it as one critical aspect of decolonial thought, which is (among other things) engaged with considering possibilities of the social and the political, especially in their relationship to land, that exceeds that which is possible or thinkable under the parameters of settler colonialism – and, in the focus of this chapter, namely US settler colonialism. In the following I also want to show that, in particular, a recent resurgence of Native literatures in the twenty-first century can offer a variety of ways, both thematically and formally, to think through these questions anew.

Blackness, Indigeneity, and the Question of the "Human"

Prominent voices in Black theory of the past ten to fifteen years have interrogated how racializing structures equate humanity with whiteness or how different bodies are ascribed their degree of humanity in relation to their whiteness or nonwhiteness. Black feminist theorist Sylvia Wynter has issued a powerful critique of this in her widely acclaimed essay "Unsettling the Coloniality of Being/Truth/Power/Freedom." In this essay she redefines the term "humanity" as historically only referring to a specific "genre of being human."[1] This genre she deliberately capitalizes as "Man" and describes it as the "present ethnoclass (i.e. Western bourgeois) conception of the human . . . which overrepresents itself as if it were the human itself."[2] A model which assigns humanity based on its belonging to a specific "ethnoclass" therefore enables gradations from the "fully human" to the "not-quite-human" and to the "non-human."[3] Black Studies theorist Alexander Weheliye picks up this point in his influential work *Habeas Viscus: Racializing Assemblages, Biopolitics, and Black Feminist Theories of the Human*, and develops it further when he observes that Wynter's theorization of the "violently tiered categorization of the human species in western modernity" opens new forms of analytical inquiry. "[W]ithout denoting race and gender to the rank of the ethnographically particular," Weheliye states how it "instead expos[es] how these categories carve from the swamps of slavery and colonialism the very flesh and bones of modern Man."[4]

Following a similar line of thought, Indigenous studies scholars have argued that dehumanization of Indigenous peoples is not an unfortunate by-product of colonization, or simply a legacy of a settler colonial past, but crucial to the foundation and the ongoing existence of a settler colonial nation-state such as the USA. Historically, an example would be the tradition of conflating Indigenous people with the "natural world," while in the present day the crisis of "Missing and Murdered Indigenous Women and Girls" in Canada and the USA speaks to the ongoing sexualization and dehumanization of Indigenous female bodies.[5]

A settler colonial nation-state, as which I just described the USA, is a state that is premised on the expropriation of land and the elimination of the Indigenous peoples inhabiting it, variously through techniques of eradication and/or through dismantling their sociopolitical structures as autonomous polities. In turn, the colonial power erects on these lands new, settler colonial structures, which are institutionalized and legalized as the settler colonial nation-state, which makes, in Patrick Wolfe's term "invasion a structure, not an event."[6] Indigenous dehumanization is an instrumental part of this process and thus constitutive of a settler colonial present that continues to operate according to Patrick Wolfe's second well-established axiom: a "logic of elimination."[7] This logic rests on the need of Indigenous disappearance in order for settler nation-states to reassert themselves and constantly reassure themselves of their unchallenged sovereignty over Indigenous lands, bodies, and peoples. Consequently, Sherene Razack argues in her study on *Inquests and Inquiries into Indigenous Deaths in Custody*:

> Viewed as abject bodies always on the brink of death, Indigenous people can be imagined as less than human, a dehumanization that gives birth to the settler as fully human and as having emerged from the state of nature in which Indigenous people are thought to be trapped. Finally, we must find the courage to name and confront dehumanization.[8]

From this perspective one can view Black people and Indigenous people as being subjected to forms of dehumanization which are used to maintain different yet related structures of subjugation – namely, anti-Black racism and white supremacy, on the one hand, and Indigenous dispossession and settler colonialism, on the other.[9] While addressing this issue from Black studies, as the brief references to Wynter and Weheliye already show, requires more of a rethinking of the category of the "human" than a mere call to rehumanize Black bodies, a further different dimension is added to this question within Indigenous studies and, oftentimes, Indigenous literatures.

Arguably, the position of Indigeneity – as a cultural, social, and political collective form of land-based belonging – requires, beyond a rethinking of the category of the human, in fact a displacement of "the human" as the sole category of reference. Displacing the human from this status puts a stronger emphasis on the human as being one form of life that exists in and through relationships to different forms of life, including the land. A sole focus on "the human" as the primary reference point, which can be found in some Black theory as a means to question a system that assigns different degrees of human worth to different bodies, risks the eclipse of Indigenous epistemologies and ontologies that rely not so much on the primacy of the "human" as an ordering device but on relationality and kinship as paradigms of constituting the social, which can further open the political horizon of an Indigenous-centered decolonization.

Beyond a mere cultural trait, such a focus on relationality figures strongly in theorizations of Indigenous peoplehood as sociopolitical formations. Lenape scholar Joanne Barker, for instance, has defined the "polity of the Indigenous" through its "system of (non)human relationships and responsibilities."[10] Similarly, the Dené Yellowknife Glen Coulthard writes in *Red Skin, White Masks: Rejecting the Colonial Politics of Recognition* of a "grounded normativity" for Indigenous peoples in Canada, the USA and other places that is characterized by "living our lives in relation to one another and our surroundings in a respectful, nondominating, and nonexploitative way."[11] Relationality, which might otherwise be read as merely spiritual or psychological, becomes the basis for the formation of a social and political collective that is constituted by its ties to the land and its habitants, and thereby, as Dakota literary scholar Chris Pexa puts it, the foundation for "the ethical norms of peoplehood."[12]

While I do not want to argue that all of Indigenous literature is focused on such questions of relationality, I do want to maintain that the political horizon of much contemporary Indigenous literature can be better assessed and analyzed through a lens on the decolonial and relational than through re-evaluating the racialized status of the "human." Extending beyond the confines of US settler colonial governance and a racial politics of the "human," such literature points to the horizon of the decolonial, a horizon in which other means of doing politics based on "ethical norms of peoplehood" including the other-than-human become thinkable and imaginable again. Indigenous literature can be a way to express this shift, but also a means to contribute to expanding this space of the political. In order to show this, I will focus on two Indigenous poets, starting with Deborah Miranda.

Deborah Miranda's *Raised by Humans*, Settler Colonial Logics, and Figures of Relationality

In 2015, Deborah Miranda, a poet of Chumash and Esselen heritage and an enrolled member of the Ohlone-Costanoan Esselen nation, of California, published her third poetry collection: *Raised by Humans*. In my focus on her work, I want to show how she uses poetic imagery and form so as to consider the human in systems of relationality, and the relational as a signifier of the political in terms of Indigenous sovereignty, self-determination, and struggles for decolonization.

In her poetry collection of 2015, the title indicates and questions the status of the "human" by suggesting a set of relations in which the "human" does not occupy the space habitually assigned to it. With the title *Raised by Humans*, Miranda references narratives of feral children being brought up by or living with wolves, bears, or other wild animals – and reverses them. Through such a shift, the "human" loses its status as an unmarked norm of behavior and interaction in the social sphere, and is instead repositioned as one form of life, one species among others.

The eponymous poem outlines a situation in which "humanity" as an unequivocal ideal is strongly challenged: "My mother abandoned me" (1) starts the poem, outlining in brief couplets a narrative of neglect, displacement, and emotional dependence.[13] The pursuit of the mother's "lovers: Alcohol, Heroin, Despair" (3) is identified as leading to her abandoning her child and leaving behind "our homeland" (4, California) for "the interior of a strange place" of "dark green firs" (5, Pacific Northwest). Taken in by an aunt and uncle who provide the child with all human necessities ("They bought me clothes, bathed me, fed me every night", 9), the child remains defined by the emotional bond to the parent who left her: "I waited for my mother to come back" (10). The reunion with the mother who returns with "Trickster/Con Artist/Coyote" (12) leads to them taking the child back up "north to the rain" (14) and a renewed history of neglect and abandonment: "They locked me in a tin house // went carousing while I huddled each night alone" (14–15).

The child is thus exposed to abandonment and solitude, and finds reprieve from these conditions by turning temporarily "feral": In the "surrounding woods" (16), the child finds escape from deprivation, nourishment partly through traditional Native foods of the region ("ate huckleberries and drank from a muddy creek," 17), and comfort among plants indigenous to the place ("slept buried in dried pine and cedar needles," 18). The "surrounding woods" (16) are rendered not so much as a place of wilderness or isolation from society, but as a space of nurturing lived relations of an expansive sociality (specifically named), which stands in contrast to the maternal patterns of return and abandonment leading to physical and emotional "starvation" (22) and the seemingly more clinical treatment of the child as an object of "humanitarian" care by their aunt and uncle. Still bound to the mother and her human family, however, the child remains a "tamed fox" (18) and goes back to "my captivity for dinner" (19). The child remains domesticated, then, by an emotional bond of love and hurt it does not know how to break: "chained // to my cage by a metal only the human heart / knows how to forge" (24–26), as the poem closes with what could be read as an allusion to William Blake's "A Divine Image" ("Cruelty has a human heart" and "the human form, a fiery forge").[14]

What is thus depicted as exceptional to humanity is not intelligence or ethical superiority, but the capacity to disregard one's responsibilities to the closest familial relation possible, and even to utterly disregard them as a fellow living being with rights and needs. Moreover, the poem suggests, only "the human heart" is able to construct out of such abuse a bond of emotional dependence. Such a bond is formally captured in a poem that contains its history of abandonment and captivity in a strict couplet-structure. However, at the same time, when the poem asserts the strength of the chain, the enjambment across the final stanza-break between "chained" and "to my cage" might also be read to indicate the possibility of breaking it, or upsetting the structures that keep it intact.

In this way, the chain and the cage, and the possibility of breaking the chain, might not only refer to the harmful patterns of abandonment and emotional dependence. The invisible/invisibilized chain and cage can also be read to index the settler colonial structures of invasion and logics of elimination that are implemented on various levels and that shape the everyday worlds of Indigenous people in ways that might not register as being linked to experiences of colonialism. One way to make these underlying structures and logics transparent is to make conditions of domestic violence and child abuse within Indigenous communities visible, as within this poem, not as evidence of Indigenous people's inability to cope in the "modern world," but as recent iterations of what Miranda, in another instance, calls "genealogies of violence" that settler logics help to perpetuate and naturalize as seemingly part of the fabric of Native social life in "Western modernity." The poem illustrates the connection of such logics to questions of (de)humanization and its limits by indicating how these logics of racialization and animalization that underlie structures of Indigenous dehumanization are themselves rooted in an idealizing and political privileging of a specific version of "humanness" as norm and normative in settler colonial formations.

In the poem, an animal-like state is ascribed to the child – "a tamed fox" (18); "wolved a meal down" (21); "whimpering" (24) – but that does not suggest an inferiority, or a state closer to nature, inherent in the child. Instead, the position of animality inhabited by the child in the poem works in two ways. Within "the surrounding woods," the child is not so much represented as a nonhuman animal as depicted through actions that evoke animality specifically through their full reliance on the given environment, in this case the woods, such as drinking from creeks or using the local vegetation as sites for rest and sleep. In other words, the child is not pictured as being denigrated to a "lower" form of existence, but rather is shown briefly inhabiting a particular place, in relation to the possibilities it offers and the forms of sustenance that can be derived from it, and thus making the place a temporary "homeland" away from home.

The politics of kinship, and their violent interruption through imposition of a settler colonial order, manifests on this intimate scale: crucially, this aspect of Native social life cannot be neatly disconnected from the abusive family dynamics taking center-stage in the poem; instead, both are intimately related. The child is likened to an animal and becomes subservient when domesticated, finding itself in conditions of "captivity"; additionally, the economies of sustenance practiced in the woods are replaced with structures of dependency. If this shows, then, without suggesting any direct equivalency between animality and indigeneity, how different forms of life and being in the world become incorporated by a settler colonial regime that distributes value and privilege in reference to an idealized version of "humanness" acting as norm, the contrary is true for the other version of animality at least hinted at in the poem as well. In contrast, it is imagined within part of a network of forms of life whose existence through reciprocal responsibilities and relationships constitutes the basis for the polity of the Indigenous – a polity conceptualized and organized through the relationships of the human and nonhuman world, thus upsetting settler colonial logics and offering the potential to decolonize political thought.

Natalie Diaz's *Postcolonial Love Poem* and the Decolonial Politics of Water

In order to situate the reading of Mojave poet Natalie Diaz, in particular "The First Water is the Body" and "*exhibits from* The American Water Museum," from her Pulitzer-winning collection *Postcolonial Love Poem*, published in 2020, it is important to revisit the NoDAPL movement in 2016–17. This is the movement of peaceful resistance by the Standing Rock Nation, the Oceti Sakowin (i.e., all nations grouped under Sioux in US federal policy), as well as their Indigenous and non-Indigenous allies against the construction of the Dakota Access Pipeline under the Missouri River on unceded territory of the Oceti Sakowin and adjacent to the Standing Rock Nation territory.

Standing Rock was the largest resistance movement of Indigenous nations since the American Indian Movement and positioned itself against the US government, US state forces, and fossil energy and security corporations. While there is much that can and has been said about it – from its importance as an environmental justice movement, to the importance of Indigenous traditions for a resistance understood as protection and ceremony, to the massive militarized police response that met the water protectors – what I want to focus on in the context of this chapter is how the central call of the movement – "Mni Wiconi" – articulates a relational politics with strong decolonial implications. Originally in Oceti Sakowin, Mni Wiconi means "water is life," and the ease through which one might agree with this statement might signal the degree to which this aspect of the movement could be communicated to a wider, non-Indigenous public. Accordingly, this call was taken up on many occasions and at many locations in order to show solidarity. The levels of meaning that were more readily evoked, however, were the ones that could be quite comfortably integrated within a liberal and environmentalist framework. In that sense, "Mni Wiconi" tended to be read then as "water is the source of life," or "without water there is (literally) no life."

Indigenous scholars discussing the protests at Standing Rock and what Melanie K. Yazzie (Diné) and Cutcha Rising Baldy (Hupa, Yurok, Karuk) call "the politics of water," though, make clear that Mni Wiconi is not that easily reduceable, asserting instead an expansive view of nonhuman life and relations that has epistemological and political dimensions.[15] Nick Estes (Lower Brule Sioux) states that Mni Wiconi "is also an affirmation that water is alive" (15) and that Mni Sose, the Missouri River, which the resistance to the Dakota Access Pipeline sought to protect, is best understood as a "nonhuman relative, who is alive, and who is also of the Mni Oyate, the Water Nation" (15).[16] Relatedly, Craig Howe (Oglala Sioux) describes MniSose as a "living being" and frames the resistance at Standing Rock in terms of relationality: "Standing Rock is where the people are gathered to protect their relative right now."[17] Extending this thought, but also emphasizing water's own autonomy, Edward Valandra (Oceti Sakowin Oyate/Sicangu Titunwan) writes: "We . . . recognize water as having personhood, independent of humans 'giving' that standing or status."[18] For Yazzie and Baldy, this notion of water's autonomy is coupled with a focus on "water view" – the perspective that water itself has on the world – which ultimately not only highlights water's agency but also puts a demand on human action in relation to water: "[O]ur theoretical standpoint is one that foregrounds *water view*, (re)claiming knowledges not just for the people, but also for the water; not just looking at our relationship to water, but our accountability to water view."[19]

When taking these water views from Indigenous scholars into account, it appears that Mni Wiconi does not so much assert that life is equal to water, or that water is important for the continuation of life. Instead, they articulate the dynamic forms of existence, the ways of being in the world that inhere to water as being meaningful in its own right, not solely because it nourishes other forms of life. This shift entails viewing how water extends beyond itself toward nonhuman and human bodies without reducing this to a resource functioning in support of a body's life. Instead, it can be appreciated as a form of communal interaction between humans and what Zoe Todd (Métis/otipemisiw) has called their "watery kin."[20] Furthermore, it points to a means of establishing, manifesting, and affirming relations between all forms of being that makes present a structure of kinship crucial to the social and political life of Indigenous communities – a relational structure that is crucial to decolonial thought as it points outside what is thinkable as politics within the given framework of US settler colonial governance.

With this in mind, I want to turn for the remainder of the chapter to Natalie Diaz's *Postcolonial Love Poem* and two poems within it: "The First Water is the Body" and "*exhibits from* The American Water Museum" which highlight the relationality of body, Native peoplehood, and water, pointing out the political implications of these relations while simultaneously signaling a moment of endangerment due to environmental degradation. In "The First Water is the Body," Diaz directly references Standing Rock in a prose passage within the poem: "in the United States, we are teargassing and rubber-bulleting and kenneling Natives trying to protect their water from pollution and contamination at Standing Rock in North Dakota."[21] In the next sentence she names possibly the most infamous case of environmental racism with Flint, in which a majority-Black community was exposed to lead-contaminated water on grounds of austerity. She states: "We have yet to discover what the effect of lead-contaminated water will be on the children of Flint, Michigan, who have been drinking it for years" (51). Putting one instance next to the other makes clear how these cases of endangering marginalized communities through polluting their water supply (or risking this pollution) are related to one another. At the same time, the poem makes clear that water can neither be separated from the Native body politic nor from the speaker's body, calling out the political potential of both and the risk that comes with such an intimate connection at the same time.

The poem begins with "The Colorado River is the most endangered river in the United States – also, it is part of my body" (46). As a member of the Mojave nation, traditionally located at the Colorado River, Diaz reflects on the colonially induced naming of "Mojave" (by the Spanish) and the name by which her people refer to themselves "Aha Makav" (46). Often translated as the "people who live by the river" (46), Diaz points out how the relationality conveyed by the name and the envisioned form of peoplehood runs much deeper than that: "When a Mojave says, Inyech, Aha Makavch ithhuum, we are saying our name. We are telling a story of our existence. *The river runs through the middle of my body*" (46). Furthermore: "Translated into English, '*Aha Makav*' means *the river runs through the middle of our body, the same way it runs through the middle of our land*" (46). If this evokes the fantasy of a Native American – or, rather, "Indian" – culture fully in harmony with nature, Diaz is aware of this and sarcastically comments: "In American imaginations, the logic of this image will lend itself to surrealism or magical realism" (47). For Diaz, this is not simply about a spiritual bond to make one feel better in relation to nature; this is about a form of interrelationality in which one life is dependent on the other, and in which, ultimately, one's existence as a body and, collectively, the existence of the people as a whole is at stake. The harm done to the Colorado River through climate-change-induced drought and mismanagement of the river-flow makes it the "epicenter of the nation's water and climate crisis," and this human- (or, rather, settler colonial- and capitalist-) induced crisis of the river calls into question the livability of the Mojave as a people.[22]

Diaz writes:

> What does 'Aha Makav mean if the river is emptied to the skeleton of its fish and the miniature sand dunes of its dry silten beds?
>
> If the river is a ghost, am I? (50)

As the body and the people of the Mojave are made through water, as they are the people for whom "*the river runs through the middle of our body*" (46), so the endangerment of that river not only makes living conditions harder, but also threatens the existence of the Mojave as a people. Diaz, however, reacts to this not solely with despair, but also with defiance and an indictment of a thinking in separation that fails to realize the vital importance of connectivity:

> We think of our bodies as being all that we are: I am my body. This thinking helps us disrespect water, air, land, one another. But water is not external to from our body, our self. (51)

She goes on:

> The water we drink, like the air we breathe, is not a part of our body but is our body. What we do to one – to the body, to the water – we do to the other. (52)

Diaz sketches a situation in which acknowledging and acting upon relationality as a ground for constituting an expansive social fabric becomes necessary and essential to life. In "*exhibits from* The American Water Museum," a poem that I want to focus on in the closing of this chapter, she includes the "prayer of an Elder Mojave woman" in which she makes the responsibilities tied to relationality explicit: "The river is my sister – I am its daughter" (68). And "I am the body kneeling at the river's edge / letting it drink from me" (68). Diaz draws a relationship of care, reciprocity, and responsibility, and the question is less how the speaker's body is assigned or denied a human status, but rather how a human body is able to meet its obligations to other forms of being and create a workable social body that acknowledges the agency and participation of other social and political actants outside of humans. Diaz provides a note to the poem in which she narrates that it is a prayer by an "Elderly Mojave woman shot in the head and throat by two rubber bullets as she sat in prayer before a tractor and a row of German shepherds barking against their leashes at the site of yet another pipeline" (68).

With this note, Diaz combines in that section of the poem the demands for a relational, decolonial politics articulated in the possible social bond with the body of water, while also bluntly illustrating the risk posed to it and those bodies advocating for it. Closing with this harsh image also illustrates that Indigenous literature invested in questions of the relational and decolonial does not leave behind or ignore issues of dehumanization. It is important to see how a protest against a racial politics of dehumanization and a settler colonial politics of elimination and dispossession can be met with the same violence by the state. At the same time, the violence against the Elder Mojave woman can be seen as a response to what is clearly – and, I would argue, rightfully – viewed as a threat to the settler status quo of the social and political order. In the final instance, the prayer of the Mojave Woman as well as Diaz's poetry articulating it call for a different kind of politics, a different way of constituting the social and political sphere than is currently the case or even conceivable within the parameters of Euro-American settler colonial rule. The image of the Mojave woman asserting her relationality to the river and other forms of being in the face of the violence directed at her can transport to us the defiance necessary to voice and uphold these demands, in ongoing forms of Indigenous resistance as well as in those of present-day Indigenous poetry.

Conclusion

Concluding this chapter with a focus on Diaz's poetry brings to mind not only the differences that a focus on Blackness and Indigeneity in relation to the human and questions of racialization might entail. It also opens a perspective on the body and that of embodiment as a category of thought and mode of being that is able to cut across what I outlined as differences at the beginning of the chapter. The racialized body that is not assigned a fully human status and is therefore exposed to danger in its bodily autonomy is ultimately linked to the colonized body of land and water which is exposed to harm as its relationality to human and other forms of human life remains unrecognized or ignored. This (willful) ignorance furthermore exposes human bodies to harm, as we can see in connection to Flint and Standing Rock, and puts them even more at risk when they put themselves on the line, as the Mojave woman does in Diaz's poem, so as to refuse and resist the policies resulting from the failure of recognizing relationality. A closer look at the differences as well as the intersections of Blackness and Indigeneity in regard to questions of the human may then afford not just a reconsidering of the human as a racialized category or a construction set apart from other forms of life. More than that, it may open a reconsideration of different forms of embodiment and bodies – human, other-than-human, of earth and water, of the environment – who are ultimately in interplay with each other and whose interplay we may understand more fully when we learn to read them as being articulated as bodies of relation, as they are in Indigenous poetry and bodies of poetry beyond it.

Notes

1. Sylvia Wynter, "Unsettling the Coloniality of Being/Power/Truth/Freedom: Towards the Human, After Man, Its Overrepresentation – An Argument," *CR: The New Centennial Review* 3, 3 (2003): 257–337, 269.
2. Wynter, "Unsettling the Coloniality of Being," 260.
3. Wynter, "Unsettling the Coloniality of Being," 301, see also Alexander G. Weheliye, *Habeas Viscus: Racializing Assemblages, Biopolitics, and Black Feminist Theories of the Human* (Durham: Duke University Press, 2014): 3.
4. Weheliye, *Habeas Viscus*, 30.

5. See, among others, Sarah Deer, *Beginning and End of Rape* (Minneapolis: University of Minnesota Press, 2015); and Joanne Barker, ed., *Critically Sovereign: Indigenous Gender, Sexuality, and Feminist Studies* (Durham: Duke University Press, 2017).
6. Patrick Wolfe, "Settler Colonialism and the Elimination of the Native," *Journal of Genocide Research* 8, 4 (December 2006): 387–409, 388; see also Wolfe, *Traces of History: Elementary Structures of Race* (London: Verso, 2016).
7. For the logic of elimination, see Patrick Wolfe, *Settler Colonialism and the Transformation of Anthropology: The Politics and Poetics of an Ethnographic Event* (London: Cassell, 1999): 27: "settler-colonialism consists in a negative articulation between invaders and the land. The cultural logic which is organic to a negative articulation is one of elimination."
8. Sherene Razack, *Dying from Improvement: Inquests and Inquiries into Indigenous Deaths in Custody* (Toronto: University of Toronto Press, 2015): 59.
9. For thinking together about questions of settler colonialism, Blackness, and Indigeneity, see, for instance, Tiffany King, "In the Clearing: Black Female Bodies, Space and Settler Colonial Landscapes" (published PhD diss., University of Maryland, 2013): www.proquest.com/docview/1461804097?pq-origsite=gscholar&fromopenview=true&sourcetype=Dissertations%20&%20Theses; Justin Leroy, "Empire and the Afterlife of Slavery: Black Anti-Imperialisms of the Long Nineteenth Century" (unpublished PhD diss., New York University, 2014); Manu Karuka "Black and Native Visions of Self-Determination" *Critical Ethnic Studies* 3, 2 (2017): 77; Iyko Day's "Being or Nothingness: Indigeneity, Antiblackness, and Settler Colonial Critique," *Critical Ethnic Studies* 1, 2 (2015): 102–121.
10. Joanne Barker, ed., *Critically Sovereign: Indigenous Gender, Sexuality, and Feminist Studies* (Durham: Duke University Press, 2017), 5.
11. Glen Coulthard, *Red Skin, White Masks: Rejecting the Colonial Politics of Recognition* (Minneapolis: University of Minnesota Press, 2014): 60.
12. Christopher J. Pexa, *Translated Nation: Rewriting the Dakhóta Oyáte* (Minneapolis: University of Minnesota Press, 2019), n.p. [Kindle ed.].
13. Miranda, Deborah. *Raised by Humans: Poems* (San Fernando: Tía Chua Press, 2015), 20–21. Hereafter, quotations from the poem "Raised by Humans" are given by line numbers in parentheses in the text.
14. William Blake, *Songs of Innocence and of Experience, 1789, 1794* (Library of Congress), electronic edition. www.loc.gov/item/48031329/.
15. Melanie K. Yazzie and Cutcha Risling Baldy, "Introduction: Indigenous Peoples and the Politics of Water," *Decolonization: Indigeneity, Education & Society* 7, 1 (2018): 1.
16. Nick Estes, *Our History Is the Future: Standing Rock Versus the Dakota Access Pipeline, and the Long Tradition of Indigenous Resistance* (London: Verso, 2019): 15.
17. Craig Howe and Tyler Young, "Mnisose," *Hot Spots, Fieldsights*, December 22, 2016, https://culanth.org/fieldsights/mnisose.

18. Edward Valandra, “Mni Wiconi: Water Is [More Than] Life,” in *Standing with Standing Rock: Voices from the #NoDAPL Movement*, ed. Nick Estes and Jaskiran Dhillon (Minneapolis: Minnesota University Press, 2019): 81.
19. Yazzie and Baldy, “Politics of Water,” 2, emphasis in original.
20. Zoe Todd, “Protecting Life Below Water: Tending to Relationality and Expanding Oceanic Consciousness Beyond Coastal Zones.” *American Anthropologist* website, October 17, 2017. www.americananthropologist.org/deprovincializing-development-series/protecting-life-below-water.
21. Natalie Diaz, *Postcolonial Love Poem* (Minneapolis: Graywolf Press, 2020): 51. Hereafter, references to poems in the volume are made through page numbers in parentheses in the text.
22. https://www.cpr.org/2022/04/18/colorado-river-drought-conservation-endangered/.

CHAPTER 10

Shades of Whiteness and the Enigma of Race

Racial In-Betweenness and American Literature

Mita Banerjee

Race, as Toni Morrison famously wrote, is the motor of the American literary imagination. Morrison argues that, from its very beginnings, American literature can be seen as a response to an "Africanist presence": White imagination constituted itself against a canvas of fabricated Blackness. This canvas became a foil onto which the fears and desires of the dominant culture could safely be projected. Two aspects are particularly significant here: First, Morrison argues that the preoccupation – obsession, even – with race and racial difference is the source of literary creativity and the literary imagination. Second, it is equally important to note that the "Blackness" described in American literature has no referent: it is less an accurate depiction of African American culture than a "fabrication" of Blackness. As Morrison goes on to observe, "the subject of the dream is the dreamer. The fabrication of an Africanist persona is reflexive."[1] For an analysis of US race relations in American literature, this insight could not be more significant. The subject of the dream, Morrison writes, is not the enigmatic Black figure that the dream is about, but it is rather the person of the dreamer themselves. Blackness in works by white American writers, in other words, tells us more about the white imagination than about African American culture and subjectivity.

In the paragraphs that follow, I would like to map these ideas onto the concept of racial in-betweenness in American literature. I will try to show that just as American literature is obsessed with racial difference, it is equally obsessed with racial in-betweenness. Racial in-betweenness reveals the fault lines of race itself: To the extent that racial groups are seen as stable and clearly defined, the idea that race is itself a social construct disappears from view.[2] By contrast, racial in-betweenness reveals the "slipperiness" of racial categories: Concepts such as "mixed-race" identity and racial hybridity emphasize that the boundaries between racial groups blur; it is impossible to decide where one racial group ends and the other begins.

Racial in-betweenness hence reveals the "slipperiness" and arbitrariness of racial definition itself.

As this chapter will show, racial in-betweenness can take various forms. First, it can take the shape of mixed-race identity; second, it can point to the historically shifting nature of racial definition as such. I will look at examples from both of these categories of racial indecision. I will analyze how literary texts negotiate the racial status of "off-white" groups such as the Irish, and I will explore the role of mixed-race characters in American fiction. At the same time, I will inquire into the relationship between literary aesthetics and racial in-betweenness. I will ask in what sense racially ambiguous characters can be seen to fuel the literary imagination at specific periods in American literary history: from naturalism to American modernism.

The Irishness of American Naturalism

The literature of American naturalism, it can be argued, was reform oriented. Writers such as Stephen Crane set out to explore the shady sides not only of American society, but of human nature itself. In keeping with European naturalism, as in the work of Émile Zolà, naturalist writers wanted to study human nature at its most animalistic. If human nature is stripped of all forms of social convention and decorum, they asked, what essence of human instinct can be revealed? As Donald Pizer has observed, naturalistic writers demonstrate "a fascination with the animal vestiges of man's evolutionary heritage."[3] In search of this baseline quality of humanity, naturalistic authors turned to the ghettoes of American cities. They argued that it was here that human instinct was most clearly revealed: in the survival of the fittest and the idea of social Darwinism which marked ghetto life.

All these ideas are part of the definition of American naturalism. What has not been remarked on, however, is the role that race and racial in-betweenness play in this exploration of human nature. In the following analysis, I will turn to Stephen Crane's novella *Maggie: A Girl of the Streets* to analyze racial in-betweenness as a driving force of American naturalism. In this reading, I will relate naturalistic politics to whiteness studies. It is symptomatic of the complexity of race that neither whiteness nor Blackness were historically "given": rather, both were subject to constant change. This is particularly true of the role of the Irish in the American social and racial fabric. In the nineteenth-century racial definition, the Irish were seen as "colored." This discrepancy points to the difference between seeing and being:[4] Both whiteness and Blackness are constructed categories. What we see as white today was seen as a clear instance of "Blackness" in the nineteenth century. As Jacobson observes, "an earlier generation of Americans *saw* Celtic . . . physiognomies where today we see only subtly varying shades of a mostly undifferentiated whiteness."[5] Historically, then, the Irish "became white" only over the course of the twentieth century. As Noel Ignatiev observes, "[W]hile the white skin made the Irish eligible for membership in the white race, it did not guarantee their admission; they had to earn it."[6]

What is important to note, however, is that the process through which the Irish became white manifests itself not only outside the pages of fiction, but inside American literature as well. Naturalistic texts such as Stephen Crane's *Maggie* can be seen as a testing ground for whiteness. If outside the pages of fiction the Irish were seen as "probationary" whites,[7] this probation was also central to the depiction of Irish characters in naturalistic texts. Nineteenth-century political rhetoric portrayed the Irish as prone to alcoholism and violence;[8] they were seen as "unfit for self-government."[9] As Jacobson notes, the new American nation was to "be an empire of law and reason, not arbitrary will or passion. . . [The] new democratic order would require of its participants a remarkable degree of self-possession."[10] Given these requirements voiced by lawmakers to describe potential American citizens, how might we assess the "fitness for self-government" on the part of the Irish? Crane and other writers addressed that question. If in nineteenth-century America the Irish were on probation, Crane's novel clearly portrays the Irish mother as undeserving of the potential of eventually being "mainstreamed" into American society.

The point that can be made here, however, is that this probation is also at the core of literary naturalism. *Maggie* maps this dilemma between the "blackness" of the Irish and their potential whiteness onto its depiction of different generations in an Irish immigrant family. Maggie, the protagonist of Crane's novella, grows up in an environment that by today's standards would be seen as dysfunctional: Her life is characterized by her mother's alcoholism, fits of rage, and violence, and the physical abuse of Maggie's younger brother, Tommie.

If the Irish are on probation in naturalistic fiction, the abusive behavior of Mary Murphy, who is unconcerned even with the eventual death of her own son, does not bode well for the racial future of the Irish:

> As the father and children filed in, she peered at them. "Eh, what? Been fightin' agin!" She threw herself upon Jimmie. The urchin tried to dart

> behind the others, and in the scuffle the babe, Tommie, was knocked down. He protested with his usual vehemence, because they had bruised his tender shins against a table leg. The mother's massive shoulders heaved with anger. Grasping the urchin by the neck and shoulder she shook him until he rattled . . . At last she tossed him into a corner where he limply lay weeping.[11]

Where, then, does the potential of Irish whiteness lie? This potential can be located in the narrative's protagonist, Maggie. It is through Maggie's eyes that we contemplate the scenes of violence and utter desolation. It is the abhorrence in her eyes that mark the potential of the Irish to become white:

> Turning, Maggie contemplated the dark, dust-stained walls, and the scant and crude furniture of her home . . . The almost vanished flowers in the carpet pattern, she conceived to be newly hideous. Some faint attempts which she had made with blue ribbon to freshen the appearance of a dingy curtain, she now saw to be piteous.[12]

The overall portrait here is of a family driven by passions, but viewed through the eyes of someone more acceptable to the so-called standards of the dominant culture.

The tragedy at the heart of Crane's text is that Maggie's potential and her moral sensibility, which is so at odds with her family's behavior, should be short-lived. It is Maggie's innocence and naiveté that marks both her potential whiteness and her doom. Having been dumped by Pete, a man she loved, yet completely oblivious to the fact that he manipulated her, Maggie has to resort to prostitution. Her own mother, learning of her fate, turns her out on the street to starve. Her mother's hypocrisy is the coffin nail in the claim of first-generation Irish immigrants to whiteness. By contrast, Maggie becomes white because she is so different from her mother: In the end, she commits suicide, unable to live a life of indecency and moral depravation. It is in her suicide that Maggie has earned her probation: She becomes white at the moment of her death: "The forlorn woman had a peculiar face. Her smile was no smile. But when in repose her features had a shadowy look that was like a sardonic grin, as if some one had sketched with cruel forefinger indelible lines about her mouth."[13] It is significant here that Maggie's face has no color. In a novel obsessed with colors, with different shades of yellow and purple and red, this colorlessness is itself evocative. In the absence of color, it is Maggie's features that we see: freed of the need to ascertain her race and racial status, we can contemplate her personality. The "cruel forefingers" that have etched lines around her mouth are society's own. In keeping with naturalism's agenda, *Maggie* shows that it is society that has driven a young woman into such a tragic fate. In finally zooming in on Maggie's features, and not on the "Irish" color that obfuscates these features, Crane's narrative portrays "how the Irish become white."[14] If the new republic required its citizens to govern their passions and to demonstrate the quality of self-possession,[15] Maggie shows precisely such a mastery of her own instincts. It is only this moral sensibility which drives her to commit suicide. It is in death that she has earned her whiteness.

Mexican Blackness in William Faulkner's *Light in August*

The fact that the protagonist of William Faulkner's novel *Light in August* (1932) should be named Joe Christmas is at once enigmatic and revealing. What is so remarkable here is that in naming his protagonist "Joe Christmas," a man unsure of his own racial ancestry, Faulkner should in fact anticipate an entire field of research which would emerge almost a century after the publication of his novel: the field of whiteness studies. As Ian Haney López has written, whiteness and Christianity have been closely connected in the history of American race relations. He describes one particular court case which took place in the nineteenth century. In this trial, an immigrant from Syria petitioned the court to grant him the right to be naturalized; he argued that given his complexion and his place of birth, he was a white man and hence eligible for naturalization. Naturalization in the nineteenth century was restricted to "free white persons."[16] The petitioner, George Dow, argued that being from Syria, he came from the same region that Jesus Christ had come from. If the court were to deny citizenship to him, George Dow, this would hence come close to denying citizenship to none other than Jesus himself. Remarkably, the judges retorted that this amounted to "emotional blackmail" of the court. However, in this act of turning down Dow's petition, the court revealed two aspects about American legal and cultural identity: First, they admitted the linkage between whiteness and Christianity on which Dow had staked his claim in the first place. Second, their verdict revealed the affective, emotional nature of this connection. As López writes, "Judge Smith refused via the rhetorical charge of emotivity to engage the question regarding the racial eligibility of Christ for citizenship, a very interesting question indeed given that in much White supremacist ideology Whiteness and Christianity are nearly synonymous."[17]

Joe Christmas's name immediately rouses suspicions about his racial status: "'Did you ever hear of a white man named Christmas?,' the foreman said."[18] Crucially, this passage speaks volumes about the complexity of whiteness as such. If whiteness and Christianity are synonymous, as the court case *Dow* v. *United States* (1915) makes clear, then this synonymy is tacit knowledge, it is never openly confessed. In fact, the court was coerced into making this synonymy explicit only when "emotionally blackmailed" by George Dow, the petitioner from Syria. Where Joe gives himself away, where he reveals his potential nonwhiteness, then, is in making this link visible. Like George Dow, Joe Christmas stakes his claim to whiteness on the relationship between whiteness and Christianity; and, like Dow, he loses the case. Hearing his name, the foreworker immediately becomes suspicious. No white man, he implies, would give himself this name. Moreover, the fact that Christmas has to invent his own genealogy at once points to his racially enigmatic status and the potential of his illegitimacy.

What makes Faulkner's literary aesthetics so remarkable is that he creates a psychogram of white supremacism: he portrays white supremacism as the psychopathology it is. Faulkner's characters in *Light in August* are obsessed with policing the boundaries of whiteness. This policing is itself based on the assumption that the boundaries of whiteness can be defined. As a figure in this racial fabric characterized by obsession and paranoia, Joe Christmas is "outrageous" on a number of counts: First, he defies racial definition: given the uncertainty of his ancestry, it is unclear whether he is white or Black. All we know, and all he himself knows, is that his mother was white; the racial lineage of his father remains unclear. Second, however, this racial enigma which surrounds Joe's birth father turns him into a racially in-between character. He is defined in the novel, and he defines himself, as mixed race.

The mastery of Faulkner's literary aesthetics, however, is that he focuses not on the solution to this racial riddle but on the enigma itself. This enigma, the fact of racial in-betweenness, becomes not only a marker of the action in *Light in August* but also the fuel for racial speculation that takes place inside the narrative. Joe Christmas is literally a canvas onto which racial definitions and racial paranoia can be projected. In *Light in August*, Faulkner locates the question of racial definition in the Southern psyche itself. Race, in Faulkner's novel, is not a biological fact that can be ascertained by looking at a man named Joe Christmas. Rather, it is a projection which tells us more about the observer than the observed. *Light in August* ideally exemplifies Morrison's dictum that the "subject of the dream is the dreamer." In the novel, each character is defined by the way they look at Joe Christmas. Because he is racially indeterminate, he serves to reflect the racial assumptions of those who look at him: "The others had not stopped work, yet there was not a man in the shed who was not again watching the stranger in his soiled city clothes, with his dark, insufferable face and his whole air of cold and quiet contempt."[19] His face is "insufferable," then, because it defies racial definition.

Joe Christmas, the racially enigmatic character, becomes a prism for race relations in the American South, and he becomes a conduit for Southern racial paranoia and its obsession with racial purity. The novel begins with Joe being disavowed by his maternal grandfather: His grandfather, never having fully acknowledged his relationship to Joe, the presumably mixed-race child, works as a janitor in the orphanage where Joe lives. His actions toward his illegitimate grandson can be described as an act of exorcism. He is torn between caring for his daughter's son and hating the Blackness inside him. As a woman at the orphanage tells him,

> "You hate him too," she said. "You've been watching him too" . . . His eyes were quite clear, quite grey, quite cold. They were quite mad too. But the woman did not notice that. . . . "You never sit here except when the children are outdoors. But as soon as they come out, you bring this chair here to the door and sit in it where you can watch them. Watching him and hearing the other children calling him Nigger."[20]

Where the novel is so masterful, then, is that it tuns the reader's perspective into a white gaze: The reader looks at Joe Christmas, the racially enigmatic child, through the *white* eyes of Joe's grandfather. In this narrative psychogram, the reader enters the mind of the white supremacist. To the extent that we are made to look at Joe Christmas through his grandfather's cold stare and racial appraisal, we, too, become complicit in white supremacist thinking. Or, rather, Faulkner's literary aesthetic forces us to consider where we stand in this system of racial surveillance, definition, and appraisal. Faulkner draws us into an abyss of racial definition and racial indeterminacy. He anticipates twenty-first-century critical race theory by drawing us deeply into the fulcrum of race: The quest for racial definition is bound to be an odyssey from which we will never return; the search for racial purity, as *Light in August* demonstrates, is doomed because race itself is a construct, not an essence.

As if this vortex of race and racial indecision were not enough, Faulkner gives one more twist to the screw of racial inquiry. Joe Christmas himself is caught up in this search for racial definition. Joe is perhaps one of the most tormented characters in American literature, and he is tormented by the specter of race. The point that the narrative makes is not only that Joe is made by the uncertainty of his racial ancestry into a canvas for racial projection; rather, he turns himself into the canvas of his own projection and his own racial paranoia.

The self-torment that Joe goes through is that he himself scrutinizes his own actions for symptoms of Blackness. *Light in August* is a psychogram of Black self-hatred: What was once his grandfather's act of exorcism now becomes Joe's own. He is torn between the fascination with the Blackness that is within him and its abhorrence. The violence which he inflicts on others is a form of self-abuse. This self-hated in turn gives rise to an obsession with Blackness. Lying next to his African American lover, Joe tries to imbue the Blackness that is within him:

> At night, he would lie in bed beside her, sleepless, beginning to breathe deep and hard. He would do it deliberately, feeling, even watching, his white chest arch deeper and deeper within his ribcage, trying to breathe into himself the dark odour, the dark and inscrutable thinking and being of negroes, with each suspiration trying to expel from himself the white blood and the white thinking and being.[21]

As this passage in the novel makes clear, the curse of hybridity is the dilemma of unbelonging; of being neither "purely" white nor "purely" Black. Lying next to his African American lover, Joe sees the whiteness of his own body heightened under his constant scrutiny. His whiteness is suspect even to himself: it is an off-whiteness, a whiteness which is uncertain and ambiguous. If the men whom he had encountered at the mill saw him as "dark" and "insufferable,"[22] he now sees his whiteness as being equally "insufferable."

The one idea that Joe refuses to entertain, however, is the absence of Blackness. What if Blackness were only in the eyes of the observer? Joanna, the white woman who loves him and whom he will eventually kill, asks Joe what he would do if the rumors about his Black ancestry turned out to be wrong and he were really a white man:

> She was still looking at him; her voice told him that. It was quiet, impersonal, interested without being curious. "How do you know that?" He didn't answer for some time. Then he said: "I don't know it." Again his voice ceased; by its sound, she knew that he was looking away, toward the door. His face was sullen, quite still. Then he spoke again, moving; his voice now had an overtone, unmirthful yet quizzical, at once humorless and sardonic: "If I'm not, damned if I haven't wasted a lot of time."[23]

The tragedy of *Light in August* is that there is no escape from racial paranoia and the obsession with racial purity and racial definition.

Faulkner's *Light in August* is a literary masterpiece because it solves the enigma of race without solving it: In the end, after Joe has fully descended into the abyss of violence and self-destruction, having committed several murders, his true ancestry is finally revealed: Joe's father was not Black, but Mexican. And yet, as the narrative has made clear from the beginning, Mexicanness, too, is a form of off-whiteness, not whiteness proper. Like the Irish, Mexicans were racially suspect in the nineteenth and early twentieth centuries.[24] In *Light in August*, the resolution of Joe Christmas's racial indeterminacy is hence only another enigma: The narrative dispels the specter of Blackness (Joe's African American ancestry) only to give rise to another enigma: the off-whiteness of Mexicans in the US. As Foley notes, Mexicans as a "race" were suspect because they were seen as racial hybrids to begin with: Joe is thus doubly or triply hybrid in Faulkner's narrative: not only is he mixed race (Mexican/white), but Mexicanness itself was seen as mixed-race category, being made up of Spanish, Mexican, and African ancestry, as Foley observes.

The signature move in *Light in August*, however, is yet to come. In the relationship between Joe and Joanna, *Light in August* imagines a liaison that is illicit in a number of ways. First and foremost, it constitutes a crime in the legal sense: In the era of segregation, miscegenation was forbidden; there could be no marriage between a white woman and a Black man. Second, however, it is indicative of the novel's complex grasp of race relations and the absurdity of racial policing that it superimposes on this idea of illegitimacy many other transgressions. The liaison between Joe and Joanna Burden transgresses not only the boundaries of race, but also those of age: the novel repeatedly stresses that Joanna is much older than Joe. Moreover, if interracial marriage is a crime in the early-twentieth-century South (and will remain a crime until segregation is overturned in 1954 in *Brown* v. *Board of Education of Topeka*), it is interesting to note that the narrative revolves around two possibilities in particular: the concepts of marriage and of miscegenation. Even though Joe and Joanna never formally marry, there is an indication that they will be separated only by death. In the end, Joanna wants to kill both Joe and herself.[25] Second, after they have been together for several years, Joanna brings up the question of children. Here, however, *Light in August* conjures up the "crime" of miscegenation only to dispel it. Even as Joanna wants to have a child, it turns out that she is too old to become a mother: "But the shadow of autumn was upon her. She began to talk about a child, as though instinct had warned her that now was the time when she must either justify or expiate. She talked about it in the ebb periods."[26]

Whiteness Under Suspicion

The novel's most striking sleight of hand, however, revolves around the racial status of Joanna herself. Joanna's whiteness in the novel is centered on her difference from African Americans: she is a white woman living in a Black neighborhood. What emerges in this context is the idea that whiteness needs Blackness for its own self-definition. Joanna becomes white only through her association to Blackness. Crucially, Joanna's racial status may thus in fact be as enigmatic as Joe's. This kinship is suggested not least by the similarity of their names. As the novel opens, we think of Joanna as a white woman, and we think of Joe as a Black man. As the novel closes, however, Joe has been revealed to be Mexican, and toward the novel's close we learn that Mexican "blood" also runs in Joanna's family.

The complexity of Faulkner's racial mapping could not be more astute here: His signature move in this context is that he not only inquires into the nature of Blackness, but that he equally questions the nature of whiteness. Faulkner's narrative thus dispels the notion of what López has called the "transparency phenomenon." López writes: "I call this the transparency phenomenon: the tendency of whites not to think about whiteness ... Transparency [is] the unnerving tendency of Whites to remain blind to the racialized aspects of [their] identity."[27] This inquiry into the construction of whiteness, in turn, is the fatal blow for the racial paranoia of the white Southerners whom Faulkner so astutely portrays: The white South is obsessed with Blackness, but it believes its own genealogy to be beyond doubt. It is this white certainty that the novel goes on to eclipse. The eclipsing of white purity starts with an investigation of the racial lineage of the Burden family. It starts with the destruction of white privilege in what may at first seem a marginal issue: the family name was changed from Burrington to Burden since Joanna's grandfather, Calvin, was "desperately illiterate."[28] This moves him, the white man, into the direction of poor whites in the American South. Crucially, poor whites have been seen, as Matt Wray has emphasized, as being "not quite white" in the American racial imagination. Poor whites, Wray writes, were often insulted as "white trash." Their economic status hence served to compromise their whiteness.[29]

Even before he gets married to a woman of questionable racial descent, then, Calvin's whiteness is itself suspect. He then proceeds to marry a Huguenot, a woman who, the novel makes clear, is quite dark-skinned. In this as in many other instances, Faulkner inquires, half a century before the birth of whiteness studies, into the shades within whiteness.

He portrays a moment of Calvin looking at his young son: "The two of them would be alone in the room: the tall, gaunt, Nordic man, and the small, dark, vivid child, who had inherited his mother's build and coloring, like people of two different races."[30] Where, Faulkner's narrative asks, does whiteness end and racial difference begin?

As if this upsetting of whiteness was not enough, Calvin's son Nathaniel, who is of "dark coloring" himself, then emigrates to Mexico; he comes back with a Mexican wife, Juana. The first wife of Joanna's father was thus in fact Mexican, even though her father and grandfather insist that she is Spanish. Joanna herself was named after this woman, Juana, after she had passed away and her father Nathaniel had taken another wife. However, this complex family tree, as well as her Mexican name, can be said to cast a shadow on Joanna's whiteness.

What is remarkable in this context is that even before Joanna is revealed to have a Mexican half-brother, she has made herself racially dubious through her actions. As the novel opens, Joanna may be white, but she is depicted as what Ian Haney López has called a "race traitor": Having deliberately shed her white privilege, she has crossed over to the Black world: "A Yankee, a lover of negroes, about whom in the town there is still talk of queer relations with negroes . . . it still lingers about her and about the place: something dark and outlandish and threatful."[31] What is so remarkable, then, is that *Light in August* cannot only be read through the concept of critical race theory, but also through the lens of whiteness studies. Joanna has clearly committed race treason; she has deliberately abandoned her white privilege. According to López, who draws on the work of Noel Ignatiev here, a "race traitor" is "someone who is nominally classified as white, but who defies the rules of whiteness so flagrantly as to jeopardize his or her ability to draw upon the privileges of white skin."[32] Seen from this perspective, Joanna Burden is a "race traitor" par excellence. She "defies the rules of whiteness" in multiple ways: by living in a Black neighborhood, by having all her business affairs conducted by a Black lawyer, and by eventually entering a relationship with a Black man, Joe Christmas.

In terms of Southern race relations, Faulkner's narrative deliberately defies closure: In the end, the line of demarcation between whiteness and Blackness remains more unclear than ever. Joe's mother had a liaison with a Mexican man from a traveling circus. This relationship, moreover, mirrors the racial mixing in Joanna's family: her father, too, had a Mexican wife. Eventually, the crime of miscegenation is thus dispelled by the narrative. Joanna is sufficiently white, even though she engages in race treason, and Joe, it turns out as the novel closes, is not quite Black. Yet, what might have been a solution to the racial enigma of Joe Christmas only turns out to be another puzzle. If modernism's project is the reconstruction of unity, the putting together of fragments, *Light in August* maps this agenda onto the study of race. It argues that race will always remain an enigma because it is itself a fiction. The Mexicanness of Joe Christmas, far from being a solution, turns out to be another blurring of lines.

What emerges from this reading of Stephen Crane's *Maggie* and William Faulkner's *Light in August* is the centrality of race to the American literary imagination. In both novels, race is both metaphorical and material. Both narratives revolve around characters that are racially ambiguous; yet, this racial ambiguity was in keeping with the race relations of their time. In the nineteenth century, at the time that Crane was writing his novella, the Irish were seen as "probationary" whites.[33] It is such probation that Crane maps onto the canvas of his literary imagination. Similarly, Mexicans were historically seen as "off-white"; this off-whiteness also marks the ambiguity of Joe Christmas in *Light in August.* In this way, literary authors, too, become chroniclers of race and of race relations. Literary texts become a census of sorts. Yet, what is significant here is not only the similarity between fiction and social reality, but also the difference between them. Literature can be seen as a form of experimental social action. Literary writers imagine not only race relations as they are, but also as they *could be.* For this reason, Stephen Crane and William Faulkner not only represent race but also offer us new ways of thinking about race and racial definition. This is the power of fiction: it can help us to reconsider not only what is but also what might be.

Notes

1. Toni Morrison, *Playing in the Dark: Whiteness and the Literary Imagination.* New York: Picador, 1992, 17.
2. Ian Haney López, *White by Law: The Legal Construction of Race.* New York: New York University Press, 1996, 111.
3. Donald Pizer, *Frank Norris and American Naturalism.* New York: Anthem Press, 2018, x.
4. Elahe Haschemi Yekani, Gabriele Dietze, and Beatrice Michaelis, "Modes of Being vs. Categories: Queering the Tools of Intersectionality." In *Beyond Gender: An Advanced Introduction to Futures of Feminist and Sexuality Studies.* Ed. Greta Olson, Daniel Hartley, Mirjam Horn-Schott, and Leonie Schmidt. London: Routledge, 2018, 117–136.

5. Matthew Frye Jacobson, *Whiteness of a Different Color: European Immigrants and the Alchemy of Race*. Cambridge: Harvard University Press, 1999, 10.
6. Noel Ignatiev, *How the Irish Became White*. New York: Routledge, 1995, 59.
7. Jacobson, *Whiteness of a Different Color*, 174.
8. Ibid., x.
9. Ibid., x.
10. Ibid., 26.
11. Crane, *Maggie: A Girl of the Streets, and Selected Stories*, 7.
12. Ibid., 23.
13. Ibid., 59.
14. Ignatiev, *How the Irish Became White*, *passim*.
15. Jacobson, *Whiteness of a Different Color*, 26.
16. López, *White by Law*, x.
17. Ibid., 75.
18. William Faulkner, *Light in August*. New York: Vintage, 2005[1932], 23.
19. Ibid., 22.
20. Ibid., 93.
21. Ibid., 166.
22. Ibid., 22.
23. Ibid., 188.
24. Neil Foley, *The White Scourge: Mexicans, Blacks, and Poor Whites in Texas Cotton Culture*. Berkeley: University of California Press, 1997, 19.
25. Faulkner, *Light in August*, 211.
26. Ibid., 194.
27. López, *White by Law*, 22 & 174.
28. Faulkner, *Light in August*, x.
29. Matt Wray, *Not Quite White: White Trash and the Boundaries of Whiteness*. Durham: Duke University Press, 2006, 3.
30. Faulkner, *Light in August*, 178.
31. Ibid., 50; Karen Andrews, "The Shaping of Joanna Burden in Light in August." *Pacific Coast Philology* 26.1–2 (1991), 5.
32. López, *White by Law*, 189.
33. Jacobson, *Whiteness of a Different Color*, 174.

CHAPTER 11

There Is Here
Immigration Law and the Literature of Belonging

Jean Pfaelzer

Immigrant authors in the USA write under the shadow of hostile laws that assure that their tales of transit are uncertain and their stories of arrival are dangerous. Expectations of political equality and emotional growth travel from their homelands, prompting them to write of acts of repudiation and resistance. But American immigration law naturalizes race and redefines identities. Countering their home countries' assumptions about birth and lineage, immigration law shapes representations of identity and alters narrative forms. It provokes migrants' terrifying tales of global transition and rejection, as well as their enduring dreams of belonging. Immigrant literature is international and intercultural.[1] Depicting both émigrés who choose to move to the USA and those who are forced to migrate, it adapts literary strategies to confront America's racialized laws; migrant characters refuse to be turned into perpetual outsiders.[2]

Immigrants, refugees, transient laborers, and victims of human trafficking challenge the scourge of laws that endanger their going forth and coming in, through fiction, poetry, and art.[3] Driven by the illusive promise of escape from poverty or political repression, immigrants' own traditions of identity and cultural belonging often conflict with the cruel restrictions of immigration policies, creating fractious endings of assimilation – a soul-destroying but tempting telos. Although migrants hope to belong, US laws spawn nightmares of confinement and expulsion, forging a literature of loss. As America's need for workers tussles with its attitudes of ethnic contempt, immigrants' representations of national identity distort illusive literary traditions of romance and domesticity.

The Immigration Act of 1790 was the first to specify that only an "alien, being a free white person," could become an American citizen.[4] Written at the birth of the nation, it declared that citizenship – civic belonging– could only pass through a father. Indentured servants and free or enslaved Blacks – those who were considered "property" rather than "persons" – could neither be nor become naturalized citizens.[5] "Naturalization" is a presumptuous word that implies a telos of normalcy. After the Civil War, the Naturalization Act of 1870 extended "naturalization" to "aliens of African nativity and to persons of African descent," but it excluded Asians and Latinos – that is to say, nonwhite immigrants.[6]

Korean mural artist David Young Kim recalls how his immigrant childhood in Los Angeles provoked an obsession with "an idea of 'home'" – a drive to document and recreate a trope of belonging: to "define it, lose it, but constantly reiterate it in paint." In the 1970s, as his "mother country" was rapidly distancing itself from its history, "never to look back," Kim migrated with his family to the USA. As Kim grew older, his personal Korea became "frozen in time," while modern Korean American society demonstrated "I am otherwise." Still, he hangs on to the idea that Korea holds the keys to his grandparents', parents', and ultimately his own identities. His images of Korean culture atrophied and became a "proxy for a more universal subject matter." In his art, Kim appropriates symbols, patterns, and colors from the culture that once felt familiar. Although he is well aware of the dissonance between lived history and nostalgia, Kim adorns his vast murals with traditional Korean patterns, "thereby making a strange place more like home." His art plays with the idea of "manufacturing nostalgia."[7] This fractious relationship between past and present, memory and history, distortion and fact, permeates American immigrant literature.

As in David Kim's murals, Edith Maude Eaton/Sui Sin Far's (1865–1914) stories depict immigrants' conflicted visions of Asian identity and American belonging. Eaton's mother was a Chinese trapeze artist who was allegedly rescued by missionaries. Her father, a British soldier and merchant, moved the family to Montreal, Canada. There he became a human smuggler.[8] One of fourteen children, Eaton was a popular syndicated journalist who wrote from Canada, Jamaica, California, and New York. Often publishing under versions of her pen name, Sui Sin Far, she is best known for her 250 short stories and essays that embed a diasporic, feminist, and Asian lens. Eaton set more than 100 of her short stories in Chinatowns.[9]

In "Its Wavering Image" Eaton tells of Pan, a "half-white half-Chinese" girl. Her white mother is dead, and she is raised by her father, a prosperous merchant in San Francisco's Chinatown.[10] Pan's racial identity "wavers" when she faces romantic pressures from an aggressive white reporter, Mark Carson, who has been sent to Chinatown to "find a story." Pan becomes that story. She introduces Carson to the segregated Chinatown rebuilt from the ashes of the devastating 1906 San Francisco earthquake. Designed by white architects, it mimics the Forbidden City in Beijing to attract white tourists and spectators such as Mark.[11]

Mark Carson thinks that, in Chinatown, he has discovered a free-spirited and childlike Eurasian girl. Marketed since the 1860s as a titillating site, here young girls who had been kidnapped from the streets of Guangdong were sold from caged brothels.[12] Journalists, ministers, and local officials used the sordid image of the enslaved prostitutes to promote anti-Chinese immigrant legislation. Eaton explores the challenges of belonging through the biracial character of Pan and the voyeuristic and commercialized gaze of Mark Carson: white tourists make Pan feel "strange and constrained" and prompt her to shrink "from their curious scrutiny as she would from the sharp edge of a sword" (61).

Pan's father is proud to display his daughter and his community to Carson, and he invites the journalist to "cross the threshold of a cool, deep room fragrant with the odor of dried lilies and sandalwood," a female erotic and exoticized space where Pan "initiates" him into the "simple mystery and history of many things." Although Pan feels "natural and at home" with her "father's people," the journalist insists that she reject the liminality of her racial and national origins and of Chinatown itself – a site, in his eyes, of "heat and dust and unsavoriness" – and accept the "white" identity of her late mother. Meanwhile, he seeks to isolate Pan, a tactic typical of abusers, and he teaches "the young girl that, all unconscious until his coming, she had lived her life alone," thus severing her from Chinatown's men's clubs and women's gatherings (62).

Ultimately, Mark Carson teaches Pan the codes of Orientalism that ideologically divide the world into the progressive, masculine, and productive "West" and the static and feminine, if decorative, "East." Orientalism is a racial ideology marked by the twin urges to liberate and to subordinate. Orientalism suggests that Asians are unable to liberate themselves and must accept "Western" powers who would discover, expropriate, and enjoy their bodies and their nation. Mark instructs "childlike" Pan to view Chinatown as backward and un-American, to accept the contradiction that Asians are both necessary and repellent to the industrial and imperial West. Through his binary lens, Asians are necessary to empire diplomacy and a capitalist economy, even as they endanger white morality.[13]

Mark Carson also tells Pan that her Chinese "race" is voluntary and, hence, performative. As a metaphor for an immigrant multiracial nation, Carson declares that she is, in fact, an impossibility and insists that she reject her biracial identity and her ties to two cultures: "Pan, don't you see that you have got to decide what you will be – Chinese or white? You cannot be both." He seals his ultimatum with lines from Longfellow: "The moon and its broken reflection" shall appear in "its wavering image here" and a kiss. In the finest tradition of sentimental evidence, Pan weeps with happiness. Carson concludes, "Those tears prove that you are white" – and, hence, American.

In the end, Carson's newspaper article degrades Chinatown and shames the family by turning Pan into a commodity, a profitable informant. Her father is horrified that he encouraged Pan to "spread" herself before a "ridiculing and uncomprehending foreigner" whose words are a phallic "sword [that] pierced through her to pierce others" – a dangerous bridge between a fantasized past and a dystopian future in which the immigrant woman is available, modern, and white (64–65).

"Its Wavering Image" marks how Orientalism shapes the literary representation of Asian American immigrants. Eaton's street scenes of Chinatown, her depictions of Chinese households, and her characters become tactics that manage gendered, racial, and national borders, even as they counter stereotypes of diseased erotic slaves and secluded merchants' wives constrained by bound feet. Mark's editor warns Carson that Pan is powerful because she can tell stories – she too is an author. Eaton's characters teeter on the liminal edge of here and there, of past and present, for, as theorist Lisa Lowe observes, an immigrant's political space is both "juridically legislated" and "culturally embodied."[14] Eaton's Chinese–American home fuses the political and territorial sites of the nation.

Facing a terrifying legal landscape during the wave of anti-Chinese hate, Eaton observed, "I have no nationality and am not anxious to claim any."[15] In the final scene, Carson visits Pan, who is "lying low," horizontal, on a settee, dressed in a "Chinese costume," while a toddler presses her head on Pan's bosom. Pan has surrendered to a performance of Chinese womanhood. The toddler interpolates the promise of Americanization through motherhood; the spirited girl who freely roamed the streets and entered spaces of both male and female purview is now comforted "as a Chinese woman," promised that she too will bear a child someday. Pan rejects her multiple identity and declares "I am a Chinese woman . . . I would not be a white woman for all the world" (66). The "It" of "Its Wavering Image" is the binary of racial hybridity and assimilation: the female immigrant is illegible to the white reader. True belonging is unlikely.

Eaton's stories followed the Page Act of 1875, the first federal immigration law to ban "undesirable" immigrants and any "Mongolian" woman who was not a merchant's wife or who entered the USA for prostitution or "lewd and immoral purposes." Although there is no history of enslaved Chinese men in the USA, the Act also banned any "Mongolian" man who came for involuntary "coolie" labor. It also removed the right of most Chinese immigrants to become citizens.[16] The infamous Chinese Exclusion Act of 1882 soon followed; it was the first US law to ban a people by race. It prohibited Chinese naturalization and outlined paths to deportation.[17] A decade later, the Geary Act required all 110,000 Chinese residents in the USA to carry photo-identification cards or face a year of hard prison labor. Most of Eaton's immigration stories appeared during the era of the Scott Act (1902), which effectively banned Asian immigration for the next forty years.[18]

By naming specific geographies and groups of people, early American immigration laws interacted with popular stereotypes to create categories of human beings targeted for low wages and ethnic cleansing. They marked Asians as diseased – docile but dangerous migrants who threatened the purity of white bodies. Legally, Chinese, Japanese, and Latin American migrants were viewed as necessary laborers, marginalized and temporary, yet, like Pan, resistant objects of desire. In 1892, 100,000 of a total of 110,000 Chinese residents refused to register for photo-identity cards – an act of mass civil disobedience against the country's first internal passport.[19]

Eaton's sentimental representation of loss is framed by an assertive rhetoric of civil rights. At the unspoken center of Eaton's stories of East–West is the cold glare of Angel Island Immigration Station, a detention center built into crumbling buildings of a military fort that opened on a windy island in San Francisco Bay – a cartography of contempt located somewhere between Ellis Island and Guantanamo Bay. The Great San Francisco Earthquake of 1906 torched much of San Francisco and most of Chinatown. Nature's upheaval burned City Hall along with all the immigration and birth records that could prove that a Chinese person had been born in the United States or was the child of a native-born Chinese–American. In the paperless interlude, thousands of Chinese rushed to California.

Between 1910 and 1940, more than 100,000 Chinese immigrants were ensnared on Angel Island. Some stayed days and weeks; many stayed years, segregated from other detainees, looking ashore toward Gold Mountain.[20] Although terrified that they would be entrapped by their own words during the interrogations, at least 135 prisoners carved poems on the walls of the men's dormitories, from floor to ceiling, under beds and behind toilets, described by one poet as "a cry of worms, chilled night."[21] Written surreptitiously, most are undated and unsigned, incised in the soft wood of the barracks.[22] Visible and unavoidable, the poems are communal expressions of rage and displacement. Some depict economic pressures to migrate:

Instead of remaining a citizen of China, I willingly became an ox.
I intended to come to America to earn a living[23]

Often isolation and injustice are foregrounded by race:

I am distressed that we Chinese are detained in this wooden building
It is actually racial barriers which cause difficulties on Yingtai Island.[24]

Bold images of orality and hunger expose poverty, deception, and regret:

Originally, I had intended to come to America last year.
Lack of money delayed me until early Autumn . . .
I ate wind and tasted waves for more than twenty days . . . .

Written in Cantonese, the language of the southern coast of China, the captive becomes angry:

How was I to know I would become a prisoner suffering in the wooden building?
The barbarians' abuse is really difficult to take.

Moving from rage to sorrow and from here to there, he writes:

When my family's circumstances stir my emotions,
A double stream of tears flow.

Yet, in a final couplet, his stance as a hopeful migrant endures:

I only wish I can land in San Francisco soon,
Thus sparing me this additional sorrow here.[25]

The Angel Island poets also call for revenge:

I will not speak of love when I level the immigration station!
An advantageous position for revenge will surely come one day.
I will certainly behead the barbarians and spare not a single blade of grass.[26]

In 1924, Congress passed the Johnson–Reed Act, which excluded Chinese, Japanese, Indians, and other Asians from entering because they were racially "ineligible" to be naturalized, while white European immigrants could follow a path to citizenship. Consequently, writes historian Mae M. Ngai, from the 1920s onward, the national, ethnic, and racial identities of Latin American and Asian immigrants were conjoined.

Racialized by law, they became permanently foreign and unassimilable "alien citizens," even if they were born in the USA.[27]

On December 7, 1941, Japan bombed the US fleet at Pearl Harbor on the island of Oahu in Hawaii, killing 3,500 American soldiers. At the time, 75,000 American citizens of Japanese ancestry and 45,000 Japanese nationals were living in the USA but were denied citizenship because of their race: 93,000 in California and 19,000 in Washington and Oregon.[28]

Ten weeks later, on February 19, 1942, President Franklin D. Roosevelt signed Executive Order 9066 and authorized the arrest and incarceration of "all persons" from any area of the country deemed vulnerable to attack or sabotage. Almost immediately, agents of the US Justice Department routed the Japanese–American communities along the West Coast. With only days to dispose of homes, cars, businesses, and pets, Japanese nationals and Japanese–American citizens were rounded up and shipped to detention centers quickly established in horse stalls at racetracks or livestock pavilions on nearby fairgrounds. Within months, more than 100,000 Japanese people were shipped to 10 desolate and remote incarceration camps, hastily built in hot wind-swept deserts in California and frigid Wyoming and swamps in Arkansas. There they were held for four years in rough barracks thrown together from raw lumber and tar paper, surrounded by barbed wire, searchlights, and guard towers.

The War Relocation Authority called the mass incarceration an "evacuation" (removal for one's safety) or a "relocation" (temporary placement) – euphemisms that disguised the forced exile, harsh economic losses, and unconstitutional terms of the concentration camps. Lieutenant General John DeWitt of the Western Defense Command defended the internment: "The Japanese is an enemy race . . . while many second and third generation Japanese born on United States soil, possessed of United States citizenship, have become 'Americanized,' the racial stains are undiluted" and make all Japanese Americans "potential enemies."[29] Even as the prisoners established schools, theaters, churches, and sports teams in the camps, they ate skimpy fare in crowded mess halls, shared cold communal bathrooms, and tried to grow their own food in the thin soil of the camps. The desert sand crept into their bedding and clothes.

Hisaye Yamamoto (1921–2011), born to Issei (first-generation) parents in Redondo Beach, California, was shipped with her family to the Poston War Relocation Center, a camp in a remote desert in Arizona. Four years after her release, Yamamoto published "The Legend of Miss Sasagawara" (1950), her only story of the detention camps. Marked as a "legend" and told through rumors, the story depicts an imprisoned ballet dancer, Mari

Sasagawara, held at Poston with her widowed father, a detached Buddhist minister.[30] Kiku, a teenage girl, narrates the trauma of the "forever foreign" woman. In the very public life of the camp, Kiku knowingly reproduces the gossip that created Miss Sasagawara as different within a world defined by difference, understanding that her preoccupation is a reaction to her own repressive, "monotonous days."

The camp authorities assign Miss Sasagawara to two rooms in a bleak and crowded barracks with her silent father, a man who "could not stop for an instant his meditation on the higher life" (239). His remoteness contrasts with the curiosity of other prisoners, who obsessively observe the 39-year-old dancer, isolated as an unmarried woman, a performer, and a prisoner. Miss Sasagawara's bold presence titillates the other inmates, who are also trapped within the limited visual space of Poston and who watch her struggle inside the fence of the barren camp.

As the other inmates strive to perform their "American-ness," they judge the lonely dancer by her refusal to assimilate. Mari endures terrifying pressure to feign loyalty, as other Japanese prisoners copy the perspective of the guards and medics and judge the dancer as exotic and irrational. Miss Sasagawara's ballet costume creates a spectacle of embodied art which affirms her status as both different and assimilated.

In a critique of Orientalism's dangerous surveillance, Yamamoto crafts a legend about watching a traumatized community watch a traumatized woman whose thin hauteur cannot mask the female trope of a "temperamental" and "crazy" lady, a sensual woman who has "had her fun" (238). Images of the camp's lack of privacy mark its bodily and cultural invasion. One night, Miss Sasagawara appears at the camp hospital complaining of severe abdominal pain, but she becomes terrorized when the medics try to examine her. Rather than enter an ambulance with a male driver, she runs five miles back to her barracks. Still in pain, she returns to the hospital, only to struggle again with the orderlies who seek to keep her "for observation." As she sits on a bed covered only by a "brief hospital apron," other patients, nurses, and aides trip "in and out abashed on some pretext or other to pass by her bed" while she freezes, "silently immune." Again voiceless, trapped by the terrifying assault of the hospital's panopticon gaze, Miss Sasagawara endures a metaphorical rape.[31] Declaring she did not want any more doctors "pawing her," Mari tries to escape (244). Two weeks later, she is sent to a state psychiatric hospital in Phoenix.

The "legend" concludes when Kiku discovers a long poem that Mari Sasagawara has published in a small magazine, introduced as "the first published poem of a Japanese–American woman who is, at present, an evacuee from the West Coat making her home in a War Relocation Center in Arizona." The magazine repeats the euphemism that the poet was an "evacuee . . . making her home" at the concentration camp, rather than an imprisoned American citizen. Mimicking the forces of complicity and historical erasure, Kiku summarizes the poem rather than quote it in the dancer's own words, again appropriating Miss Sasagawara's voice (251).

The poem itself is a sardonic depiction of her father and Buddhist minister, Rev. Sasagawara, who paradoxically feels free inside the site of "sheer imprisonment," where he can "extinguish within himself all unworthy desire" and become "evil, deaf and blind to the human passions rising, subsiding and again rising, perhaps in anguished silence." He aptly performs the role of an ideal convict, seduced, as was the nation, into an eroticized pleasure of denial and brutality. Yet Yamamoto gives the last word to Miss Sasagawara, who describes her father's repression "as a sort of madness, the monstrous sort" that brings "troublous scented scenes to recur in the other's sleep" (251).

In what direction lies return? Is homeward bound a welcoming or a rejecting transit? Crossing the border or the bridge in either direction leads to a hall of mirrors, versions of here and there, of now and then, of multiple selves.

Immigrant characters resist categorization and survive in spaces of confinement and dehumanization. The poets of Angel Island describe the trap of the migrant's "in between" world outside of home yet barred from the real and fantasized American geography: "I am like the pear blossoms which have already fallen" – a wavering space that mocks the latent beauty of springtime and hides its fruition.[32]

Immigrant authors often question America's contact zones that are usually depicted as knowable. By their very existence, as well as their rhetoric, they counter the stereotype of the silent Asian immigrant. Despite the precarity of immigrant life or the promise of assimilation, they refuse to be complicit in their historical erasure.[33] Each story rejects its own silencing. Each author repudiates the gaps in the official accounts of immigration history.[34]

Texts by refugees and exiles depict immigrants' power to change their new destination. American migration literature inevitably reveals the dialectic between character and environment – the touchstone of realism in which characters' ability to choose location, rather than location itself, becomes the narrative's determining energy. Place is a metonym for power; place beckons and repels. In the liminal space between there and here, at some level all migration literature is global literature which positions characters through collective identities: nation, race, religion, and gender.[35]

Nevertheless, the tension between difference and belonging, migrant and citizen, endures. Chinese–American poet Nellie Wong (1934–) insists:

> Our bowls are rimmed with bats and fire flies
> Our feet pedal sewing machines making blue denim jeans . . .
> Our ancestors memorized the number of doors and windows in the home village, whether our fathers had more than one wife
> We are immigrants at home all over the world . . .
> We are natives, born in Eureka, Augusta, Oakland, Phoenix, Flushing
> We dispense herbs, make soup to heal our bodies
> Harvest chrysanthemums, grapes, pea shoots, taro
> Oh yeah, we yakety yack, we jitterbug and jive, play flutes and drums.[36]

A collective "we" – a shared Chinese–American voice – assertively chants difference: "We eat chicken feet." Four crisp syllables follow and insist on collective survival: "we are not dead." Wong rejects the idea that an immigrant's telos of erasure is inevitable. While refusing to disregard cultural differences, she claims a global commonality and appeals to national citizenship. Yet Eureka, California, like Seattle, Washington, was the site of the expulsion of the entire Chinese population in 1885 when hundreds of residents were marched from Chinatown to the dock at Humboldt Bay. Only taking what they could pack on a cold February Lunar New Year, they were shipped in two small boats to San Francisco.

Immigrant authors often portray physical labor, especially that of women who work and live outside the safety of their community. When Wong depicts modern sweatshop workers locked in clothing factories in Chinatowns, she sets Americans' consumption of blue jeans against comforting memories of Chinese "chrysanthemum tea, grapes, pea shoots and taro." Painted Chinese dishes filled with healing herbs and soups – food and orality – mark collective narrators' Chinese-ness, which Wong decorates with American slang and images of dance, play, and, ultimately, writing. Her narrator is a hero, a healer who transforms soup and herbs into medical rescue and cultural salvation.

As the narrator pedals an old sewing machine stitching denim, her repetitive labor, her underpaid ordinariness, and, in particular, her tired feet morph into the feet of a Chinese woman who can jitterbug and jive, a woman who can live in two worlds. She is multiple; she is "we." Culturally ambiguous, "we" are women who still play their Chinese flutes and drums. "We" are community. Together "We ... yakety yack" – and turn inside out and upside down the stereotype of silent and subservient Asian women: "We dream and we praise and steam and we write."

The impact of immigrant literature often hinges on a paradox: characters deprived of civic access are emotionally and ethically equivalent to citizens, entitled to belonging not only because it is just but because they share typical human sentiments. Thus, their core appeal is to empathy. Like Eaton and Wong, many immigrant authors turn to the tactical power of sentimental representation to reinvent others in their own image. Sentimental discourse claims that human identification can cross racial and national borders so that both readers and characters can transcend fears of otherness and then connect. Through fantasies of shared emotions, if not shared experiences, readers can imagine themselves in others' positions, welcome the migrant, and promote belonging.[37]

To reset the terms for reading "outsiders," immigration literature alters traditional forms of American realism and sentimentalism. By depicting forced and voluntary acts of transport and mobility, it redefines the relationship between character and place. People on the move or on the run are driven by forces that transcend traditional literary quests. American immigration literature explores the forces that send people across the sea and represents how society reacts to migrants, exiles, and refugees who reveal its diversity.[38] Tropes of displacement engage sensibilities of nostalgia and attitudes toward return. Migration transforms plots of family relationships, often located in idealized endings. Immigration literature tells of communities lost and communities created, of diasporas that include immigrants, exiles, refugees, free, and enslaved.[39] It is impossible to extract the migrant from a history that is inevitably multicultural, "intercultural," and often postcolonial.[40] Here forces of displacement shape the telling as testimony, memory, or dream, often marked, as critic Corinna Stan notes, by water and walls – landscapes of trauma.[41] The urge to be visible and the urge to hide, the desire to belong and still to affiliate with a homeland, are literary tropes by immigrants who know that national belonging is defined by resistance to law and public policy.

Writes Nellie Wong,

> We dream and we braise and steam and we write
> We eat chicken feet and we are not dead.[42]

Notes

1. Elien Declercq, "'Écriture migrante', 'littérature (im)migrante', 'migration literature' : réflexions sur un concept aux contours imprécis', Revue de litterature comparee, n°339.3 (2011), 301–310, 310. Cited in Amy Burge, "What Can Literature Tell Us About Migration?" *Iris Working Paper Series*, No. 37/2020.
2. For a capacious and thoughtful view of the fraught relationship of migration to texts in "the greater literary traditions," see Ha Jin, *The Writer as Migrant* (Chicago: University of Chicago Press, 2008).
3. I am indebted to Amy Burge for the definitions of various forms of migration in "What Can Literature Tell Us About Migration," *Iris Working Paper Series*, NO. 37/2020. 5–6.
4. A Bill to Establish a Uniform Rule of Naturalization, 1790. H. R. 40, *Records of the US Senate, National Archives and Records Administration.*
5. A Bill to Establish a Uniform Rule of Naturalization, 1790. H. R. 40, *Records of the US Senate, National Archives and Records Administration.*
6. An Act to Amend the Naturalization Laws and to Punish Crimes against the same, and for other Purposes; 16 Stat. 254–256.
7. https://oaklandnorth.net/2019/05/17/muralist-dave-young-kim-uses-art-to-tap-into-his-korean-roots/.
8. See Mary Chapman, "Introduction," in *Becoming Sui Sin Far: Early Fiction, Journalism, and Travel Writing by Edith Maude Eaton* (Montreal: McGill-Queen's University Press, 2016), xiii–lxxvi.
9. Ibid.
10. All quotations from "Its Wavering Image" are from Sui Sin Far (Edith Maude Eaton), *Mrs. Spring Fragrance and Other Stories* (Urbana: University of Illinois Press, 1995), 61–65.
11. Caroline Porter, "The Illegible Pan: Racial Formation, Hybridity, and Chinatown in Sui Sin Far's 'Its Wavering Image,'" *Asian American Literature: Discourses and Pedagogies* 6 (2015), 10–26, 18. For discussion of the impact of the devastating San Francisco earthquake of 1906, see Mae Ngai, "How Chinatown Rose from the Ashes," *New York Times*, April 17, 2006, www.nytimes.com/2006/04/17/opinion/how-chinatown-rose-from-the-ashes.html; and Bonnie Tsui, *American Chinatown: A People's History of Five Neighborhoods* (New York: Free Press, 2009), 284,
12. Jean Pfaelzer, *California: A Slave State* (New Haven: Yale University Press, 2023).
13. Vijay Prashad, "Orientalism," in Bruce Burgett and Glenn Hendler (ed.), *Keywords for American Cultural Studies* (New York: New York University Press, 2007), 174–177.
14. Lisa Lowe, *Immigrant Acts, Immigrant Acts: On Asian American Cultural Politics* (Durham: Duke University Press, 1996), 2.
15. Edith Maude Eaton, "Leaves from the Mental Portfolio of an Eurasian." *Independent.* January 21, 1909.

16. 22 Stat 58; 22 Stat. 214.
17. The Naturalization Act of 1790. 1 Stat. 103; Page Act of 1875 (Sect. 141, 18 Stat. 477).
18. The 1917 Immigrant Act (39 Stat. 874) created an "Asiatic Barred Zone" that covered all of British India, most of Southeast Asia, and most of the Middle East, and anyone over the age of sixteen, illiterate or not capable of learning to read. In 1921 the Emergency Quota Act began the ongoing process of setting admission quotas for each nationality. That template has endured. President Franklin D. Roosevelt's 1941 Executive Order 9066 Evacuation and Segregation shipped more than 120,000 Japanese Americans into "relocation" or concentration camps. The federal government only modified these acts to provide for temporary migrant workers, such as farmworkers, to create a pool of transient workers who are not entitled to wage or safety protections, and who may not bring their families and hence not create a permanent population with lineage or citizenship. In 1906, knowledge of English became a requirement for citizenship. The Emergency Quota Act of 1921, 42 Stat. 5, limited migrants from most countries based on 3 percent of those already in the USA – apparently selecting by nationality, but inevitably selecting by race. In 1965, national quotas were replaced by a migrant's relationship to a resident family member, and/or by the needs of a US employer. For the next fifty years, Congress occasionally modified these laws to grant relief to immigrants from states reigned by dictators or, conversely, to exclude migrants by broadening the definition of terrorism.
19. Act to Prohibit the Coming of the Chinese 27 Stat. 25.
20. Jeffrey Thomas Leong, *Wild Geese Sorrow: The Chinese Wall Inscriptions at Angel Island* (Calypso Editions, 2021) xv.
21. Leong, *Wild Geese Sorrow*, 13.
22. Ibid., xi–xii.
23. Ibid.
24. Cited in Cary Nelson, *Anthology of Modern Poetry* (New York: Oxford University Press, 2000), 492.
25. Poem #7, from Him Mark Lai, Genny Lim, and Judy Yung, *Island: Poetry and History of Chinese Immigrants on Angel Island, 1910–1940* (Seattle: University of Washington Press, 1980), 38–39.
26. Authorship is given as "By One from Taishan"; Nelson, *Anthology of Modern Poetry*, 492.
27. Mae M. Ngai, *Impossible Subjects: Illegal Aliens and the Making of Modern America* (Princeton: Princeton University Press, 2004), 8.
28. Lawson Fusao Inada, *Only What We Could Carry: The Japanese Internment Experience* (Berkeley: Heyday Books, 2000), VI.
29. Quoted in "Commission on Wartime Relocation and Internment of Civilians." *Personal Justice Denied.* Seattle: University of Washington Press, 1997. Also quoted on the Digital History site, under the title "Personal Justice Denied."

www.digitalhistory.uh.edu/active_learning/explorations/japanese_internment/personal_justice_denied.cfm.

30. Quotations from Hisaye Yamamoto "The Legend of Miss Sasagawara" in Inada, *Only What We Could Carry*, 237–251.
31. Sung Yook, "Hisaye Yamamoto's "The Legend of Miss Sasagawara": The Collective Silence of Japanese Internees and Its Literary Representations," *Studies in Modern Fiction*, 19, 3, 2012, 193–210.
32. Nelson, *Anthology of Modern Poetry*, 492.
33. Mathew Elliott, "Sins of Omission; Hisaye Yamamoto's Vision of History," *Melus*, Spring 2009, 34, 1, 47–68, 48.
34. Hisaye Yamamoto joined Dorothy Day's Catholic Worker's Movement and lived a life of direct action in voluntary poverty and nonviolence. She participated in the civil rights actions of the Committee on Racial Equality (CORE) and wrote about racial politics for *The Los Angeles Tribune*. Elliott, "Sins of Omission," 52.
35. See Gallien, "Forcing Displacement," 743, 747.
36. Nellie Wong, *We Eat Chicken Feet and We Are Not Dead*. www.radicalwomen.org/about/culture.shtml#chicken-feet-Wong.
37. Elizabeth Barnes, *States of Sympathy: Seduction and Democracy in the American Novel* (New York: Columbia University Press, 1997), 2.
38. Paul White, "Geography, Literature and Migration," in *Writing Across Worlds: Literature and Migration*, ed. Russell King, John Connell, and Paul White (London: Routledge, 1995), 1–19, 10.
39. Russell King, John Connell, and Paul White, "Preface," in *Writing Across Worlds: Literature and Migration*, ed. Russell King, John Connell, and Paul White (London: Routledge, 1995), ix–xvi, x; Corina Stan, "A Life without a Shoreline: Tropes of Refugee Literature in Jenny Erpenbeck's *Go, Went, Gone*," *Journal of Postcolonial Writing*, 54.6 (2018), 795–808.
40. Agnes Woolley, *Contemporary Asylum Narratives: Representing Refugees in the Twenty-First Century* (London: Palgrave Macmillan, 2014), 3, 7–10.
41. Stan, "A Life without a Shoreline," 59.
42. Wong, *We Eat Chicken Feet*; Fusao Inada, *Only What We Could Carry*.

PART IV

Rethinking American Literature

CHAPTER 12

Race, Revision, and William Wells Brown's Miralda

Brigitte Fielder

Nineteenth-century literature was interested in the representation of race and the social issues that attended it, and it also provided space to interrogate popular understandings of race and racialization. By the antebellum era, literature about mixed-race people (and particularly mixed-race Black women) had become a popular site for recognizing race's complexity and its reproduction. Nineteenth-century mixed-race heroine fiction both reflected and contributed to US constructions of race. In its antislavery iterations, this genre critiqued the race-based system of slavery by emphasizing the slipperiness of racial categories. Race was not always visually apparent, and mixed-race Black people were enslavable. Because children inherited their mothers' status – regardless of their fathers' race – enslavers profited from the sexual assault of Black women. Enslavers targeted Black women for sexual violence and hypersexualized them, imagining them as always sexually available to white men. Depictions of mixed-race Black heroines in antislavery fiction addressed these problems for various audiences. Authors of this genre critiqued both slavery and racism – including that of white abolitionists – revisiting and revising this genre and its tropes even after emancipation.

William Wells Brown, who had escaped slavery as a young man, took up the mixed-race heroine genre with his first foray into fiction and revised his rendition of this genre in three subsequent iterations. After his first, London-published novel, *Clotel; or the President's Daughter* (1853), Brown revised its basic narrative three times: serialized in the Black press as *Miralda; or, the Beautiful Quadroon. A Romance of American Slavery Founded on Fact* (1860–1) and in two monographs published in the United States, *Clotelle: A Tale of the Southern States* (1864) and *Clotelle; or the Colored Heroine* (1867).[1] Although some scholars have treated these four versions of the novel together, more have prioritized Brown's first iteration; his earliest novel has received far more scholarly attention than the other three combined. Likely reasons for this include the celebrated "firstness" of the 1853 text, currently believed to be the first (known, at this time) African American-authored novel to be published. But Brown's later revisions reveal important shifts in his renderings of race, which speak also to shifts in audience and focus. In Brown's revisions, we see his subtle reframing of interracial kinship refigured away from mixed-race Black women's sexual relationships with and sexual violence by white men and toward relationships to white fathers. These small changes and their attendant generic shifts evidence Brown's reimagining of interracial kinship's limitations and possibilities.

This chapter reads Brown's first revision of the novel, *Miralda; or, the Beautiful Quadroon*, serialized in the *Weekly Anglo-African* between December 1860 and March 1861, as an important revision of Brown's theorization of race in the United States. This iteration better anticipates further developments in mixed-race heroine fiction, including writing by Black women whose work has been given less attention than Brown's or that of white antislavery authors, skewing literary perceptions of this genre. I begin with a brief discussion of *Clotel*, to frame the literary trajectory that follows. I more fully discuss *Miralda*, to highlight how Brown revised his original theorizations of race. I then situate this shift within a longer history of mixed-race heroine fiction that illustrates why scholars ought to give more attention to subsequent versions of this novel, which seem in closer conversation with other Black writers within this genre, particularly Black women writers.

Clotel as Racial Prequel; or, an Incomplete Novel

Given their many similarities, there is a good argument for reading Brown's four novels as a single text. Laura Soderberg offers this apt summary of the novels' basic similarities in plot:

> [T]he outline of all four books is much the same. An enslaved woman's two adolescent daughters are abruptly auctioned off, both to infatuated white men who father one or two daughters with the women before dying or growing unfaithful and returning the women and their children to the slave market. In each novel, one woman from these various generations will fall in love with a black revolutionary and eventually reunite with him in the freedom of Europe. Another will find herself trapped on a bridge by slave hunters and drown herself in the Potomac. Yet, the figure who will bear these fates is changeable, as are the details of the lives running alongside her, so that each of Brown's *Clotel* novels offers its own set of characters, but each

> of these sets overlaps with the others, changing and unwriting the characters that have gone before.[2]

This plot outline relays Brown's repetitions across genre but obscures much about his revisions. Despite their similarities, the shifts Brown makes across the four novels are significant, representing shifting rhetorics of race and slavery. These allow us to better read Brown's fiction not only among larger genres of antislavery writing, but also in closer keeping with African American fiction and its continuing repetition and revision of genres and tropes.[3] I begin by outlining some of *Clotel*'s key generic and rhetorical moves in order to show where Brown later departed from these to reframe his novel for different audiences and contexts. Disaggregating these later iterations from the original connects them generically, rather than just intertextually.

Clotel's plot frames its mixed-race heroine within what has most often been called the "tragic mulatta" trope, constituting the most overrepresented subgenre of mixed-race heroine fiction. Clotel drowns herself in the Potomac rather than be re-enslaved and subjected to the sexual violence that accompanied enslavement for a woman marketable in what was called the "fancy trade." Brown's heroine embodied slavery's history of sexual violence and evidenced the instability of a race-based system that could not fully account for its own essentialist self-justification. Via this first mixed-race heroine, Brown reinforced a genre that staged tragedy as an inevitable result of racial essentialism and racism: in a world of Black and white, the mixed-race heroine was doomed to die, her romantic relationship to a white man thwarted by an oppressive system that refused to legitimate their marriage. In antislavery fiction, the mixed-race heroine's existence revealed both the illogic of a race-based system of slavery and its hypocrisy. Enslavers enacted various forms of sexual violence against and exploitation of enslaved people, producing mixed-race people who were difficult to categorize according to racial essentialist ideas of who was and who wasn't enslavable. Some mixed-race heroine narratives were not pro-amalgamation stories so much as cautionary tales, demonstrating slavery's evils via the suffering of mixed-race Black women.

The mixed-race heroine trope appeared throughout antislavery fiction as evidence of slavery's sexual immoralities and its untenability. If racist (though antislavery) white readers were more liable to sympathize with light-skinned Black people like Clotel and her family members, they might also be unsettled by the slipperiness of race itself, which rendered racial difference difficult – at times impossible – to determine, thus undermining any race-based system. Here, mixed-race heroine antislavery fiction also critiqued the theorizations of race upon which this system was built, exposing the sexual violence white men perpetrated against enslaved women and the ridiculousness of a system that produced people who were difficult to categorize because their appearance did not match their enslaved status. Such readers remained subject to colorism: the form of anti-Black racism that would continue to overrepresent and prioritize light-skinned mixed-race Black people (including those who might, intentionally or unintentionally, pass as white). Still, these stories trouble ideas about proximity to whiteness, showing that even biological relation to white people was not *necessarily* advantageous to people of African descent, particularly because slavery's inheritability disregarded paternity.

Brown also framed his novel as a national critique. This, too, was familiar among antislavery literature, but *Clotel* located slavery's racial, sexual, and moral nexus in the nation's founding. Like other antislavery writers, Brown critiqued the nation by noting racism as hypocritically inconsistent with American democracy and freedom. In *Clotel*, these points are intertwined, as Brown ties his heroine explicitly to the nation's founding. The "president's daughter" of Brown's subtitle alludes to former president Thomas Jefferson's enslavement of Sally Hemings and his own children borne by her.[4] Despite Jefferson's musings on slavery and freedom, interracial sexual mixing, racism, and particular disparagement of Black women, his personal history as an enslaver, sexual history with a woman he enslaved, and enslavement of his own biological children were an "open" secret, known during Jefferson's lifetime and into the antebellum era. Brown names the "founding father" explicitly, embedding into his novel the hypocrisies of American democracy as evidenced by the immoral practices of one of its originators. Brown's realism, then, is dependent upon this situating as a specifically nationally-oriented historical fiction.

Previous scholarship has clarified *Clotel*'s importance within US histories of slavery and in relation to prominent antislavery literary texts and genres. We might also regard this text as a prequel to Brown's experimentation with mixed-race heroine fiction. Despite its vast historical and literary influence, its prominence, and its importance for the African American literary canon, Brown – in some way – treated the novel as unfinished, continuing to repeat and revise its themes and tropes in subsequent years. Framing *Clotel* as prequel allows us to set it aside, so to speak, to displace it from its centrality by considering it as one incomplete part of the longer arc of his work. Considering Brown's revisions across time is an opportunity for tracing his development of mixed-race heroine fiction and its attending tropes. The changes he makes between texts allow us to see his subtle shifting of the mixed-race heroine genre and thereby his shifting theorizations of race and relation.

If we consider Brown's first novel as an incomplete beginning of sorts for his subsequent repetitions and revisions, we might also understand his shifting characterizations as a shifting focus for theorizing race. Elsewhere, I have read incomplete African American fiction as sites for comprehending late-nineteenth-century African American women writers' mixed-race heroine fiction.[5] In my turn to *Miralda*, I approach *Clotel*, often touted as a "first" of African American long fiction, as an incomplete text, an unfinished beginning, a fragment of sorts in the longer development that Brown himself would produce not only as a serialized novel but a series of novelistic revisions. It is perhaps odd (and definitely unusual) to regard *Clotel* as incomplete. We have a complete monograph of Brown's 1853 novel. No chapters are missing and some of the text seems almost extraneous. We are more likely to read *Clotel* for its superfluity, overflowing with repetitions and revisions of earlier antislavery writing. But reading *Clotel* as Brown's unfinished rendering of this genre and tracing *Clotel*'s trajectory to *Miralda* illustrates Brown's departure from the "tragic mulatta" centering that most interested white antislavery audiences and his contribution to genres of African American literature with which he would overwhelmingly be contrasted rather than compared.

Scholars including Anna Nelson, M. Giulia Fabi, and Jennifer James have discussed the political differences between Brown's novels, parsing their comparative conservatism or radicality. These differences are significant. Comparing *Clotel* and *Clotelle* (1867), for example, Jennifer James writes that "Brown actually has written two very different novels posing as one."[6] Alternately reading Brown's novels in terms of their collective seriality and the possibility of their overlapping readerships, Soderberg argues that *Clotel* "becomes most comprehensible when understood as homologous to the sequence of its published variants as a whole."[7] But it would be a mistake to understand this sequence as simple continuity with Brown's original text. The series illustrates, rather, its endless potential for revision. Derrick Spires connects the serial sketch's "air of incompletion" (a characteristic shared by serialized and serially revised novels) and "resistance to stasis" to Bakhtin's notion of "potentiality" (50). Brown's revisions show that *Clotel* similarly resists stasis and allows for the potential to move beyond the prominent generic tropes most often associated with it, such as the "tragic" mixed race heroine. In these revisions, we see also shifts in Brown's characterizations of fathers.

Miralda's Racial Revisions

Brown's *Miralda; or, the Beautiful Quadroon, A Romance of Slavery Founded on Fact* was serialized in the *Weekly Anglo-African* between December 1860 and March 1861. The placement of *Miralda* in the *Weekly Anglo-African* – an African American newspaper – necessitates a shift in usual readings of Brown's original plot, most often framed with white antislavery readers in mind. The *Weekly Anglo-African* (like its sister periodicals, the *Anglo-African* and the *Anglo-African Magazine*) was founded by Robert and Thomas Hamilton and known for its rich array of prominent Black contributors in a variety of genres.[8] Considering the newspaper's Black readership, we might differently understand Brown's treatment of race.

Miralda begins in an unrecovered issue of the newspaper. Its opening chapters are missing, leaving the version we now have incomplete. Nelson provides fascinating context for the novel's first three chapters, reading an account of the *Weekly Anglo African*'s now-missing December 1, 1860 installment that was mentioned in the January 23 issue of the white newspaper, the Washington DC *Evening Star*. This account explains that a white enslaver found this issue of the Black newspaper among the people she held enslaved in Georgetown, who thereupon refused to account for its presence when she confiscated it from them. The *Evening Star*'s report describes some of the texts that were originally published alongside *Miralda*, which included articles on "Negro Nationality" and the "Anniversary of the Martyrdom of John Brown," and linked the circulation of the newspaper in the nation's capital (where slavery was legal) to the underground railroad's work to emancipate enslaved people. Noting this publication context, Nelson writes that *Miralda*'s "very context within the *Anglo-African* was highly politicized."[9] Considering this context, Nelson argues that Brown's consecutive editions of the novel are thus not progressively more or less radical versions, but rather rhetorically adaptive manifestations of his politics.[10]

Most often read alongside *Clotel*, *Miralda* has received relatively little attention on its own. Without the issues of the newspaper in which its early chapters appeared, readers can only surmise how the novel began. Christopher Mulvey's electronic edition of all four novels does just this, offering a synopsis of the opening six-and-a-half chapters that could have made up the missing December 1st and 8th installments of the newspaper.[11] Of course, Mulvey bases this synopsis on Brown's earlier and later novels. Other readers of *Miralda* would similarly position the novel in this way. *Miralda* would (like other serialized nineteenth-century African American fiction) remain unrecovered in its entirety and be habitually read not on its own but as part of the larger genre Brown would continue to revise.

Though not Brown's first foray into this genre, *Miralda*'s particular repetitions and revisions are useful for considering the work of generic revision. We might consider *Miralda* as a doubly serial novel, its seriality explicit both in its original publication form and its generic positioning in a clear line of texts that would repeat and revise the original's tropes of race and gender. Though its similarities to Brown's first novel have been highlighted, these have too often been critiqued as unoriginal rather than rigorously examined for their nuance. Because the changes Brown makes between these two novels are slight, what changes he did make require further contemplation. Brown's revision includes significant moves that reframe his novel's representation of race and racialization. These revise its titular character's relationship to a white US president, shift the plot's suicide away from the novel's titular character, and reimagine the racial presentation of the couple at the novel's end.

The most obvious of Brown's revisionary changes involves the shifting roles of his titular characters. Importantly, Brown revises the "tragic" status of his mixed-race heroines as he reorients his protagonists' ultimate fates around his title. Clotel is the heroine who commits suicide in order to avoid re-enslavement in the novel's climactic chapter, "Death is Freedom." Clotel's daughter Mary is the focus of the novel's denouement. Occupying the same position as Mary in the novel's genealogical structure, Miralda (like both Clotelles who would follow her) not only survives but is shifted to the novel's center, becoming its clear protagonist. This recentering also serves to develop Miralda's relationship to her father, a move that revises Brown's commentary on racial genealogies.

Part of Brown's narrative recentering involves reframing his heroine's white genealogy via the removal of Thomas Jefferson as its patriarchal touchstone. Jefferson never appears in Brown's first novel and is therefore a bit of a red herring. He is truly an absentee father, notable in name only. Brown tempers his critique of Jefferson by noting that he is unexceptional. "Sad to say," he writes, "Jefferson is not the only American statesman who has spoken high-sounding words in favour of freedom, and then left his own children to die slaves."[12] Miralda is not the president's daughter, but we read that her mother was "a descendant of" Jefferson. And Clotelle (in both later versions) is not directly tied to this founder, but to a US senator. Shifting attention away from his protagonist's relationship to a specific and prominent white man, Brown does not, however, downplay his critique of white fathers. Rather, he develops Miralda's relationship to her father more fully even while leaving other elements of his mixed-race heroine plot intact.

Horatio Green, the lover who has abandoned Clotel, is embarrassed when his new, white wife notices a "beautiful child" near Clotel's cottage and learns of their connection to her husband.[13] In Brown's second novel, it is Miralda herself who reveals her duplicitous father's secret. Seeing Henry and his wife ride by in their carriage, the girl calls out to him "Papa!" thus making her relationship to him apparent.[14] Miralda knows her father. She recognizes him, and likely feels the pain of his abandonment. She is not simply an unacknowledged child, but one who this man initially acknowledges then later rejects. The nuance of this distinction allows us to see her father's actions not as inevitable, but as a choice – one that might have been otherwise and a course which might yet be changed.

Horatio sees his daughter enslaved and abused in his own house. Not only unable but unwilling to protect Mary, we read that "Horatio Green had lost all feeling for his child" (210). This is not so of Miralda's father. Miralda was not enslaved by her own father but by her father's vengeful mother-in-law, with whom Mary's treatment was a point of contention, although Henry is ineffectual in protecting her. In *Miralda*'s closing chapters (which depart significantly from the earlier novel) we learn that this man regrets both his unfaithfulness to Miralda's mother, Isabella, and his neglect of his child. After Miralda is reunited with her long-lost love, Jerome, in Europe, they encounter another hotel guest who is distraught with guilt. They hear him through his door, crying out "She's dead – yes, she's dead; but I did not kill her. She was my child – my own daughter; I loved her, and yet I did not protect her."[15] This man is Miralda's father, Henry Linwood. Miralda (unlike Clotel), is not dead and she and her father weep and recall "other days" – when she could call him "papa."[16] Miralda sobs at this reunion, waits at her father's bedside as he recovers, and inquires after his affairs. Although she makes no outward statement of forgiveness, she is happy to have her father with her.

But this reconciliation is not simple. Neither is Miralda's legacy. Horatio's father is the enslaver of George Green, the man Mary marries at the book's close. In an ironic web of slavery's inheritances, Mary weds a man who bears the surname of her biological father's family, even though she has no meaningful kinship relationship to this father-in-name-only.

What Miralda inherits is neither name nor property, but she uses this reunion as an opportunity to influence her father: She and Jerome convince him to free the people he still holds enslaved. This antislavery resolution is significant. Still, this light-skinned mixed-race daughter does not ignore her father's racism. We learn that "[i]t was long before Miralda's father could eradicate from his mind, the belief of the inferiority of the negro race."[17] Her father disapproves of her marriage to a dark-skinned Black man. In Brown's first book, Mary's love interest, George, is "so white as easily to pass for a white man" and is even "somewhat ashamed of his African descent."[18] But Jerome is a man whose "black complexion excited astonishment in those who met him" in Europe.[19] He cannot "pass" for white, nor is he apparently related to his enslavers. When he escapes with only a first name, he determines not to take the name of the family who had held him in bondage.

Jerome's blackness works in tandem with Miralda's mixed-race Black identity in the text. With him, she becomes less able to "pass" (even unintentionally) as white.[20] Brown's shifting representation of his heroine's husband makes visible the workings of race that might align her with Black people despite her previous marriage to the white European man who had purchased her freedom, and despite whatever relationship she might have to a white enslaver father. When Henry Linwood returns to the United States, his daughter and her family remain in Europe. The interracial family is partially reconciled but remains fractured at the end of Brown's novel.

The ending of *Miralda* turns from this fictional family to the author's own interracial kinship ties. Brown himself was a mixed-race child of an enslaved woman and a white man whose acknowledgment of paternity prevented neither his son's enslavement nor his sale to various enslavers. As Brown closes *Miralda*, he seems to justify his complex treatment of enslaver characters such as Henry Linwood, explaining, "If I have sometimes seemed to favor the slaveholder, I may be pardoned upon the ground of my connection with men and women, who are extensive owners in the staple product of my native State, yet I have tried to do justice to both master and slave; knowing I must meet both in the world to come."[21] M. Giulia Fabi notes that this paragraph represents a conspicuous revision across Brown's novels. While the text of his 1864 *Clotelle* much resembles *Miralda*, it omits this closing paragraph. Fabi reads this revision as Brown's move to close on "the more optimistic note of a father-daughter, master-slave reconciliation on earth."[22] But reading this alongside Brown's genealogical "connection" to enslavers and the larger, national implications of such racial genealogies, this ending reads also as a realist problem of earthly nonreconciliation.

Through these three somewhat minor revisions – of characters' genealogical relationships to tragedy, of the novel's relationship to white national histories, and of relations of racial reproduction via white fathers – the novel explores not only racial pasts but also racial futures. This first revision of Brown's novel aligns his later mixed-race heroines more closely with the mixed-race heroines of writers such as Julia C. Collins, Frances Ellen Watkins Harper, and Charles Chesnutt than with *Clotel*. I turn now to African American women's mixed-race heroine fiction that follows on the heels of Brown's *Miralda*.

Miralda's Racial Futures

Reading Miralda serially, in terms of its publication history and its broader generic positioning, allows us to understand the novel's place in a larger genre of African American authored mixed-race heroine fiction, some of which would deliberately depart from the "tragic mulatta" trope of antislavery writing. The generational shift Brown enacts between *Clotel* and *Miralda* would be sustained in his subsequent two novels. Neither the 1864 nor the 1867 Clotelle drown themselves in the river. Taking the place of Miralda – rather than that of the original Clotel – both Clotelles live to their stories' ends. Brown's last three novels can be best understood among a larger array of mixed-race heroine fiction that would repeat and revise the genre. These reveal a deliberate shift away from the "tragic mulatta" genre that was so prominent in the midcentury. Brown's multiple revisions are hereby fitting with other African American literary revisions of mixed-race heroine fiction. Looking beyond *Clotel* and viewing *Miralda* as an early shift in that longer literary future, we better understand late-nineteenth century mixed-race heroine fiction.

Later African American fiction allows us to see Brown's repetition and revision within a broader genre; the explicit revisionary work he does in these novels is part of African American literary traditions that similarly make that work explicit. An individual author's multiple revisions within the mixed-race heroine genre also occur in Frances Harper's fiction. Although sharing some basic elements of plot and literary tropes, the differences between Harper's 1869 serialized novel *Minnie's Sacrifice* and her 1892 monograph *Iola Leroy; or, Shadows Uplifted* represents another deliberate reworking of mixed-race heroine fiction. These novels are more distinct from one another than Brown's but they have been similarly misread, flattened by both early readers and scholars who have refused to attend to their nuances. An early review complains that literature depicting "the quadroon and creole girl, suffering the misfortunes and hardships incident to slavery, has become a totally worthless subject to set before the public in the name of Afro American well being," thereby dismissing Harper's novel and this vein of African American fiction.[23] P. Gabrielle Foreman shows how mixed-race heroine fiction has often been misread as "passing" literature, associated with light-skinned characters who willingly pass for white, when it is more accurately understood as "anti-passing" literature, as these characters pass only unknowingly and, once their Black genealogies are revealed, embrace Black family, identity, and community.[24]

Minnie's Sacrifice revises the tragic trope. This mixed-race heroine was raised as white and free but learns in early adulthood that she is the enslaved daughter of an enslaved mother. Minnie does not pursue relationships with white men, either in her biological family or as suiters. Like *Clotel*'s Mary, Minnie marries a light-skinned Black man (also raised as white and learning of his Black ancestry in adulthood, though under differing circumstances) and embraces African American identity, choosing to live in a Black community of the South and work (as Harper did) as an activist and educator. Most importantly, Minnie does not kill herself, although her story does end tragically: she is lynched by the Ku Klux Klan in retaliation for her and her community's Black suffrage work, leaving her husband and community to continue without her.

While Brown's revisions were subtler, enacted across a series of novels that were more structurally similar and more explicitly connected in their representations of plotlines and passages, Harper's was more drastic. Her final novel, *Iola Leroy*, begins somewhat like *Minnie's Sacrifice*, with a mixed-race woman who learns she is Black in adulthood, but its heroine does not die. Iola is under threat of enslavement, and she is pursued by – but rejects – a white suitor, refusing to pass as white and citing the possibility of her potential children's inability to pass as an "insurmountable barrier" to their union.[25] Like Minnie, Iola situates herself firmly as a member of the African American community, marrying a Black man and committing herself to uplift work, though without bearing the brunt of white supremacist retaliation.

This series of revisions rejects tragedy as the definitive frame for mixed-race Black heroines. Rather, interracial and Black familial futures are negotiated and explored through these characters. Reading Brown's novels among these later iterations within the genre, we might better understand the stakes of these shifts. Read across texts, we see that the genre either departs from tragedy or revises its cause, via national stakes that are central to US democratic foundations as well as to the ordinariness of people far removed from those genealogies, toward an interrogation – and ultimately a decentering – of white lovers and white fathers.

***

Brown's critique of slavery cannot be fully understood separately from his own fugitivity. A self-emancipated man, Brown escaped his enslavers in 1834, and in the late 1830s and early 1840s successfully helped other fugitives escape to Canada. He published his memoir, the *Narrative of William W. Brown, a Fugitive Slave, Written by Himself*, in 1847. In 1849, he left the United States with his two daughters, Clarissa and Josephine, remaining abroad until 1854, when Brown's freedom was officially purchased by English abolitionists. This purchase (though a controversial strategy among abolitionists) ensured Brown and his family a greater degree of security, particularly following the passage of the 1850 Fugitive Slave Act. *Clotel* was published not in the United States but in London, during Brown's time abroad.

Miralda leaves its heroine's family in Europe, estranged from a nation and a family that was unfit to safely support them. But the later Clotelles and their families – like Brown and his daughters would – return to the United States at their novels' endings. These revisions, contemporary with Collins' and Harper's novels, articulate a project of national and racial reconstruction, with varying degrees of skepticism about the viability of that project. Reading Brown as a serial writer working within the breadth of this genre, we can better perceive his shifting readings of race and kinship. These subtle changes illuminate Brown's reorientation toward an African American audience and further alignment with other African American authors in this genre, whose work cannot be understood as static texts but work toward perpetual revision.

Brown's revisions allow us also to see how writers like him used literature to theorize and retheorize race, noting its instability and the complexity of its (sometimes contradictory) alignments with slavery, freedom, kinship, and identity. Just as Black people's negotiation of their relationship to the United States has not followed a clear, progressive trajectory, so too has fiction about relationships between race and nation reflected a recursive and continually revisionary project. This was true even for Black people with clear biological ties to white people, revealing the instability of race's construction. The necessity of race's continual reconstruction and renegotiation is played out in these literary revisions.

Notes

1. On comparisons between these editions, see *Clotel: An Electronic Scholarly Edition*, ed. Christopher Mulvey (Charlottesville: University of Virginia Press, 2006) and Samantha Marie Sommers, "A Tangled Text: William Wells Brown's *Clotel* (1853, 1860, 1864, 1867)." Unpublished undergraduate thesis, Wesleyan University, 2009.
2. Laura Soderberg, "One More Time with Feeling: Repetition, Reparation, and the Sentimental Subject in William Wells Brown's Rewritings of *Clotel*," *American Literature* 88.2 (June 2016): 245.
3. My reading of genre as "repetition and revision" is informed by research by scholars such as Frances Smith Foster, who discusses the often overlooked complexities of African American women's mixed-race heroine fiction, and authors like Suzan Lori Parks, whose concept of "Rep & Rev" likens the revision of Black literary genres to the musical repetitions and revisions of jazz. See Frances Smith Foster, "Gender, Genre and Vulgar Secularism: The Case of Frances Ellen Watkins Harper and the AME Press." In *Recovered Writers/Recovered Texts: Race, Class,and Gender in Black Women's Literature*, ed. Dolan Hubbard (Knoxville: The University of Tennessee Press, 1997), 54; and Suzan Lori-Parks, *The America Play* (New York: Theatre Communications Group, 1995), 8–9.
4. On Jefferson's enslavement of Hemings and their children, see Annette Gordon-Reed, *Thomas Jefferson and Sally Hemings: An American Controversy* (Charlottesville: University of Virginia Press, 1997).
5. See Brigitte Fielder, "Embracing the Incomplete: Speculative Reading in *The Curse of Caste*, *Minnie's Sacrifice*, and the *Christian Recorder*," *African American Review* 55.1 (Spring 2022): 1–16.
6. Jennifer James, *A Freedom Bought with Blood: African American War Literature from the Civil War to World War II* (Chapel Hill: University of North Carolina Press, 2007), 48.
7. Soderberg, "One More Time with Feeling," 246.
8. The *Weekly Anglo-African* was published from 1859–1861. Due to financial troubles, in March 1861 (following the publication of *Miralda*) the Hamiltons sold the newspaper to James Redpath, at which point it was (nominally) edited by George Lawrence, Jr. and renamed as the *Pine and Palm*, which ran from 1861 to 1862. Unhappy with the paper's new direction under Redpath's leadership, the Hamiltons revived the *Anglo-African* in July 1861. On this transition, see Brigitte Fielder, Cassander Smith, and Derrick Spires, *Weekly Anglo-African* and *Pine and Palm*, excerpts from 1861 to 1862, Just Teach One – Early African American Print. https://jtoaa.americanantiquarian.org/welcome-to-just-teach-one-african-american/weekly-anglo-african-and-the-pine-and-palm/.
9. Anna Nelson, "William Wells Brown's Miralda and the Missing Issue No. 72 of the *Weekly Anglo-African*," *African American Review* 51.1 (Spring 2018): 2.
10. Nelson, "William Wells Brown's Miralda and the Missing Issue," 3.
11. See Brown, *Clotel: An Electronic Scholarly Edition*.

12. William Wells Brown, *Clotel; or, the President's Daughter*, ed. Robert S. Levine (New York: Bedford/St. Martin's, 2000), 158.
13. Brown, *Clotel; or, the President's Daughter*, 122.
14. William Wells Brown, *Miralda; or, the Beautiful Quadroon. A Romance of American Slavery, Founded on Fact*, ed. Christopher Mulvey (Marlborough: Adam Mathew Publications, 2003), 56.
15. Brown, *Miralda*, 222.
16. Ibid., 225.
17. Ibid., 232.
18. Brown, *Clotel; or, the President's Daughter*, 217.
19. Brown, *Miralda*, 234.
20. In this respect, Miralda's and Jerome's racialized relationship resembles that of Ellen and William Craft.
21. Brown, *Miralda*, 237.
22. M. Giulia Fabi, "The 'Unguarded Expressions of the Feelings of the Negroes': Gender, Slave Resistance, and William Wells Brown's Revisions of *Clotel*," *African American Review* 27.4 (1993): 648.
23. See Rev. J. C. Embry, "Publications Reviewed," *Christian Recorder*, January 12, 1893. In Frances Harper, *Iola Leroy; Or, Shadows Uplifted*, ed. Koritha Mitchell (Ontario: Broadview Press, 2018), 332.
24. See P. Gabrielle Foreman, "Who's Your Mama? 'White' Mulatta Genealogies, Early Photography, and Anti-Passing Narratives of Slavery and Freedom," *American Literary History*, 14.3 (2002): 505–539.
25. Frances Harper. *Iola Leroy; Or, Shadows Uplifted*, ed. Koritha Mitchell (Ontario: Broadview Press, 2018), 138.

CHAPTER 13

"Here's to Chicanos in the Middle Class!" Culture, Class, and the Limits of Chicano Literary Activism

José Antonio Arellano

In 1984, the novelist Tomás Rivera wrote an essay reflecting on the accomplishments of Chicano literature and the institutional conditions that brought it into being,[1] noting that "In 1965, there were few works written by writers of Mexican extraction in the United States. There were no courses being taught in Chicano literature. Today there are courses taught in Chicano literature in a total of 135 universities at the undergraduate and graduate levels. It is recognized as a body of literature."[2] He takes this retrospective look and tallies the institutional gains because he was reviewing Richard Rodriguez's notorious memoir *Hunger of Memory* (1981), in which Rodriguez takes a far less optimistic view of Chicano literature and its role within higher education. Rodriguez characterizes Chicano literature and higher education as middle-class enterprises that do not advance the needs of the poor. Whereas Rivera operated within the Chicano literary tradition as one of its creators and advocates, Rodriguez stood outside of it as one of its most vocal critics.

In this chapter, I show how the fundamental disagreement between their views centers on competing visions of the value of culture. I analyze their competing positions to explain why the topic of Mexican American culture, as made available through Chicano literature, became especially urgent during the 1960s and 1970s, but why the emphasis on culture came under question during the 1980s. I show how, by providing more nuanced characterizations of Mexican Americans, the Chicano literary intervention was crucial for exposing the reductive caricatures that always appear to beset their lives. I summarize Rodriguez's controversial criticism of Chicano literature, however, because he argues that literary writers – novelists in particular – tend to foreground the perspective of the middle class precisely by highlighting a shared culture that occludes class inequality.

I use Rodriguez's critique as a lens to analyze novels by José Antonio Villarreal and Arturo Islas, whose texts emphasize the value of a shared ethnic identity at the expense of foregrounding class inequality. Yet, because Rodriguez prompts writers to reconsider their ability to represent the poor and the working class unproblematically, his criticism highlights a view of literature that takes Mexican American humanity as a given and directs readers' critical attention toward the problems that arise from a society organized by class. I conclude by analyzing the novel *We Happy Few* (2006), by Tomás Rivera's friend and fellow Chicano writer Rolando Hinojosa. Hinojosa's novel, I argue, heeds Rodriguez's critique and reconsiders the legacy of Chicano activism by disarticulating the novel's meaning from cultural unity and reconnecting it to the needs of workers.

Chicano Culture and Workers

We can begin to register what is at stake in Rivera and Rodriguez's disagreement when we note the very labels they use to describe those whom Rodriguez calls "the poor"[3] and whom Rivera calls "Mexican families ... from rural communities."[4] Rodriguez describes meeting a group of undocumented Mexican workers hired for the day to perform strenuous manual labor. He highlights how he could have talked to them in Spanish, established a sense of familiarity based on a shared culture, and thereby attempted to bridge the gap between their positions (he was a college student at Stanford at the time). He chooses *not* to bridge this gap and instead emphasizes the workers' profound silence. His staccato description of their encounter – "I stood there. Their faces watched me." – emphasizes this silence, his repeated reference to the men as "the faces" going beyond synecdoche and bordering on objectification.[5] While it may seem that their objectification is a result of Rodriguez's failure to represent them complexly, for him, "Their silence is more telling" of their "disadvantaged condition."[6] The men are temporarily hired to be manual laborers and thus not provided a living wage, healthcare, or safe working conditions. Their silence is an emblem of the structural divisions that capitalism produces. These workers are objectified because of their place within aneconomy and not because of Rodriguez's feelings toward them or his failure to adequately represent them.

In Rivera's review of Rodriguez's memoir, he refers to his own "struggle" when trying to write about "this phenomenon ... the impenetrable face/masks and their silence."[7] Unlike Rodriguez, he does more than simply register their silence. His novel *... y no se lo trago la tierra* (1971) captures their voices. As José F. Aranda describes, the novel "tells the stories of a migrant community shaped by one hundred years of cultural displacement, neglect, and loathing. And yet, the beauty of Rivera's narrative is that these people also shape themselves."[8] That is to say, Rivera's novel acknowledges and represents what Rivera calls the "worldview and perceptions" *behind* the "face/masks" of the people.[9] He recognizes the dignity of the poor by acknowledging their cultural agency as expressed in their Spanish language.

Rodriguez, notoriously, did not support bilingual education because he was in favor of empowering Spanish-speaking students to learn "the English of public society."[10] Rivera could thus conclude that Rodriguez denies his "cultural root, the native tongue" that binds him to a culture he rejects. And this rejection risks perpetuating the long history of dehumanization of Mexicans and Mexican Americans (including their stereotyping and objectification) that Chicano literature as such was meant to counteract.[11]

Rivera operated within the Chicano literary tradition, the emergence of which was especially important during the second half of the twentieth century. For decades, existing works of American literature had formed an image of "the" Mexican American that tended to be a facile caricature.[12] Moreover, too many existing works of midcentury sociology and anthropology had provided unfavorable explanations of what it meant to be a Mexican American. Social scientists identified Mexican and Mexican American culture as creating unproductive values that precluded assimilation and active participation in politics.[13] The culture was blamed for Mexican American poverty, the school drop-out rates, and the high instances of teenage pregnancy.[14] Against these depictions, mid-1960s initiatives celebrated the positive, constructive nature of Mexican and Mexican American culture. The term "Chicano" circulated as an assertion of a collective sensibility based on a shared culture. Self-proclaimed Chicanos proudly established their own means of publication through which they could produce their own academic journals that focused on the social sciences, literature, and the arts.[15]

Artistic production was understood as liberating, enabling even a working-class movement benefiting Chicanos who were subjected to unsafe working conditions. In California during the mid-1960s, César Chávez and Dolores Huerta helped organize farmworkers with the help of the playwright Luis Valdez.[16] Valdez's one-act plays encouraged union organizing through didactic theatrical performance. His play *Los Vendidos* (meaning both "the sold ones" and "the sellouts"), for example, exposes the prevailing typifying caricatures of Chicanos by demonstrating the underlying humanity behind the reductive types. Valdez's play depicts the necessity of college-educated Chicanos not to betray their community and instead use their voices to advocate for workers' needs by calling for labor organizing. In the play, the exclamations, "¡Viva la raza!" and "¡Viva la huelga!" ("Long live the race!"; "Long live the strike!") assert an underlying homology uniting ethnic solidarity and labor organizing.[17]

Despite the arguments for an organic form of college leadership that remained attuned to the needs of the working class,[18] for Rodriguez this Chicano emphasis on a shared ethnic culture tends to lead to the middle-class advancing its own self-interest at the expense of workers. He writes, "I also heard academic officials say that minority students would someday form a leadership class in America. (From our probable positions of power, we would be able to lobby for reforms to benefit others of our race.)"[19] Yet, for him, the production and maintenance of a "leadership class" is part of the structural problem the strategy would occlude by claiming to make strides toward a solution. Activist efforts including the advocacy of affirmative action, for example, help those individuals *already* in a position to take advantage of higher education.[20] Students from low-income neighborhoods with underfunded public schools would most likely not attend college. Rodriguez thus critiques the Chicano creative class for foregrounding ethnicity instead of highlighting the "disadvantage" resulting from class.[21] For him, undocumented workers are "Persons apart. People lacking a union obviously, people without grounds."[22] Redress, for him, should thus involve efforts to ensure job security, safe working conditions, living wages, health care, and legal protection against labor abuse. In contrast, when one looks at Aranda's litany of the ills of migrant work I quoted earlier – "cultural displacement, neglect, and loathing" – the list fails to make explicit their poverty, thereby psychologizing the solution to their situation. Poverty becomes a stigma to be neutralized through empathy instead of a condition to be addressed with political and economic reform. Poverty, in short, becomes something like a culture to be respected, aestheticized by "the beauty of Rivera's narrative," represented by Chicano literature.

Markets and Chicanos

When, in the 1970s, a "group of eight or ten Hispanic students" approached Rodriguez in his office at UC Berkeley "to teach a 'minority literature' course at some barrio community center," he turned them down because he disagreed with their guiding assumptions.[23] Although the students argued that access to literary representation in the form of ethnic literature led to empowerment, Rodriguez asks his readers to consider the following: Who has access to the resources necessary to develop the skills to write novels, and who has the leisure to read them? From his perspective, Chicano literature amounts to a decidedly middle-class phenomenon, one which claims that the beneficiaries of upward class mobility remain "unchanged" from their working-class "community" and thus share and advance their political interests.[24]

With Rodriguez's critique in mind, we could consider José Antonio Villarreal's novel *Clemente Chacón* (1984). Villarreal sets the novel in 1972, during the height of Chicano activism and around the time Rodriguez would have turned away the Hispanic students. Like Rodriguez's contentious meeting, Villarreal delineates a charged confrontation between the protagonist Clemente and a group of Chicanos who also come to his office to make a request. "The boys from the University – from MACHOS" (the "Militant Arm of the Chicano Organization for Students") ask Clemente to "come out in the open" as a self-proclaimed Chicano.[25] A satire of actual student organizations such as the Mexican American Youth Organization (MAYO) and the Movimiento Estudiantil Chicano do Aztlán (MEChA), MACHOS demand that Clemente "serve as an example of what our young people can aspire to, [sic] you have shown that you can compete alongside the Anglo in an Anglo endeavor."[26] Taken together, the confrontational requests referenced by Rodriguez and Villarreal highlight the most salient intuition of the Chicano Movement: community empowerment via positive forms of representation. Both Rodriguez and Villarreal, writing in the early 1980s, assess the Chicano intuitions and reject their efficacy.

Unlike Rodriguez, however, Villarreal does so from a neoliberal perspective that underscores individual gumption. Villarreal's character Clemente declines the students' request and disagrees with their position because they dismiss the possibility of a meritocracy. In their account, white supremacy amounts to a seemingly insurmountable obstacle, Mexican American upward class mobility thus rarely occurring and thereby remarkable. Clemente, though, believes that his exemplary career is the result of his wily industriousness and ambition. The characters' disagreement thus centers on the status of Clemente's representativeness. He either typifies the bootstrap narrative in which anybody willing to work can make it (as he puts it "that it can be done by *anyone*"),[27] or he provides what the Chicanos want: "an example of what our young people can aspire to."[28] What is immediately evident about the confrontation is the virtual emptiness of the disagreement between the Chicanos' argument and Clemente's neoliberal one. Whether companies hire Mexican employees because the employers "actually" "believe in democracy" (as those in MACHOS would like) or whether they simply hire the best person for the job (like Clemente, who sold more than a million dollars in insurance for his company), both positions lead to the companies' profits. The winner of their debate is *business*, whether it is "good business" (as Clemente puts it) not to discriminate against competent Mexicans or whether it is "good business" (as those in MACHOS put it) to pretend to like Mexicans through tokenism.[29] The logic of the market prevails when discrimination does not interfere.

This logic is developed in the free-market economist Gary Becker's *The Economics of Discrimination* – republished in 1971, the year before the events of *Clemente Chacón* are supposed to take place. Becker argues that employers pay a price for their discriminatory hiring practices, which operate as a form of market intervention.[30] "Articulating a stereotype is cheap, while acting on it can be costly," is how Becker's University of Chicago graduate student Thomas Sowell makes the point in a chapter also titled "The Economics of Discrimination" from his book *Markets and Minorities*, published in 1981, just three years before *Clemente Chacón*.[31] For Becker and Sowell, discrimination functions as a form of market intervention because individuals *not* discriminated against could, in effect, charge a premium for their labor.[32]

Both Clemente's and the Chicanos' perspectives are entirely compatible with – indeed, historically coterminous with – the free market, or "neoliberal," economic theory that came into prominence during the 1970s and became the dominant political ideology of the 1980s. "This entire situation is a matter of economics," is how a character in *Clemente Chacón* puts it. This character, however, highlights what the free-market economists do not: the economic benefits of racist market intervention. "Racial bigotry is the result of an economic condition" that benefits capital by keeping groups of people "in ignorance," thereby ensuring "a source of cheap labor."[33] So, while employers benefit from abundant sources of cheap labor, they also benefit from the large, varied pools of ambitious, qualified employees. What the victims of racism should do, this account implies, is enlighten themselves about the reality of racism's role in the market. They should become like Clemente and pull themselves out of poverty. And they could do *that*, the novel implies, by maintaining the integrity of their identity. *Clemente Chacón* thus exemplifies the very logic of neoliberalism's insistence that upward class mobility is made possible by individual responsibility and hard work – which is to say, without the assistance of state-sponsored safety nets and the market intervention of union organizing.

The neoliberal logic can help explain why, initially, the novel places two types of plots at odds: the plot concerning Clemente's identity, wherein he will realize that he is, proudly, a Mexican (embodying, as he does, Mexico's mestizo history),[34] and its bootstrap "rags to riches" plot, wherein "work, ingenuity and smarts" enables "the American dream achieved in the American way with just enough ruthlessness."[35] "He, Clemente Chacón, was Horatio Alger, even if he *was* Catholic and brown,"[36] is how the novel describes its protagonist in the opening pages, immediately setting up a narrative tension between "being brown" and being upwardly mobile. Being Mexican, in Clemente's mind, stands inferior to the class position he seeks. As a boy, he and his single mother were poor, so he left Mexico and refused to return because he was ashamed. "I could not afford to associate with semi-literate or illiterate campesinos [farmers] if I were to achieve my meta [goal]," he explains, yet this justification mistakenly conflates a cultural identity with a class position; "I always believed that when I achieved success I would rise above old customs and traditions,"[37] he states, equating being "Mexican" and being destitute. By the novel's conclusion, however, Clemente realizes that being Mexican need not be an obstacle to becoming rich, and becoming rich should not lead to one's being a snob and thinking one is better than other Mexicans. Instead, Mexican and Mexican Americans should, as Clemente puts it, "retai[n] their pride" like "the Indians." By remaining true to who they are, "Indians" have retained their existential foundation even when dispossessed of their land. "They are not out for the dole; those sonsabitches fight."[38] Stated differently, the integrity of the Native Americans' identity rejects the government's aid for the poor in the form of welfare. This rejection of welfare articulates one of the guiding principles of neoliberalism.

By delineating a resolution to the presumed tension between class ascendancy and ethnic identity, *Clemente Chacón* mitigates the difference class produces by emphasizing a shared culture. Whereas class mobility forms a separation between those who have "made it" and those who have not (a result that the novel portrays as meritocratically justified), *Clemente Chacón* highlights a sustainable ethnic connection that is threatened by the sins of condescension and snobbery. The novel reminds its readers that so long as those who "make it" remember who they are (foregoing snobbery and condescension), they will not be all that different from those who have not.

Migrant Souls Instead of Migrant Workers

Published the same year as *Clemente Chacón*, Arturo Islas's novel *The Rain God* (1984) also characterizes the problems arising from economic inequality as those of condescension and snobbery. The novel opens with the protagonist, Miguel Angel, considering his relationship with his family. By distancing himself from his family, Miguel, now a college professor and novelist, risks exhibiting the same kind of "arrogance" and sense of "superiority" as his grandmother Encarnación Olmeca ("Mama Chona").[39] Mama Chona believes that she is "better than the illiterate riffraff from across the river."[40] She rejects Mexicans and Native Americans as inferior, a rejection made ironic by her "Indian cheekbones" and "aquiline nose."[41] Mama Chona's real name, Encarnación Olmeca, doubly registers the irony, her name alluding to her embodiment (*incarnation*) of the Olmecs, the oldest known Mesoamerican civilizations. This snobbery, differently articulated, is reinforced by his family's American education. "After his first year in school [Miguel's cousin] JoEl learned to be ashamed of the way his mother abused the language,"[42] and "Home economics classes at school" taught Miguel's other cousins that "the brilliant colors" their mother used to paint their home's rooms were not in "good taste."[43] In *The Rain God*, an education enables upward class mobility, and this class ascendence is represented as producing condescension.

By the end of the novel, however, Miguel learns that the supposedly "illiterate" Mexicans and "Indians" are neither inferior nor are they persons apart because they constitute his family's genealogy (however much this lineage is denied). His family, in turn, determines him. *The Rain God* thus emphasizes the irreducibility of a shared identity and produces the narrative grounds for self-pride in which this shared identity could be affirmed.

Islas's second novel, *Migrant Souls* (1990), a sequel to *The Rain God*, elaborates on Mama Chona's self-denial, which has contributed to the Angel family's existential state of uncertainty. Miguel's cousin Rudy mocks the Angel family during a satirical toast: "Here's to Chicanos in the middle class!" exclaims Rudy, a Berkeley graduate and lawyer. Rudy toasts those who have "finally made it into the middle class. Hated by the workers and taxed to death by the Great White Fathers!" Although he is sending up the Angel family, the liminal state he describes the Angels occupying – between "workers" and "White Fathers" – quickly and unironically transitions into an account of their spiritual and geographic dislocation:

> Just like our souls are between heaven and earth, so are we in between two countries completely different from each other. We are Children of the

> Border . . . This was Mexico before it was the land of liberty and equality for some. And before that it was Indian territory. They knew how to live in it. So where are we? . . . We are on the border between a land that has forgotten us and another land that does not understand us . . . So what are we educated wetbacks and migrant souls to do . . . Let's keep the border and give both lands back to the Indians![44]

The novel's titular "migrant souls" are thus not those whom one might expect – the Mexican and Mexican American migrant workers toiling in the field for very little pay. Instead, the "migrant souls" belong to those Mexican Americans in the middle class who complain about paying the taxes that could fund social services ("taxed to death"). Notice how the explicit *class position* Rudy invokes (the middle class) disappears as such and becomes a vertiginous psychological *identity* (the migrant souls). In the novel, ascending to the middle class could entail the forfeiture of an important part of one's cultural history, ensuring one's continued psychological displacement. This is why another of Miguel's cousins, Ricardo, teaches his children "to ignore their Mexican heritage and to live according to the myths of North America."[45] Ricardo's "dream was to be a respected member of the middle class on the north side of the river,"[46] an ambition he achieves, yet he starts going by the name "Richard" (like Richard Rodriguez, I should add) and is soon (ironically) called "Dick" by his friends.[47] Dick's problem is that he is a snob who denies who he is. So, although he has much more money than those to whom he condescends, he should realize that, deep down, they are not at all different because they share his ethnic identity. He should, in short, stop being a "Dick" and remember he is Ricardo.

These novels effectively replace the economic reality of class distinction, which cannot help but be strictly hierarchical, with an ethical call for anti-snobbery and respect. Class distinction (in which university professors enjoy certain material benefits) is rearticulated as mere difference (wherein those that have more money learn to respect those that do not). The fact of economic inequality is replaced with the commonality of a shared identity. Ultimately, novels such as *Migrant Souls* and *Clemente Chacón* offer a sense of solace to those in the middle class who have had the great fortune of upward class mobility but may now find themselves wondering if their class ascendance negates their identity. It need not, these novels suggest. All the Mexican Americans in the middle class need to do is remember where they came from so that they do not forget who they really are.

Twenty-First-Century Chicano Activism

The point of this final section, as it is for Rodriguez's critique, is not that the novelists should have written about the poor instead of focusing on the middle class. Even when they are about the poor, argues Rodriguez, novels as such cannot help but register the deep disparity between the writer (who has access to resources) and the depicted subject (whose access is far more limited).[48] Indeed, we might extend Rodriguez's brief observation about the "relationship of the novel to the rise of the middle class" to suggest that the genre reinforced the ideal of the bourgeois individual as such through its depictions of complex interiority and particular concrete characters.[49] The novel has been the genre that enables the very subjectivity of the middle class by providing a picture of what this subjectivity looks like. The genre would thus appear as a poor instrument for enabling social change today.

Yet, seemingly contradictorily, Rodriguez refers to "the fat novels" of Charles Dickens as examples of how the middle class *could* be in a position to bring about social change.[50] Dickens, he argues, "wr[ote] for a middle-class audience"[51] but made them "aware of their ability to effect social reform."[52] Dickens made readers "mindful of [their] social position and privilege." Rodriguez does not develop these brief observations to show how this dynamic works, but I would like to conclude by turning to Rolando Hinojosa's novel *We Happy Few* (2006), which does.

The novel's opening scene features a college student quietly reading "a fat book" outside of a professor's office. A group of workers has just finished painting; one painter notices the student and asks, "And what you reading there? [sic]," to which the student responds by "shrug[ging] and show[ing] him the book: *Great Expectations*." The student says, "Mostly about dreams, filled and unfilled, retribution, justice, memories, remembrances . . . " The difference between the painter's question and the student's answer is not lost on the worker, who responds "Wow. Too deep for me, kid."[53] Insofar as somebody learns about retribution and justice from Dickens's novel, it is the college student. But this college student appears incapable of conveying the sense of that importance to the worker. It is as if Hinojosa includes this scene concerning one of Dickens's "fat novels" to respond to Rodriguez and show how his own novel indeed has an important role to play. If instead of reading Dickens the student read Hinojosa's much slimmer *We Happy Few*, perhaps he would learn something about his relation to the working painter that Dickens could not teach him.

Instead of developing characters imbued with complex psychological interiorities, Hinojosa divides the novel into short sections with the titles of occupations, including "The Dean," "Regents," and "The Bankers." A shorter section titled "The Faculty" consists entirely of snippets of overheard conversations among university professors. Taking Chicano humanity as a given that does not require narrative proof, Hinojosa provides his readers with seemingly one-dimensional characters that appear as placeholders (such as "the student") within a social structure. His novel thus asks readers to consider how institutions (including banking and universities) interact to produce a world in which the class differences among these occupations matters.

Hinojosa's novel continually highlights the difference between workers and students – even though many of the students also work while attending school. The novel is set in the 1990s in a university located in Texas. Just as Rivera offers a celebratory litany of the gains of Chicano literature, the novel regularly lists similar statistics, noting how the majority of the students are Mexican American, many being the first in their families to attend college. The number of Mexican American professors has quadrupled. And the students benefit from the cultural centers that Chicano activism created. Yet, the students appear utterly self-absorbed. There is the "Chicano Cultural Club" who argues with the "Mexican American Cultural Committee" in the Aztec/Maya Cultural Center.[54] While they have these arguments, the "university's employees . . . have to clean up the mess after every meeting." Referring to these workers, one student admits, "I haven't said hello to any of those women who clean up after us."[55] Tellingly, the novel does not contain sections titled "Custodians" or "Groundskeepers." Those who hold these positions do not speak for themselves *as* characters within the novel. Readers are made aware of their presence, but, like the students, we do not know the workers' names.

With *We Happy Few*, Hinojosa – one of the most recognized Chicano novelists of the 1970s – provides a representation of the waning efficacy of a radicalism that has lost sight of a unifying goal based on workers' rights. In the novel, students experiment with the forms of activism that were effective in the 1960s. They barge into the university president's office to announce their occupation of the academic building, but they do not have an agenda or concrete demands. Unperturbed, the president politely invites them to have a seat and welcomes them to proceed with their protest. "Occupy away," he tells them. But, before leaving to attend his scheduled meetings (i.e., before carrying on with business as usual), he warns them in a more authoritative tone:

> whatever trash is left in the offices and hallways is your responsibility. I will not have the men and women who clean your dorms, the classrooms, the labs, the offices, the libraries, restrooms, the Student Union, in short, every building on campus and the grounds on which they stand. I will not have them clean up after you. They're overworked, they're people in their fifties and sixties, and they do their jobs daily and nightly so you may enjoy a clean place in which to work.[56]

Here, too, the students are presented as self-absorbed, their actions potentially resulting in overburdening the workers. The novel prompts readers to ask *why* are people in their fifties and sixties "overworked," as the university president describes? According to him, it is the students' fault. *They* are making too much of a mess. But note how he claims that people in their fifties and sixties work as custodians not to sustain their own lives and those of their families, but to benefit students who are in school, presumably, to *avoid* such low-paying jobs. Could it be that they are overworked because they are insufficiently compensated for their labor?

"What needs to be done?" asks the Liberal Arts Dean when the students occupy his building, "What are we to do?"[57] The students appear not to have considered the questions or what might count as answers. The novel shows how even the professors who actively claim to be doing something helpful are misguided. One professor, whose "PhD is six years old," has yet to publish a peer-edited article or book because he will not "stop politicking." According to him, his activism remains "important to the community," but his colleagues remind him that "This isn't the sixties or the seventies, man. We have more kids in school, some are sharper than we were at that age." To his colleagues, his activism, because no longer as urgent, amounts to a form of procrastination: "the community expects us to work, just like they do."[58] Just who gets to count *as* this community remains unclear. (Do the older custodians?) Unclear, too, is how these interlocutors seem to have access to this community's collective expectations. The professor "politicks" on the community's behalf, and his colleagues assure him that his efforts are not exactly what this community wants, all while the purported community hovers in the background while its interlocutors debate what it might want and need.

Hinojosa prompts us to consider how the gains made by the Chicano Movement remain crucial. But unless these gains are continually reconnected to the rights of the working class and to the struggles of the poorest members of our society, they will simply result in a slightly more diverse middle class. As crucial as this inclusion remains, those who will not have access to this inclusion will continue to be left behind. Those of us (*we happy few*) fortunate enough to be the beneficiaries of the Chicano Movement's efforts to diversify academia risk congratulating ourselves on our achievement. The conclusion we risk drawing from reading Hinojosa's novel is that what we must do is remember where we came from (so we are not sell-out snobs) and humanize the custodians of our colleges (by learning their names and saying hello). Such a gesture of compassion would certainly be a start. But unless we come up with an answer to the question "What are we to do?" we might be like the university president who acknowledges overworked people in their fifties and sixties for their work ethic while doing nothing to ameliorate their situation.

Notes

1. A note about terminology: The term "Chicano" effectively means "Mexican American," but it differs in its self-conscious declaration of cultural pride and ethnic solidarity. "Chicano" became historically significant during the 1960s when there was the need to declare an identity that was based on more than the contingent facts about one's ancestry and geography. More recent uses of the term tend to appear in the more inclusive form "Chicanx" to avoid the lexical genders of Spanish nouns. The broader term "Latinx" avoids the problems of exclusionary nationalism, referring to people from Latin America more generally.
2. Tomás Rivera, "Richard Rodriguez' *Hunger of Memory* as Humanistic Antithesis," in *Tomás Rivera: The Complete Works* (Houston: Arte Público Press, 2008), 347.
3. Richard Rodriguez, *Hunger of Memory: The Education of Richard Rodriguez: An Autobiography* (New York: Dial Press, 2005), 121.
4. Rivera, "Richard Rodriguez' Hunger of Memory," 342.
5. Rodriguez, *Hunger of Memory*, 145.
6. Ibid., 149.
7. Rivera, "Richard Rodriguez' *Hunger of Memory*," 342.
8. José F. Aranda, *When We Arrive: A New Literary History of Mexican America* (Tucson: University of Arizona, 2003), xv.
9. Rivera, "Richard Rodriguez' *Hunger of Memory*," 342.
10. Rodriguez, *Hunger of Memory*, 11.
11. Ibid., 342.
12. See Edward Simmen, *The Chicano: From Caricature to Self-Portrait* (New York: New American Library, 1971).
13. For examples of such contested scholarship, see Munro Edmonson, *Los Manitos: A Study of Institutional Values* (New Orleans: Middle American Research Institute: 1957); and Celia S. Heller, *Mexican-American Youth: Forgotten Youth at the Crossroads* (New York: Random House, 1968).

14. For an account of this dynamic, see Lucius F. Cervantes, *The Dropout: Causes Plus Cures* (Ann Arbor: The University of Michigan Press, 1966).
15. One prominent example is the foundation of the Chicano publishing house Quinto Sol in 1967, which began to publish the journal *El Grito: A Journal of Mexican-American Thought* that year.
16. Luis Valdez and Stan Steiner (eds.), *Aztlán: An Anthology of Mexican American Literature* (New York: Knopf, 1972).
17. Luis Valdez and Teatro Campesino, "Los Vendidos," in *Luis Valdez: Early Works: Actos, Bernabe, and Pensamiento Serpentino* (Houston: Arte Publico Press, 1990), 51.
18. See Juan Gómez-Quiñones, "On Culture," *Revista Chicano-Riqueña* 5, 2 (spring 1977), 35–53.
19. Rodriguez, *Hunger of Memory*, 5.
20. Ibid., 165.
21. Ibid., 27.
22. Ibid., 149.
23. Ibid., 173.
24. Ibid., 6.
25. José Antonio Villarreal, *Clemente Chacón: A Novel* (Binghamton: Bilingual, 1984), 52.
26. Villarreal, Clemente Chacón, 53. For an account of the MAYO and MECha, see *Making Aztlán: Ideology and Culture of the Chicano Movement* (Albuquerque: University of New Mexico Press, 2014).
27. Villarreal, *Clemente Chacón*, 103 (emphasis in original).
28. Ibid., 53.
29. Ibid., 54.
30. Gary Becker, *The Economics of Discrimination* (Chicago: University of Chicago Press, 1971).
31. Thomas Sowell, *Markets and Minorities* (Oxford: Basil Blackwell, 1981), 29.
32. For an elaboration of this point see the first chapter, the section titled "The Affairs of the World," of Walter Benn Michaels, *The Beauty of a Social Problem: Photography, Autonomy, Economy* (Chicago: University of Chicago Press, 2016). See also Michaels's essay, "Dude, Where's My Job?," *PMLA*, Vol. 127, No. 4, October 2012.
33. Villarreal, *Clemente Chacón*, 101–102.
34. Clemente's father, who originates from "the region [in Spain] that had sent the conquistadores," rapes Clemente's mother, a violence that produces Clemente who will in turn leave his family to seek his fortunes abroad. Villarreal, *Clemente Chacón*, 24.
35. Ibid., 7.
36. Ibid., 8 (emphasis in original).
37. Ibid., 139.
38. Ibid., 103.
39. Arturo Islas, *The Rain God* (Palo Alto: Alexandrian, 1984), 128.
40. Ibid., 15.

41. Ibid., 27.
42. Ibid., 119.
43. Ibid., 120.
44. Arturo Islas, *Migrant Souls: A Novel* (New York: Morrow, 1990), 163.
45. Ibid., 204.
46. Ibid., 202.
47. Ibid., 204.
48. Rodriguez, *Hunger of Memory*, 173.
49. Ibid., 173. A student at Standford, Rodriguez would have certainly been familiar with Stanford Professor Ian Watt's influential *The Rise of the Novel: Studies in Defoe, Richardson, and Fielding*. (Berkeley: University of California Press, 1957).
50. Rodriguez, *Hunger of Memory*, 67.
51. Ibid., 167.
52. Ibid., 177.
53. Rolando Hinojosa, *We Happy Few* (Houston: Arte Publico, 2006), 2.
54. Ibid., 40.
55. Ibid., 33.
56. Ibid., 30–31.
57. Ibid., 29.
58. Ibid., 60.

CHAPTER 14

Pulping the Racial Imagination

Kinohi Nishikawa

Published in the pulp magazine *Weird Tales* in January 1927, "The Horror at Red Hook" follows New York City police detective Thomas Malone as he pieces together the strange affairs of one Robert Suydam, a "lettered recluse of ancient Dutch family ... inhabiting the spacious but ill-preserved mansion which his grandfather had built in Flatbush when that village was little more than a pleasant group of Colonial cottages." Suydam is involved in shady business, but the authorities cannot pinpoint his crime, even as a "kidnapping epidemic" plagues Red Hook. The mystery deepens when Suydam and his new wife turn up dead on a honeymoon cruise. Malone subsequently investigates the mansion's basement, and there he discovers a secret chamber in which fiends perform occult rituals, practice human sacrifice, and reanimate Suydam's corpse. The ceiling collapses on Malone, but he survives and uncovers the truth of Suydam, whose necromancy overlays "extensive man-smuggling operations."[1]

H. P. Lovecraft's short story is at once a touchstone of modern horror writing and a mouthpiece for reactionary racial ideology. From Malone's perspective of a "Celt's far vision of weird and hidden things," Lovecraft speaks of escaping "the polyglot abyss of New York's underworld," of reeling from Red Hook's "babel of sound and filth," and of suspecting that the "blear-eyed and pockmarked young men" on the streets are "heirs of some shocking and primordial tradition; the sharers of debased and broken scraps from cults and ceremonies older than mankind." In this way, Lovecraft shows evil permeating the city through foreigners who exert their influence over a scion of old Dutch ancestry. No surprise, then, that Suydam's associates "coincided almost perfectly with the worst of the organized cliques which smuggled ashore certain nameless and unclassified Asian dregs wisely turned back by Ellis Island," and that these cliques were "of Mongoloid stock, originating somewhere in or near Kurdistan ... land of the Yezidees, last survivors of the Persian devil-worshipers."[2] Suydam is thus less an agent of nefariousness than a victim himself – of the anonymous illegal immigrants taking over New York. This is Lovecraft's true horror of Red Hook.

Though it may be tempting to dismiss Lovecraft out of hand for his xenophobia and racism, doing so would risk ignoring the popularity of stories such as "The Horror at Red Hook" in their time, as well as the influence they have had on literary and cultural production over the last century. Debuting in 1923, *Weird Tales* specialized in fantasy and horror stories – a genre niche within the larger pulp market. But in honing the genre codes of pulp fiction, the magazine's writers established themes, character types, and narrative devices that have become part and parcel of popular culture writ large. Robert E. Howard, for example, introduced the world to Conan the Barbarian in a *Weird Tales* story from December 1932. Since then, the hero's adventures have been adapted into books, comics, television series, and, most notably, a movie franchise starring Arnold Schwarzenegger. Seabury Quinn's detective of the supernatural, Jules de Grandin, is less of a household name, but his revelation of the all-too-human causes behind eerie, otherworldly crimes forms the crux of episodic narratives from *The Twilight Zone* to *Scooby-Doo*.

Pulp fiction reached millions of readers as print magazines were disseminated across the country and as short stories and novellas were adapted into other media. Yet pulp's long-term influence has been difficult to track because these magazines were produced for quick and easy consumption: something to buy from the newsstand, read in a sitting or two, and then toss out or hand off to another reader when you are done. Thus, while the imaginative resources of pulp fiction undoubtedly endured, the physical formats in which they originally appeared did not. This paradox of influence – widespread in its time yet obscured in hindsight – informs what it means to study pulp today.

This chapter surveys how pulp fiction at once reflected and shaped the racial ideologies of their time. To begin, it considers pulp magazines that flourished in the first half of the twentieth century. It then addresses the successor of this format, the mass-market paperback, which took the medium affordances and genre codes of magazine literature and (re)packaged them as books. In moving from magazines to paperbacks, the chapter shows how pulp fiction lay at the heart of how Americans viewed, and changed their views about, race from the Jim Crow and immigrant exclusion eras through the civil rights and Black Power movements. While it was a signal achievement for writers of color to break into the pulp industry and diversify its ranks, this chapter suggests that the masculinist bent of pulp fiction necessarily constrained its racial imagination, even when it had been wrested away from white authors' control.

***

"The pulps," print culture scholar Erin A. Smith writes, "were direct descendants of nineteenth-century dime novels, cheaply produced fiction published by Beadle & Adams, Street & Smith, and other companies that targeted the urban working classes."[3] A vehicle for emergent crime and Western genre writing, dime novels were sold at newsstands and dry goods stores for a dime or a nickel apiece. Pulp magazines built on dime novels' success with a digest format that was suited for industrialized print production and circulation. Beginning with Frank Munsey's transformation of *Argosy* into a short-story magazine in 1896, the pulps became the new century's most accessible medium for popular fiction. Instead of single-issue paperbound stories, pulp magazines stuffed multiple stories into each issue, giving readers more bang for their buck. "During their heyday in the 1920s, '30s, and '40s," Smith concludes, "hundreds of pulp titles crowded newsstands, their garish covers competing for the attention of their 10 million regular readers."[4] Pulps also could be distributed by mail – an advantage that, in an increasingly networked country, finally put dime novels out of business.

Publishers conceived the typical reader of pulp magazines to be "a young, married man in a manual job who had limited resources and lived in an industrial town."[5] Many of those who fit this profile would have been recent immigrants to the United States, so the pulp industry targeted their products to a demographic of ethnic whites. Operating under these assumptions, pulp magazines embraced storylines that privileged action over plot, sensation over intellectuality, and whiteness over all other forms of racial identification. Publishers' ability to turn a profit required a blunt approach to the market: give boys and young men what they want. The predictability of this approach downplayed girls' and women's tastes, relegating the romance genre to token status in a world dominated by horror stories, adventure tales, and science fiction. It also excluded nonwhite readers from the presumptive standpoint of pulp's imaginary worlds. For instance, when H. L. Mencken and George Jean Nathan needed to prop up their prestigious but money-losing magazine the *Smart Set*, they considered publishing a "Negro pulp," only to conclude that "there was not enough money in the black community to support one."[6] Instead, Mencken and Nathan cofounded *Black Mask* magazine, which appealed to a white working-class readership in rendering "black" merely synonymous with thrilling, paranormal elements.

It was precisely this blinkered profit motive that led pulp magazines to entertain the most reactionary causes of the day. In fact, from June 1923 to the end of that year, *Black Mask* published stories about the Ku Klux Klan (KKK) and hosted a forum on its back pages in which readers voiced their opinions about the white-supremacist group. As literary historian Sean McCann notes, the magazine tolerated the KKK's "nativist defense of 'Americanism' against various 'strangers' – especially Catholics, Jews, and immigrants" – because membership in the group was at its peak, and it was understood that pulp's readers overlapped in sentiment, if not in actual numbers, with Klansmen. *Black Mask* thus came uncomfortably close to fostering sympathy for racial terrorism. The cover of the June "Ku Klux Klan Number" special issue, for example, shows a hooded figure, dressed in full regalia, holding a burning cross and using his other hand to peer out from behind a curtain. Though the figure's intentions are unclear, the fact that the cover leaves it an open question – he could be acting villainously or righteously – rhymes with the magazine's intention to provide the "only open, free, absolutely unbiased discussion for and against the Invisible Empire published anywhere in America."[7] In other words, *Black Mask* invited readers to see the KKK as a just cause.

Hewing to this "both sides" approach, the magazine did not shy away from depicting the KKK as a front for "narrow forms of self-interest and foolish longings for outmoded kinds of social control." It did so through Carroll John Daly's stories featuring Race Williams, a go-it-alone tough guy who would become a model for the modern industrialized city detective. Williams's debut in the KKK special issue opposes a masculinist urban individualism to a masculinist rural communitarianism, with the former prevailing over the latter. Piercing the KKK's veil of honor, Williams uncovers the "corruption of popular rule that actual Klansmen indicted in their attacks on economic and political elites." In this way, Daly sets forth the parameters of hard-boiled pulp fiction to come, with the rugged individual pointing out the rank hypocrisy and moral degeneration of the world. Yet what to make of Daly naming his protagonist Race? If the KKK espouses a distinct racial chauvinism – hewing to an ideology that aligns white Anglo-Saxon Protestantism with American identity – Williams, for McCann, epitomizes "something like an antinativist racialism, or a racially legitimated opposition to ethnic separatism."[8] In other words, Williams represents a better version of whiteness ("racialism"), one that looks past racial signifiers for the deeper rot within all men.

As generous as this reading is, it remains debatable why Williams's perspective has to be "racially legitimated" in the first place. What does *whiteness* do for the pulp reader?

Cultural historian Gail Bederman addresses this question by way of the pulp adventure series *Tarzan of the Apes*. Originally published in *All-Story* magazine in 1912, *Tarzan* was the creation of Chicago-born writer Edgar Rice Burroughs. The story begins with mutineers casting off a British diplomat and his pregnant wife on the shores of Africa. They perish, but their son is rescued and raised by apes in the jungle. Named Tarzan by his simian family, the boy grows up to become a fearsome hunter, in part because he is able to use the knife his father left behind. Combining the purity of his Anglo-Saxon bloodline with the savagery of the untamed jungle, Tarzan embodies a revitalized white manhood. The racial implications of this characterization are unnerving. For example, after the African warrior Kulonga kills Kala, his ape mother figure, Tarzan exacts revenge by "stealthily lowering a rope noose round his head, and then jerking him, struggling, up into the treetops." To complete what Bederman refers to as a "lynching," Tarzan stabs Kulonga in the heart with his trusty knife. Far from an exception, this killing is the prelude to Tarzan becoming a "one-man lynch mob, a proud murderer of African men" who employs the "standard method of hanging."[9] Burroughs makes Tarzan's homicidal streak palatable by representing these tribal figures as beneath contempt – cannibals who exist on a civilizational scale lower than even that of apes. The rampant dehumanization of Black masculinity has a specific symbolic purpose. Soon after he lynches another Mbongan warrior, Tarzan meets Jane Porter, the white woman who will become his love interest. The proximity of events suggests that Tarzan will defend white womanhood not only against the beasts of the jungle but against the Black men who threaten to violate Jane.

Thus, even when pulp stories touched on the fantastical, their white protagonists stood for and held up a racial hierarchy in which Black people were violently subjugated. McCann concedes as much when considering the "exotic stories of foreign adventure – tales of white men beset by tropical dangers – that drew on the recent Tarzan vogue." In a time when Black men were still being lynched across the American South and Midwest, pulp magazines tapped into the racial blood lust by displacing the action to foreign locales. The connection was hardly a matter of coincidence. A writer who had penned a Klan-sympathetic piece in one issue of *Black Mask* simply "retold that story by infusing its concerns with the romance of the exotic" in a later issue. In so doing, the "Invisible

Empire's anxiety about local control and native community became . . . the melodrama of racial conflict that was always implicit in Klan rhetoric": Black brutes competing with heroic men for the right to claim white womanhood.[10]

This formula of displaced racial animus proved so popular that it outlasted the KKK fascination and populated the pages of pulp well into the 1940s, which was the tail-end of the format's widespread circulation. Indeed, the Tarzan copycat Ki-Gor, so-called White Lord of darkest Africa, appeared in the magazine *Jungle Stories* from 1938 to 1954. In one episode from 1946, Ki-Gor pummels a Black guard whose tribe has held the hero's love interest, Helene, captive:

> His fingers dug into the native's throat, wrenched deep as though to choke the life from him. The black's eyes bugged out, his dark face puffed and twisted, and he bucked in futile, agonized desperation. Then as Ki-Gor saw the life draining from the man, he released his grip slightly, allowed the Wasuli to gasp a breath into his aching lung.
>
> "Quick, dango!" he snarled. "Where is the white girl? Speak or you die!"[11]

His grotesquerie emphasized by having the breath squeezed out of him, "the black" of this episode is figured as the opposite of all that is right and true: Ki-Gor's protection of "the white girl." Helene's virtue is not merely a narrative device but a symbolic impetus for vigilante action. In this register, adventure stories came perilously close to justifying the affective coordinates of the racial hierarchy that subtended Jim Crow segregation.

If Black characters in pulp magazines reflected an imagined internal threat to America's white citizenry, Asian characters in the same posed a more straightforward external threat to Western civilization at large. No other author popularized this anti-Asian ideology in the early twentieth century more than the English novelist Sax Rohmer, the pseudonym of Arthur Henry Ward. From 1913 to 1917, Rohmer introduced readers on both sides of the Atlantic to Chinese criminal mastermind Dr. Fu Manchu in three novels that were serialized by *Story-teller* and *New Magazine* in Britain and by *Collier's* in America. Though *Collier's* was not a pulp rag, its zealous promotion of Rohmer's pulp fiction meant that, by the second novel, it preceded British outlets in serial publication. Pitted against the Sherlockian duo of Sir Denis Nayland Smith (as the Holmes figure) and Dr. Petrie (as Watson), Fu Manchu arrives in London with dark designs on the British Raj. Traveling with Indian henchmen as well as an enslaved Arab girl named Kâramanèh, Fu Manchu embodies both yellow peril fears and orientalist fantasies. On one hand, his murderous crime spree, carried out by a cadre of thugs, feeds into jingoistic beliefs about foreign threats to imperial and national identity. On the other hand, Fu Manchu's association with opium and Kâramanèh's ability to seduce Petrie tap into the alluring, yet dangerous, qualities of the same group of outsiders. In both guises, Fu Manchu constitutes a threat to Western civilization: "We are dealing with a Chinaman," says Smith, "with the incarnate essence of Eastern subtlety, with the most stupendous genius that the modern Orient has produced."[12]

After a hiatus of nearly fifteen years, Rohmer returned to the series with *Daughter of Fu Manchu* (1931) and went on to publish six more installments over the next decade. Nativist sentiment had intensified since the passage of the Chinese Exclusion Act in 1882, and American pulp writers saw an opportunity to replicate Rohmer's success among the white working class. New York's Popular Publications, for example, "gave readers the most memorable Fu Manchu imitations with Robert J. Hogan's pulp title, *The Mysterious Wu Fang*, and its successor, Donald Keyhoe's *Dr. Yen Sin*." The resemblance to Rohmer's series rested not just on the by-now clichéd Chinese supervillain but on the Sherlockian duo – federal agent Val Kildare and news correspondent Jerry Hazard in Hogan's series; Michael Traile (another G-man) and Eric Gordon (another correspondent) in Keyhoe's – that worked together to uncover the foreign menace. Popular Publications banked on readers' identification with the original by hiring the illustrator of Rohmer's serialization in *Collier's*, John Richard Flanagan, to provide the art work for its series. *The Mysterious Wu Fang* ran between 1935 and 1936, halting publication only after its publisher "received a cease and desist letter from Rohmer's attorneys." *Dr. Yen Sin* was a short-lived reboot that nonetheless indexed how commonplace anti-Asian stereotypes had become.[13]

The yellow peril motif underwent its own adjustment when Japan flexed its imperial muscle on the world stage. In light of the Japanese invasion of Manchuria in 1931, which eventuated in the outbreak of full-scale war between China and Japan in 1937, the Chinatown schemes of Fu Manchu were counterbalanced by the militancy of an Asian country with global ambitions. Take, for instance, Arthur Leo Zagat's *Tomorrow* series of novelettes, which ran in *Argosy* from 1939 to 1941. Rather than revive the anti-immigration sentiment of previous eras, Zagat's stories dovetailed with growing fears of Japan's place in the geopolitical contest for power. The dystopian fiction presents an America taken over by an Afro-Asian coalition of nonwhites, where Black people provide the brute force needed to execute Asians' dastardly plans. With entire cities "leveled by bombs" and white Americans "enslaved in work camps," Zagat's vision of a race hierarchy turned upside down inspires a band of underdogs, led by the fearless Dikar (born Dick Carr), to overthrow their persecutors.[14] Stoking fears of both foreign invasion and domestic insurgency, Zagat draws a clear line between heroic Americanism and racial and ethnic subversion.

At the same time that *Argosy* released these stories, developments in the American publishing industry were about to hasten pulp magazine' demise. The rise of the paperback book in the 1940s made reading material even more accessible to the masses. On one hand, fiction that had only appeared in hardcover or other editions could now be repackaged for a fraction of the cost, at around twenty-five cents per copy. This led to a vast democratization of middlebrow and highbrow works. But paperbacks competed with pulps on the other end, too, insofar as they vied for readers' attention in the very outlets – newsstands and drugstores – where magazines were bought and sold. This retail competition pushed pulp magazines' razor-thin profit margins to the breaking point. "In the autumn of 1950," writes pulp historian Ron Goulart, "you could have walked up to almost any newsstand in the country and bought the latest issues of *Dime Detective*, *Black Mask*, *Detective Tales*," and the like. "Just three years later," however, "every one of these titles was dead and gone."[15] But this market shift in format did not signal the demise of the pulp imagination. Instead, pulp adapted to paperbacks, whose covers replicated magazines' sensationalistic imagery and whose content continued to traffic in racial stereotypes, though in notably different ways.

With the USA emerging victorious from World War II, the yellow peril fears of previous decades subsided in print and popular culture. Instead of posing external threats, Asians were more often portrayed as pliant, feminized subjects who bowed to American directives. Take Ted Pittenger's *Warrior's Return*, published by Signet in 1955. Signet was an imprint of New American Library, a paperback firm founded in 1948 by Victor Weybright and Kurt Enoch after both had worked at Penguin Books' American branch. Like many of Signet's offerings, *Warrior's Return* was a paperback original, meaning that it had been written for this format and had not appeared previously in hardcover. Like pulp magazines, paperback originals were intended for quick and easy consumption; this mass-market format prioritized sales over quality. That may explain why Pittenger's story about an American serviceman stationed in Japan during the war reads like a down-market cousin to James A. Michener's *Sayonora* (1954). Having published a story with the same title in *Atlantic Monthly* in 1953,

Pittenger – a copy chief at a Los Angeles advertising firm – may have wanted his book to ride on *Sayonara*'s success.

Reflective of changing American attitudes toward Asians, the protagonist of *Warrior's Return*, Terry Wright, recalibrates his white masculinity while serving in the Pacific theater. Having achieved the trappings of success with a high-paying magazine job and a glitzy marriage, Terry realizes during the war that these are illusions that exploit his trust, routinize his labor, and undermine his virility. Crucial to arriving at this realization is his relationship with three Japanese sisters who welcome him into their family home in Yokohama. Deferential to Terry and to their father, the sisters model a "proper" femininity that affirms the natural order of things. Pittenger spells this out in no uncertain terms when one sister is confused by a phrase she sees in a Japanese–English dictionary: "Woman Suffrage." Terry thinks, "My God, how can I explain this one so she'll understand?" After establishing their gender differences – "I man; you, woman; is that not so?" – Terry explains:

> "We are equal . . . "
> Myoko said no, that was not so; Itsuko said she was crazy. Toyoko said: "We do not understand your interpretation, Elder Brother."
> Terry sat ramrod straight, folded his arms across his chest, looked at them with mock seriousness and growled: "MacArthur says so."
> "Ah, McOsser," Itsuko said; and the three sisters spoke in excitement.[16]

Having declined Terry's explanation for women's equality, the sisters punctuate the exchange with a ringing endorsement of General Douglas MacArthur, who accepted the surrender of Japan aboard the USS *Missouri* on September 2, 1945. For Terry, patriarchal authority and American military might are confirmed by Japanese daughters who seem to know their place quite well.

Pulp's Black characters also underwent a shift in the postwar years. The civil rights movement's fight against Jim Crow fostered more liberal attitudes toward race. The question for paperback originals was how to frame this social, political, and legal transformation in ways that spiked sales. Their solution was crude: since sex sells, what better way to explore racial issues than through sexual taboos? The most successful titles in this vein were titillating historical romances set in the slavery era. The fad began with the appearance of Kyle Onstott's *Mandingo* in 1957. A former dog breeder, Onstott imagined plantation slavery as a system where the economics of enforced reproduction yielded scenarios of sexual control and illicit desire. The independently published novel became an unexpected hit. Fawcett picked up the rights to *Mandigo*, and its paperback edition sold upward of three million copies. The book's popularity alerted Fawcett to the sales potential of a series based at Falconhurst, the fictional plantation where much of the action is set. Between 1962 and 1988, a combination of Onstott and two other authors added fourteen books to the series, immersing millions of readers in a world where the brutality of slavery was intertwined with the pleasures of sex.[17]

Consider the fourth book in the series, *Falconhurst Fancy*, published by Fawcett as a paperback original in 1966. Dovie Verder, the white mistress, has purchased Colt, an enslaved Black man primed to "stud," or copulate with other enslaved people to increase their owner's holdings. After tamping down her attraction to Colt on several occasions, Dovie finally decides to lie with him. Though the scene is characterized by extreme inequality, such that any notion of Colt's choice or agency is rendered moot by his enslaved status, the novel recounts their coupling as an equalizing tryst: "During the night their positions became reversed. She was no longer the mistress and he the slave. In this close communion he became the master and she the willing slave doing his bidding as he became more emboldened and threw off all restraint. It was he who ordered and she who obeyed willingly, finding a new joy in his mastery over her." The fantasy that Dovie's and Colt's positions may be "reversed" through sex is one of the series' primary means of obscuring the racial hierarchies instituted by plantation slavery. As the novel has it, "Her eyes refused to envisage him as the servant who followed her about in the daytime, as the servant she had purchased in Warren Maxwell's barn ... as a n[*****]."[18] Premised on Colt's enslaved status, this illusion of mutual desire ultimately satisfies Dovie's lust, tinged by the sense that her transgression is an act of beneficence.

As this example suggests, paperbacks' replacement of magazines in the pulp business meant that publishers catered to a slightly older audience and sensibility. The sensationalism that story magazines had cultivated in the first half of the century was now the province of paperback originals that pushed the envelope of obscenity for adult readers. As the profit motive to transgress took hold, genre fantasies steadily shaded into pornographic fare. The Los Angeles pulp publisher Holloway House, for example, envisioned Asia as a mystical land of sexual conquest. It did so, first, by reprinting Victorian erotica set in imperial outposts like India, Turkey, and Persia.[19] The works were of dubious credibility, but their widespread popularity in the age of empire inspired Holloway House's appeals to a white American masculinity staring down global Cold War threats.

The company followed up on the erotica with supposed memoirs of Asian women who have sex for pay: Su-Ling's *The Nine Holes of Jade* (1967), Iolana Mitsuko's *Honolulu Madam* (1969), and Tami Miyoshi's *The Cherry Dance* (1969). Though fictionalized, these books' claim to veracity (something the old pulps would not have done) assured readers that the women's exploitation at the hands of men was something they had braved and in fact enjoyed. This fantasy of willing submission, as ventriloquized through Asian femininity itself, kept yellow peril fears during the conflict in Vietnam at bay.

At the time of these developments, Holloway House brought out a book that seemed to invert the pulp imagination's racial hierarchy. Iceberg Slim's *Pimp: The Story of My Life* (1967) was pitched as a confessional, but its first-person narrative resembled the dramatic arc of a coming-of-age novel. Slim was the pseudonym of a middle-aged exterminator named Robert Beck who looked back on his youthful forays into the criminal underworld of the 1930s and 1940s with equal parts nostalgia and regret. As Slim's fictionalized persona learns how to hustle from older Black men on the streets of Milwaukee and Chicago, pimping crystallizes as a means of not only earning a good living but also sticking it to the man. His mentor Sweet Jones explains that, after emancipation, white men continued to subjugate Black men, whether in Northern cities or on Southern farms. But some opportunity-minded Black men saw that white men were "still ramming it into the finest black broads," while Black women "still freaked for free with the white man." To secure their own means of uplift, then, these men "started hipping the dumb bitches to the gold mines between their legs. They hipped them to stick their mitts out for the white man's scratch." By creating a market around what Sweet says was a free-for-all practice, pimps became America's first self-made Black men, the "only N [*****] big shots in the country."[20] With a legend like that motivating him, Slim comes to view the running of his prostitution ring as both a lucrative and a righteous enterprise.

Subtending this fantasy of uplift is a wide-ranging misogyny that treats Black women as expendable commodities for men's profiteering and pleasure. The verbal and physical abuse visited upon women is a constant refrain in *Pimp*. Yet far from making Slim a pariah, the novel turned him into a minor celebrity, identifying in the process a new market for Holloway House's books: Black readers. Noting the buying power of this demographic, Holloway House recast its catalog around Black-oriented pulp, copying Slim's formula in books such as Donald Goines's *Whoreson: The Story of a Ghetto Pimp* (1972) and Charlie Avery Harris's

Macking Gangster (1976) and exploiting stereotypes of inner-city violence in novels of crime, espionage, and adventure fiction. While the effect of these efforts was to diversify the pulp marketplace, bringing Black authors and readers together in what I term a "black literary underground," there can be no mistake that the worldview the company promoted through its products was that of the pimp. Holloway House's white ownership, I argue, "cultivated the fantasy that it was inherently a man's world, and that, for black men in particular, 'It was better to be a taker than one of those who got took!'"[21] After a remarkably long run, the independent publisher closed its doors in 2008. However, Slim's influence on popular culture's image of Black masculinity is secure, with examples ranging from rapper-cum-actor Ice-T (whose moniker is an homage to the author) to stand-up comic Dave Chappelle (whose 2017 Netflix special *The Bird Revelation* contains a prolonged shoutout to Slim).

***

If Holloway House represented the pulp imagination's excesses taken to the extreme, mainstream publishers in the 1980s and 1990s forged a different path for genre writing by welcoming diverse talent into their rosters. Decoupled from a down-market format such as pulp magazines or paperback originals, genre fiction underwent a multicultural turn that did away with the presumption that white readers were the default audience of popular literature. This decades-long process has seen all the major genres fundamentally changed – in style, storyline, and narrative perspective – by writers of color. Walter Mosley and Henry Chang, for example, have transformed the detective novel into piercing depictions of what it means to be racially and culturally other in America. Set in Black neighborhoods in Los Angeles and in New York City's Chinatown, respectively, their mysteries shed light on questions of law and criminality from within the context of urban minority communities. Meanwhile, Samuel R. Delany and Octavia E. Butler have tapped into the worldmaking genre codes of science fiction to examine the unsettling overlap between utopian and dystopian racial futures. Their novels explore stigmatized identities and skewer moral and political hypocrisies, and, in so doing, have helped establish the artistic and cultural movement known as Afrofuturism.

Building on these meaningful efforts at diversification, a younger generation of writers and artists has actively engaged with one of pulp's towering figures, H. P. Lovecraft, in order to subvert the legacy of racist stereotypes he left behind. N. K. Jemisin, for example, began her Great Cities series of urban fantasy novels with a scene in which a giant tentacled creature, reminiscent of Lovecraft's mythic monster Cthulhu, destroys half of the Williamsburg Bridge in Brooklyn. The plot of *The City We Became* (2020) follows a group of outcasts who, in the face of such destruction, aim to save the city as a sanctuary for the excluded. In a different medium, showrunner Misha Green, actor and filmmaker Jordan Peele, and producer J. J. Abrams created *Lovecraft Country*, a television series based on Matt Ruff's 2016 novel of the same title. Set in 1950s America, the series represents how Jim Crow segregation facilitated a kind of racial terror that collapses the distinction between the supernatural and the all-too-real. Finally, there is the signal achievement of *The Ballad of Black Tom* (2016), in which author Victor LaValle rewrites "The Horror at Red Hook" from the perspective of Charles Thomas Tester, a young Black man in Jazz Age Harlem. Tom's encounter with Robert Suydam's dark arts is mirrored by a lamentably familiar kind of horror: that of police brutality against unarmed Black men. *The Ballad of Black Tom*, whose upending of Lovecraft's vision is inspired by the rise of the Black Lives Matter movement, garnered a slew of accolades and won the Shirley Jackson Award for best novella.

This wave of revision suggests that while the era of printing fiction on processed wood pulp has long past, the legacy of pulp's racial imagination extends into the twenty-first century. Jemisin, Green, and LaValle, among many others, evidence how that legacy need not repeat the cultural erasures or symbolic violences of pulp's magazine and paperback heyday. It also need not resort to masculinist sexual fantasy as a rationale for including different voices in the pulp pantheon. Working against the grain of pulp's traditional racial and gender politics, today's writers and creators of color are embracing some of the least welcoming of genres – horror, fantasy, and supernatural thrillers – and insisting on their constitutive openness to the new, the marginalized, and the unknown. While there has been blowback from some white male fans of genre writing, the change is already underway, representing pulp's potential for reimagining itself.

Notes

1. H. P. Lovecraft, "The Horror at Red Hook," *Weird Tales*, January 1927, 62, 66, 71.
2. Ibid., 60, 61, 62, 64.
3. Erin A. Smith, *Hard-Boiled: Working-Class Readers and Pulp Magazines* (Philadelphia: Temple University Press, 2000), 19.
4. Ibid.
5. Quoted in Smith, *Hard-Boiled*, 23.

6. Smith, *Hard-Boiled*, 27.
7. Quoted in Sean McCann, *Gumshoe America: Hard-Boiled Crime Fiction and the Rise and Fall of New Deal Liberalism* (Durham: Duke University Press, 2000), 44, 42.
8. McCann, *Hard-Boiled*, 59, 57, 61. For an account of the ideological variance of the KKK issue, see Felix Harcourt, *Ku Klux Kulture: America and the Klan in the 1920s* (Chicago: University of Chicago Press, 2017), 75–99.
9. Gail Bederman, *Manliness and Civilization: A Cultural History of Gender and Race in the United States, 1880–1917* (Chicago: University of Chicago Press, 1995), 224, 222, 225.
10. McCann, *Hard-Boiled*, 63, 63–64. The author of these stories, Herman Petersen, is misnamed "Peterson" by McCann. For a reading of *Tarzan* in light of white fears of urban social contamination, see Catherine Jurca, "Tarzan, Lord of the Suburbs," *Modern Language Quarterly* 57.3 (1996): 479–504.
11. John Peter Drummond, "The Monsters of Voo Doo Isle," *Jungle Stories*, February–April 1946, 41.
12. Sax Rohmer, *The Insidious Dr. Fu-Manchu* (New York: McBride, Nast, 1913), 55. For a contextualization of Fu Manchu and Kâramanèh in interwar popular culture, see Nathan Vernon Madison, *Anti-Foreign Imagery in American Pulps and Comic Books, 1920–1960* (Jefferson: McFarland, 2013), 41–87.
13. William Patrick Maynard, "Popular Yellowed Perils," *PulpFest*, June 28, 2019, www.pulpfest.com/tag/yellow-peril/.
14. Samuel Wilson, "Real Pulp Fiction: ARGOSY, May 27, 1939," *Mondo 70: A Wild World of Cinema*, May 29, 2014, http://mondo70.blogspot.com/2014/05/real-pulp-fiction-argosy-may-27-1939.html. For an account of Zagat in the context of American anti-Japanese sentiment, see Madison, *Anti-Foreign Imagery*, 96–98.
15. Ron Goulart, *The Dime Detectives* (New York: Mysterious Press, 1988), 231.
16. Ted Pittenger, *Warrior's Return* (New York: Signet, 1955), 105.
17. Two useful surveys of the Falconhurst phenomenon are Earl F. Bargainnier, "The Falconhurst Series: A New Popular Image of the Old South," *Journal of Popular Culture* 10.2 (1976): 298–314; and Paul Talbot, *Mondo Mandingo: The "Falconhurst" Books and Films* (Bloomington: iUniverse, 2009).
18. Lance Horner and Kyle Onstott, *Falconhurst Fancy* (New York: Fawcett, 1966), 387. Horner worked on the series as soon as Onstott moved to mainstream publishing, serving in an uncredited role for the second and third books. He and Onstott were credited with co-writing *Falconhurst Fancy*. After Onstott died in 1966, Horner went on to write the next five installments on his own.
19. Charles Devereaux, *Venus in India* (Los Angeles: Holloway House, 1967); anonymous, *The Harem Omnibus:* A Night in a Moorish Harem *and* The Lustful Turk (Los Angeles: Holloway House, 1967). For an account of Holloway House's cut-and-paste practices for publishing erotica, see

Kinohi Nishikawa, *Street Players: Black Pulp Fiction and the Making of a Literary Underground* (Chicago: University of Chicago Press, 2018), 29–37.

20. Iceberg Slim, *Pimp: The Story of My Life* (Los Angeles: Holloway House, 1967), 195.
21. Nishikawa, *Street Players*, 223. The quotation is from Donald Goines, *Black Gangster* (Los Angeles: Holloway House, 1972), 119.

CHAPTER 15

Recognition, Urban NDN Style
The Social Poetics of Pre-1980s Intertribal Newspapers

Siobhan Senier

In every conceivable way, 2020 was awful, but it was arguably the year that Indigenous poetry arrived. It was the year that Joy Harjo (Muscogee), the first Native American poet laureate of the United States, published *When the Light of the World Was Subdued, Our Songs Came Through: A Norton Anthology of Native Nations Poetry*. Backed by the massive power of one of US literature's premiere canon-makers, W. W. Norton & Company, *The Light of the World* cinched access for Indigenous poets to some of the most important mechanisms of dissemination and prestige: university classrooms, academic libraries, and scholarly publications. The book made multiple bestseller lists and was lauded in every major reviewing outlet. It even got Oprah Winfrey's Queen Midas touch.[1]

So 2020 did some good for the world – or, at least, for the world of Indigenous literature. It introduced a broader than ever public to the great diversity and richness of Indigenous poetry. It enshrined now-canonical poets such as Harjo herself, N. Scott Momaday (Kiowa), and Simon Ortiz (Acoma) alongside up-and-coming younger poets including Michael Wasson (nimíipuu/Nez Perce) and Lara Mann (Choctaw). It showed that Indigenous people have been writing poetry for centuries, and, moreover, that they have often done so with prestigious presses and accolades. Perhaps most importantly, *The Light of the World* reaffirmed that Indigenous poets have written with a deep consciousness of their specific tribal nations. This is a fact still lost on many Americans: that Indigenous people are not a race, but political entities – sovereign nations with their own claims to territory, governance, and citizenship.

As previous chapters in this collection have demonstrated, despite their status as political formations, Indigenous nations have been racialized, deracinated, and reracialized throughout US history. This history has made Indigenous people perhaps especially vulnerable to ethnic identity fraud, which is attracting profound anger these days on both social and professional media. Harjo was forced to address the problem directly in the introduction to her book:

> We editors do not want to arbitrate identity, though in such a project we are confronted with the task . . . The question "Who is Native?" has become more and more complex as culture lines and bloodlines have thinned and mixed in recent years. We also have had to contend with an onslaught of what we call "Pretendians," that is, nonindigenous people assuming a Native identity. DNA tests are setting up other problems involving those who discover Native DNA in their bloodline. When individuals assert themselves as Native when they are not culturally indigenous, and if they do not understand their tribal nation's history or participate in their tribal nation's society, who benefits? Not the people or communities of the identity being claimed. It is hard to see this as anything other than an individual's capitalist claim, just another version of a colonial offense. We note that there are some poets who have cycled through varying tribal claims from their first appearance in print. Some claim identity by tenuous family story and some are perpetrating outright fraud. We do not want to assist in identity crimes.[2]

"Tenuous family story" might refer to someone like Elizabeth Warren, whom some saw as trading on her Cherokee "family lore" before she finally had to admit that she is not in fact a tribal member; and "outright fraud" would describe someone like the "Navajo memoirist" Nasdijj, who turned out to be a white writer named Timothy Patrick Barrus who was unashamedly lying.[3] Without question, ethnic fraud is a serious problem. It's distressingly widespread in Indian country; too many teachers have had to remove at least one "Pretendian" from the Native American literature syllabus after discovering that the writer built a career on bogus claims. Above all, these cases are incredibly damaging and painful for Indigenous people themselves: they take resources away from people who could have had that job or that publishing contract; and they create mistrust and fear within communities and between friends and colleagues. So the arguments about alleged Pretendians go beyond just outing scurrilous individuals; they call for publishers, universities, and other institutions to do a better job of verifying Indian identity claims.

Accordingly, some are pulling now toward a specific and complicated benchmark: enrollment in a federally recognized tribe. That is precisely where Harjo says she landed in choosing writers for the Norton volume.[4] It's a move that acknowledges the critical importance of tribal specificity and political citizenship, and is thus a necessary corrective to vague appeals to "Indianness" or "family lore." At the same time, it's worth remembering that federal recognition is itself a mixed bag. Today, the USA recognizes 574 tribal nations. Most of those had long-standing relationships with the federal government through treaties or war, but many others are unrecognized thanks to what the Diné attorney Faith Roessel calls an "historical twist of fate" – they made treaties with colonial or state governments, or they were small enough that they literally escaped recognition.[5] Thus, federal recognition has become, for many tribal nations, a legal fight and process – often an extremely expensive and protracted process – especially since the 1970s, when the Bureau of Indian Affairs codified the procedures and criteria for being "granted" recognition. The Choctaw historian Brian Klopotek explains that "recognition overflows with potential benefits," including new opportunities for economic development, and a sense of community pride and well-being; at the same time, he cautions, it "bears hidden risks to what might be called traditional tribal configurations," limiting tribes' exercise of self-determination within a federal framework of "domestic dependent nations."[6]

Federal recognition is not something we can dismiss out of hand as a colonial fabrication, but it's also not unproblematic, as observers will know if they have followed even a single circuitous case, such as that of the Mashpee Wampanoag.[7] With respect to Native American and Indigenous literary study, which turned decades ago, fruitfully, to tribally specific approaches to texts, it's worth thinking about how an over-emphasis on federal recognition might be shaping the ways we understand Indigenous literary canons and literary history – how an insistence on individual enrollment in federally recognized tribes can foreclose possibilities as much as it can enable them.

To think through this, I turn to poetry published by lesser-known, sometimes anonymous Indigenous writers in two pan-tribal newspapers from the 1970s – the eve and early days of new federal recognition processes and fights. *Talking Leaf*, published in Los Angeles, and *The Circle*, published in Boston, provide unique insight into how Indigenous people at that time recognized *each other*, alongside or outside of settler state acknowledgment. They show that, for Native nations experiencing ethnocide, state detribalization, and outright rejection of their recognition claims, poetry and print culture have been vital ways that tribal members find each other, remember their histories and collectively imagine their futures. These newspapers pursued what the poet Mark Nowak calls *social poetics*: a practice that "seeks the transition of the pen or the laptop from the 'committed' author (be they journalist, academic poet, novelist, playwright, or other writing professional) to working people themselves in a new conjunction of aesthetic practice and political action." Amid the 1970s efflorescence of urban Indigenous political action and publishing, these newspapers and their poets created what Nowak would call "new spaces and new organizations for new chroniclers and new narrators."[8]

Los Angeles: *Talking Leaf* (1972–1986)

One reason why some tribes had to seek recognition in the first place was that they had been *de*-tribalized by earlier legislation, including the 1950s push for what was then called Indian termination. Under this policy, some tribal governments were dissolved, so-called entitlements were eliminated, and many Native people were relocated to major urban centers including Los Angeles, Chicago, Seattle, Denver, and others.[9] This policy, like earlier polices of Removal and Allotment before them, *intended* to make Indians disappear. But as scholars including Laura Furlan and Renya Ramirez (Winnebago) have shown, cities became places of great political and cultural renewal for Indigenous people, as people from far-flung reservations met each other, sharing and producing new knowledge.[10]

They often did so in print. Historians of print culture have shown that not only is community "an effect of print" (in the old Benedict Anderson argument), it's also the *cause* of print.[11] In many cities, growing populations of relocated Indigenous people founded urban Indian centers, which in turn had a practical need for regular publications that could inform the community of their offerings. The Los Angeles Indian Center, for instance, was founded in 1935, and is one of the longest running urban Indigenous organizations in the country.[12] Beginning in the 1970s, it started publishing a newspaper called *Talking Leaf*, which covered Indian Center news, including proceedings of the Center's board meetings, and announcements for services provided by the center, such as legal advice and housing assistance. It also ran pieces about elders or veterans in hospital, notices of weddings and deaths, sports coverage, and announcements for powwows and other community events. Like many community newspapers, *Talking Leaf*'s format and typeface changed regularly, while its publication schedule was somewhat less regular: it appeared every 3 or 4 months, and seems to have depended heavily on a small cohort of volunteer correspondents. Subscriptions were $4 a year, and it reached a distribution of some 3,000 copies monthly.[13]

Talking Leaf did not support much poetry, but it did publish some during the tenure of its first editor, Sandy Osawa (Makah), whom many literary scholars know for her career as a filmmaker. Her name appeared on the masthead from the second issue of 1972 through the first three issues of 1973. She wrote quite a bit of content herself, while her husband, Yasu Osawa, contributed photography and layout. In the October–November 1972 issue, *Talking Leaf* gave an entire page to three short, stanza-conscious poems by Ginger Turner: an untitled one whose first line is "sister"; another called "circles" (a common image/metaphor in intertribal papers of this period); and one called "spirit."[14] Ginger Turner is not identified in the paper by tribal affiliation, nor is the artist whose work accompanies the poems, Clifford Suathojame.[15] The poems themselves generally eschew specific references to tribal nation or even place until the third, "sister," which takes the form of a direct address from one Indigenous woman to another:

> tribal ways
> run strong and deep
> as the Rio Grande
> (white ways plague us both)[16]

Who is this speaker, and who is her interlocutor? The reference to the Rio Grande suggests a relationship to land or lands outside of Los Angeles, and it carries that relationship into this urban space, much as Renya Ramirez has described "Native hubs," wherein tribal members bring their distinct cultural knowledges and histories into the city, and bring the knowledge and experience they gain there back out to their respective homelands again. Whether Ginger Turner relocated to Los Angeles from someplace further east, or had been living in California for all her life, her poem brings Indigenous women together across space and time: what unites these two sisters is their shared experiences of "tribal ways," and their mutual oppression under settlers' "white ways." Printed in Los Angeles and circulated as far afield as Korea,[17] this poem generates a ripple effect of intertribal, cross-spatial identifications.

Another poem in *Talking Leaf* was written by June Leivas, identified on the page as Chemehuevi.[18] She too is writing about intertribal concerns. "Song for Yellow Thunder" refers to the murder of Raymond Yellow Thunder in South Dakota, where he was kidnapped, beaten, and stripped, brought to a bar and mocked, and then left for dead. The shocking hate crime spurred the American Indian movement into action and made national news, as Leivas recounts:

> I remember your face so well
> Your picture was in Life magazine
> But that's not where I remember it from

I saw it smashed between the pages
Of a history book
From a poster tacked upon a wall
  Lined with shadow and light
  Your pain so well concealed
  Your eyes so piercingly real
  Your beauty something to feel
  And your spirit said "go on"
  And I was not real
  As I vowed "I will"[19]

Pan-tribal newspapers and the poets who wrote for them were acutely conscious of mainstream press representations of Indigenous people, and acutely conscious of their role as counter-narrators. For Leivas, the importance of Yellow Thunder is not the sensationalism of his murder but the vicarious trauma – and resilience – she experiences as she contemplates his story and his image. That image, in the world of the poem, recirculates from national media (*Life*) to a private space (a wall, presumably her own or another Indigenous space) to preservation in the pages of the books that Indigenous people are reading to educate themselves. Leivas's style of writing recalls the activist, archivally oriented work of Muriel Rukeyser, Richard Wright, and other 1930s documentary poets. To Mark Nowak, documentary poetics is "not so much a movement as a modality within poetry whose range I see along a continuum from the first-person auto-ethnographic mode of inscription to a more objective third person documentarian tendency."[20] Leivas's poem, falling closer to the auto-ethnographic end of that continuum, also serves a reportorial function in the newspaper; poetry, in this instance, acts as a democratic form of correspondence.

These newspaper poets, sometimes tribally unaffiliated, usually "unprofessional," often more concerned with pan-tribal identification than tribal specificity, complicate the present moment, in which we have come to understand Indigenous poets as representative of distinct tribal nations. In the early 1970s, many tribal nations in California were as yet unrecognized.[21] This undoubtedly affected the way Indigenous identification(s) played out in the region. That is not to say that tribal affiliation or enrollment, or even federal recognition, were unimportant; on the contrary, the *Talking Leaf* was highly aware and supportive of federal recognition cases, including that of the Bridgeport Indian colony, who finally received it in 1974.[22] What's intriguing about the paper's *own* recognition of local Indigenous communities and individuals is that it was edited by people who were not themselves indigenous to California, who came from tribal nations that *were* at that time already recognized. Sandy Osawa's Makah had been recognized since 1934. Her successor, Jack Haikey, was Creek, a nation whose recognition was also long established. And yet these editors appeared ready to acknowledge that the city into which they moved was *already* Indigenous space. They seemed to create a print community that was able to encompass nonrecognized tribes and individuals alongside those with federal acknowledgment.

It's also worth noting that most of the poets in *Talking Leaf* and *The Circle*, discussed below, were women, and that they express what Molly McGlennen finds in her study of contemporary intertribal Indigenous feminist poetry: it "maps a different type of Indigenous citizenship that has less to do with nation-state-sponsored documentation, blood quantum politics, or reservation life, and more to do with community engagement and broader Indigenous affiliations."[23] In the 1970s and 1980s, at least, urban Indigenous social poetics appeared to de-emphasize tribal political citizenship in favor of intertribal unity and connection.

Boston: *The Circle* (1976–1984)

A similar dynamic played out in Boston. Thanks to their colonization well before the US federal government even came into being, *all* of the tribes in Massachusetts and the broader New England region were "unrecognized" in the 1970s. Will Basque (Mi'kmaq), first president of the Boston Indian Council (BIC), said that "[b]ecause of state and federal non-recognition, we are treated . . . as statistics, but not as people . . . [O]n one side, we know who and what we are; we know that we are Indian. But on the other side, we are forced to live in a society that tells us that we do not exist, that we have disappeared."[24] Those words appeared in an early issue of the Council's paper, *The Circle*, published between 1976 and 1984. Established in 1969 in Jamaica Plain (and still there, as the North American Indian Center of Boston), the BIC has published numerous bulletins and newsletters throughout its history. For those eight years, though, it ran a full-fledged newspaper. Like *Talking Leaf*, this paper served as an organ of the Council, publishing announcements about its offerings in adult education, job-seeking assistance, substance-abuse counseling, and child welfare; it also ran stories of national Indigenous interest, including the trial of Leonard Peltier and the fire at John Trudell's home.

A fun fact for literary scholars is that the now-famous author Louise Erdrich (Turtle Mountain Chippewa) worked briefly for *The Circle*.[25] She and most of the other newspaper staff, like Sandy Osawa and Jack Haikey in Los Angeles, were not Indigenous to the city or region. *The Circle*'s first editor, Jack Hayes, had no tribal affiliation noted; the next major editor, Helen M. Blue, was Upper Sioux from Minnesota.[26] Like their LA counterparts who came to the city from places further away, these editors kept a close eye on – and voiced explicit support for – regional federal recognition struggles, including the Mashpee and Maine Indian land claims cases.

The Circle published far more poetry than *Talking Leaf.* The Boston paper included poems in almost every issue, often devoting entire pages to verse. The paper actively encouraged its readers and community members to think of themselves as writers. It published work by some writers who are today quite well known: Mi'kmaq educators Elsie Basque and Isabelle Knockwood, and Anishinaabe activist Winona LaDuke. The paper published notices of opportunities for writers, including one event where they could "Read Poems for Money" at the Huntington Avenue YMCA, suggesting that poets could earn 10 dollars by reading for 10 minutes.[27]

The Circle did two other important things to build, and recognize, its Indigenous community's literary capacity. First, it put out calls for people not only to contribute their own writing, but also to get involved in the work of the paper itself. In October 1977 editor Jack Hayes issued a notice seeking an assistant editor.[28] Two months later the paper advertised an adult education class in newspaper production, encouraging people to learn everything from writing to photography to layout.[29] Second, the paper published work by BIC staff. Tom McDonald, a maintenance worker and elder survivor of the Shubenacadie residential school, had a regular humor column called "Tom Talks." Kim McDougall, an Ojibwe woman from Ontario, hired to work with the teen program, published some of her poetry. In other cases, BIC staff submitted poetry on behalf of anonymous writers. For instance, this prose poem, "Walking Up and Down that Lonely Street," was "written by an Indian teenager, name withheld":

> Walking up and down that lonely street wondering what I am going to do, wondering where I am going to stay tonight. Here I sit in the cold, wondering how I am going to survive tonight. I did a crime so I could do some time, so I could have some shelter, food and protection. I found the food and shelter but never found the protection I was always looking for. Here I sit behind the walls of prison wondering what I am going to do when I get out.[30]

Like June Leivas's rumination on Raymond Yellow Thunder, this poem provides auto-ethnographic *reportage* on the realities of Indigenous life in the city. While BIC staff wrote announcements of their programs and offerings, and collated coverage of local and national news, they also made room for "new chroniclers and new narrators," à la Nowak, to describe the lived experience of Indigenous youth, Indigenous elders, and others, often people on the margins who would have been using the Center's services.

Numerous pieces, sometimes anonymous, recount struggles with alcoholism. One, a six-line, heartfelt poem asking readers to recognize the speaker's humanity, was titled simply "I Am an Alcoholic" and attributed to Thomas N. Sock.[31] Not all of the paper's poets are easy to track down, but a 2018 obituary for a Thomas N. Sock says that he "lived in Boston for many years," that he was born in Molus River, New Brunswick, and he died in Presque Isle, Maine.[32] Molus River is close to the Elsipogtog First Nation, and Presque Isle is the seat of the Aroostook Band of Micmacs, so it is highly possible that Sock was Mi'kmaq. In fact, Boston has a long history of Mi'kmaq movement in and out of the city, and the BIC was run largely by Mi'kmaq people while *The Circle* was being published. In the 1980s, anthropologist Jean Forward found that 80 percent of the Indigenous population of the Greater Boston area was Mi'kmaq from Maine and the Maritimes.[33] In her estimation, Mi'kmaq people at the BIC maintained a strong sense of tribal identity and influence, but they were also keenly interested in building identification with people from other tribal nations. When visitors arrived in the reception area, she says, they were "first asked what tribe," and then invited into a conversation about "common friends and/or relatives in the Indian community."[34] The infrequency with which *Talking Leaf* and *The Circle* specifically mention tribal identifications may simply mean that everybody already knew who belonged to what nation, so there was no need to mention it in a small community paper. But it might also reflect the ease with which tribally specific identities sat alongside broader Indigenous identities – and the efficacy of those community-based, face-to-face conversations in determining who was Indian.

The Circle's most-published poet was also unidentified by tribal nation: his byline was simply "Coleman A. Gurley, a Senior Citizen." The BIC had a robust elders' program whose activities were often reported in paper. Gurley acted as something of a poetic correspondent for the group. He wrote a tribute in verse, "Our Chauffeur Steve," which was signed by five other elders and published alongside the beloved

Steve's photograph.[35] He also loved to play with stanzas and rhymes, sometimes verging on doggerel:

'Tis true we are aging,
But let this one thing be said,
Though the storms now are raging,
We are far from being dead.[36]

Gurley also wrote about events of major political importance, including The Longest Walk, the 1978 American Indian Movement–led civil rights march from Alcatraz to Washington, DC. Many BIC members joined the march, and *The Circle* printed photographs and reports from the field. To these, Gurley added a four-stanza celebration:

The Longest Walk is the road back home,
It leads far into our long ago,
Where up and down its hills we did roam,
The joy we had, only we can know.[37]

Without the larger context of the paper, this poem's reference point could easily be missed; it could be taken, indeed, for a stereotype of Indigenous people as nomadic and rooted in the distant past. It's unclear whether Gurley and other elders were able to participate in this walk themselves (he's not referenced in any of the articles about BIC participation), so it's interesting to consider the affective dimensions of his witnessing from afar. As an older man, watching younger Native people enthusiastically reporting about a dramatic political and spiritual renewal, he does write with an element of mourning ("for some it is like December/For them the past has lost all its glow"). But he also writes with a sense of unity. This poem treats the walk not just as a singular historical event but also as a metaphor for a transhistorical, transcontinental, collective Indigenous identity: "The joy we had" is something with which Indigenous people identify, *as* Indigenous people, whether they are youth in the streets at the Capitol or elders reading these accounts in their community paper.

Though the term "pan-Indian" is now considered a bit dated, it captures the spirit of much of the writing in *The Circle*. The first several issues included the following statement:

> This paper is called The Circle.
>
> It is more than a name, it's a symbol. For centuries, the circle has represented the unbroken unity and harmony of our people. It stands for the many Indian nations, joined together from time past to time to come. It is both our heritage and our religion. The wholeness of Indian life.

> The purpose behind this newspaper is to express that sense of unity. It is for all Native people. Just as the BIC is open to any Native person in this city, so too is the paper in the hands of the people it serves.

Empowerment through inclusivity and openness: that is the feeling of *The Circle* overall. If some of the poetry feels "detribalized," this doesn't mean that people shucked their tribal identities, or were understood to have done so, as that front-desk check-in dialogue at the BIC suggests. Intertribal cooperation, Laura Furlan points out, was hardly unique to the 1970s and 1980s; it's something Indigenous people have pursued since time immemorial. She adds: "While governmental and tribal requirements for tribal enrollment are often the standards by which identity is determined, Indian identity for many has been decided by other factors, such as participation in a Native community and acceptance by tribal members."[38] That ethos of participation and acceptance was proudly displayed on the very front of the Boston Indian Center, where a large banner proclaimed "AMERICAN INDIAN SPOKEN HERE."[39] In turn, Native community and acceptance were kept alive on the pages of *The Circle*, where professional writers identified by their membership in federally recognized tribes found common cause with everyday chroniclers who may or may not have been able to show a government-issued Certificate of Degree of Indian Blood (CDIB).

***

Lest this all sound naively utopic, calls for CDIBs did in fact appear in *Talking Leaf*.[40] The problem of people trying to horn in on scant resources, whether they are "Pretendians" or garden-variety white settlers, is nothing new; and while it's not the overriding tenor of either paper, this threat does rear its head from time to time. On the one hand, these editors knew how to call foul when they saw it. A reader of *Talking Leaf*, for instance, reported that "Several months ago Cher announced that she was part Indian and ever since then there have been repeated references [on the Sonny and Cher show] for squaw, wooden Indian and other derogatory language."[41] Whatever Cher's blood quantum or tribal membership, it was obvious that she was not enacting the Indigenous values the *Talking Leaf* was trying to foster. On the other hand, fraudulent individuals did sometimes slip through the cracks. *Talking Leaf* reported the advocacy of Iron Eyes Cody (the Pretendian of all Pretendians) in calling for better representation of Indians in the media; and *The Circle* published a poem about the Mashpee land claims case written by none other than Jimmie Durham – the self-proclaimed Cherokee artist/activist who is the subject of a special issue of the *American Indian Culture and Research Journal* on ethnic fraud.[42]

My argument, then, is emphatically not that, unfettered from the colonial constraints of federal recognition and enrollment, Indigenous people somehow magically knew how to recognize each other. This is precisely what's so devastating about ethnic fraud. Besides stealing material resources, it has too often led even Indigenous people into supporting people who are unsupportable. My argument, rather, is that teachers, scholars, and promoters of Indigenous writing should remain mindful that our canons are shaped, for better or worse, by very particular criteria for adjudicating Indigenous identity – and that these criteria are often historically and politically contingent.

No one knows this better than Indigenous writers themselves. The statement by a new organization, Indigenous Nations Poets, reads

> The work of In-Na-Po supports the sovereignty of Native Nations determining their citizenship, and we understand Native identity and citizenship to be a complex and evolving matter. We are inclusive of Native writers who are citizens of their Native Nation or community, as well as those who may not be enrolled but are actively participating and working towards the survival and continuance of their Nation(s) and who can demonstrate a familial connection, or descent through lineage.[43]

One of their prominent advisory board members is Joy Harjo.

Talking Leaf and *The Circle* practiced what Mark Nowak describes as the foundation of social poetics:

> In an era when many communities of poetry continue to embed themselves deeper and deeper into elite institutions (private colleges and elite universities, costly academic conferences and writers retreats, black-tie book award ceremonies, and the like), social poetics remains a radically public poetics, a poetics for and by the working-class people who read it, analyze it, and produce it within their struggles to transform twenty-first-century capitalism into a more equitable, equal, and socialist system of relations.

It's an indisputable good that Indigenous poets are now more deeply embedded in elite institutions. Still, the long histories of Indigenous poetry in all kinds of venues – from propagandistic boarding school newspapers to the office of the US Poet Laureate – show us a whole panoply of ways that Indigenous people have determined different forms of belonging, both political and aesthetic. Urban Indigenous newspaper poetry gives us a unique window onto how these communities have constructed and reconstructed themselves based on kinship both tribal and intertribal – on relations to land and to each other that pre-exist and exceed US-tribal government to government relations. That is not to say what transpires on their pages is perfect, or even "better" than a collection of poetry by people enrolled in federally recognized tribal nations, only that it could be, that it sometimes has been, otherwise.

Notes

1. Leigh Haber, "Oprah Shares the Seven Books That Help Her Through Tough Times," *Oprah Magazine*, October 26, 2020, www.oprahmag.com/entertainment/books/a34473594/oprah-books-tough-times-list/. Winfrey promoted these books on her Oprah's Book Club and Apple social platforms during the early days of the COVID-19 pandemic.
2. Joy Harjo, *When the Light of the World Was Subdued, Our Songs Came Through: A Norton Anthology of Native Nations Poetry* (New York: W. W. Norton & Company, 2020), 4.
3. See "Syllabus: Elizabeth Warren, Cherokee Citizenship, and DNA Testing," *Critical Ethnic Studies*. www.criticalethnicstudiesjournal.org/blog/2018/12/19/syllabus-elizabeth-warren-cherokee-citizenship-and-dna-testing; Matthew Fleischer, "Navahoax," *LA Weekly*, January 23, 2006, www.laweekly.com/navahoax/. Other widely publicized cases include that of the novelist Joseph Boyden, as recounted in Jorge Barrera, "Author Joseph Boyden's Shape-Shifting Indigenous Identity," *APTN News* (blog), December 23, 2016, www.aptnnews.ca/national-news/author-joseph-boydens-shape-shifting-indigenous-identity/; and the scholar Andrea Smith, as reported in "The Native Scholar Who Wasn't," *The New York Times* (May 25, 2021). www.nytimes.com/2021/05/25/magazine/cherokee-native-american-andrea-smith.html.
4. She finesses this by saying "we have included only indigenous-nations voices that are known tribal members or live and work directly within their respective communities" (p. 4); still, the book includes no contemporary poets from nonfederally recognized nations.
5. Faith Roessel, "Federal Recognition – A Historical Twist of Fate," *NARF Legal Review* (1989), 16.
6. Brian Klopotek, *Recognition Odysseys: Indigeneity, Race, and Federal Tribal Recognition Policy in Three Louisiana Indian Communities* (Durham: Duke University Press, 2011), 238. For an excellent bibliographic essay on sovereignty, see Stephanie Nohelani Teves, Andrea Smith, and Michelle Raheja, eds., *Native Studies Keywords* (Tucson: University of Arizona Press, 2015).
7. In academic circles, the Mashpee case became a famous example of the problems of settler governments adjudicating cultural authenticity, thanks to James Clifford, *The Predicament of Culture: Twentieth-Century Ethnography, Literature and Art* (Cambridge: Harvard University Press, 1988).
8. Mark Nowak, *Social Poetics* (Minneapolis: Coffee House Press, 2020).
9. A lucid overview of the so-called termination era can be found in Donald Fixico, *Termination and Relocation: Federal Indian Policy, 1945–1960* (Albuquerque: University of New Mexico Press, 1990).

10. Laura M. Furlan, *Indigenous Cities: Urban Indian Fiction and the Histories of Relocation* (Lincoln: University of Nebraska Press, 2017); Renya Ramirez, *Native Hubs: Culture, Community, and Belonging in Silicon Valley and Beyond* (Durham: Duke University Press, 2007).
11. Lara Langer Cohen, "The Emancipation of Boyhood," Common-place: the Journal of Early American Life. http://commonplace.online/article/the-emancipation-of-boyhood/.
12. Larry Smith, "Story Map: Indigenous Urbanity in Los Angeles: 1910s–1930s," Mapping Indigenous LA, undated, www.arcgis.com/apps/MapJournal/index.html?appid=385eb4f3432442eab8bcffb19109f92e.
13. Joan Weibel-Orlando, *Indian Country, L.A.: Maintaining Ethnic Community in Complex Society* (Chicago: University of Illinois Press, 1999), 93.
14. *Talking Leaf* (October–November 1972), 8.
15. A Hualapai painter and portraitist, according to "Clifford Suathojame," Heard Museum | ARGUS.net (Final). https://5019.sydneyplus.com/Heard_Museum_ArgusNET_Final/Portal/Portal.aspx?component=AAAM&record=4b38a624-17e8-4ca8-ad2d-2782a4223391.
16. *Talking Leaf* (October–November 1972), 7.
17. Nicolas G. Rosenthal, *Reimagining Indian Country: Native American Migration and Identity in Twentieth-Century Los Angeles* (Chapel Hill: University of North Carolina Press, 2012), 117.
18. *Talking Leaf* 2.2 (1973), 16. In 2015, she was a tribal council member and language instructor at the CRIT reservation, according to Kevin Baird, "Learning the Language: The Tribe Is Working to Have More Children Learn Chemehuevi as Few Adults Speak It Fluently," *Havasu News* (July 27, 2015): www.havasunews.com/learning-the-language-the-tribe-is-working-to-have-more-children-learn-chemehuevi-as-few/article_460e3396-341c-11e5-bf91-2f846cd0d8ae.html.
19. *Talking Leaf* 2.2 (1973), 15.
20. Poetry Foundation, "Documentary Poetics by Mark Nowak," Poetry Foundation (Poetry Foundation, January 1, 2022), www.poetryfoundation.org/harriet-books/2010/04/documentary-poetics.
21. There were many reasons for this, including Congress's refusal to ratify treaties made in the nineteenth century, and the "termination" of some 44 tribes during the 1950s and 1960s. For more on this "distinctive history," see Section XIV of Carole Goldberg and Duane Champagne, "UCLA AISC, A Second Century of Dishonor" (Los Angeles: UCLA American Indian Studies Center, March 27, 1996), www.aisc.ucla.edu/ca/Tribes.htm.
22. *Talking Leaf*, 2.1 (1973), 8.
23. Molly McGlennen, *Creative Alliances: The Transnational Designs of Indigenous Women's Poetry* (Norman: University of Oklahoma Press, 2014), 41.
24. *The Circle* 1.3 (June 1976), 6.
25. I have been able to find Erdrich on the masthead for only one issue: Late Winter 1980; the largest collections of the paper are at Cornell University and the University of Connecticut, but there is not a full run between these two collections.

26. Jean Forward believes that Jack Hayes was non-Native (email conversation 1/7/2022). Helen Blue is not identified in the paper by tribal affiliation, but I found her in Peter Slevin, "Standing for Change Upper Sioux Chairman Helen Blue-Redner '85 Speaks Her Mind to Help Her Tribe," *Princeton Alumni Weekly*, March 9, 2005, www.princeton.edu/~paw/archive_new/PAW04-05/10-0309/features.html.
27. *The Circle* 2.1 (April 1977), 7.
28. *The Circle* 1.7 (October 1977), 11.
29. *The Circle* 2.8 (December 1977), 3. This was obviously not an easy project to sustain. In what may have been the paper's final issue, Helen Blue issued a plea for assistance, noting that the paper cost $1,000 per month to produce (and, contextualizing this, "the universal poverty of Indian publications all over the country") and repeating the offer to teach readers how to contribute writing, editing, photography, pasting up, and other skills. *The Circle* 8.8 (January 1986), 2 and 11.
30. *The Circle*, 8.6 (November 1985), 9.
31. *The Circle* 2.1 (April 1977), 7.
32. "Thomas N. Sock," *The County*, March 7, 2018, https://thecounty.me/2018/03/07/obituaries/thomas-n-sock/.
33. Jean S. Forward, "*Ethnicity and Education: The BIC Innovative Culture Broker*" (PhD, Amherst: University of Massachusetts, 1985), 30.
34. Ibid., 152. Additionally, many of the Indigenous people in northern Maine at that time identified less as Mi'kmaq or Maliseet than as "Aroostook Indians"; and they created a vibrant intertribal print culture that dissolved after some tribes and not others succeeded in federal recognition cases. See Siobhan Senier, "Rethinking Recognition: Mi'kmaq and Maliseet Poets Re-Write Land and Community," *MELUS: Multi-Ethnic Literature of the US* 37.1 (2012): 15–34.
35. "Our Chauffeur Steve," by Coleman Gurley, "signed by Elders Helen Spengler, Reginald Spengler, Rebecca LaBillois, Betty Demers, and Gladys McDonald." *The Circle* 2.10 (March–April 1978), 8.
36. "Senior Citizens," *The Circle* 2.6 (October 1977), 3.
37. "The Longest Walk," *The Circle* 3:1 (July–August 1978), 16.
38. Ibid., 17.
39. Photograph in *The Circle*, October 1985, front page.
40. A community member in Los Angeles circulated a petition requiring all Indian Center board members to provide the documentation; *Talking Leaf* (March–April 1972), 2.
41. *Talking Leaf* 2.1 (1973), 4.
42. "Minorities Petition Federal Communications Commission," *Talking Leaf* 2.2. (1973), 29. Untitled poem attributed to Jimmy Durham, *The Circle* (March–April 1978), 9. On Durham as a case of ethnic fraud, see Nancy Mithlo, "Decentering Durham," *American Indian Culture and Research Journal* 43.4 (2019), 25–28.
43. Indigenous Nations Poets (In-Na-Po), "Statement on Indigenous Identity," Indigenous Nations Poets. https://sites.uwm.edu/in-na-po/about-us/.

PART V

Case Studies

CHAPTER 16

Uncle Tom's Cabin *and the Question of Race*

Claire Parfait

"For better or for worse, it was Mrs. Stowe who invented American Blacks for the imagination of the whole world."[1] While the claim made by literary critic Leslie Fiedler in the late 1970s might seem somewhat exaggerated, it cannot be denied that, as Richard Yarborough has argued, *Uncle Tom's Cabin* "played a major role of establishing the level of discourse for the majority of fictional treatments of the Afro-American that were to follow – even for those produced by blacks themselves."[2] *Uncle Tom's Cabin* (1852), an antislavery novel written by Harriet Beecher Stowe, a white woman from New England, came out in the context of the debate over slavery[3] and in the wake of a much-debated Fugitive Slave Law passed by Congress in 1850. It was a tremendous success and the source of intense polemic when it first appeared. Since then, and in spite of ups and downs in its popularity and critical reputation, the novel has never entirely disappeared from the scene. In the more than 150 years that have elapsed since its first publication, *Uncle Tom's Cabin* has never been out of print; it has had countless adaptations and rewritings, and as a result has remained the locus of heated discussion on the representation of race and on race relations in the USA. Its eponymous hero is firmly inscribed in the American imagination and lexicon, albeit in a way that Stowe could hardly have predicted when she had Tom die at the end of the novel for refusing to give away the hiding place of two fugitive slaves. Indeed, the Merriam-Webster online dictionary defines "Uncle Tom" as "a black person who is overeager to win the approval of whites (as by obsequious behavior or uncritical acceptance of white values and goals)." As a term of abuse, "Uncle Tom" has been used against many public figures, including Martin Luther King, Clarence Thomas, and Barack Obama.

This chapter will attempt to trace the role *Uncle Tom's Cabin* – Stowe's novel, but also its rewritings, tie-ins, and adaptations – has played in discussions of race in the United States since the 1850s. The first part will investigate the inception of the novel, its strategies, publishing circumstances, and immediate reception. The second part will focus on the afterlife of *Uncle Tom's Cabin*, in terms of both scholarly commentary and popular appropriations.

Inception and Serialization of *Uncle Tom's Cabin*

Harriet Beecher Stowe, the daughter of a well-known Presbyterian minister, had been writing short pieces and sketches for magazines and gift books for some twenty years when she started working on *Uncle Tom's Cabin*. Few of her productions dealt with slavery until 1850 and the passage in Congress of the Fugitive Slave Act. The act reinforced a 1793 law and imposed harsh penalties on anyone – including those citizens who lived in free states – who helped fugitive slaves. The 1850 law made it clear that the whole country was involved in the system of slavery and, like many northerners, Stowe was incensed. This anger led her to start what would become her first novel, *Uncle Tom's Cabin*.[4] She initially planned to write "a series of sketches" about slavery for the *National Era*, an antislavery weekly published in Washington, DC. She had long been reluctant to tackle the topic, both because she was aware that the subject was seen as unfit for a woman and because she feared for her sanity. Yet she felt that the "peril and shame" of slavery were such that "even a woman or a child who can speak a word for freedom and humanity" was bound to speak. The "series of sketches" developed into a full-blown novel, which the antislavery paper serialized over the course of some ten months, between June 5, 1851 and April 1, 1852. Readers' letters printed in the *National Era* indicate the great interest they took in the story, which they found thrilling (as one reader put it, "We don't get sleepy reading it") and moving ("Some of the passages . . . go straight into the depths of the soul, stirring up its purest, best emotions"). Readers felt it was a true account of slavery and that it would "do more good to the antislavery cause than a score of ordinary volumes."[5]

Plot, Main Characters, and Authorial Strategies

Uncle Tom's Cabin unfolds a double plot and a double journey. The first is the South–North journey typical of slave narratives, which takes fugitives Eliza, George, and their son Harry from slavery in Kentucky to freedom in Canada. The second plot follows the opposite trajectory as the main protagonist of the novel, Uncle Tom, is sold always further down South.

Tom is a pious slave who lives rather comfortably on the Shelby plantation in Kentucky with his wife and children; unfortunately, Shelby has to sell slaves to pay off his debts. Because Tom is the most valuable slave on the plantation, he has to go, together with Little Harry, Eliza's son. On the boat which takes him to the deep South, Tom saves young Eva St. Clare from drowning. Eva's grateful father buys Tom, who spends a few not unhappy months in New Orleans, growing always fonder of the child, who is as pious as he is. But she dies of consumption, in one of those protracted death scenes common in Victorian fiction. St. Clare, who had promised to emancipate Tom, is killed while trying to stop a fight between two drunken men (Stowe was also a temperance writer). Tom is then sold to the real villain of the story, Simon Legree, a Yankee who takes him to his cotton plantation on the Red River. Legree vainly tries to get Tom to whip slaves and has him beaten to death when he refuses to reveal the hiding place of two fugitives. Tom dies a Christian death, forgiving the men who killed him.

Eliza is a young quadroon who also belongs to the Shelbys. When she overhears the conversation between Shelby and the slave trader, she decides to escape with Harry. In a scene that was to become a staple of illustrations, tie-ins, and adaptations, she crosses the Ohio river on blocks of ice, and is taken in by a family of Quakers, where her husband George, who also fled his plantation, meets her quite by accident. They make their way to Canada before deciding to move to Liberia. In addition to these main characters and plots, the novel abounds in secondary characters (such as Topsy, a little Black girl whom many critics have seen as the typical "pickaninny," a stereotyped Black child, in the minstrel show tradition[6]) and subplots.

Uncle Tom's Cabin calls upon all the staples of antislavery literature: the inhumanity of slavery, the separation of families caused by the domestic slave trade, at a time when family was considered sacred, the violation of the nation's founding principles – the courage displayed by George and his fighting spirit are equated with those of the American patriots who freed the colonies from the British yoke. Tom is a Christ-like figure pilloried by the "peculiar institution." Stowe embodied the evils of slavery in vivid characters and mixed realism with the sentimental and domestic fiction that was familiar to the readers to make them "*feel right*" on the topic of slavery, and thus operate what Joan Hedrick calls "a revolution in sentiment."[7] Shirley Samuels locates sentimentality, "a set of cultural practices designed to evoke a certain form of emotional response," at the core of nineteenth-century American culture.[8] Philip Fisher has explained how by extending humanity to slaves, sentimentality "exactly reverses the process of slavery itself which has at its core the withdrawal of human status from a part of humanity."[9] Stowe's first objective was to humanize African Americans in the eyes of American readers by forcing the reader to identify and empathize with, for example, a female slave like Eliza who, because she was a quadroon, looked much like the white reader who was Stowe's intended audience, and shared the same values of purity and domesticity. Should this fail, Stowe frequently addressed her audience within the text of the novel to invite them to feel right, and in closing paragraphs threatened the nation with God's wrath for the sin of slavery. The writer also included comic interludes so that there is an alternation of melodrama, comedy, irony, sarcasm and sermonizing. She attempted to strike a delicate balance between fiction and documentary account of slavery, and devoted part of the final chapter – a kind of coda or afterword to the novel – to explaining that many of the characters and incidents were derived from either her personal experience or that of friends.[10] Part of her strategy was to show that even a "good" master such as Shelby did not make the system right: the master could die or run into debt, and slaves would have to be sold and families would be separated. She was careful not to antagonize the South,[11] and she took pains to attack the system rather than individuals.

Uncle Tom's Cabin as a Book: Initial Reception

Finding a publisher was no easy task, evidence that American publishers approached antislavery literature with extreme caution. Leading Boston publishers Phillips, Sampson & Company rejected it partly out of fear of alienating their Southern customers, and partly because they doubted the success of an antislavery novel serialized in an antislavery journal. John P. Jewett, another Boston publisher, agreed to bring out *Uncle Tom's Cabin*. He was an antislavery man and his catalog already included a few antislavery works.

To ensure the success of the work, Jewett created a genuine marketing blitz which would later be widely imitated. Thus, for instance, before the book came out he used ads to create a degree of suspense over the date of publication, promised but not guaranteed to be March 20 (1852). The publication itself of what Jewett touted as "The Story of the Age," or "The Great American Tale," was thus turned into an event. After *Uncle Tom's Cabin* came out, and when an extraordinary 10,000 copies had been sold in a week, then an astounding 50,000 copies in 8 weeks, Jewett purchased entire pages to boast of the sales in the press. Newspaper articles also kept readers informed of the prodigious numbers of copies sold, of binders (between 125 and 200) and machines (3 or 4 of Adam's power presses) working round the clock without quite meeting the demand, and of the incredible quantity and weight (90,000 pounds) of the paper consumed in the enterprise.[12] After all, all this was news. And, of course, it further enhanced the sales. In March 1853, a year after the first publication of the novel, Jewett announced that 305,000 copies had been sold in the USA.[13] The sales figures for Stowe's novel far outstripped those of books that were published in the same period and that were also considered bestsellers:[14] about 11,000 copies of Hawthorne's *The Scarlet Letter* were sold within 5 years of its first publication in 1850; in 1851, Elizabeth Stuart Phelps's semiautobiographical novel *The Sunny Side; or, the Country Minister's Wife*, which was very popular, sold 100,000 copies within a year. The 305,000 copies of *Uncle Tom's Cabin* sold in the USA were indeed unprecedented numbers.[15]

The publisher also initiated one of the first (if not *the* first) of many tie-ins to the novel by commissioning a poem from antislavery poet John Greenleaf Whittier, then paying a composer to write the music to the song, entitled "Little Eva." This was followed – though the next byproducts were not commissioned or inspired by the publisher – by other songs, engravings, statues, spoons, plates, scarves printed with scenes from the novel, puzzles, card games in which children had to bring the slave families together, and other kinds of artifacts, as well as well as stage adaptations.[16]

After the work came out in book form, criticism of the novel was as strong as praise. It was said to offer an exaggerated portrait both of the horrors of slavery[17] and of the moral qualities of slaves: Tom was too good, George and Eliza too intelligent to be true. Stowe was charged with fueling the hatred between North and South, encouraging slaves to rebel and murder their masters. In addition, she had proved herself to be "unladylike" by writing on a topic that a proper woman should have avoided. The polemic was abundantly relayed in the day's periodicals, and further ensured that the book would be talked about.[18] It came at precisely the right time to furnish or revive arguments in the antislavery debate. Stowe's novel was a national (or at least Northern and Western)[19] phenomenon and became part and parcel of the ongoing debate about slavery. It was deemed sufficiently dangerous to produce a host of anti-*Uncle Tom* novels in which masters were benign and slaves affectionate.[20] For abolitionists, as Manisha Sinha notes, *Uncle Tom's Cabin* was "a godsend, a mass conversion tool," the best possible weapon in the fight against slavery. However, its ending, with Stowe sending George off to Africa, seemed like an endorsement of the hotly contested colonization scheme.[21] Its depiction of slaves also raised a number of issues: as critics have shown, Stowe's novel drew upon and reproduced popular stereotypes and was heavily influenced by "romantic racialism," which George Frederickson has defined as "a doctrine which acknowledged permanent racial differences but rejected the notion of a clearly defined racial hierarchy."[22] Thus, Anglo-Saxons were superior in intellect, for instance, but African Americans were better Christians, as is best exemplified in the character of Uncle Tom.

Some contemporary commentators objected to Tom's Christian forbearance; thus, Black abolitionist William Allen noted that Tom "had too much piety." While Frederick Douglass praised the novel in the *Frederick Douglass' Paper*, his 1853 novella *The Heroic Slave* can be seen as a rewriting of Uncle Tom: the novella's hero, Madison Washington, leads a slave revolt.[23] Martin Delany was extremely critical of Stowe, particularly her colonizationist stance and the fact she borrowed from slave narratives, especially Josiah Henson's, who Delany argued should get a part of the profits made from the sale of the book.[24]

Stowe's novel owed its success to, among others, the topicality of the work, authorial strategies, publisher's hype, and intense controversy as to the truth of the portrayal of the system of slavery. Whether the novel played a part in bringing about the Civil War has long been debated and raises a question that can never be fully answered: the power of fiction to influence historical events. What can safely be argued, however, is that the immense popularity of *Uncle Tom's Cabin* showed the power of fiction in the antislavery fight,[25] and placed slavery at the center of the national debate as no other work had previously done.[26] Byproducts also played a part in its success, providing countless reminders of the novel and its characters, while also transforming them as they were reappropriated in popular culture. The very success of the novel turned its characters into archetypes which later writers, whether Black or white, had to contend with when proposing their own representations of African Americans.

The Afterlife of *Uncle Tom's Cabin*

When investigating the relation of Stowe's novel with questions of race and representations, it should first be noted that whatever the era, it was reread in the light of changing contexts. Thus, after the end of Reconstruction, new editions and critical literature tended to downplay the polemic the work had caused upon publication and present it as a testimony to a bygone past. When the rights fell into the public domain in the early

1890s, the flurry of new editions, which presented the work both as a classic and a popular read, showed that the novel was still viewed as a profitable commodity. At the same time, it was increasingly interpreted as a plantation novel, partly owing to theatrical adaptations. Plays based on the novel were performed from 1852 well into the twentieth century, and they developed into a veritable industry. According to David Reynolds, there were two types of Tom shows: those that emphasized the liberation plot and those that minimized it and instead offered a romanticized vision of the plantation, in keeping with the myth of the Lost Cause.[27] As David Blight and others have shown, the last decades of the nineteenth century witnessed a wave of nostalgia for the antebellum days, partly prompted by the momentous changes American society was undergoing (fast industrialization and urbanization, massive waves of immigration), and partly by the desire for sectional reconciliation. At a time when segregation was becoming institutionalized and the number of racially motivated lynchings was increasing in the South, when all kinds of demeaning stereotypes of African Americans pervaded the nation's newspapers, plantation literature – in the works of Thomas Nelson Page, for instance – depicted slavery as essentially benign. Mainstream history provided a scholarly basis for this interpretation of history.[28] In the Tom shows modeled after plantation literature, minstrelsy "quickly cannibalized Stowe's novel," and Tom, who in the novel is presented as a strong man with small children and thus relatively young, became old and feeble.[29] This was also the way he was portrayed in many of the cheap editions of the turn of the century. as well as ads for all sorts of consumer goods – tobacco, sugar, and brooms, among others.[30] Between the 1930s and the 1950s, like its eponymous hero, Stowe's novel seemed to become increasingly irrelevant and dated. Literary scholarship dismissed the work as too sentimental, and the cartoons based on the novel contributed to its degraded reputation.[31] Yet, as Barbara Hochman has shown, between the late nineteenth century and the civil rights movement, Black readers "devoured" *Uncle Tom's Cabin*. At a time when slave narratives were largely out of print and forgotten, they turned to Stowe's novel to learn about slavery.[32] In the twentieth century, especially from the 1930s, both Black and white intellectuals increasingly rejected the novel as racist and many African Americans felt the work was in need of rewriting. This is what Richard Wright, for instance, set out to do with *Uncle Tom's Children* (1938), and later with *Native Son* (1940), whose hero, Bigger Thomas, is the polar opposite of Stowe's Uncle Tom.[33] In an influential 1949 essay, African American author James Baldwin labeled *Uncle Tom's Cabin* racist, while also calling it "a very bad novel." Stowe, Baldwin argued, had turned her hero into "a man who has been robbed of his humanity and his sex."[34] In an introduction to a 1952 edition, Langston Hughes voiced a rare dissenting opinion when he defended the novel as "a moral battle cry," not to be confused with its adaptations.[35]

The civil rights movement gave Stowe's novel a new relevance, as is evidenced in the number of essays on the book and new editions which, more often than not, invited readers to use *Uncle Tom's Cabin* in order to understand the state of race relations in contemporary America. Much as had been the case when it was first issued, there was heated debate and disagreement among commentators. Thus, while most preface writers underlined the impact of the novel on American history, historian Dwight L. Dumond argued that the idea that *Uncle Tom's Cabin* had caused the war was absurd, while another historian, John William Ward, asked "In what sense does a novel have the power to move a nation to battle?"[36] The literary evaluation of the work was diverse, and ranged from complete revaluation to complete condemnation, with a few more moderate assessments in between. The interpretation of the characters was influenced by both historiography and current events. Slavery was being rewritten as brutal, and historians such as John Hope Franklin were exploring slave culture and religion as resistance. In the ongoing civil rights movement, "Uncle Tom" was widely used as a term of abuse, and Malcolm X criticized "the white man's puppet Negro 'leaders,'" and first of all Martin Luther King.[37] Depending on critics, servility was inscribed in the main protagonist of Stowe's – racist – novel or was an unfair avatar of theatrical adaptations; Tom's Christian forbearance was viewed as merely pathetic or, conversely, the most effective form of defiance.

Since then, the discussion on *Uncle Tom's Cabin* has also been influenced by new approaches; feminist readings of the novel, starting in the 1960s but gaining speed in the 1970s and 1980s, contributed to the reassessment of the novel,[38] while also showing that Stowe had invested Tom with "feminine" qualities, thus making him a "motherly black Christ."[39] Over the past decade or so, reader reception theories, book history, childhood studies, visual studies and material culture studies have led to new explorations of the novel, its characters and their various avatars.[40] The issue of the representation of race in the novel continues to divide, even if most of today's critics agree that to a certain extent Stowe's novel is indeed racist. Richard Yarborough convincingly contends that, "Like most white writers of her day, Harriet Beecher Stowe was not especially committed to (or equipped to present) a complex, realistic depiction of blacks." This "tragic failure of imagination" made it impossible for her to envision truly equal races – thus, George's manly qualities are inherited from his white father – or a real interracial society, hence George's departure to Africa.[41] According to Toni Morrison, Stowe needed to reassure herself and her white readership that the "slave's natural instinct" was "toward kindness." As a result, the slavery depicted in *Uncle Tom's Cabin* is "sexually and romantically sanitized and perfumed." This, Morrison argues, is particularly evident in the sentimentalized relationship between Topsy and Eva ("another prime example of the romance of slavery").[42] Stephen Railton invites us to read *Uncle Tom's Cabin* to understand "how racial difference is constructed, how hard it has been for white Americans to see the other inside the dark shadows cast by their desire."[43]

While continued discussion is one of the hallmarks of classics, the rewritings of *Uncle Tom's Cabin* show that the novel still has the power to rankle. And the work has kept being retold, in dance (Bill T. Jones's 1990 *Last Supper at Uncle Tom's Cabin/The Promised Land* ends with slaves' defeating Legree through nonviolent resistance), theater (e.g., Robert Alexander's *I Ain't Yo' Uncle: The New Jack Revisionist Uncle Tom's Cabin*),[44] fiction (such as Ishmael Reed's 1976 *Flight to Canada*), and art (e.g., Kara Walker's 1995 *The End of Uncle Tom and the Grand Allegorical Tableau of Eva in Heaven*). As Samuel Otter notes, such rewritings often represent an attempt "to liberate Stowe's characters through satire and parody."[45]

Conclusion

Episode eight of the HBO series *Lovecraft Country*, which aired in early October 2020, has *Uncle Tom's Cabin*'s Topsy step out of the book cover to become a ghoul that, together with her twin Bopsy, persecutes Black teenager Dee. Earlier in 2020, a documentary movie provocatively entitled *Uncle Tom* claimed that Stowe's Uncle Tom was a hero and defended Black conservatives, often called "Uncle Toms."[46] However one interprets the documentary or the scene in the series – for instance, as a rejection of racist stereotypes associated with minstrel shows which continue to plague Black children in the 1950s, when the series is set, or yet another attempt to get rid of Stowe's troublesome classic – it is significant that more than a century and a half later, *Uncle Tom's Cabin* still plays a role in representations of race in the United States. This chapter has shown that this was partly due to the prodigious success of the novel when it first appeared, and partly to the very many adaptations and rewritings of *Uncle Tom's Cabin* and its various characters. The *Annotated Uncle Tom's Cabin*, edited by Henry Louis Gates Jr. and Hollis Robbins,[47] juxtaposes Stowe's text and some of its avatars, thereby providing readers with a complex approach to a multilayered text. A stage adaptation performed in New York in December 1997 and January 2010 adopted a similar strategy, and offered spectators extracts from *Uncle Tom's Cabin* together with excerpts from slave narratives and nineteenth- and twentieth-century reviews and theatrical adaptations of the novel.[48] In sum, it is next to impossible today to approach *Uncle Tom's Cabin* innocently, as it were, and ignore more than 150 years of debate and discussion over the text and its representations of African Americans, complicated by visual, material, and other types of artifacts. Ultimately, the continued relevance of a nineteenth-century novel in today's debate about race and representations has much to do with the fact it "addresses itself to a nation that remains bitterly divided by racism, race consciousness, and the unresolved memory of slavery."[49]

Notes

1. Leslie Fiedler, *The Inadvertent Epic: From Uncle Tom's Cabin to Roots* (Toronto: Canadian Broadcasting Corporation, 1979), 26.
2. Richard Yarborough, "Strategies of Black Characterization in *Uncle Tom's Cabin* and the Early Afro-American Novel," in Eric J. Sundquist, ed., *New Essays on Uncle Tom's Cabin* (Cambridge: Cambridge University Press, 1993 [1986]), 45–84.
3. For a comprehensive history of the antislavery movement, see Manisha Sinha, *The Slave's Cause* (New Haven: Yale University Press, 2016).
4. For a biography of Stowe, see Joan Hedrick 's superb *Harriet Beecher Stowe: A Life* (New York: Oxford University Press, 1994). Also see her essay "Stowe's Life and *Uncle Tom's Cabin*": http://utc.iath.virginia.edu/interpret/exhibits/hedrick/hedrick.html.
5. *National Era*, November 7, 1851; August 28, 1851 for the last two quotes. The excellent website "Uncle Tom's Cabin and American Culture," directed by Stephen Railton at the University of Virginia, which provides a wealth of information, primary sources, and essays on the publication, reception, and afterlife of the novel, reproduces several of the readers' letters: http://utc.iath.virginia.edu/sitemap.html. On the serialization of *Uncle Tom's Cabin*, see, among others , Claire Parfait, *The Publishing History of* Uncle Tom's Cabin, *1852–2002* (Aldershot: Ashgate, 2007), chapter 1.
6. Topsy had been hardened by the brutalities of slavery, but she is transformed by Little Eva's love and death. While Robin Bernstein agrees that Topsy is a "minstrel-influenced caricature," she also contends that Stowe "created in

Topsy an extraordinarily sophisticated and powerful argument for enslaved children's essential innocence and their susceptibility to suffering": Robin Bernstein, *Racial Innocence: Performing American Childhood from Slavery to Civil Rights* (New York: New York University Press, 2011), 44–48.

7. *Uncle Tom's Cabin* (Boston, John P. Jewett, 1852), vol. 2, 317; italics in the original. Joan D. Hedrick, ed. *The Oxford Harriet Beecher Stowe Reader* (New York: Oxford University Press, 1999), 77.
8. "Introduction," in Shirley Samuels, ed., *The Culture of Sentiment. Race, Gender, and Sentimentality in 19th-Century America* (New York: Oxford University Press, 1992), 4.
9. Philip Fisher, *Hard Facts. Setting and Form in the American Novel* (New York: Oxford University Press, 1985), 100.
10. Stowe had Black servants in Cincinnati, and Hedrick rightly notes that her knowledge of African Americans "was garnered mainly in domestic settings in which her position as white mistress to black servants radically compromised her perceptions" (Hedrick, *Harriet Beecher Stowe*: 209). Stowe read a few slave narratives, most notably the story of Josiah Henson (whom she had met, according to her son, http://utc.iath.virginia.edu/articles/n2escesb1t.html), and most likely those of Henry Bibb and Frederick Douglass; she wrote to Frederick Douglass to obtain information on cotton plantations: Charles Edward Stowe and Lyman Beecher Stowe, *Harriet Beecher Stowe, The Story of Her Life* (Boston: Houghton Mifflin, 1911), 144; 149–155.
11. Stowe was aware that antislavery publications were censored or banned in the South (see, for example, Sinha, *The Slave's Cause*, 250–51); furthermore, she believed alienating Southerners would only make them more eager to defend slavery.
12. A contemporary commentator explained that the "miracle" of *Uncle Tom's Cabin* had been made possible by the improvements in printing technology and transportation, as well as the increasing number of readers in the United States: Unsigned article (Charles Briggs), "Uncle Tomitudes" (*Putnam's Monthly*, January 1853), 97–102.
13. It should be noted, however, that because Jewett's archives seem to have disappeared, there is no archival evidence as to the real sales of the novel.
14. The word "bestseller" itself did not appear until the last decade of the nineteenth century; see, for example, John Sutherland, *Bestsellers: Popular Fiction of the 1970s* (Abingdon: Taylor & Francis, 2010 [1981]), 8.
15. On the publishing history of *Uncle Tom's Cabin*, see Parfait, *Publishing History*, and Michael Winship's essay "*Uncle Tom's Cabin*: History of the Book in the 19th-Century United States": https://utc.iath.virginia.edu/interpret/exhibits/winship/winship.html.
16. A number of these early byproducts, as well as later ones, can be viewed at http://utc.iath.virginia.edu/tomituds/tohp.html; also see Louise L. Stevenson, "Virtue Displayed: The Tie-Ins of *Uncle Tom's Cabin*," http://utc.iath.virginia.edu/interpret/exhibits/stevenson/stevenson.html, and Sarah Meer, *Uncle Tom*

Mania: Slavery, Minstrelsy and Transatlantic Culture in the 1850s (Athens: University of Georgia Press, 2005).

17. This led Stowe to produce *A Key to Uncle Tom's Cabin* (Boston: John P. Jewett, 1853), a volume which gathers documentary evidence of the cruelties of slavery.
18. On the reception of the novel, see Thomas F. Gossett, *Uncle Tom's Cabin and American Culture* (Dallas: Southern Methodist university Press, 1985). Primary sources can be found at http://utc.iath.virginia.edu/reviews/rehp.html and http://utc.iath.virginia.edu/africam/afarticles.html.
19. The novel was quickly banned in the South but continued to circulate secretly. See Parfait, *Publishing History*, 94–98. *Uncle Tom's Cabin* was also a global phenomenon. On the international career of Stowe's novel and its uses and reappropriations in various parts of the world, see Tracy C. Davis and Stefka Mihaylova, eds., *Uncle Tom's Cabins. The Transnational History of America's Most Mutable Book* (Ann Arbor: University of Michigan Press, 2018).
20. Thomas Gossett lists twenty-seven pro-slavery fictional responses to Stowe's novel in his Uncle Tom's Cabin *and American Culture* (chapter XII); for a sample of this type of fiction, see http://utc.iath.virginia.edu/proslav/antitoms.html.
21. Sinha, *Slave's Cause*, 443.
22. George Frederickson, *The Black Image in the White Mind: The Debate on Afro-American Character and Destiny, 1817–1914* (New York: Harper & Row, 1971), 107.
23. Robert B. Stepto, "Sharing the Thunder: The Literary Exchanges of Harriet Beecher Stowe, Henry Bibb, and Frederick Douglass," in Eric J. Sundquist, ed., *New Essays on Uncle Tom's Cabin* (Cambridge: Cambridge University Press, 1993 [1986]), 135–153.
24. On the Douglass–Delany debate on Stowe's novel, see Robert S. Levine, *Martin Delany, Frederick Douglass, and the Politics of Representative Identity* (Chapel Hill: The University of North Carolina Press, 1997), chapter 2.
25. There seem to have been about a dozen antislavery novels before *Uncle Tom's Cabin*, but they have hardly left a mark, save perhaps for white historian Richard Hildreth's *The Slave; or Memoirs* of *Archie Moore*, which Hildreth published anonymously in 1836, and which purported to be a slave narrative; there were even fewer novels penned by African Americans before the Civil War. At a time when the authors of slave narratives went to great lengths to prove their authenticity, the use of fiction to denounce the horrors of slavery may have seemed counterproductive. See Claire Parfait, "Fiction and the Debate over Slavery," in Michaël Roy, Marie-Jeanne Rossignol, and Claire Parfait (eds.), *Undoing Slavery: American Abolitionism in Transnational Perspective (1776–1865)* (Paris: Éditions Rue d'Ulm, 2018), 75–92.
26. Solomon Northup and his publishers were to capitalize on the popularity of *Uncle Tom's Cabin*, as Michael Roy demonstrates in "Cheap Editions, Little

Books, and Handsome Duodecimos: A Book History Approach to Antebellum Slave Narratives," *MELUS: Multi-Ethnic Literature of the United States* (vol. 40, no. 3, 2015), 69–93.

27. David S. Reynolds, *Mightier than the Sword: Uncle Tom's Cabin and the Battle for America* (New York: W. W. Norton, 2011): see chapter 5 on Tom shows, chapter 6 on movie adaptations.
28. David Blight, *Race and Reunion: The Civil War in American Memory* (Cambridge: Harvard University Press, 2001). As to mainstream history, the interpretation of slavery as benign finds perhaps its best interpretation in white historian Ulrich Bonnell Phillips 's *American Negro Slavery* (New York: D. Appleton, 1918), which was to hold sway until the 1950s, when slavery was rewritten as a brutal institution.
29. Meer, *Uncle Tom Mania*, 59. On theatrical adaptations, see Meer, ibid.; Gossett, Uncle Tom's Cabin *and American Culture*, chapters XIV (especially pp. 278–280 on the "aging" of Tom) and XIX; Patricia A. Turner, *Ceramic Uncles and Celluloid Mammies: Black Images and Their Influence on Culture* (New York: Anchor Books, 1994); Adena Spingarn, *Uncle Tom: from Martyr to Traitor* (Stanford: Stanford University Press, 2018); also see primary sources at http://utc.iath.virginia.edu/onstage/oshp.html and John Frick's interpretive essay at http://utc.iath.virginia.edu/interpret/exhibits/frick/frick.html, as well as Reynolds, *Mightier.* Unlike other scholars, Reynolds contends that Tom shows, which in the early 1870s started using Black performers rather than whites in blackface, actually represented a form of empowerment for African American actors and spectators, that they disseminated African American culture, especially spirituals, and that minstrel shows allowed Black minstrels to spread subversive messages.
30. Parfait, *Publishing History*, 167–175.
31. Ibid., 180–181.
32. Barbara Hochman, *Uncle Tom's Cabin and the Reading Revolution: Race, Literacy, Childhood and Fiction, 1851–1911* (Amherst: University of Massachusetts Press, 2011), 231–251.
33. On this and other rewritings of Stowe's characters by African American writers, see Yarborough, "Strategies." The novel was also rewritten from a white Southern point of view in the twentieth century, most notably by Thomas Dixon, whose 1903 novel *The Clansman* served as the basis for D. W. Griffith's monumentally successful and controversial movie *Birth of a Nation* (1915); Dixon had attended a Tom show in 1901 and wrote a trilogy meant to revise Stowe's novel; Margaret Mitchell's *Gone With the Wind* (1936) was also partly meant as an answer to *Uncle Tom's Cabin*: see Reynolds, *Mightier*: chapter 6.
34. Baldwin provides a scathing criticism of both *Uncle Tom's Cabin* and Wright's novel *Native Son* in "Everybody's Protest Novel," *Partisan Review* 16 (June 1949), 578–585.
35. Langston Hughes, Introduction, *Uncle Tom's Cabin* (New York: Dodd, Mead & Co., Great Illustrated Classics, 1952).

36. Dwight L. Dumond, Introduction, Classic Collier Books (1962), 10; John William Ward, Afterword, Signet Classics (1966), 480.
37. See chapter 6 in Reynolds, *Mightier*, for a fascinating exploration of the use of "Uncle Tom" as a term of abuse in the twentieth century; *The Autobiography of Malcolm X* (London: Penguin, 2001 [1965]), 349.
38. Thus, Jane Tompkins and Nina Baym, among others, explained that Stowe and other female writers had been excluded from the canon because the latter had been defined by (white) men: see their essays (Tompkins, "Sentimental Power, *Uncle Tom's Cabin* and the Politics of Literary History," 81–104; Baym, "Melodramas of Beset Manhood – How Theories of American Fiction Exclude Women Authors," 63–80) in Elaine Showalter, ed., *The New Feminist Criticism: Essays on Women, Literature, and Theory* (New York: Pantheon Books, 1985).
39. Elizabeth Ammons, "Stowe's Dream of the Mother-Savior: Uncle Tom's Cabin and American Women Writers Before the 1920s," in Eric J. Sundquist, *New Essays on Uncle Tom's Cabin* (Cambridge: Cambridge University Press, 1993 [1986]): 155–195.
40. See, among others, Hochman, *Uncle Tom's Cabin and the Reading Revolution*; Bernstein, *Racial Innocence*; Jo-Ann Morgan, *Uncle Tom's Cabin as Visual Culture* (Columbia: University of Missouri Press, 2007).
41. Yarborough, "Strategies," 65.
42. Toni Morrison, *The Origin of Others* (Cambridge: Harvard University Press, 2017), 9–14, 10, 14.
43. Stephen Railton, "Black Slaves and White Readers," in Elizabeth Ammons and Susan Belasco, eds., *Approaches to Teaching Stowe's* Uncle Tom's Cabin (New York: Modern Language Association of America, 2000), 104–110.
44. Woodstock, Ill.: Dramatic Pub., 1996.
45. Samuel Otter, "*Uncle Tom's Cabin* and Race," in Cyndy Weinstein, ed., *The Cambridge Companion to Harriet Beecher Stowe* (Cambridge: Cambridge University Press, 2004), 15–38, 19.
46. *Uncle Tom: An Oral History of the American Black Conservative*, directed by Justin Malone, produced by Larry Elder, 2020.
47. New York: W. W. Norton, 2007.
48. *Uncle Tom's Cabin or Life Among the Lowly*, adapted by Floraine Kay and Randoph Curtis Rand, directed by R. C. Rand, Greenwich House Theater; In 2010, the Metropolitan Playhouse in New York put up a production of George Aiken's 1850s adaptation which, according to Gossett, was the most important, albeit not the first, stage adaptation of the novel (Gossett, Uncle Tom's Cabin *and American Culture*, 262), www.metropolitanplayhouse.org/uncletomscabin.
49. Daniel R. Vollaro, "Lincoln, Stowe, and the 'Little Woman/Great War' Story: The Making, and Breaking, of a Great American Anecdote," *Journal of the Abraham Lincoln Association*, vol. 30, no. 1 (winter 2009), 18–34.

CHAPTER 17

The Legacy of Toni Morrison
Black Writers, Invisibility, and Intimacy

Stephanie Li

After reading Ralph Ellison's *Invisible Man* (1952), Toni Morrison famously asked, "Invisible to whom? Not me."[1] For decades following the publication of Ellison's masterpiece, invisibility functioned as the dominant metaphor by which to understand Black subjectivity. To be Black was to be discounted and dismissed by mainstream society. To be Black was to exist outside the field of vision. However, as Morrison implies in her sharp response, Ellison's conception of Blackness is entirely dependent on a white gaze. The Invisible Man is invisible because white people cannot see him; they only see the stereotypes that define Blackness. To be invisible is to be constructed through whiteness and to long for the validation of a society built upon the plunder of Black bodies.

By contrast, Morrison always understood herself to be visible to her community, her family, and her people as a whole. Where Morrison presumes intimacy and belonging, Ellison's protagonist languishes in the solitude derived from his demand to be seen by white peers. Morrison's response to *Invisible Man* begs a question Ellison entirely avoids: What has happened to this man's people? How could his mother and father, his sisters and brothers, cousins, and, of course, his grandfather allow their child to hole himself up in some underground lair and let him believe that his identity is premised only upon the blindnesses of white people? But such speculations are impossible to contemplate within the narrow scope of Ellison's novel. These other characters, as vital as they must have once been to the formation of this iconic narrator, are not just invisible, they are all but nonexistent. By focusing entirely on the plight of a lone individual, Ellison portrayed a man effectively devoid of all ties to family and a meaningful past. There is no room in his magisterial novel for the very community that might have freed the Invisible Man from the despair of his invisibility.

The difference in how Ellison and Morrison conceived of Black subjectivity has profound consequences for how we understand the audience of African American literature in the contemporary period. Who are twenty-first-century Black authors writing for? Do they assume invisibility or intimacy? How do they contend with the aspects of Black life that still remain opaque to white readers while also asserting the community that grounds Black literature in a complex network of intertextual exchange? Ellison and Morrison represent twin poles of such considerations, from the implicit desire for white validation to the bold expectation that Black life not be explained to outsiders. However, these concerns are also complicated by the continued need to enlist white readers in the political and cultural change necessary to transform the racist hierarchies and institutions that undergird American society. Evidence of Ellison's and Morrison's respective approaches to Black literature is reflected in two recent texts by prominent African American writers. Ta-Nehisi Coates's *Between the World and Me* (2015)[2] and Imani Perry's *Breathe: A Letter to My Sons* (2019) both highlight how key aspects of Black life remain invisible to white observers while also using readerly intimacy as a potent force for social change. These texts demonstrate the continued tension of presenting Black writing within a national landscape dominated by white hegemonic power.

Morrison's Visibility

In her writing as in her life, Morrison had no patience for the self-imposed isolation of men like the Invisible Man and his creator. Following the publication of his novel, Ellison cultivated a disciplined solitude in which to write and rewrite a long-awaited second novel that was only published posthumously.[3] During these very decades, Morrison was just beginning her own literary career but never failed to enthusiastically champion the voices of young Black writers. While an editor at Random House, she helped launch the careers of Henry Dumas and Gayl Jones, and also convinced both Angela Davis and Muhammed Ali to pen their autobiographies. If Ellison would come to define the Black experience by invisibility and his own writerly life by isolation, Morrison actively refuted such choices by exulting in a community of Black writers and activists. She and her peers may have been invisible or misunderstood by white onlookers but such ignorance was secondary to the unity and purpose of their collective sense of self.

The solitude of the Invisible Man is not just a condition of his hibernation but a reflection of the audience Ellison ultimately sought to address. Just as the Invisible Man longs to be seen by whites, Ellison implicitly craved the validation of white readers and inclusion in a decidedly Western canon. In one of his most famous essays, "The World and the Jug," he distinguished between writers he identified as his literary "relatives" and others he called his "ancestors." "Relatives," he explained, included contemporaries such as Langston Hughes and Richard Wright, who he was associated with due to a shared cultural heritage and historical experience, while literary "ancestors" were those he chose – writers such as Ernest Hemingway and T. S. Eliot, who he identified as significantly impacting his own writing style. Ellison asserted "while one can do nothing about choosing one's relatives, one can, as artist, choose one's 'ancestors.'"[4] Despite the importance of writers exercising the freedom to identify their own primary influences, it is impossible to ignore the conspicuous racial divide in the examples Ellison provides. Even as *Invisible Man* is clearly indebted to the music of the blues and other aspects of the African American literary tradition, Ellison continually looked to non-Black sources to validate the experience of his protagonist as well as his own artistic reputation.

Like Ellison, Morrison speaks glowingly of white authors who have influenced her approach to literature, but she does not make such sharp distinctions between literary relatives and ancestors. Instead, her work welcomes comparison to a host of different writers from a variety of racial and historical backgrounds. Morrison wrote her masters' thesis on William Faulkner and Virginia Woolf, and it is impossible not to see connections between her work and those esteemed writers. Countless articles have been written on the relationship between Morrison and a number of key white male writers, such as Nathaniel Hawthorne, Ernest Hemingway, Philip Roth, John Updike, and many others. Morrison has also written of her admiration for the work of Herman Melville and Henry James. These writers are less ancestors for her than touchstones for the kind of cultural specificity and critical inquiry she demonstrates in her novels. However, when she turned to African American authors, she was often frustrated by their tone and condescending approach to Black life. While Ellison objected to comparisons between his work and other Black writers simply on the basis of race, Morrison found that many of these authors, especially those most celebrated by white critics, did not provide useful models of address. She took issue not with being aligned with literary "relatives" but instead with how these "relatives" presented their work:

> I was preoccupied with books by black people that approached the subject, but I always missed some intimacy, some direction, some voice. Ralph Ellison and Richard Wright – all of whose books I admire enormously – I didn't feel were telling me something. I thought they were saying something about *it* or *us* that revealed something about *us* to *you*, to others, to white people, to men . . . When I began writing I was writing as though there was nobody in the world but me and the characters, as though I was talking to them, or us, and it just had a different sound to it.[5]

Morrison's concern about audience has been a long-standing point of contention since the inception of African American print literature. Ironically, Black writers and intellectuals have championed the importance of crafting literature specifically for African Americans for decades. Early in the twentieth century, W. E. B. Du Bois lamented how Black writers "are handing everything over to a white jury," decrying a system in which "[i]f a colored man wants to publish a book, he has got to get a white publisher and a white newspaper to say it is great; and then you and I say so." Du Bois instead affirmed that "[w]e must come to the place where the work of art when it appears is reviewed and acclaimed by our own free and unfettered judgment."[6] Despite this impassioned call to empower both Black writers and audiences, the major African American authors of the day continued to fulfill artistic expectations defined by white standards. While pioneering authors such as Langston Hughes and Zora Neale Hurston certainly longed to craft a more independent voice, their financial struggles and dependence on such white patrons as Charlotte Osgood Mason – or Godmother, as she insisted on being called – complicated any simple claim to artistic freedom. Echoing Du Bois a generation later, Richard Wright was also impatient for Black writing that would be directed solely to Black readers, asking, "Today the question is: Shall Negro writing be for the Negro masses, molding the lives and consciousness of those masses toward new goals, or shall it continue begging the question of the Negroes' humanity?"[7] And yet, as Baldwin famously observed, *Native Son* (1940), Wright's most famous novel, reinforces destructive stereotypes about Black violence and animality.[8] Many viewed such depictions as yet another concession to white conceptions of Black subjectivity.

In sharp contradiction to these postwar male authors, Morrison long insisted that she wrote explicitly for Black people. She began her first novel by conceiving of it as a book she herself wanted to read. Then a single mother in upstate New York with no extended family nearby, Morrison turned to fiction writing to create the community she lacked in the flesh. When she began drafting sections of *The Bluest Eye* (1970), texts by early-twentieth-century women writers like Zora Neale Hurston, Jessie Fauset, and Ann Petry were out of print. Morrison found herself most energized by the work of African writers such as Chinua Achebe, Aime Cesaire, and Camara Laye, who "did not explain their black world." These African writers took their Blackness as central and the whites were the 'other.'"[9] Morrison's admiration for this approach fundamentally influenced her lifelong commitment to writing for a Black audience. Unlike Ellison, she assumes her own visibility and that of her characters as she explores the inner workings of an independent and deeply complex Black social structure. This difference in literary approach has stark ramifications for the narrative effects of these two consequential writers and demonstrates how Morrison has fundamentally transformed contemporary Black writing.

Audience Address in *Invisible Man* and *The Bluest Eye*

The opening lines of both *Invisible Man* and *The Bluest Eye* can be read as confessions, but while Ellison's protagonist speaks to an abstract other who is seemingly removed from his personal circumstances, Claudia MacTeer, Morrison's young narrator, assumes intimacy with her addressee. Ellison begins:

> I am an invisible man. No, I am not a spook like those who haunted Edgar Allan Poe; nor am I one of your Hollywood-movie ectoplasms. I am a man of substance, of flesh and bone, fiber and liquids – and I might even be said to possess a mind. I am invisible, understand, simply because people refuse to see me. Like the bodiless heads you see sometimes in circus sideshows, it is as though I have been surrounded by mirrors of hard, distorting glass. When they approach me they see only my surroundings, themselves, or figments of their imagination – indeed, everything and anything except me.[10]

The Invisible Man vividly describes what it is like to encounter white people who project their stereotypes and false expectations of Blackness onto him. He does not specify that the people who "refuse to see me" are white because whiteness is the precondition of his sense of self. He is not visible without them. Similarly, to explain this dynamic between white observers and Black subjects is to affirm a white audience, and specifically readers at a remove from his personal experience. Will these readers understand what the Invisible Man describes? Ellison instills no assumption of trust; he remains alone in his narration, writing to an audience that becomes as much of an abstraction as the family that created him.

While Ellison effectively writes to a stranger, Morrison begins *The Bluest Eye* in an entirely other kind of register: "*Quiet as it's kept, there were no marigolds in the fall of 1941.*"[11] The intimacy between text and reader is immediate as the narrator divulges a type of secret knowledge. The voice speaks in a private, hushed tone to an audience that is consequently figured as a confidant, someone who is worthy of the trust necessary to comprehend the tragic story of a little girl's demise. In "Unspeakable Things Unspoken," Morrison elaborates on the dynamic she aimed to capture in this opening sentence:

> First, it was a familiar phrase, familiar to me as a child listening to adults; to black women conversing with one another; telling a story, an anecdote, gossip about someone or event within the circle, the family, the neighborhood. The words are conspiratorial . . . It is a secret between us and a secret that is being kept from us. The conspiracy is both held and withheld, exposed and sustained. In some sense it was precisely what the act of writing the book was: the public exposure of a private confidence.[12]

Where Ellison sought to explain the experience of Blackness confronted by a white gaze, Morrison establishes what she terms "instant intimacy."[13] She assumes that the reader can and will occupy an insider position in her texts. This is not to suggest that white audiences cannot appreciate her work, but as the novel unfolds it is clear that Claudia operates in a world that is almost exclusively African American. With the exception of an irritating girl in her neighborhood, she does not speak to white characters; she does not presume that they understand her or her world. Claudia's disgust for the white dolls that Black girls receive indicates that she is deeply impacted by the ideals of whiteness but individual whites are peripheral to her emerging sense of self. It's not that she doesn't care about white people; rather, given the dynamic community around her, they simply don't register as particularly important or noteworthy. The same might be said of Morrison's approach to white readers. Even as they may read her work, they are marginal to the world she portrays.

Fifty years since the publication of *The Bluest Eye*, issues of audience are still paramount to conceptions of African American literature. Morrison's specific address to Black audiences does not imply that all contemporary Black writers follow in her stead. Rather, the difference between her work and that of Ellison is a dynamic that continues to shape Black letters. Morrison wrote her novels keenly aware of the print origin of the Black literary tradition which emerged from a marketplace and social economy defined by white political power. In "The Site of Memory," she explains that the authors of slave narratives wrote with an explicit political agenda: to end chattel slavery. As a result, their texts were directed specifically at Northern white readers with the power to bring about abolition. This address led to omissions and rhetorical indulgences that flattered nineteenth-century audiences convinced of their own righteousness despite the mass horrors that enabled the success of the nation. Morrison observes of formerly enslaved narrators:

> In shaping the experience to make it palatable to those who were in a position to alleviate it, they were silent about many things, and they "forgot" many other things. There was a careful selection of the instances that they would record and a careful rendering of those that they chose to describe . . . But most importantly – at least for me – there was no mention of their interior life.

Morrison wrote *Beloved* (1986) specifically to fill a historical record left vacant by the silence of enslaved men and women. Aware of the limitations of slave narratives, she explains that as "a writer who is black and a woman . . . [m]y job becomes how to rip that veil drawn over 'proceedings too horrible to relate'"[14] to expose the psychological and emotional violence endured by Black slaves. Morrison's project in *Beloved* affirms a freedom made possible by a nation that is no longer dependent upon the enslaved labor of an entire people. And yet the political imperative that drove writers such as Frederick Douglass, Harriet Jacobs, William Wells Brown, and many others to tell their stories has not vanished nearly 200 years later. Slavery has been abolished but African Americans hardly enjoy the freedoms and privileges of their fellow white citizens.

Between the World and Me and *Breathe*

The precarity of the contemporary Black body is at the center of Ta-Nehisi Coates's acclaimed nonfiction narrative, *Between the World and Me*. Presented as a letter to his teenage son Samori, Coates describes what it means to be a Black man in twenty-first-century America. Despite the book's purportedly singular Black audience, Coates has admitted that the epistolary address is a rhetorical device. *Between the World and Me* operates much like James Baldwin's essay "Letter to My Nephew," which was first published in *The Progressive* in 1962; it is a staged confidence made public with significant political implications for non-Black readers. Both Baldwin and Coates construct their audience as a kind of eavesdropper on a deeply intimate exchange. And yet such intimacy is a manufactured conceit.

Though Coates, like Baldwin, may be passing down vital advice to a young male relative, he hardly needs to publish a bestselling book that was lauded on the pages of nearly every national newspaper to do so. As Jon Stewart wryly noted to Coates on *The Daily Show*, there is genuine cause for concern if Coates believes this is the best way to reach his son.[15] But of course, Coates is not writing to his son in the pages of the book; there is even some question as to whether he is addressing a Black audience at all, for, as Simon Abramowitsch notes, "the racism documented here will surprise no black reader."[16] Who, then, is Coates addressing as he adopts this rhetorical device?

Throughout *Between the World and Me*, Coates describes key moments in his personal development while also providing deeply historicized reflections on American triumphalism. As befits the comments of an adult man speaking to a child, his thoughts are instructive, even educational in their academic sourcing. And yet Coates's son no doubt already knows all these lessons, has heard his father's stories of Howard or the Mecca countless times, and can likely recite his father's thoughts on Bellow and Tolstoy. Repetition is not the point; Samori Coates need never read this book because it is not for him. Instead, its lessons and wisdom are for others, for those who don't know why Coates did not comfort his son following the acquittal of Darren Wilson, the officer who shot eighteen-year old Michael Brown Jr. in Ferguson, Missouri in 2014, nor mourn the dead of 9/11. The book's particular address affords Coates a mode of reflection that circumvents accusation in favor of hard-won parental wisdom. No one can deny the right, if not the actual necessity, of a father passing down his experience and insight to his child. Coates's address to his son thus aligns him with what Dana A. Williams describes as his "secondary audience" – that is "white people"[17] – through a desire that operates independently of race: to provide advice and counsel to one's child. This appeal through the parental bond has precedent in nineteenth-century African American literature.

In *Incidents in the Life of a Slave Girl* (1861), Harriet Jacobs makes a direct plea to women of the North to aid the enslaved Black women of the South. Throughout her slave narrative, Jacobs highlights her experiences as a mother to elicit the empathy of white women who are repeatedly asked to imagine being separated from their children or watching their brothers and cousins horrifically abused by slavemasters. By defining herself primarily as a mother and as a woman who draws her strength and resistance to the slave system most acutely from a desire to protect her children, Jacobs powerfully enjoins white readers to recognize the humanity of Black women. A similar dynamic is at play in *Between the World and Me*, in which Coates, from the opening word of the book, "Son," identifies himself most potently as a father. What does it mean to father a Black son at this historical moment? Although the book presents itself as a statement about what Black boys need to know to survive in America, it is most powerfully an exposition of Black parenting at a time in which Claudia Rankine has described Black life as a condition of mourning.[18] Even as Coates addresses his son with the tenderness and wisdom of a loving father, he effectively rips another "veil drawn over 'proceedings too horrible to relate'" – that is, the proceedings of what it means to raise a child amid such immediate dangers. This is information otherwise unavailable to non-Black audiences: the anguish of sending a son into a world in which he is vulnerable to the casual but lethal mistakes of police force, and the daily disregard of a society founded on white supremacy.

Coates begins his book by describing his interview with a popular news show: "the host wished to know why I felt that white America's progress, or rather the progress of those Americans who believe that they are white, was built on looting and violence" (5–6). Coates explains that "[t]he answer to this question is the record of the believers themselves" (6), clarifying that the false belief of this population is whiteness: "Difference in hue and hair, the notion that these factors can correctly organize a society and that they signify deeper attributes, which are indelible – this is the new idea at the heart of these new people who have been brought up hopelessly, tragically, deceitfully, to believe that they are white" (7). Much of *Between the World and Me* is dedicated to describing people who "believe that they are white" and what Coates identifies as the "Dream" that sustains this illusion. The Dream is "perfect houses with nice lawns. It is Memorial Day cookouts, block associations, and driveways." The Dream mirrors the aspirations of the American Dream, a suburban, patriarchal fantasy that is built both on the false premise of American meritocracy and willful ignorance of the nation's violent history of slavery, genocide, and institutionalized racism. Coates admits that the Dream is seductive, but it is ultimately an impossibility for African Americans:

> And for so long I have wanted to escape into the Dream, to fold my country over my head like a blanket. But that has never been an option because the Dream rests on our backs, the bedding made from our bodies. And knowing this, knowing that the Dream persists by warring with the known world, I was sad for the host, I was sad for all those families, I was sad for my country, but above all, in that moment, I was sad for you. (11)

Although Coates does not specifically define the Dream as a racialized category, it is best understood as a compelling metaphor for whiteness. Those who believe themselves to be white are in thrall to the Dream.

While *Between the World and Me* lacks the overt address to white readers evident in slave narratives by Harriet Jacobs, Frederick Douglass, and many others, it participates in a Black literary tradition that affirms the political utility of educating a white audience. In this way, Coates departs from the primary focus on Black readers demonstrated by Morrison. However, this does not suggest that Morrison's model is the only or the most important way of defining Black letters. In fact, Morrison helped make *Between the World and Me* one of the most read and debated books of 2015 with her prominently printed blurb on the text's cover: "This is required reading." And yet, there remains in Coates's work a remnant of Ellison's plea for visibility. What has shifted is that while the Invisible Man longs to be seen by white people, Coates longs for the Dreamers to awaken from their pernicious illusions. For Coates to be seen, the Dream must be vanquished. The Dream threatens all people; it does not just erase the humanity of African Americans, but it also undermines the viability of our collective future as humans on this planet:

> [S]hould the Dreamers reap what they had sown, we would reap it right with them. Plunder has matured into habit and addiction; the people who could author the mechanized death of our ghettos, the mass rape of private prisons, then engineer their own forgetting, must inevitably plunder much more. This is not a belief in prophecy but in the seductiveness of cheap gasoline.[19]

Coates writes with the urgent address of a parent desperate to protect his child, but while Ellison closes *Invisible Man* with the question "Who knows but that on the lower frequencies, I speak for you?,"[20] *Between the World and Me* does not rest on some universal conflation between Black and white. Coates does not speak for whites even as he implicitly speaks to whites.

Imani Perry's *Breath* might simplistically be understood as a feminist response to *Between the World and Me*. The mother of two sons, Freeman Diallo and Issa Garner, Perry addresses her book to them. Again, a private correspondence is made public and the conceit of intimacy allows for a rich exploration of Black life in the twenty-first century. However, unlike Coates, Perry does not immediately begin her epistolary text with a direct address to her children. Instead, she opens by meditating on one of the book's epigraphs: "It must be terrifying to raise a Black boy in

America," which she credits as spoken by "Everybody and their mother (and father too)":

> Between me and these others – who utter the sentence – the indelicate assertion hangs mid-air. Without hesitation, they speculate as if it is a statement of fact. I look into their wide eyes. I see them hungry for my suffering, or crude with sympathy, or grateful they are not in such a circumstance. Sometimes they are even curious. It makes my blood boil, my mind furnace-hot. I seldom answer a word.
>
> I am indignant to their pitying eyes. I do not want to be their emotional spectacle. I want them to admit that you are people. Black boys. People. This fact, simple as it is, shouldn't linger on the surface. It should penetrate. It often doesn't. Not in this country anyway.[21]

This frame, which is followed on page three by the start of Perry's letter (she begins "Sons,"), reminds readers that the text's epistolary form operates in a larger political and social context than a letter from a parent might suggest. Perry is taking deliberate aim at people who understand the raising of Black sons as defined by fear. While Coates highlights again and again his fear of violence, Perry, though not diminishing such immediate concerns to the Black body, confronts another kind of misperception. Like Coates, Perry describes an encounter with white people who fail to understand Black subjectivity. For Coates this is an experience rooted in his body or, as he opens his book, "Last Sunday the host of a popular news show asked me what it meant to lose my body."[22] By contrast, Perry's sense of alienation emanates from her relationship to her sons and the assumption that raising Black boys is terrifying. Defining herself through her children, Perry presents an experience of Blackness that is inextricable from family. Of course, Coates is writing to his son and in that way he affirms his parental connection, but in his encounter with the news anchor he remains alone, isolated from community and family.

This difference draws attention to the opening phrase of Perry's *Breath*, "Between me and these others," which must be read as an implicit critique of the title of Coates's book. *Between the World and Me* is a direct allusion to the Richard Wright poem of the same name that describes a man who comes upon the remains of a lynching: "the sooty details of the scene rose, thrusting themselves between the world and me."[23] The man is gripped by fear as he catalogs the gin-flask, cigarette butts, peanut shells, and broken clothes left by the violence wrought. Terror lies then between the man and the world, the constant threat of harm and death suffered by the lynching victim. Consistent with this sensibility, Coates describes his obsessive vigilance that leads him to distrust a friendly stranger in France and to nearly come to blows with a man over a woman who pushes his son. It is precisely this fear which Perry counters in the opening of *Breathe*. She challenges the belief that fear is at the root of Black parenting. Instead, she heeds her mother's observation, "Mothering Black boys in America – that is a special calling," and examines in the book an answer to the questions "How do I meet it? What is it like?" For Perry, what lies between her and the world is not fear but layers of voices, both familial and literary. There are the words of her relatives which punctuate the text but also a lattice of allusions to African American writers. In addition to gesturing to Coates and Wright in her opening line, she immediately responds to the question of how she meets the special calling of raising Black sons with a series of queries that recall Langston Hughes's poem, "What Happens to a Dream Deferred?" She writes, "Is it like cultivating diamonds? Pressure that is so tight that it turns you, Black, into something white and shiny and deemed precious and valuable: That is no good. Do I fuel it like coal, something that is to be burned up and used for the warmth of others? Or the consolation prize on Christmas? That's no good either."[24]

Perry's numerous literary allusions formally demonstrate how her voice emanates from a community of beloved predecessors. She is no lone speaker of invisibility but a woman constituted through a diverse array of personal and artistic influences. Even as she too participates in a rhetorical strategy that belies a broader form of address, Perry continually returns to her own story as the foundation for the wisdom she wishes to impart to her son. While Coates is especially animated by describing the pernicious effects of "the Dream" and the illusions of whiteness, Perry explains to her sons that "[g]iving you the space to know me, gives you space to become you."[25] In this way, Perry provides a more intimate description of her upbringing, her closest relatives and the stories that defined her childhood. Though Perry effectively appeals to white parents as Coates does in *Between the World and Me*, the substance of her book reflects a more Morrisonian approach. Perry is less concerned with awakening whites from the dream of racialized privilege than with celebrating the joy of her mothering. While Coates and Ellison write of their invisibility with a palpable sense of fear – fear of not being recognized and fear of the vulnerability of their Black bodies – Perry and Morrison approach Blackness with the intimacy of community and love. This is not to suggest that they are ignorant or dismissive of fear, or that these Black male writers do not also express great love; rather, in their textured mode of address, Perry and Morrison make their vibrant families and communities central. Though invisibility and fear are foundational to Black subjectivity, their writings affirm the ties, both literary and familial, that root Black life in a rich past that reaches toward a brighter future even amid the grief of our present moment.

Notes

1. Pam Houston, "Pam Houston Talks with Toni Morrison," in *Toni Morrison: Conversations*, ed. Carolyn C. Denard (Jackson: University Press of Mississippi, 2008), 262.
2. Ta-nehisi Coates, *Between the World and Me* (New York: Spiegel and Grau, 2015).
3. *Juneteenth* was published in 1999. The 368 page novel was edited and condensed by Ellison's friend and biographer John F. Callahan from more than 2,000 pages written over 4 decades. A longer version of the book was published in 2010 under the title *Three Days Before the Shooting*, and was coedited by Callahan and Adam Bradley.
4. Ralph Ellison, "The World and the Jug," in *Shadow and Act* (New York: Vintage Books, 1964), 140.
5. Charles Ruas, "Toni Morrison," in *Conversations with Toni Morrison*, ed. Danille Taylor-Guthrie (Jackson: University Press of Mississippi, 1994), 96.
6. W. E. B. Du Bois, "Criteria of Negro Art," in *The Norton Anthology of African American Literature*, 2nd ed., Henry Louis Gates, Jr. and Nellie Y. McKay (New York: W. W. Norton Company, 2004), 783–784.
7. Richard Wright, "Blueprint for Negro Writing" in *The Norton Anthology of African American Literature*, 2nd ed., Henry Louis Gates, Jr. and Nellie Y. McKay (New York: W. W. Norton Company, 2004), 1405.
8. See "Everybody's Protest Novel" in James Baldwin, *Notes of a Native Son* [1955] (Boston: Beacon, 1984).
9. Claudia Dreifus, "*Chloe Wofford Talks about Toni Morrison*," in *Toni Morrison: Conversations*, ed. Carolyn C. Denard (Jackson: University Press of Mississippi, 2008), 102.
10. Ralph Ellison, *Invisible Man* (New York: Vintage Books, 1952), 3.
11. Toni Morrison, *The Bluest Eye* (New York: Vintage International, 1970), 3.
12. Toni Morrison, "Unspeakable Things Unspoken: The Afro-American Presence in American Literature," in *The Norton Anthology of African American Literature*, 2nd ed., Henry Louis Gates, Jr. and Nellie Y. McKay (New York: W. W. Norton Company, 2004), 2313.
13. Morrison, "Unspeakable," 2313.
14. Toni Morrison, "The Site of Memory," in *The Norton Anthology of African American Literature*, 2nd ed., Henry Louis Gates, Jr. and Nellie Y. McKay (New York: W. W. Norton Company, 2004), 2293.
15. See www.cc.com/video/yy2dzc/the-daily-show-with-jon-stewart-ta-nehisi-coates; season 20, airdate 7/23/2015.

16. Simon Abramowitsch, "Addressing Blackness, Dreaming Whiteness: Negotiating 21st-Century Race and Readership in Ta-Nehisi Coates's *Between the World and Me*." *CLA Journal*, 60:4 Special Issue: Democratizing the Black Public Intellectual: The Writings of Ta-Nehisi Coates (June 2017): 459.
17. Dana A. Williams, "Everybody's Protest Narrative: *Between the World and Me* and the Limits of Genre." *African American Review*, 49:3 (2016), 182.
18. Claudia Rankine, "The Condition of Black Life Is One of Mourning," in *The Fire This Time: A New Generation Speaks about Race*, ed. Jesmyn Ward (New York: Scribner, 2016), 145–156.
19. Coates, *Between the World and Me*, 150.
20. Ellison, *Invisible Man*, 581.
21. Imani Perry, *Breathe: A Letter to My Sons* (Beacon Press: Boston, 2019), 1.
22. Coates, *Between the World and Me*, 5.
23. Richard Wright, "Between the World and Me," in *American Negro Poetry*, rev. ed., ed. Arna Bontemps (New York: Hill and Wang, 1974), 103.
24. Perry, *Breathe*, 2.
25. Ibid., 73–74.

Further Reading

Race Studies

Cheng, Anne, *The Melancholy of Race*. New York: Oxford University Press, 2001.

Fielder, Brigitte, *Relative Races: Genealogies of Interracial Kinship in Nineteenth-Century*. Durham: Duke University Press, 2020.

Jerng, Mark C., *Racial Worldmaking: The Power of Popular Fiction*. New York: Fordham University Press, 2018.

Melamed, Jodi, *Represent and Destroy: Rationalizing Violence in the New Racial Capitalism*. Minneapolis: University of Minnesota Press, 2011.

Mills, Charles W., *The Racial Contract*. Ithaca: Cornell University Press, 1997.

Omi, Michael and Howard Winant, *Racial Formation in the United States from the 1960s to the 1990s*, 2nd ed. New York: Routledge, 1994.

Reddy, Chandan, *Freedom with Violence: Race, Sexuality, and the US State*. Durham: Duke University Press, 2011.

Rusert, Britt, *Fugitive Science: Empiricism and Freedom in Early African American Culture*. New York: New York University Press, 2017.

Schuller, Kyla, *Biopolitics of Feeling: Race, Sex, and Science in the Nineteenth Century*. Durham: Duke University Press, 2018.

Snorton, C. Riley, *Black on Both Sides: A Racial History of Trans Identity*. Minneapolis: University of Minnesota Press, 2018.

Post/Colonialism Studies

Anderson, Warwick, *Colonial Pathologies: American Tropical Medicine, Race, and Hygiene in the Philippines*. Durham: Duke University Press, 2006.

Eittreim, Elisabeth M., *Teaching Empire: Native Americans, Filipinos, and US Imperial Education, 1879–1918*. Lawrence: University Press of Kansas, 2019.

Hong, Grace Kyungwon and Roderick A. Ferguson, eds., *Strange Affinities: The Gender and Sexual Politics of Comparative Racialization*. Durham: Duke University Press, 2011.

Jacobs, Margaret D., *White Mother to a Dark Race: Settler Colonialism, Maternalism, and the Removal of Indigenous Children in the American West and Australia, 1880–1940*. Lincoln: University of Nebraska Press, 2009.

Mignolo, Walter, *Local Histories/Global Designs: Coloniality, Subaltern Knowledges, and Border Thinking*. Princeton: Princeton University Press, 2000.

Ponce, Martin Joseph, *Beyond the Nation: Diasporic Filipino Literature and Queer Reading*. New York: New York University Press, 2012.

Rodríguez-Silva, Illeana M., *Silencing Race: Disentangling Blackness, Colonialism, and National Identities in Puerto Rico*. New York: Palgrave Macmillan, 2012.

Wexler, Laura, *Tender Violence: Domestic Visions in an Age of US Imperialism*. Chapel Hill: University of North Carolina Press, 2000.

Comparative and Multiracial Studies

Chiles, Katy L., *Transformable Race: Surprising Metamorphoses in the Literature of Early America*. New York: Oxford University Press, 2014.

Gracia, Jorge J. E., ed., *Race or Ethnicity? On Black and Latino Identity*. Ithaca: Cornell University Press, 2007.

Le, Nhu, *Unsettled Solidarities: Asian and Indigenous Cross-Representations in the Américas*. Philadelphia: Temple University Press, 2019.

Ngai, Mae M., *Impossible Subjects: Illegal Aliens and the Making of Modern America*. Princeton: Princeton University Press, 2004.

Prashad, Vijay, *Everybody Was Kung Fu Fighting: Afro-Asian Connections and the Myth of Cultural Purity*. Boston: Beacon Press, 2001.

Rana, Swati, *Race Characters: Ethnic Literature and the Figure of the American Dream*. Chapel Hill: University of North Carolina Press, 2020.

African American Studies

Berry, Daina Ramey and Kali Nicole Gross, *A Black Women's History of the United States*. Boston: Beacon Press, 2020.

Diggs Colbert, Soyica, *Black Movements: Performance and Cultural Politics*. New Brunswick: Rutgers University Press, 2017.

Ellis, Nadia, *Territories of the Soul: Queered Belonging in the Black Diaspora*. Durham: Duke University Press, 2015.

Ernest, John, *Chaotic Justice: Rethinking African American Literary History*. Chapel Hill: University of North Carolina Press, 2009.

Freeburg, Christopher, *Black Aesthetics and the Interior Life*. Charlottesville: University of Virginia Press, 2017.

Gates, Henry Louis, *The Signifying Monkey: A Theory of Afro-American Literary Criticism*, 25th anniversary ed. New York: Oxford University Press, 2014.

Hartman, Saidiya, *Lose Your Mother: A Journey Along the Atlantic Slave Route*. New York: Farrar, Straus, and Giroux, 2007.

James, Jennifer, *A Freedom Bought with Blood: African American War Literature from the Civil War to World War II*. Chapel Hill: University of North Carolina Press, 2007.

Morrison, Toni, *Playing in the Dark: Whiteness and the Literary Imagination*. Cambridge: Harvard University Press, 1992.

Nishikawa, Kinohi, *Street Players: Black Pulp Fiction and the Making of a Literary Underground*. Chicago: University of Chicago Press, 2018.

Sharpe, Christina, *In the Wake: On Blackness and Being*. Durham: Duke University Press, 2016.

Ward, Jesmyn, ed., *The Fire This Time: A New Generation Speaks about Race*. New York: Scribner, 2016.

Warren, Kenneth, *What Was African American Literature?* Cambridge: Harvard University Press, 2011.

Weheliye, Alexander G., *Habeas Viscus: Racializing Assemblages, Biopolitics, and Black Feminist Theories of the Human*. Durham: Duke University Press, 2014.

Asian American Studies

Chen, Tina, *Double Agency: Acts of Impersonation in Asian American Literature and Culture*. Stanford: Stanford University Press, 2005.

Chuh, Kandice, *Imagine Otherwise: On Asian Americanist Critique*. Durham: Duke University Press, 2003.

Eng, David L. and Shinhee Han, *Racial Melancholia, Racial Dissociation: On the Social and Psychic Lives of Asian Americans*. Durham: Duke University Press, 2018.

Hong Sohn, Stephen, *Inscrutable Belongings: Queer Asian North American Fiction*. Stanford: Stanford University Press, 2018.

Huang, Betsy, *Contesting Genres in Contemporary Asian American Fiction*. New York: Palgrave Macmillan, 2010.

Kyung-Jin Lee, James, *Pedagogies of Woundedness: Illness, Memoir, and the Ends of the Model Minority*. Philadelphia: Temple University Press, 2021.

Lee, Robert G., *Orientals: Asian Americans in Popular Culture*. Philadelphia: Temple University Press, 1999.

Lowe, Lisa, *The Intimacies of Four Continents*. Durham: Duke University Press, 2015.

Maeda, Daryl Joji, *Chains of Babylon: The Rise of Asian America*. Minneapolis: University of Minnesota Press, 2009.

Maeda, Daryl Joji, *Rethinking the Asian American Movement*. New York: Routledge, 2012.

Miyung Joo, Rachael and Shelley Sang-Hee Lee, eds., *A Companion to Korean American Studies*. Leiden: Brill, 2018.

Ninh, Khuê, *Passing for Perfect: College Imposters and Other Model Minorities*. Philadelphia: Temple University Press, 2021.

Palumbo-Liu, David, *Asian/American: Historical Crossings of a Racial Frontier*. Stanford: Stanford University Press, 1999.

Park Hong, Cathy, *Minor Feelings: An Asian American Reckoning*. New York: One World, 2020.

Pfaelzer, Jean, *Driven Out: The Forgotten War Against Chinese Americans*. Berkeley: University of California Press, 2008.

Schlund-Vials, Cathy, ed., *Keywords for Asian American Studies*. New York: New York University Press, 2015.

Tang, Amy C., *Repetition and Race: Asian American Literature After Multiculturalism*. Oxford: Oxford University Press, 2016.

Thanh Nguyen, Viet, *Race and Resistance: Literature and Politics in Asia America*. New York City: Oxford University Press, 2002.

Tsou, Elda E., *Unquiet Tropes: Form, Race, and Asian American Literature*. Philadelphia: Temple University Press, 2015.

Ty, Eleanor, *Asianfail: Narratives of Disenchantment and the Model Minority* Urbana: University of Illinois Press, 2017.

Indigenous Studies

Barker, Joanne, ed., *Critically Sovereign: Indigenous Gender, Sexuality, and Feminist Studies*. Durham: Duke University Press, 2017.

Brooks, Lisa, *The Common Pot: The Recovery of Native Space in the Northeast*. Minneapolis: University of Minnesota Press, 2008.

Coulthard, Glen, *Red Skin, White Masks: Rejecting the Colonial Politics of Recognition*. Minneapolis: University of Minnesota Press, 2014.

Estes, Nick, *Our History is the Future: Standing Rock versus the Dakota Access Pipeline, and the Long Tradition of Indian Resistance*. New York: Verso, 2019.

Fixico, Donald, *Termination and Relocation: Federal Indian Policy, 1945–1960*. Albuquerque: University of New Mexico Press, 1990.

Furlan, Laura M., *Indigenous Cities: Urban Indian Fiction and the Histories of Relocation*. Lincoln: University of Nebraska Press, 2017.

Gilio-Whitaker, Dino, *As Long as Grass Grows: The Indigenous Fight for Environmental Justice, from Colonization to Standing Rock*. Boston: Beacon Press, 2019.

Goeman, Mishuana, *Mark My Words: Native Women Mapping Our Nations*. Minneapolis: University of Minnesota Press, 2013.

Lopenzina, Drew, *Red Ink: Native Americans Picking up the Pen in the Colonial Period*. Albany: SUNY Press, 2012.

McGlennen, Molly, *Creative Alliances: The Transnational Designs of Indigenous Women's Poetry*. Norman: University of Oklahoma Press, 2014.

Ramirez, Renya, *Native Hubs: Culture, Community, and Belonging in Silicon Valley and Beyond*. Durham: Duke University Press, 2007.

Razack, Sherene, *Dying from Improvement: Inquests and Inquiries into Indigenous Deaths in Custody*. Toronto: University of Toronto Press, 2015.

Rifkin, Mark, *When Did Indians Become Straight?* Oxford: Oxford University Press, 2011.

Rosenthal, Nicolas G., *Reimagining Indian Country: Native American Migration and Identity in Twentieth- Century Los Angeles*. Chapel Hill: University of North Carolina Press, 2012.

Saunt, Claudio, *Unworthy Republic: The Dispossession of Native Americans and the Road to Indian Territory*. New York: W. W. Norton, 2020.

Smithers, Gregory D. and Brooke N. Newman, eds., *Native Diasporas: Indigenous Identities and Settler Colonialism in the Americas*. Lincoln: University of Nebraska Press, 2014.

TallBear, Kimberly, *Native American DNA: Tribal Belonging and the False Promise of Genetic Science*. Minneapolis: University of Minnesota Press, 2013.

Teves, Stephani Nohelani, Andrea Smith, and Michele Raheja, eds., *Native Studies Keywords*. Tucson: University of Arizona Press, 2015.

Wilkins David Eugene, and Shelby Hulse Wilkins, *Dismembered: Native Disenrollment and the Battle for Human Rights*. Seattle: University of Washington Press, 2017.

Latinx Studies

Aranda, José F., *When We Arrive: A New Literary History of Mexican America*. Tucson: University of Arizona, 2003.

Beltrán, Cristina, *The Trouble with Unity: Latino Politics and the Creation of Identity*. New York: Oxford University Press, 2010.

Burnett, Christina Duffy and Burke Marshall, eds., *Foreign in a Domestic Sense: Puerto Rico, American Expansion, and the Constitution*. Durham: Duke University Press, 2001.

Caminero-Santangelo, Marta, *On Latinidad: US Latino Literature and the Construction of Ethnicity*. Gainesville: University Press of Florida, 2009.

Cutler, John Alba, *Ends of Assimilation: the Formation of Chicano Literature*. New York: Oxford University Press, 2015.

Dalleo, Raphael and Elena Machado Sáez, *The Latino/a Canon and the Emergence of Post Sixties Literature*. New York: Palgrave Macmillan, 2007.

Guidotti-Hernández, Nicole M., *Archiving Mexican Masculinities in Diaspora*. Durham: Duke University Press, 2021.

Hudson, Renee, *Latinx Revolutionary Horizons: Form and Futurity in the Americas*. New York: Fordham University Press, 2024.

Irizarry, Ylce, *Chicana/o and Latina/o Fiction: The New Memory of Latinidad*. Urbana: University of Illinois Press, 2016.

Latinx Lives in a Hemispheric Context, special issue *of English Language Notes* 56, no. 2 (October 2018).

LatinX Studies: Variations and Velocities, special issue of *Cultural Dynamics* 31, no. 1–2 (February–May 2019).

Milian, Claudia, *Latining America: Black-Brown Passages and the Coloring of Latino/a Studies*. Athens: University of Georgia Press, 2013.

Milian, Claudia, *LatinX*. Minneapolis: University of Minnesota Press, 2019.

Muñoz, José Esteban, *The Sense of Brown*. Durham: Duke University Press, 2020.
Ortiz, Ricardo, *Latinx Literature Now: Between Evanescence and Event*. New York: Palgrave Macmillan, 2019.
Román, Miriam Jiménez and Juan Flores, eds., *The Afro-Latin@ Reader: History and Culture in the United States*. Durham: Duke University Press, 2010.
Sáez, Elena Machado, *Market Aesthetics: The Purchase of the Past in Caribbean Diasporic Fiction*. Charlottesville: University of Virginia Press, 2015.
Theorizing LatinX, special issue of *Cultural Dynamics* 29, no. 3, August 2017.
Vázquez, David, *Triangulations: Narrative Strategies for Navigating Latino Identity*. Minneapolis: University of Minnesota Press, 2011.

Whiteness Studies

Allen, Theodore W., *The Invention of the White Race: The Origin of Racial Oppression in Anglo-America*. New York: Verso, 1997.
Babb, Valerie, *Whiteness Visible: The Meaning of Whiteness in American Literature and Culture*. New York: New York University Press, 1998.
Foster, Travis M., *Genre and White Supremacy in the Postemancipation United States*. New York : Oxford University Press, 2019.
Frye Jacobson, Matthew, *Whiteness of a Different Color: European Immigrants and the Alchemy of Race*. Cambridge: Harvard University Press, 1999.
Haney López, Ian, *White by Law: The Legal Construction of Race*. New York: New York University Press, 1996.
Hill, Mike, *Whiteness: A Critical Reader*. New York : New York University Press, 1997.
Ignatiev, Noel, *How the Irish Became White*. New York: Routledge, 1995.
McIntosh, Peggy, "White Privilege: Unpacking the Invisible Knapsack," *Peace and Freedom Magazine*, July/August 1989: 10–12.
Roediger, David R., *The Wages of Whiteness: Race and the Making of the American Working Class*. New York: Verso, 1991.
Wray, Matt, *Not Quite White: White Trash and the Boundaries of Whiteness*. Durham: Duke University Press, 2006.

Index

Cambridge Companions To . . .

AUTHORS

Edward Albee edited by Stephen J. Bottoms
Margaret Atwood edited by Coral Ann Howells (second edition)
W. H. Auden edited by Stan Smith
Jane Austen edited by Edward Copeland and Juliet McMaster (second edition)
James Baldwin edited by Michele Elam
Balzac edited by Owen Heathcote and Andrew Watts
Beckett edited by John Pilling
Bede edited by Scott DeGregorio
Aphra Behn edited by Derek Hughes and Janet Todd
Saul Bellow edited by Victoria Aarons
Walter Benjamin edited by David S. Ferris
William Blake edited by Morris Eaves
Boccaccio edited by Guyda Armstrong, Rhiannon Daniels, and Stephen J. Milner
Jorge Luis Borges edited by Edwin Williamson
Brecht edited by Peter Thomson and Glendyr Sacks (second edition)
The Brontës edited by Heather Glen
Bunyan edited by Anne Dunan-Page
Frances Burney edited by Peter Sabor
Byron edited by Drummond Bone (second edition)
Albert Camus edited by Edward J. Hughes
Willa Cather edited by Marilee Lindemann
Catullus edited by Ian Du Quesnay and Tony Woodman
Cervantes edited by Anthony J. Cascardi
Chaucer edited by Piero Boitani and Jill Mann (second edition)
Chekhov edited by Vera Gottlieb and Paul Allain
Kate Chopin edited by Janet Beer
Caryl Churchill edited by Elaine Aston and Elin Diamond
Cicero edited by Catherine Steel
John Clare edited by Sarah Houghton-Walker
J. M. Coetzee edited by Jarad Zimbler
Coleridge edited by Lucy Newlyn
Coleridge edited by Tim Fulford (new edition)
Wilkie Collins edited by Jenny Bourne Taylor
Joseph Conrad edited by J. H. Stape
H. D. edited by Nephie J. Christodoulides and Polina Mackay
Dante edited by Rachel Jacoff (second edition)
Daniel Defoe edited by John Richetti
Don DeLillo edited by John N. Duvall

Charles Dickens edited by John O. Jordan
Emily Dickinson edited by Wendy Martin
John Donne edited by Achsah Guibbory
Dostoevskii edited by W. J. Leatherbarrow
Theodore Dreiser edited by Leonard Cassuto and Claire Virginia Eby
John Dryden edited by Steven N. Zwicker
W. E. B. Du Bois edited by Shamoon Zamir
George Eliot edited by George Levine and Nancy Henry (second edition)
T. S. Eliot edited by A. David Moody
Ralph Ellison edited by Ross Posnock
Ralph Waldo Emerson edited by Joel Porte and Saundra Morris
William Faulkner edited by Philip M. Weinstein
Henry Fielding edited by Claude Rawson
F. Scott Fitzgerald edited by Ruth Prigozy
F. Scott Fitzgerald edited by Michael Nowlin (second edition)
Flaubert edited by Timothy Unwin
E. M. Forster edited by David Bradshaw
Benjamin Franklin edited by Carla Mulford
Brian Friel edited by Anthony Roche
Robert Frost edited by Robert Faggen
Gabriel García Márquez edited by Philip Swanson
Elizabeth Gaskell edited by Jill L. Matus
Edward Gibbon edited by Karen O'Brien and Brian Young
Goethe edited by Lesley Sharpe
Günter Grass edited by Stuart Taberner
Thomas Hardy edited by Dale Kramer
David Hare edited by Richard Boon
Nathaniel Hawthorne edited by Richard Millington
Seamus Heaney edited by Bernard O'Donoghue
Ernest Hemingway edited by Scott Donaldson
Hildegard of Bingen edited by Jennifer Bain
Homer edited by Robert Fowler
Horace edited by Stephen Harrison
Ted Hughes edited by Terry Gifford
Ibsen edited by James McFarlane
Kazuo Ishiguro edited by Andrew Bennett
Henry James edited by Jonathan Freedman
Samuel Johnson edited by Greg Clingham
Ben Jonson edited by Richard Harp and Stanley Stewart
James Joyce edited by Derek Attridge (second edition)
Kafka edited by Julian Preece

Keats edited by Susan J. Wolfson
Rudyard Kipling edited by Howard J. Booth
Lacan edited by Jean-Michel Rabaté
D. H. Lawrence edited by Anne Fernihough
Primo Levi edited by Robert Gordon
Lucretius edited by Stuart Gillespie and Philip Hardie
Machiavelli edited by John M. Najemy
David Mamet edited by Christopher Bigsby
Thomas Mann edited by Ritchie Robertson
Christopher Marlowe edited by Patrick Cheney
Andrew Marvell edited by Derek Hirst and Steven N. Zwicker
Ian McEwan edited by Dominic Head
Herman Melville edited by Robert S. Levine
Arthur Miller edited by Christopher Bigsby (second edition)
Milton edited by Dennis Danielson (second edition)
Molière edited by David Bradby and Andrew Calder
William Morris edited by Marcus Waithe
Toni Morrison edited by Justine Tally
Alice Munro edited by David Staines
Nabokov edited by Julian W. Connolly
Eugene O'Neill edited by Michael Manheim
George Orwell edited by John Rodden
Ovid edited by Philip Hardie
Petrarch edited by Albert Russell Ascoli and Unn Falkeid
Harold Pinter edited by Peter Raby (second edition)
Sylvia Plath edited by Jo Gill
Plutarch edited by Frances B. Titchener and Alexei Zadorojnyi
Edgar Allan Poe edited by Kevin J. Hayes
Alexander Pope edited by Pat Rogers
Ezra Pound edited by Ira B. Nadel
Proust edited by Richard Bales
Pushkin edited by Andrew Kahn
Thomas Pynchon edited by Inger H. Dalsgaard, Luc Herman and Brian McHale
Rabelais edited by John O'Brien
Rilke edited by Karen Leeder and Robert Vilain
Philip Roth edited by Timothy Parrish
Salman Rushdie edited by Abdulrazak Gurnah
John Ruskin edited by Francis O'Gorman
Sappho edited by P. J. Finglass and Adrian Kelly
Seneca edited by Shadi Bartsch and Alessandro Schiesaro
Shakespeare edited by Margareta de Grazia and Stanley Wells (second edition)

George Bernard Shaw edited by Christopher Innes
Shelley edited by Timothy Morton
Mary Shelley edited by Esther Schor
Sam Shepard edited by Matthew C. Roudané
Spenser edited by Andrew Hadfield
Laurence Sterne edited by Thomas Keymer
Wallace Stevens edited by John N. Serio
Tom Stoppard edited by Katherine E. Kelly
Harriet Beecher Stowe edited by Cindy Weinstein
August Strindberg edited by Michael Robinson
Jonathan Swift edited by Christopher Fox
J. M. Synge edited by P. J. Mathews
Tacitus edited by A. J. Woodman
Henry David Thoreau edited by Joel Myerson
Thucydides edited by Polly Low
Tolstoy edited by Donna Tussing Orwin
Anthony Trollope edited by Carolyn Dever and Lisa Niles
Mark Twain edited by Forrest G. Robinson
John Updike edited by Stacey Olster
Mario Vargas Llosa edited by Efrain Kristal and John King
Virgil edited by Fiachra Mac Góráin and Charles Martindale (second edition)
Voltaire edited by Nicholas Cronk
David Foster Wallace edited by Ralph Clare
Edith Wharton edited by Millicent Bell
Walt Whitman edited by Ezra Greenspan
Oscar Wilde edited by Peter Raby
Tennessee Williams edited by Matthew C. Roudané
William Carlos Williams edited by Christopher MacGowan
August Wilson edited by Christopher Bigsby
Mary Wollstonecraft edited by Claudia L. Johnson
Virginia Woolf edited by Susan Sellers (second edition)
Wordsworth edited by Stephen Gill
Richard Wright edited by Glenda R. Carpio
W. B. Yeats edited by Marjorie Howes and John Kelly
Xenophon edited by Michael A. Flower
Zola edited by Brian Nelson

TOPICS

The Actress edited by Maggie B. Gale and John Stokes
The African American Novel edited by Maryemma Graham
The African American Slave Narrative edited by Audrey A. Fisch

African American Theatre edited by Harvey Young
Allegory edited by Rita Copeland and Peter Struck
American Crime Fiction edited by Catherine Ross Nickerson
American Gothic edited by Jeffrey Andrew Weinstock
The American Graphic Novel edited by Jan Baetens, Hugo Frey and Fabrice Leroy
American Horror edited by Stephen Shapiro and Mark Storey
American Literature and the Body edited by Travis M. Foster
American Literature and the Environment edited by Sarah Ensor and Susan Scott Parrish
American Literature of the 1930s edited by William Solomon
American Modernism edited by Walter Kalaidjian
American Poetry since 1945 edited by Jennifer Ashton
American Realism and Naturalism edited by Donald Pizer
American Short Story edited by Michael J. Collins and Gavin Jones
American Travel Writing edited by Alfred Bendixen and Judith Hamera
American Women Playwrights edited by Brenda Murphy
Ancient Rhetoric edited by Erik Gunderson
Arthurian Legend edited by Elizabeth Archibald and Ad Putter
Australian Literature edited by Elizabeth Webby
The Australian Novel edited by Nicholas Birns and Louis Klee
The Beats edited by Stephen Belletto
The Black Body in American Literature edited by Cherene Sherrard-Johnson
Boxing edited by Gerald Early
British Black and Asian Literature (1945–2010) edited by Deirdre Osborne
British Fiction: 1980–2018 edited by Peter Boxall
British Fiction since 1945 edited by David James
British Literature of the 1930s edited by James Smith
British Literature of the French Revolution edited by Pamela Clemit
British Romantic Poetry edited by James Chandler and Maureen N. McLane
British Romanticism edited by Stuart Curran (second edition)
British Romanticism and Religion edited by Jeffrey Barbeau
British Theatre, 1730–1830, edited by Jane Moody and Daniel O'Quinn
Canadian Literature edited by Eva-Marie Kröller (second edition)
The Canterbury Tales edited by Frank Grady
Children's Literature edited by M. O. Grenby and Andrea Immel
The City in World Literature edited by Ato Quayson and Jini Kim Watson
The Classic Russian Novel edited by Malcolm V. Jones and Robin Feuer Miller
Comics edited by Maaheen Ahmed
Contemporary African American Literature edited by Yogita Goyal
Contemporary Irish Poetry edited by Matthew Campbell
Creative Writing edited by David Morley and Philip Neilsen

Crime Fiction edited by Martin Priestman
Dante's "Commedia" edited by Zygmunt G. Barański and Simon Gilson
Dracula edited by Roger Luckhurst
Early American Literature edited by Bryce Traister
Early Modern Women's Writing edited by Laura Lunger Knoppers
The Eighteenth-Century Novel edited by John Richetti
Eighteenth-Century Poetry edited by John Sitter
Eighteenth-Century Thought edited by Frans De Bruyn
Emma edited by Peter Sabor
English Dictionaries edited by Sarah Ogilvie
English Literature, 1500–1600 edited by Arthur F. Kinney
English Literature, 1650–1740 edited by Steven N. Zwicker
English Literature, 1740–1830 edited by Thomas Keymer and Jon Mee
English Literature, 1830–1914 edited by Joanne Shattock
English Melodrama edited by Carolyn Williams
English Novelists edited by Adrian Poole
English Poetry, Donne to Marvell edited by Thomas N. Corns
English Poets edited by Claude Rawson
English Renaissance Drama edited by A. R. Braunmuller and Michael Hattaway, (second edition)
English Renaissance Tragedy edited by Emma Smith and Garrett A. Sullivan Jr.
English Restoration Theatre edited by Deborah C. Payne Fisk
Environmental Humanities edited by Jeffrey Cohen and Stephanie Foote
The Epic edited by Catherine Bates
Erotic Literature edited by Bradford Mudge
The Essay edited by Kara Wittman and Evan Kindley
European Modernism edited by Pericles Lewis
European Novelists edited by Michael Bell
Fairy Tales edited by Maria Tatar
Fantasy Literature edited by Edward James and Farah Mendlesohn
Feminist Literary Theory edited by Ellen Rooney
Fiction in the Romantic Period edited by Richard Maxwell and Katie Trumpener
The Fin de Siècle edited by Gail Marshall
Frankenstein edited by Andrew Smith
The French Enlightenment edited by Daniel Brewer
French Literature edited by John D. Lyons
The French Novel: from 1800 to the Present edited by Timothy Unwin
Gay and Lesbian Writing edited by Hugh Stevens
German Romanticism edited by Nicholas Saul
Global Literature and Slavery edited by Laura T. Murphy
Gothic Fiction edited by Jerrold E. Hogle

The Graphic Novel edited by Stephen Tabachnick
The Greek and Roman Novel edited by Tim Whitmarsh
Greek and Roman Theatre edited by Marianne McDonald and J. Michael Walton
Greek Comedy edited by Martin Revermann
Greek Lyric edited by Felix Budelmann
Greek Mythology edited by Roger D. Woodard
Greek Tragedy edited by P. E. Easterling
The Harlem Renaissance edited by George Hutchinson
The History of the Book edited by Leslie Howsam
Human Rights and Literature edited by Crystal Parikh
The Irish Novel edited by John Wilson Foster
Irish Poets edited by Gerald Dawe
The Italian Novel edited by Peter Bondanella and Andrea Ciccarelli
The Italian Renaissance edited by Michael Wyatt
Jewish American Literature edited by Hana Wirth-Nesher and Michael P. Kramer
The Latin American Novel edited by Efraín Kristal
Latin American Poetry edited by Stephen Hart
Latina/o American Literature edited by John Morán González
Latin Love Elegy edited by Thea S. Thorsen
Literature and Animals edited by Derek Ryan
Literature and the Anthropocene edited by John Parham
Literature and Climate edited by Adeline Johns-Putra and Kelly Sultzbach
Literature and Disability edited by Clare Barker and Stuart Murray
Literature and Food edited by J. Michelle Coghlan
Literature and the Posthuman edited by Bruce Clarke and Manuela Rossini
Literature and Religion edited by Susan M. Felch
Literature and Science edited by Steven Meyer
The Literature of the American Civil War and Reconstruction edited by Kathleen Diffley and Coleman Hutchison
The Literature of the American Renaissance edited by Christopher N. Phillips
The Literature of Berlin edited by Andrew J. Webber
The Literature of the Crusades edited by Anthony Bale
The Literature of the First World War edited by Vincent Sherry
The Literature of London edited by Lawrence Manley
The Literature of Los Angeles edited by Kevin R. McNamara
The Literature of New York edited by Cyrus Patell and Bryan Waterman
The Literature of Paris edited by Anna-Louise Milne
The Literature of World War II edited by Marina MacKay
Literature on Screen edited by Deborah Cartmell and Imelda Whelehan
Lyrical Ballads edited by Sally Bushell
Medieval British Manuscripts edited by Orietta Da Rold and Elaine Treharne

Medieval English Culture edited by Andrew Galloway
Medieval English Law and Literature edited by Candace Barrington and Sebastian Sobecki
Medieval English Literature edited by Larry Scanlon
Medieval English Mysticism edited by Samuel Fanous and Vincent Gillespie
Medieval English Theatre edited by Richard Beadle and Alan J. Fletcher (second edition)
Medieval French Literature edited by Simon Gaunt and Sarah Kay
Medieval Romance edited by Roberta L. Krueger
Medieval Romance edited by Roberta L. Krueger (new edition)
Medieval Women's Writing edited by Carolyn Dinshaw and David Wallace
Modern American Culture edited by Christopher Bigsby
Modern British Women Playwrights edited by Elaine Aston and Janelle Reinelt
Modern French Culture edited by Nicholas Hewitt
Modern German Culture edited by Eva Kolinsky and Wilfried van der Will
The Modern German Novel edited by Graham Bartram
The Modern Gothic edited by Jerrold E. Hogle
Modern Irish Culture edited by Joe Cleary and Claire Connolly
Modern Italian Culture edited by Zygmunt G. Baranski and Rebecca J. West
Modern Latin American Culture edited by John King
Modern Russian Culture edited by Nicholas Rzhevsky
Modern Spanish Culture edited by David T. Gies
Modernism edited by Michael Levenson (second edition)
The Modernist Novel edited by Morag Shiach
Modernist Poetry edited by Alex Davis and Lee M. Jenkins
Modernist Women Writers edited by Maren Tova Linett
Narrative edited by David Herman
Narrative Theory edited by Matthew Garrett
Native American Literature edited by Joy Porter and Kenneth M. Roemer
Nineteen Eighty-Four edited by Nathan Waddell
Nineteenth-Century American Literature and Politics edited by John Kerkering
Nineteenth-Century American Poetry edited by Kerry Larson
Nineteenth-Century American Women's Writing edited by Dale M. Bauer and Philip Gould
Nineteenth-Century Thought edited by Gregory Claeys
The Novel edited by Eric Bulson
Old English Literature edited by Malcolm Godden and Michael Lapidge (second edition)
Performance Studies edited by Tracy C. Davis
Piers Plowman edited by Andrew Cole and Andrew Galloway
The Poetry of the First World War edited by Santanu Das

Popular Fiction edited by David Glover and Scott McCracken
Postcolonial Literary Studies edited by Neil Lazarus
Postcolonial Poetry edited by Jahan Ramazani
Postcolonial Travel Writing edited by Robert Clarke
Postmodern American Fiction edited by Paula Geyh
Postmodernism edited by Steven Connor
Prose edited by Daniel Tyler
The Pre-Raphaelites edited by Elizabeth Prettejohn
Pride and Prejudice edited by Janet Todd
Queer Studies edited by Siobhan B. Somerville
Race and American Literature edited by John Ernest
Renaissance Humanism edited by Jill Kraye
Robinson Crusoe edited by John Richetti
Roman Comedy edited by Martin T. Dinter
The Roman Historians edited by Andrew Feldherr
Roman Satire edited by Kirk Freudenburg
The Romantic Sublime edited by Cian Duffy
Science Fiction edited by Edward James and Farah Mendlesohn
Scottish Literature edited by Gerald Carruthers and Liam McIlvanney
Sensation Fiction edited by Andrew Mangham
Shakespeare and Contemporary Dramatists edited by Ton Hoenselaars
Shakespeare and Popular Culture edited by Robert Shaughnessy
Shakespeare and Race edited by Ayanna Thompson
Shakespeare and Religion edited by Hannibal Hamlin
Shakespeare and War edited by David Loewenstein and Paul Stevens
Shakespeare on Film edited by Russell Jackson (second edition)
Shakespeare on Screen edited by Russell Jackson
Shakespeare on Stage edited by Stanley Wells and Sarah Stanton
Shakespearean Comedy edited by Alexander Leggatt
Shakespearean Tragedy edited by Claire McEachern (second edition)
Shakespeare's First Folio edited by Emma Smith
Shakespeare's History Plays edited by Michael Hattaway
Shakespeare's Language edited by Lynne Magnusson with David Schalkwyk
Shakespeare's Last Plays edited by Catherine M. S. Alexander
Shakespeare's Poetry edited by Patrick Cheney
Sherlock Holmes edited by Janice M. Allan and Christopher Pittard
The Sonnet edited by A. D. Cousins and Peter Howarth
The Spanish Novel: from 1600 to the Present edited by Harriet Turner and Adelaida López de Martínez
Textual Scholarship edited by Neil Fraistat and Julia Flanders
Theatre and Science edited by Kristen E. Shepherd-Barr

Theatre History edited by David Wiles and Christine Dymkowski
Transnational American Literature edited by Yogita Goyal
Travel Writing edited by Peter Hulme and Tim Youngs
The Twentieth-Century American Novel and Politics edited by Bryan Santin
Twentieth-Century American Poetry and Politics edited by Daniel Morris
Twentieth-Century British and Irish Women's Poetry edited by Jane Dowson
The Twentieth-Century English Novel edited by Robert L. Caserio
Twentieth-Century English Poetry edited by Neil Corcoran
Twentieth-Century Irish Drama edited by Shaun Richards
Twentieth-Century Literature and Politics edited by Christos Hadjiyiannis and Rachel Potter
Twentieth-Century Russian Literature edited by Marina Balina and Evgeny Dobrenko
Utopian Literature edited by Gregory Claeys
Victorian and Edwardian Theatre edited by Kerry Powell
The Victorian Novel edited by Deirdre David (second edition)
Victorian Poetry edited by Joseph Bristow
Victorian Women's Poetry edited by Linda K. Hughes
Victorian Women's Writing edited by Linda H. Peterson
War Writing edited by Kate McLoughlin
Women's Writing in Britain, 1660–1789 edited by Catherine Ingrassia
Women's Writing in the Romantic Period edited by Devoney Looser
World Literature edited by Ben Etherington and Jarad Zimbler
World Crime Fiction edited by Jesper Gulddal, Stewart King and Alistair Rolls
Writing of the English Revolution edited by N. H. Keeble
The Writings of Julius Caesar edited by Christopher Krebs and Luca Grillo

Printed in the United States
by Baker & Taylor Publisher Services